ISBN 978-1-331-05544-0
PIBN 10138962

This book is a reproduction of an important historical work. Forgotten Books uses
state-of-the-art technology to digitally reconstruct the work, preserving the original format
whilst repairing imperfections present in the aged copy. In rare cases, an imperfection in
the original, such as a blemish or missing page, may be replicated in our edition. We do,
however, repair the vast majority of imperfections successfully; any imperfections that
remain are intentionally left to preserve the state of such historical works.

1 MONTH OF
FREE
READING

at

www.ForgottenBooks.com

By purchasing this book you are
eligible for one month membership to
ForgottenBooks.com, giving you
unlimited access to our entire
collection of over 1,000,000 titles via
our web site and mobile apps.

To claim your free month visit:

www.forgottenbooks.com/free138962

THE HISTORY AND FATE

OF SACRILEGE.

By SIR HENRY SPELMAN.

EDITED, IN PART FROM TWO MSS., REVISED AND CORRECTED, WITH A
CONTINUATION, LARGE ADDITIONS, AND

An Introductory Essay.

BY TWO PRIESTS OF THE CHURCH OF ENGLAND.

Fourth Edition.

WITH AN APPENDIX BRINGING THE WORK UP TO THE PRESENT DATE BY

THE REV. C. F. S. WARREN, M.A.

JOHN HODGES,

BEDFORD STREET, STRAND, LONDON,

1895.

𝔗𝔢𝔟𝔬𝔯𝔰:
SOUTH COUNTIES PRESS LIMITED.

THE

History and Fate

OF

SACRILEGE,

Discover'd by EXAMPLES

OF

SCRIPTURE,

OF

HEATHENS,

AND OF

CHRISTIANS;

From the Beginning of the WORLD, continually to this Day.

By Sir *HENRY SPELMAN*, Kt.
Wrote in the YEAR 1632.

A Treatise omitted in the late Edition of his *Posthumous
Works,* and now Published for the *Terror of Evil Doers.*

LONDON, Printed for *John Hartley,* over-
against *Gray's Inn,* in *Holborn,* 1698.

He that buildeth his house with other men's money, is like one that gathereth himself stones for the tomb of his burial.

Ecclus. xxj. 8.

CONTENTS.

CHAPTER I.

CHAPTER II.

CHAPTER III.

CHAPTER IV.

CHAPTER V.

CHAPTER VI.

CHAPTER VII.

CHAPTER VIII.

CHAPTER IX.

EDITORS' PREFACE.

[To Edition of 1846.]

ı _____

The History of Sacrilege, now for the first time reprinted, was commenced by sir Henry Spelman about the year 1612. He has related the motive that induced him to undertake its composition. Possessed of the sites of Blackborough and Wormgay Abbeys, in Norfolk, he was involved in continual and expensive lawsuits, and when they were finally given up by him he found that he had been "a great loser, and not beholden to fortune, yet happy in this, that he was out of the briars, but especially that hereby he first discerned the infelicity of meddling with consecrated places."

He appears to have carried on his collections till the year 1632, when he began to arrange them ; the last date of any fresh entry in his memoranda is November 22, 1634. On his death, the papers were entrusted to the care of the rev. Jeremy Stephens, himself an author of some reputation, and who had evidently been acquainted with, and interested in, the progress of the work.* The Great Rebellion rendered publication, for many years, impossible. "At length, in the year 1663," says à Wood, "Mr. Stephens began to print the *History of Sacrilege.*" Bishop Gibson tells us, "I have been informed by a learned divine, since a prelate of our Church" (Dr. Simon Patrick is perhaps meant), "that Mr. Stephens was forbidden to proceed in an edition of that work, lest the publication of it should give offence to the nobility and gentry. But whatever was the occasion of its continuing in the press till the fire of London, it has been taken for granted, that the whole book was irrecoverably lost ; and I was satisfied of the same, upon Mr. Wood's relation of the matter ; till examining some MSS. which were given to the Bodleian Library, by the late bishop of Lincoln,"—Dr. Thomas Barlowe,—"I met with a transcript

* He left behind him, according to à Wood, in MS., "The design of the Cormorants upon the Church Lands, defeated in the time of K. Hen. 5, effected in the time of K. Hen. 8."

B

of some portion of it. Upon further inquiry, I found other
parts in other places; so that the work now seems to be
pretty entire."

Mr. Gibson was then preparing for the press his edition
of Spelman's Remains; and would have included this among
his other posthumous works, " but that some persons," he
says, " in the present age would be apt to interpret the mention of their predecessors, in such manner, and upon such
an occasion, as an unpardonable reflection upon their
families." Gibson was a " safe " man, and attained to
three bishoprics.

Thus, a second time, the *History of Sacrilege* seemed con-
signed to oblivion. Before this period, indeed, Clement
Spelman, puisne baron of the exchequer in the time of
Charles II., had, in the Preface to the *De Non Temerandis
Ecclesiis*, made a kind of abstract of the *History of Sacrilege*,
inserting some further particulars, which we shall notice in
their place. But immediately after Gibson's publication of
the Remains, an unknown editor became possessed of a true
copy of our work. He calls himself " a less discreet person "
than Mr. Gibson, " who will e'en let the world make what
use of it they please." And so, in 1698, the *History of
Sacrilege* was published for the first time. For, though
Watt speaks of an edition of 1693, it is evident that he
must be mistaken, because Gibson's publication bears date
January, 1698; when, as we have seen, there is direct
evidence from Gibson that it was unpublished.

The original title-page concludes, " To which is added,
the Beginners of a Monastic Life, in Asia, Africa, and
Europe, by sir Roger Twisden, knt. and bar." Some few
copies have this treatise at the end of the volume; in some
it does not occur. As this pamphlet has but little connexion
with the work itself, and is possessed of but small merit
(other than its excellent spirit), its addition to the History
seems to point out some member of the family of Twisden as
the editor of the latter. Since that time there has been no
reprint of the work ; and, in consequence, it has become so
scarce that comparatively few have seen it, out of the many
who have heard of it.

It is more than four years since the present editors conceived the idea of reprinting the *History of Sacrilege ;* and
during that time they have constantly kept the subject before
them, and collected, during a somewhat multifarious course
of reading, whatever seemed to bear upon the point. The
work was sent to press, when they received from the rev.
F. E. Paget, rector of Elford, a large parcel of MS., pur-

porting to be a portion of sir Henry Spelman's original copy. They compared it with the authenticated MSS. of sir Henry preserved in the Public Library at Cambridge; among which is a glossary of contractions drawn up for the use of his children. The hand is undoubtedly the same. And, by a curious coincidence, there is an entry in the *History of Sacrilege*, dated November 11, 1624;—while a letter exists in the Public Library, written by sir Henry, of almost the same date;—and the paper appears to be the same.

Our MS. consists of eighty pages of small foolscap, and contains almost the whole of the chapters numbered by us V. and VI. Its verbal differences from the printed edition are numerous; and have been followed by us. This, and other considerations, prove that a transcript only was used in the first edition. Blanks are, in the printed copy, left for words that could not be deciphered; but which, in the original MS., are very clear.

We have also collated, so far as seemed necessary to our purpose, the MS. preserved in the Bodleian Library, and to which bishop Gibson refers. It is contained in three small folios, of fifty-four, sixty-four, and forty-five pages respectively. It is beautifully written, though in different hands, and is apparently that copy which Jeremy Stephens prepared for the press. There are directions to the printer as to type, and in one place, an insertion at the end of a chapter. A great part of this MS. is lost. It is observable that the last folio, which contains Spelman's observations on Norfolk, is entitled *Henricus Spelmannus de successu Sacrilegii,* as if a different book. All that is left a blank in the printed edition, is also a blank in this MS. In the same volume that contains it, though not immediately following it, is *The Beginners of a Monastic Life.*

On a careful consideration of the whole subject, we come to this conclusion: that our own MS., in sir Henry Spelman's hand, was never sent to press; that Jeremy Stephens's copy of this is that of which part remains in the Bodleian, and of which Gibson saw the rest elsewhere; and that there was a transcript of this last from which the edition of 1698 was printed. For between the Bodleian MS. and the printed text several verbal discrepancies exist. After all, it is extremely doubtful if part of the work be not irrecoverably lost. For example, a fragment preserved by Hearne, is given by us at p. 243, and more such may exist.

On applying ourselves to our task of editing, we found that it was one of unusual difficulty. The first chapters of the book were, indeed, in a tolerably correct and perfect state. But further on, sheets of the original MS. seem to have been misplaced ; irrelevant insertions constantly occur ; many paragraphs are, with slightly varied words, twice repeated; text and annotations are mixed in a most curious manner; there is no distinction of sections ; and Chapter I. is followed by Chapter VI. We have endeavoured to reduce this confused mass to some degree of order; though its very nature precluded the possibility of a perfect arrangement. The notes and references gave us little less trouble ; in some cases, when the fact which they were quoted to prove was notorious, and the author of inferior credit, we have entirely omitted them ; in the others, we have endeavoured to verify them, and to quote with greater minuteness of reference. The orthography of proper names was also a source of difficulty. Spelman, translating from authors of different ages, calls the same place, in the course of his history, by different names. We have followed him implicitly (except where he is evidently mistaken), even though his expression be singular or unusual. Thus, we have allowed him to speak of the " king of *Suessons* " and of " the chief city of *Avernia*," the latter name occurring in mediæval authors.

Of our own part in the work we have little to say. We have omitted no opportunity that lay open to us of acquiring correct information ; and, where the names of our informants do not appear, we nevertheless are in possession of them. We beg leave to thank all those who have replied to our inquiries as to the fate of those abbeys on which county historians are silent. And our gratitude is more particularly due to the rev. C. J. Lyon, the author of the *History of S. Andrew's*, to whom we owe all the facts connected with Scotch sacrilege, which we have been able to present to the reader; to the rev. F. E. Paget, for the MS. to which we have referred; to the rev. W. Scott, incumbent of Christ Church, Hoxton, London; to the rev. W. Wheeler, vicar of Old and New Shoreham ; and the rev. W. Rankin, priest at Old Deir, Scotland.

The publication of the *History of Sacrilege* does not seem to have attracted much attention, or to have exerted much influence. But Spelman's treatises, *De Non Temerandis Ecclesiis*, and on *Tithes*, and the MS. of this History, which seems to have been pretty widely read, appear to have been very useful. We reprint, from the beginning of the Oxford edition of the *De Non Temerandis Ecclesiis*, an account of some of its good effects, as taken out of the epistle to the *History of Tithes* :—

"If any demand what success the labours of this worthy knight found among the gentlemen of Norfolk, and other places, where he lived long in very great esteem, and publicly employed always by his prince and country in all the principal offices of dignity and credit, it is very observable to allege some particular testimonies worthy to be recorded to posterity, and with all honour to their na. os, who were persuaded presently upon the reading of this treatise, to restore and render back unto GOD what was due unto Him.

"And first, the worthy knight practised according to his own rule: for having an impropriation in his estate, viz., Middleton in Norfolk, he took a course to dispose of it for the augmentation of the vicarage, and also some addition to Congham, a small living near unto it: himself never put up any of the rent, but disposed of it by the assistance of a reverend divine, his neighbour, Mr. Thorowgood, to whom he gave power to augment the vicar's portion, which hath been performed carefully; and having a surplusage in his hands, he waits an opportunity to purchase the appropriation of Congham, to be added to the minister there, where himself is lord and patron.

"Next, sir Ralph Hare, knight, his ancient and worthy friend in that country, upon reading of this book offered to restore a good parsonage, which only he had in his estate, performing it presently, and procuring licence from the king; and also gave the perpetual advowson to S. John's College in Cambridge, that his heirs might not afterwards revoke his grant: wherein he was a treble benefactor to the Church: and the College hath deservedly honoured his memory with a monument of thankfulness in their library, and also wrote a respective letter of acknowledgment to this excellent knight, to whom they knew some part of the thanks to be due, for his pious advice and direction.

"Sir Roger Townsend, a religious and very learned knight, of great estate in that country, restored three impropriations to the Church, besides many singular expressions of great respect to the Clergy, having had a great part of his education together with sir John Spelman (a gentleman of incomparable worth), eldest son to sir Henry, and by his direction both attained great perfection and abilities.

"The like I have understood of others in that country, but cannot certainly relate their names, and all particulars at this present, that shire abounding with eminent gentlemen of singular deserts, piety, and learning, besides other ornaments, as Cambden observeth of them.

" In other parts divers have been moved with his reasons to make like restitution, whereof I will mention some : as sir William Dodington, knight, of Hampshire, a very religious gentleman, restored no less than six impropriations out of his own estate, to the full value of six hundred pounds yearly and more.

" Richard Knightly of Northamptonshire, lately deceased, restored two impropriations, Fansley [Fawsley] and Preston, being a gentleman much addicted to works of piety, charity, and advancement of learning, and showing great respect to the clergy.*

" The right honourable Baptist lord Hicks, viscount Cambden, besides many charitable works of great expense to hospitals and churches, as I find printed in a catalogue of them in the *Survey of London,* restored and purchased many impropriations.

" 1. He restored one in Pembrokeshire, which cost £460.

" 2. One in Northumberland, which cost £760.

" 3. One in Durham, which cost £366.

" 4. Another in Dorsetshire, which cost £760.

" He redeemed certain chantry lands, which cost £240. And gave pensions to two ministers, which cost £80. Besides legacies to several ministers.—The particulars more fully recited in the *Survey,* to which I refer, p. 761.

" Mrs. Ellen Gulston, relict of Theodore Gulston, doctor of physic, a very learned man, being possessed of the impropriate parsonage of Bardwell in Suffolk, did first procure from the king leave to annex the same to the vicarage, and to make it presentative ; and having formerly the donation of the vicarage, she gave them both thus annexed freely to S. John's College in Oxon., expressing many godly reasons in a pious letter of her grant, to advance the glory of GOD to her power, &c. Thus with devout prayers for a blessing from GOD upon those which should be chosen rectors there, she commendeth the deeds and conveyances of the parsonages for ever to the College.

" The right honourable lord Scudamore, viscount Sligo, hath very piously restored much to some vicarages in Herefordshire, whereof yet I cannot relate particulars fully.

" Divers colleges in Oxon., having been anciently possessed of impropriations, have of late years taken a course to reserve a good portion of their tithe-corn from their tenants, thereby to increase the vicars' maintenance : so that the best learned divines are willing to accept the livings, and yet the College

[* These livings are still in the gift of the Knightleys.—EDD.]

is not diminished in rents, but loseth only some part of their fine, when the tenants come to renew their leases.

"In particular, Christ-Church in Oxon. hath been very careful in this kind. Likewise New College, Magdalene College, and Queen's College, have done the like upon their impropriations, and some others have made augmentations also.

"Certain bishops have also done the like; as Dr. Morton, while he was bishop of Lichfield, did abate a good part of his fine to increase the portion of the minister in the vicarage of Pitchley in Northamptonshire, belonging to his bishopric, and so did his successor, Dr. Wright, for the vicarage of Towcester also in the same shire: which was very piously done, considering what great lands and manors were taken away from that bishopric among others, and some impropriations given in lieu of them.

"And while sir Henry Spelman lived at London, there came some unto him almost every term to consult with him, how they might legally restore and dispose of their impropriations to the benefit of the Church: to whom he gave advice as he was best able, according to their particular cases and inquiries; and there wanted not others, that thanked him for his book, promising that they would never purchase any such appropriate parsonages to augment their estates."

So that Clement Spelman might well say,—"although he was not so happy as with S. Peter at once to convert thousands, yet was he not with him so unsuccessful as to fish all night and catch nothing; for some were persuaded with what was written, neither can I say that others believed not; but rather think that, like the young man in the Gospel, they went heavy away, because they had too great possessions to restore."

It now only remains to mention the works to which we are principally indebted. Of county historians :—Ormerod's Cheshire; Hitchin's Cornwall; Jefferson's Cumberland; Polwhele's Devon; Prince's Worthies of Devon; Hutchins's Dorsetshire; Surtees's Durham; Morant's and Wright's Essex; Atkyns' Gloucestershire; Rudder's Gloucestershire; Chauncey's, Clutterbuck's, and Salmon's Hertfordshire; Hasted's Kent; Baines's Lancashire; Nichols' Leicestershire; Blomfield's Norfolk; Baker's Northamptonshire; Morton's Northamptonshire; Hodgson's Northumberland; Thoroton's Nottinghamshire; Blore's Rutlandshire; Collinson's Somersetshire; Shaw's Staffordshire; Manning's Surrey; Dallaway's Sussex; Dugdale's Warwickshire; sir

R. C. Hoare's Wiltshire; Nash's Worcestershire; Meyrick's
Cardiganshire; Jones's Brecknockshire. Of local histories,
principally, Stow's Survey; Aungier's Sion House; Ferrey's
Christchurch; Jacob's Faversham; Sketches of Moray (Edin-
burgh, 1839); Dunsford's Tiverton; Yate's Bury; Bullock's
Man; Plee's Jersey; Sharp's Hartlepool; Sturt's Gains-
borough; Miller's Doncaster; Young's Whitby; History of
Newbury (Speenhamland, 1839); Savage's Hundred of Car-
hampton; Hunter's Doncaster; Bennet's Tewkesbury;
Hay's Chichester; Hindewell's Scarborough; Pricket's
Bridlington; Clarke's Ipswich; Steinman's Croydon; May's
Evesham. Of French local histories: Blordier-Langlois,
Angers; Gerusez, Rheims; Dorville, Seez; Environs de
Paris (4 vols., Paris, 1839); Dusevil, Amiens; Guipon,
Nantes; Henry, Rousillon; Histoire de Toulouse (Paris,
4 vols., 1775); Benoit, Toul; Menard, Nismes; Simon,
Vendôme; Martin and Jacob, Soissons; Bernard, Forez.
Of works on monastic history: Dugdale's Monasticon, of
which we always quote the noble Oxford edition by Ban-
dinel; Tanner's Notitia Monastica, of which we quote
Nasmith's edition, Cambridge, 1787; Burton's Monasticon
Eboracense; Oliver's Monasteries of Devonshire; Taylor's
Monasteries of East Anglia. For genealogies, we have
principally trusted to Banks' Extinct Baronage, Burke's
Extinct Baronetcies, Debrett's Baronetage, Debrett's Peerage, with an occasional reference to Dugdale. Of auxiliary
works, such as Walker's Sufferings of the Clergy, Weever's
Funeral Monuments, and the like, it does not seem necessary
to speak. We should remark that we quote S. Ambrose
from the Paris edition of 1632; S. Jerome, from the Verona
edition of 1704; Calvin, from the Amsterdam edition of
1621; and Soto, from the Lyons edition of 1585.

We thus send out this history into the world, praying for
His blessing on it, to Whose glory it is intended to minister,
and Who is able, if He so will, to make it the means of
opening the eyes of sacrilegious persons to their danger, and
of procuring the restoration of defrauded right to His own
poor, and to His own Church.

Lent, 1846.

INTRODUCTORY ESSAY.

And it came to pass, when Ahab saw Elijah, that Ahab said unto him, Art thou he that troubleth Israel? And he answered, I have not troubled Israel, but thou and thy father's house, in that ye have forsaken the commandments of the Lord.

1 Kings xviii. 17, 18.

INTRODUCTORY ESSAY.

I.

AMONG the changes which the last five years have wrought in public opinion, none is more remarkable than the alteration of its tone with respect to Religious Houses, and their suppression in the sixteenth century. The lighter literature of the day, that weathercock which veers with every change of popular breath, amply proves the fact. Time was when the Dissolution of Monasteries was mentioned as an event, grievous indeed to the fanciful and the romantic, but to them only; an event full of solid benefits to the moral and social condition of England, and approving itself fully to the calm judgment of the man of reason. Now the case is altered. The suppression is lamented as an irreparable blow to literature, or an irrecoverable loss to the poor. Newspapers will rebuke the destroyer of a monastic ruin, not only as Vandalic in his taste, but as irreligious in his feelings. Novels, the surest indices of public opinion, no longer bring forward, as stock subjects of amusement and ridicule, an ignorant priest or a knavish monk. Travellers acknowledge—in a patronizing way, it may be, but still they do acknowledge, the inestimable benefits that the theory of monasticism engendered and encouraged.

And yet, even from the time of the Dissolution, there have always been those that have, in a greater or less measure, done justice to this wonderful system. "There are some, I hear," says Camden, "who take it ill that I have mentioned monasteries and their founders. I am sorry; but (not to give them any just offence) let them be angry if they will. Perhaps they would have it forgotten that our ancestors were, and we are, Christians; since there were never more certain indications and glorious monuments of Christian piety and devotion to GOD, than were those; nor were there any other seminaries for the propagation of the Christian religion and true literature; however it came to pass that in a loose age some rank weeds ran up too fast, which required rooting out." In the same strain, Somner and Lambard, and all the school of Elizabethan antiquaries, were wont to write. The noble labours of Dugdale, imperfect though they necessarily were, if compared with that fulness with which modern research has invested them, laid the foundation of the study of English monastic antiquities. Stevens, following in the steps of his master, brought to light no small portion of forgotten history; while Erdeswicke, and sir Simon Digge, and Prince, and Plot, and Atkyns, caught something of the same reverent spirit, and each, in his own way, added to the discoveries of his predecessors. Tanner, though a man of far inferior genius and research, popularized, to a certain degree, the labours of Dugdale, and (so miserably ignorant was the close of the seventeenth century) seems to have anticipated no other reward than contempt and neglect. Burton, in his *Monasticon Eboracense*, and Willis, in his *Mitred Abbeys*, are both deserving of high praise. Archdall has the credit of having attempted—though only attempted—a Monasticon for Ireland; and, in our own times, Taylor and Oliver have successfully laboured in elucidating the monastic antiquities of East Anglia and Devonshire.

Amidst these inquiries into the history of Religious Houses, and the investigations of county historians into the fate of their lands subsequently to the Dissolution, it was not easy to avoid noticing another fact. Let us give it in Southey's beautiful words :—

"The merciless destruction with which this violent transfer of property was accompanied, as it remains a lasting and ineffaceable reproach upon those who partook the plunder, or permitted it; so would it be a stain upon the national character, if men when they break loose from restraint, were not everywhere the same. Who can call to mind without grief and indignation, how many magnificent edifices were overthrown in this undistinguishing havoc!—Malmsbury, Battle, Waltham, Malvern, Lantony, Rievaulx, Fountains, Whalley, Kirkstall, and so many others ; the noblest works of architecture, and the most venerable monuments of antiquity : each the blessing of the surrounding country, and, collectively, the glory of this land ! Glastonbury, which was the most venerable of all, even less for its undoubted age, than for the circumstances connected with its history, and which in beauty and sublimity of structure was equalled by few, surpassed by none, was converted by Somerset, after it had been stript and dilapidated, into a manufactory, where refugee weavers, chiefly French and Walloons, were set up in their trade.

"The persons into whose hands the abbey-lands had passed, used their new property as ill as they had acquired it. The tenants were compelled to surrender the writings by which they held estates for two or three lives, at an easy rent, payable chiefly in produce; the rents were trebled and quadrupled, and the fines raised in even more enormous proportion—sometimes even twenty-fold. Nothing of the considerate superintendence which the monks had exercised, nothing of their liberal hospitality, was experienced from these 'step-lords,' as Latimer in his honest indignation denominated them. The same spirit which converted Glastonbury into a woollen-manufactory, depopulated whole domains for the purpose of converting them into sheep-farms ;

the tenants being turned out to beg, or rob, or starve. To such an extent was this inhuman system carried, that a manifest decrease of population appeared.

" The founders had denounced a perpetual curse upon anyone who should usurp, diminish, or injure its possessions. The good old historian, William of Malmsbury, when he recorded this, observed, that the denunciation had always up to this time been manifestly fulfilled, seeing no person had ever thus trespassed against it, without coming to disgrace, without the judgment of God. By pious Protestants, as well as Papists, the abbey-lands were believed to carry with them the curse, which their first donors imprecated upon all who should divest them from the purpose to which they were consecrated ; and in no instance was this opinion more accredited, than in that of the protector Somerset."

It is difficult to name with certainty the writer who first applied to the church-lands confiscated under Henry VIII. this great truth of the temporal punishment of sacrilege. But we probably shall not be far wrong if we award the honour to Dr. Feckenham, last abbot of S. Peter's, at Westminster. By that writer, in his *Caveat Emptor*, a solemn warning was given to the then possessors of abbey-lands, a warning to which if they had listened, well had it been for them and for their children !

Sir Henry Spelman, at a distance of seventy years, re-stated and historically proved the principle, Once the Church's, always the Church's. What his *History of Sacrilege* might have been, had its author been spared to complete and to arrange it, those may judge, who are acquainted with the works that were carried through the press under his own superintendence. But in the fragments which remain to us, and which Providence was pleased to preserve through so many dangers, we have all Spelman's learning, all his vehemence and fire, his noble ruggedness, his contempt of everything like style, his piling fact upon fact, regardless of the beauty, so he

THE HISTORY AND FATE OF SACRILEGE.

might add to the conspicuousness, of his monument
—and lastly, his indifference to the possibility of a
charge of personality, that most invaluable quality,
or rather constitution, of mind, in one who shall
arise as a reformer in an age calling for reform.

Sir Henry Spelman, in his *History of Sacrilege,*
seems to have contemplated but one species of argument, that *de facto,* in support of his thesis.   And
even here the task which he proposed to himself
would, even had it been completed, have been, as
regards our times, most imperfect.   Such a history
should now embrace eight principal epochs, which it
may be as well to particularize :—

I. The suppression of such alien priories, in the
reigns of Edward III. and Henry V., as were not
endenizened.   There were many extenuating circumstances in this outrage on the Church.   Several
of the endenizened priories had their wealth and
privileges increased ;—several new foundations, as
for example, Sion House, arose out of the revenues
of the old.   But it was the first opening of that
door by which afterwards such tyranny of sacrilegious rapine burst in on the Church.   On this
branch of our subject Spelman treats at some
length.

II. The ravages committed in Bohemia by John
Huss, Zisca and his partisans, the Taborites, and the
like sects.   Of these sir Henry says nothing ; and
with more interesting and more important themes for
our consideration, we have not thought it necessary
to dwell on this topic.

III. The popular destruction of monasteries
throughout the continent consequent on the spread
of the reformation.   On this, also, Spelman is
silent ; perhaps on account of the popular prejudice
which then prevailed in England in favour of Luther,
Calvin, and their disciples.

IV. The suppression of religious houses throughout Great Britain, and its consequences.   These may
be divided into six heads : 1. The dissolution of the

lesser monasteries; 2. Of the greater; 3. That of chantries, free chapels, and hospitals, together with the confiscation of church ornaments; 4. The dissolution of religious houses in Ireland; 5. In Scotland; and 6. The Elizabethan sacrilege of the forced exchanges of bishops' lands, and the appropriation of the revenues of sees kept vacant for that purpose.

V. The outrages committed by the Calvinists and, in some instances, by Catholicks, in France, antecedently to, and during, the wars of the League.

VI. The sale of cathedral-lands, and profanation, or destruction, of churches, during the Great Rebellion. *Walker's History of the Sufferings of the Clergy* is a store-house of information on this head.

VII. The suppression of monasteries throughout France at the period of the Revolution. On this point it is difficult to obtain a satisfactory answer to inquiries. County-histories, as such, are unknown in France; and histories of cities, which do not give the same scope for investigating the fate of sacrilege, too often have for their authors men deeply imbued with a rationalistic spirit, and regarding monasteries not with passive contempt only, but with active hatred.

VIII. The suppression of monasteries throughout Spain, Portugal, and their dominions, at the time that the Constitution was forced on their respective governments. This epoch is almost too near to have become, at present, matter of history.*

The historical argument, then, is, as we have said, that to which sir Henry Spelman almost entirely confines himself. And doubtless, to the common reader, it is by far the strongest. But the moral argument also is not without its weight; and it is that which is principally considered in the following essay. Our continuation and Appendices,

* To this enumeration might be added (were it of any importance for this Essay to do so) as IX.: The secularization of monasteries in Naples (1861); in the other provinces of the newly-formed kingdom of Italy (1866 and 1867); and in Rome itself (1873).—[E.]

n the contrary, aim at supplying historical details to the grand argument of our author's work.

We have, for several years, steadily kept our object in view; we have pursued it through numerous and formidable difficulties; it has been uppermost in our mind in every kind of reading; and while we are aware, that, from its very nature, our task is incapable of perfection, we are sadly conscious that it has fallen very far short of that which we had once hoped to make it.

But none, probably, who have not tried an investigation of the same kind for themselves, are aware of the difficulties by which it is attended. To trace the annals of one family, or the fate of one abbey-manor, the inquirer will be sent from the county historian to the genealogical table, from the Church Notes of Weever to the Extinct Baronetage, from the last volume of the Peerage to the ponderous tomes of Gough; he must consult manorial documents and party pamphlets, biographical memoirs and topographical descriptions; he must, at one moment, be deep in the worm-eaten folios of the *Germanicæ Historiæ Scriptores,* at the next, skim the flippant pages of the watering-place guide; he must plunge into the abyss of inquisitions and escheats, of taxations and augmentations; must glance into the modern tour, and grope in the Dictionary of Heraldry; he must copy the epitaph in the country church, and listen to the anecdotes of the country sexton. And frequently a long day's work will supply him with scarcely a single new fact for addition to his list. Nor has our labour ended here. We have applied by letter to the Incumbents of very many of the parishes which contained a religious house, of the first grantee or subsequent owners of which we could not otherwise gain information; and the result of that inquiry we have incorporated in our pages.

We do not mention these facts by way of boast; for in so noble a cause as the vindication to the

Church of that which is her own, who would not
very willingly spend and be spent? But we desire
to prove that in an undertaking which, without
accuracy, must be worse than valueless, no endeavour
on our part has been wanting to ensure truth.
That perfect correctness has been attained is morally
impossible. But this we believe—that in any de-
partures from it which may be discovered by the
local genealogist or topographer, we shall be found
to have understated our argument; and to have
deduced from it consequences less favourable to
ourselves than a fuller investigation might have
enabled us to draw.

II.

WE are about, then, to attempt a proof of the following thesis :—

Property, consecrated to GOD *in the service of His Church, has generally, when alienated to secular purposes, brought misfortune on its possessors; whether by strange accidents, by violent deaths, by loss of wealth, or, and that chiefly, by failure of heirs male; and such property hardly ever continues long in one family.*

It is plain, that to dwell on the above statement at length, would require a volume, instead of a short introductory essay. We can only throw out a few hints, which our readers must follow out for themselves. We shall attempt to prove our thesis thus :—

I. *À priori.*
    1. By the analogy of Scripture.
    2. By the general consent of all nations.
    3. From the curse actually pronounced on Church-spoilers.
    4. From the very nature of the crime.

II. *De facto*, inductively.
    1. In general history.
    2. More especially,—as a more practical subject of inquiry,—in England; where sacrilege has been followed, in the family of the perpetrator, by
        ɪ. Violent deaths.

    II.   Strange and unusual accidents.
    III. The commission of detestable crimes.
    IV. Great poverty.
    V.   Unnatural hatred and domestic variance.
    VI. Rapid passing of estates.
    VII. Failure of issue, especially of heirs male, and consequent extinction of families.

III. Statistically.

The same things cannot be predicated of families not involved in sacrilege.

IV. *De facto*, deductively.

By a consideration of the most remarkable and signal judgments which English history records, it will be found that they almost universally have occurred in sacrilegious families.

V. From the testimony,
    1. Of enemies.
    2. Of friends.

We shall thence proceed to a consideration of the objections, that
    1. The suppression of abbeys was not sacrilege.
    2. The rule of punishment is not universal.
    3. The Church, at various times, has allowed of alienations.
    4. More especially during the English reformation.
    5. The prosperity of England has never been greater than since the Dissolution.
    6. The whole inquiry is uncharitable.

I. The argument *à priori*.

1. It is likely, from the analogy of Scripture, that, even in this world, a curse will attach itself to Sacrilege.

Sir Henry Spelman has so ably pointed out the temporal punishment which, in Scripture History has been allotted to the sin of sacrilege, that we need not dwell long on this branch of our subject. He has, however, omitted to point out the remarkable analogy between the kind of fate which befel sacrilegious persons among the Jews, and that which we assert to have befallen similar offenders in our own country, and in our own times.

That there is any other than an arbitrary connection between failure of heirs male and the commission of sacrilege might, at first sight, be denied. We hope in a short time to prove the contrary. At present, however, we are only concerned to remark, that this same connection cannot be denied to exist in Holy Scripture.

To take, for example, the instance of the destruction of the roll by Jehoiakim, one of the most daring acts of sacrilege that was ever committed. The sentence pronounced against him is this:—"Write ye this man childless, a man that shall not prosper in his days." Now, had we to describe, in a few brief words, the fate of those who have sacrilegiously meddled with GOD's property in this land, we could hardly choose any expression more strikingly and exactly applicable to it.

Again, the rebuilding of Bethel was an express act of sacrilege. How was it punished? By the death of the builder's children. "He laid the foundation thereof in Abiram his first-born, and set up the gates thereof in his youngest son Segub;" his other children dying in the intermediate time.

Jeroboam, to take another instance, sacrilegiously erected an altar at Bethel and at Dan;—made priests of the lowest of the people, and appointed a new feast,—a parody on those which all Israel were commanded to attend at Jerusalem. What follows? "This thing," says Holy Scripture, "became sin unto the *house* of Jeroboam, even to cut it off, and to destroy it from the face of the earth." And accordingly, Abijah the eldest, and promising, son of that monarch was almost immediately taken from the world, and the rest of his posterity utterly destroyed by Baasha.

Again, in the sacrilegious attempt of Korah, from which so many remarkable inferences may be drawn, one of the most striking is the gradation, so to speak, of punishment, wherewith the various degrees of sacrilege in the conspirators was punished. All were guilty of the sacrilege; and all, accordingly, swallowed up in an unheard-of and most fearful manner. Nevertheless, the sin of the three rebels was not equal. Korah was of the tribe of Levi, and therefore, in a manner, invested with a minor ecclesiastical dignity:—Dathan and Abiram were of the tribe of Reuben, and were completely without part or lot in the matter. The crime, therefore, of the latter was greater than that of the former; and their punishment was proportionably heavier. Their families were utterly destroyed by the visitation in which they themselves perished; whereas, we are expressly told,—Notwithstanding the children of Korah died not. (Numbers xxvi. 11.)

To the same purpose, also, is the story of Achan. It was not enough that his own death should expiate his appropriation of the accursed possessions of Jericho; his sons and his daughters were stoned together with him in the valley of Achor. On the other hand, other offences committed during the immediate theocracy of the Jews were not thus punished; the father died for his own sin; but the family were spared.

Solomon is, in his peculiar way, a remarkable instance of the same thing. As GOD had promised that the Messiah was to descend from David, and through that son, a total failure of male heirs, notwithstanding his sacrilegious erection of idol temples and shrines in places holy to GOD, was in this case impossible. But, by his seven hundred wives and three hundred concubines, he left but one son; and in that son the better part of his kingdom was lost.

In like manner, Gideon, after his victories, made an ephod from the spoils of the Midianites, and placed it in his native city Ophrah. Thither all Israel " went a whoring after it," that is, sought it with idolatrous worship. Here, then, partly through ignorance, partly through thoughtlessness, was an act of sacrilege committed by Gideon; and it " became a snare "—not to him only, which it would have been natural to expect, but also—as it is particularly recorded—" *to his house.*" Hence we are justified in regarding the destruction of all his seventy sons, except the youngest, by their illegitimate brother, as a judgment for this sacrilege.

The sons of Eli afford an example of the same thing. They were guilty of sacrilege in two, if not in more, ways; in appropriating to themselves that part of the sacrifices which more immediately belonged to GOD; and in their acts of fornication committed within the precincts of the tabernacle. " There shall not be an old man *in thine house* for ever," was the sentence pronounced, and it was followed by the total extinction of the sacrilegious family.

Saul, again, is proposed as a warning to us in the commission of four sacrilegious acts. He usurped the priest's office in offering the sacrifice which it was the intention of Samuel to offer; he spared the Amalekites, who were devoted by GOD to destruction; he commanded a general massacre of the priests; and he attempted the destruction of the Gibeonites. For this he was in a remarkable way punished in his children and posterity. First, three of his sons were slain with himself on Mount Gilboa. Mephibosheth, his grandson, from an accident in infancy, was a cripple to the end of his days. Ishbosheth, another son of Saul, was murdered by two of his own servants; and finally, seven of his other sons were slain, that GOD might be appeased in the time of the great famine.

These instances,—and more might be given,—are perhaps sufficient to prove the fact that the crime of

Sacrilege is, in Scripture History, visited on the family of the original perpetrator.

In like manner, that virtue which is the opposite of sacrilege, namely, giving to GOD that which has been devoted to Him, is rewarded in Scripture with long continuance of posterity. Idolaters were, by the Divine command, devoted to death ; and the tribe of Levi, by executing that command, and slaying, without pity, the worshippers of the golden calf, were established in Israel. So when Phinehas had slain Zimri and Cosbi, the reward bestowed on him was the promise of the long continuance of his posterity in the priesthood. Again, the purpose of David to build the temple was rewarded by the declaration, " Thine house and thy kingdom shall be established for ever before Me." In like manner, disobedience to parents, a sin which approaches in its nature to that of sacrilege, is similarly punished ; as the signal obedience of the Rechabites to a remote ancestor is illustriously rewarded by a continuance of their descendants to the present day ; and the fifth commandment is honoured by the annexation of a temporal promise.

We see but one reply which can be made to these arguments ; and that we will next proceed to consider.

It was likely, it may be said, that in an immediate Theocracy GOD should supernaturally interfere to punish the sacrilegious criminal ; but no argument can be drawn from a state altogether in a miraculous position.

It is true that in certain respects, miraculous interferences were to be expected in the Jewish state, such as it would be vain and presumptuous to look for now. But, on the whole, the difference was by no means so great as to preclude analogy. Crimes may be divided into those only known to, and therefore only punishable by, GOD; and those manifest to, and so cognizable by, man. In the former class, we may allow that GOD, under the Old Testament dispensation, did interfere in a way peculiar to that dispensation. The uncircumcised soul was to be cut off from his people; a fact only known to the party concerned and for disobedience in which he was unamenable to human laws. Yet, in many cases, GOD, in a remarkable manner, refrained from interfering with human inquiry. In the case of the man found dead, when the elders had used their utmost endeavours to discover the guilty person, no supernatural revelation followed, and they were compelled to rest content with a prayer that the land might be freed from blood-guiltiness. Why then should we imagine, that if, in a case like this, GOD would not miraculously interfere, His punishments of Sacrilege are to be considered miraculous, and peculiar to His own people?

Again, these punishments continued long after the Theocracy ceased. Antiochus Epiphanes, Heliodorus, and Lysimachus, were as notoriously visited as Uzziah or Korah.

And should it be urged that temporal rewards and punishments formed the groundwork of the Jewish polity, we confess that this argument appears to us vastly overstated. If we allow that they occupied a more prominent situation than they hold under the Christian dispensation, we allow enough. Constantly, and throughout the whole range of the Old Testament, there are references and allusions to a higher system of punishment and recompense. It is the wicked who "prosper in the world," whose "eyes swell out with fatness," who "have wealth at their desire;" it is to the righteous, and it is as a promise, not a threat, that the declaration is made, "Though the LORD give thee bread of affliction and the water of affliction, yet shall not thy teachers be removed into a corner any more;" it is the ungodly who are seen "in great power, and flourishing like a green bay tree;" to "keep innocency," and to "do the thing that is right, shall bring a man," not temporal prosperity, but "peace *at the last.*" In the same manner we read of "a place and a name better than of sons and daughters;" though that was the highest temporal blessing to a Jewish mind.

Again,—it seems hardly necessary to show that sudden and unusual accidents are often, in Scripture History, at once sent to avenge sacrilegious guilt. Korah's case is, as it were, a pattern and a type of such crime and such punishment. It had been enough, one might have thought, had these offenders perished, even had it been by an usual and customary ending. But no. "If these men die the death of all men, or if they be visited after the visitation of all men, then the Lord hath not sent me; but if the Lord make a new thing, ... then ye shall understand that these men have provoked the Lord." So the men of Bethshemesh, that sacrilegiously looked into the ark, were at once smitten with a sudden and hitherto unknown disease; just as the Philistines had previously been for its sacrilegious detention in a foreign land. For a similar offence, though with a purer intention, Uzzah was struck dead on the spot. Uzziah, who intruded into the temple, with the design of burning incense on the altar of incense, was smitten with leprosy in the act, and remained till the day of his death a miserable leper. Belshazzar, again, is a perpetual monument of the same fate. Doubtless he had often given himself up to the indulgence of his own heart's lusts; he had often praised the gods of gold and of silver, of brass, of iron, of wood, and of stone; he had often gloried in his own wealth and honours, and reviled the children of the captivity. But one fatal night, he sent for the vessels that had been taken in the sack of the temple; that he, his wives, and his concubines might drink therein. *In that same hour* he was weighed in the balance, and found wanting; in that *same hour* God numbered his kingdom, and finished it. And so ends the record of his life. " In that night was Belshazzar, the king of the Chaldæans, slain."

Nor is the case different in the New Testament. The destruction of Ananias and Sapphira was signal, sudden, miraculous. The punishment of Elymas was no less wonderful. That of Simon Magus, though not recorded in the Canon of Scripture, was a fitting close for him who thought the gift of GOD purchasable by money.

If we leave examples, and attend to the practical teaching of the Scripture, the case is the same:— " O my GOD," exclaims the Royal Prophet, " make them like unto a wheel, and as the stubble before the wind !—Make them and their princes like Oreb and Zeb : yea, make all their princes like as Zeba and Salmana ; who say, Let us take to ourselves the houses of GOD in possession." And doubtless there was something more peculiarly sacrilegious in the attempt of these Midianitish invaders, which rendered the denunciation of the Psalmist particularly applicable to these cases. In like manner the prophecy of Haggai is a solemn warning against negative sacrilege; and that of Malachi might almost be applied to the condition of England at this time. " Will a man rob GOD ? Yet ye have robbed Me. But ye say, Wherein have we robbed Thee ? In tithes and offerings. Ye are cursed with a curse ; for ye have robbed me, even this whole nation."

Another curious analogy may be, though less decidedly, traced out, between a popular belief of our own day, and a similar belief among the Jews, sanctioned by the express authority of Scripture. It is well known that abbeys, ruined churches, and desecrated chapels, are almost universally held to bring misfortune on their possessors.* A like persuasion existed among the Jews with respect

---

* We experienced a curious proof of the truth of this statement not long ago. One of the Editors of this work being in Yorkshire, observed, near the house where he was staying, an ancient building, now used as a stable. In answer to his inquiry what it was, " That, sir," replied a poor man, " was a chapel once on a time ; now it is Mr. ——'s stable ; but it is an odd thing that the horses there are never lucky."

to Jericho, the city founded by Sacrilege. "The water was naught;" and though the situation of the town was pleasant, it was cursed with "death," *i.e.* unusual mortality, and barren land. And the supernatural curse was supernaturally removed. And, as an opposite instance, the mere presence of the Ark, though neither intended for, nor (it would seem) particularly desired by, Obed-edom, brought a blessing on his house.

These few remarks are to be taken in conjunction with, and as supplementary to, those of sir Henry Spelman, with reference to the scriptural testimony against Sacrilege. We conclude then that from the analogy of Scripture, as displayed both under the Jewish and under the Christian dispensations, the crime of Sacrilege may be expected to be followed by temporal punishment. We now proceed to the next branch of our argument.

I.—2. It is likely, from the general consent of all nations, that a temporal punishment would attach itself to sacrilege.

It is not improbable that, on a perusal of sir Henry Spelman's work, the reader may be induced to complain of the great space which he devotes to a consideration of heathen sacrilege. And, perhaps, if the mere fact, that profanation of idol temples and impiety towards idols themselves has usually been punished in this world, were all that we could gather from the recital, this complaint would be just. But the thing that is of real importance is this; not whether pagan sacrileges were divinely and illustriously punished; but whether, in pagan times, sacrilege were believed to be so punished. The former consideration is not unimportant in itself, and is capable of yielding an *à fortiori* argument in defence of our own·position; but the latter is of unspeakable moment in the inquiry.

An universal belief, held at all times, by all nations, under all religions, must, to say the least, have its foundation in truth. The *quod semper*, *quod ubique*, *quod ab omnibus*, is true in the world as well as in the Church. In the fate of Pompey, Marcus Crassus, and Antiochus Epiphanes, *we* may discern the punishment of their sacrilegious acts. But how infinitely is our argument strengthened when we can show that the very heathen took the same view of the subject!

If by writers on the evidences of Christianity the consent of all nations in the belief of a GOD has been thought a powerful argument, from the same unanimous voice we may derive some confirmation for our own position. From the beginning Sacrilege has been held to be pursued by an avenging Fury. Prometheus sacrilegiously stole fire from heaven; and his reward was the rock and the chain, and the ever-growing vitals, and the ever-gnawing vulture. When the poet is accounting for the destruction of the companions of Ulysses, it is by their sacrilege :—

Αὐτῶν γὰρ σφετέρῃσιν ἀτασθαλίῃσιν ὄλοντο
Νήπιοι, οἳ κατὰ βοῦς ὑπερίονος Ἠελίοιο
Ἤσθιον· αὐτὰρ ὁ τοῖσιν ἀφείλετο νόστιμον ἦμαρ.

Orestes was guilty of sacrilegious murder; and the shade of his mother hunted him from land to land, till in the temple of the Eumenides he found an asylum. If we descend to historical times, the instances of Xerxes, and Himilco, and Cambyses, and Dionysius, and Brennus, and Agathocles, and Fulvius Flaccus, and Onomarchus, and Phayllus, are standing witnesses on our side. Three other instances are not mentioned by Spelman. Cleomenes of Sparta had, in an invasion of Attica, injured a temple and its sacred precinct; he had burnt a sacred grove in Argos; and had, by sacrilegious fraud, obtained a partial response at Delphi. To these crimes his fate was, by the voice of Greece, attributed. He became frenzied, and, deliberately cut himself piecemeal. Again, Megacles had tempted the followers of Cylon

from the temple of Athene by the promise of
quarter. Then, when he had them in his power,
he butchered them in cold blood. He was shunned
as an accursed man; his posterity was avoided as
infamous; the plague spot of sacrilege clung to him
and his for ever. Peisistratus, though unprincipled
and irreligious, preferred running the risk of losing
his tyranny, to mixing his blood, in the fourth
generation, with that of an accursed house. And
thus, too, the Ionians, when hardest pressed by the
Persian powers, would not apply the treasures of
the gods to the maintenance of human liberty. And,
if from facts we come to writings, the same principle
dictated the law, *Sacrum sacrove datum qui dempserit
rapueritve, parricida esto;* and the proverb, *Aurum
Tolosanum,* applied to unfortunate property.

The expression in Acts xix. 37, οὔτε ἱεροσύλους,
οὔτε βλασφημοῦντας τὴν θεὰν, as though these were the
worst of crimes, points out the general pagan feeling on this subject. Lucian, too, whose writings
are the most popular and dramatic records of the cur-
rent sentiment and actual life of heathenism, abounds
with allusions to the abhorrence entertained for
Sacrilege. In nearly twenty passages he uses ἱεροσυλία and its cognates, as proverbially equivalent to
the blackest sin. In the two rhetorical declamations,
the Phalaris Prior et Alter (vol. ii. pp. 187-207,
ed. Heinstech.), much curious matter may be found
on the sin of Sacrilege; and in one place, speaking
of the possible rejection of an offering at Delphi,
the orator is made to say—ἀνάθημα αὖθις ἀποπέμ-
πειν, ἀνόσιον ἤδη εἶναι νομίζω· μᾶλλον δὲ, οὐδ' ὑπερβολὴν
ἀσεβείας ἀπολελοιπέναι· οὐδὲν γάρ 'ἀλλ' ἢ ἱεροσυλία τὸ πρᾶγμά
ἐστι. (Phalar. Alt. 2.) This is remarkable as the ordinary and natural topic which must suggest itself
to any orator, for the pieces on Phalaris are mere
fictitious exercises in sophistical rhetoric, even in
the judgment of Lucian, who disbelieved all religion.
" The Voltaire of Paganism," as he has been neatly
called, when seeking for his most pointed stigma,

cannot get beyond calling an action—Sacrilege (ἱεροσυλία.)

It was the same feeling which dictated the care of the dead, and the sanctity of cemeteries. Injury to the departed, was sacrilege against the infernal gods. The most contemptuous, the most insulting epithet that the Latin language afforded, was that applied to him who snatched from the tomb the viands which friends had there provided for the spirit of the departed. And the plot of that most perfect of Grecian dramas, the *Antigone* of Sophocles, turns on the same subject;— that tragedy is the tragedy of Sacrilege.

And the same belief has existed in barbarous as well as in civilized nations. Let one instance suffice. Nobunanga,* who, towards the close of the sixteenth century, was the most powerful prince in Japan, had spread the terror of his arms far and wide, had subjugated one kingdom after another, had become, so to speak, feudal head of the whole empire. In an evil hour he desired to be adored as. a god. He reared a magnificent temple to his own honour; he set therein a statue of himself; he commanded, under the severest temporal and eternal penalties, that his subjects, on an appointed day, should come and worship the image. The number of those that came up was prodigious. The city overflowed. Multitudes abode in tents in the surrounding country; and multitudes in the vessels that rode on a neighbouring lake. The first that worshipped the statue was the eldest son of Nobunanga. A few days afterwards, a conspiracy was formed against this hitherto invincible monarch; and he, and this eldest son, were burnt alive in their own palace. And this was regarded as the just punishment of one who was guilty of sacrilege in its highest sense.

And if the case were thus among heathens, how much more strong must the feeling have been among Christians! We know that Charles Martel, both in his life and in his end, was considered a memorable

* Crasset, L'Eglise du Japon, i. 485-487.

warning of the recompense of sacrilege. "He gave
the holy right of tithes* to military men, and permitted his soldiers to sweep away and to plunder
things sacred with things profane, more than the
Visigoths ever did; the sees of Lyons and Vienne
were for many years deprived of their bishops, the
one dying by military violence, the other driven into
a monastery." After the death of this prince, the
great defender, be it remembered, of the Church
against the Saracens, "S. Eucherius, bishop of
Orleans, being warned thereof in a vision, took
Fulrade, abbot of S. Denys, to Martel's tomb, where
he had been but lately buried; and they found only
a serpent in the grave, otherwise empty, and no
marks of a human body there, but all within black,
as if it had been burnt." We may notice that this
popular belief is more to our purpose, if false, than
it would be if true.

Again, we know that at the Reformation country
workmen would not, in many instances, give their
assistance in pulling down consecrated buildings :—
hardened villains from London accompanied the con-
tractor, and completed the work. In one instance,—
that of the Priory of the Holy Trinity, in the ward
of Aldgate,—"church and steeple were proffered to
whomsoever would take it down and carry it from
the ground, but no man would undertake the offer."†
We have Spelman's authority,—(who lived, be it
remembered, as near to the time of the Dissolution,
as we to that of the French Revolution),—that for
many years subsequently to the suppression, the
churches pertaining to monasteries were not inhabited; and, indeed, to this day there seems an
objection against this particular species of Sacrilege.
Stukeley in his *Itinerarium Curiosum* (Iter vi.),
speaking of Glastonbury, informs us that in his time
he observed frequent instances of the townsmen

* Paulus Æmilius, Vita Chilperici, iii. 67, ap. Johnston's As-
surance.
† Stow's Survey, p. 58 (fol. ed.).

being generally afraid to purchase any of the ruins
of the Abbey, as thinking that an unlucky fate
attends the family when these materials are used;
and they told him many stories and particular
instances of it; others that were but half religious
would venture to build stables and outhouses therewith, but by no means any part of the dwelling-
house.   It is well known, that for some time after
the late Dissolution of Monasteries in Spain and
Portugal, it was difficult, in many instances, to find
a purchaser for church-lands.

And even now, after centuries of legalized sacrilege, a belief that it never thrives is, as we have
hinted, strong among our peasantry.   Abbey sites
are "unlucky;" Abbey buildings are haunted; it is
"unfortunate" to have anything to do with them;
they will not "stick by" any family.   On the supposition that the hypothesis which we are supporting
is ungrounded and superstitious, how impossible is
it, and must it remain, to account for this general
belief!   Allow it to be the voice of GOD, and it
ceases to be inexplicable.   Therefore we conclude,
with S. Ambrose: That which is above nature proceeds from the Author of Nature.

I.—3. It is likely from a consideration of the
curse pronounced on church spoilers, that Sacrilege
would be attended by temporal punishment.

It is well known that property, given to the Church,
was, at its dedication, guarded by the imprecation of
the most fearful calamities and ruin to such as should
violate or alienate it.   Specimens of this solemn
curse we have given in Appendix IV.   The question,
however, arises, 1. Whether those who denounced
it had any right thus to invoke GOD's vengeance:
and, 2. Whether the curse itself was a vain demon-
stration of impotence,—or a living, acting thing,
that had power to make itself felt long after its pro-
nouncers had mouldered in the grave.

It cannot be denied that men have the power of

binding their unborn descendants to that, of which possibly, could they have had a voice in the matter, they would have disapproved. The whole theory of the Church is based on this right. The unconscious child enters into a covenant at the Font; and is as much bound by it as if he had set his hand and seal to it of his own free accord. Civil polity, indeed, without such a right acknowledged, could not exist: the deed of the father binds the son, and oftentimes, remote descendants. In Scripture History there are innumerable instances of this: not only in things immediately appointed by GOD, as when Abraham, for himself and his posterity, entered into the Covenant of Circumcision, or Israel bound themselves and their children to serve the LORD at Shechem:— but also in matters that were perfectly optional, as when the princes engaged to take the Gibeonites under their protection. A violation of this compact, nearly four hundred years after, by Saul, led to a three years' famine, only to be ended by the death of seven sons of that monarch.

In like manner, it has been held that a simple command is sufficient to bind the descendants of him by whom it was given. The direction of Jonadab the son of Rechab would, in itself, appear unwise; yet obedience to it was in the highest degree rewarded. Now such a curse as that now under consideration is only a command with the denunciation of vengeance to the transgressors of that command. And therefore a curse pronounced by one who had authority to order that, the disobeying of which he thus threatened, has oftentimes produced fearful effects. Joshua pronounced a curse on the rebuilders of Jericho: Hiel the Beth-elite defied it: his eldest son died when the foundation was laid: his youngest when the gates were set up. But this, it may be said, was the immediate effect of Divine Inspiration. We will therefore take an instance from the history of Saul, which can in no wise be said to have been so. Engaged in pursuit of the Philistines,

and fearing that the tempation of plunder might
draw off his army from the destruction of their enemies, he denounced a curse on all who should taste
of food till the evening.   The command would have
been preposterous; the curse might almost have
been pronounced blasphemous.   Did it take effect
or not?   Jonathan, knowing nothing of the matter,
by tasting a little honey, violated his father's commands.   On being informed of the circumstance, he
dwelt on the unreasonableness of the royal edict,
and appears to have felt no further uneasiness.   But
that night the oracle of GOD would return no answer.
There was guilt in the camp; whose, must be determined by lot.   And by lot, Jonathan was pointed out
as he whose offence had precluded the manifestation
of the Divine Will to the priest.*

Again, for the same reason the adjuration was
allowed, in the Jewish courts (and under the title
of the *question ex officio* it long remained in our
own), as a last resort for the discovery of the truth.
To adjure a person, implies a curse in case of refusal.
And our Blessed LORD's conduct with respect to
this adjuration is very remarkable.   Accused of
many things, He answered nothing.   But when the
high priest, *ex officio*, said, " I adjure Thee by the
Living GOD, that Thou tell us whether Thou be the
CHRIST, the SON of GOD," He at once replied.   And
that in this action He proved His obedience to
the civil law of the Jews, is plain from a comparison of the original statute,—though somewhat
unintelligible in our translation : " If a soul sin, and
hear the voice of swearing, and is a witness, whether
he hath seen or known it; and he do not utter it,
then he shall bear his iniquity."   And, in Solomon's

* In the same manner, the story of Micah is well worthy our
consideration.   His mother had devoted eleven hundred shekels
of silver to the formation of two images,—a capital crime; yet
the curse which she pronounced against those who had deprived
her of it, operated to the ruin of her son's property, and almost to
the loss of his life.

dedication-prayer, the principle is the same : " If any man trespass against his neighbour, and an oath be laid upon him to cause him to swear, and the oath come before Thine altar in this house : then hear Thou in heaven, and do, and judge Thy servants, condemning the wicked."

It would appear, then, that when a man has a right to command, he has a right to enforce that command with a curse. And in a certain and vague sense, this is true; as true, that is, as it would be to say, that what a man has a right to assert, he has a right to swear. Three conditions are required to make both an oath and a curse lawful. In the former there must be perfect accuracy in the statement, great weight in the subject-matter—and an impossibility of discovering the truth by any other method. In the latter there must be full authority in the denouncer, deep importance in that which is denounced, and an impossibility of employing any other method of guarding against its violation.

These conditions, when perfectly fulfilled, render a curse, by whomsoever pronounced, fearful indeed. It is the first which gives such terror to that of a parent, the last to that of a widow or orphan.

But, to render a curse entirely formidable, another element is yet wanting. It is part of the priest's office to bless ; and though the blessing of the poor and fatherless is valuable, a peculiar dignity is attached to that pronounced by sacerdotal lips. So it is with a curse. Nay, in the latter case the intervention of a priest is even more essential than in the former. The act of blessing is, in itself, apart from other considerations, salutary to the mind; the act of cursing, under the same restrictions, the reverse. It is, therefore, more essential that so fearful a weapon should be entrusted to hands that will use it aright, and that will not prostitute, to purposes of mere revenge, that which it is unlawful to use in such a way.

All these elements meet in the curse pronounced

on the violators of Church property.   The authority
of the denouncer; legally unquestioned; morally
indubitable; sacerdotally complete.   The importance of the thing guarded; a means of performing
the service of GOD, and accomplishing the salvation
of souls.   The impossibility of any other defence;
for how can a man protect a donation for centuries
to come?

We perceive that we shall be thought to have
proved too much.   Then, it will be replied, a man
has a right to preserve property in his own family,
by denouncing a curse on those who shall wrest it
from his descendants; and the curse will in this case
be less formidable than in the other, only by how
much the continuance of property to the rightful
heirs is of less importance than its continuance to
the Church.

We reply, that our first condition is not fulfilled.
A man has but a life interest in his estate.   Over its
possession after his death he has no right; therefore, he has no right to threaten those that shall
injure it, because they have done him no wrong.
He must let that alone for ever.   His posterity
must defend themselves.   The curse of the then
possessor may be formidable; not that of one who
is not possessor.

But, with respect to Church property, the case is
different.   The Church is a corporation, and a corporation never dies.   The durability of her claim
to any given property is commensurate with her
existence, and that is for ever.   Her right, therefore, of defending that property exists also for ever;
because through her, it is offered to Him of Whom,
through all ages, "it is witnessed that He liveth."

It may, however, be asserted, that cursing is a
weapon, the use of which is altogether forbidden.
" Bless them that persecute you; bless, and curse
not."

If we are to take this command literally, at all
times, and under all circumstances, we are bound to

take similar commands in an equally literal sense.
Thus we are bound not to resist an action at law;
not to defend ourselves from personal injury; and
to yield all that, and more than, an oppressor should
demand from us. That the holiest of men have
pronounced curses on their own, and on GOD's
enemies, we know; nay, we find a command to do
so.   " Curse ye Meroz, said the Angel of the LORD,
curse ye bitterly the inhabitants thereof."

And in what sense are we to receive the formula-
ries of cursing delivered to us in that most awful of
Psalms, the hundred and ninth?   No one, surely,
will assert,—it were fearful to think it,—that they
were the mere expressions of anger and hatred on
the part of the Psalmist. If he speaks in his own
person, his words must be received in a modified and
conventional sense.   But that they have a far wider
range than this, is expressly testified by S. Peter, who
applies the imprecation, "his bishopric let another
man take," to the traitor Judas.   David is, undoubtedly, to be regarded as speaking in the person
of the Church; and vindicating to her that solemn
right which is indeed hers.   That the English Church
still claims this function is amply proved by the
Commination Service.

Again, it is remarkable that three of the most
solemn curses of Scripture are pronounced on crimes
that had in them the nature of Sacrilege. Noah was
not only the father of the human race, but (as under
the Patriarchal dispensation) GOD's High Priest and
Vicegerent upon earth. An insult offered to him was
sacrilege.   And the words follow,—Cursed be
Canaan : a servant of servants shall he be unto his
brethren.—In like manner, Elisha, the LORD's Prophet, was mocked by the children of Bethel. On his
curse there came two she-bears out of the wood, and
tore forty and two children of them. And Jeremiah's
curse on the man that putteth his trust in man, is
similar in its tendency and its nature.

We are bound therefore to conclude that cursing,

in the spirit of revenge, or on an unworthy occasion, is forbidden by our LORD. And if such an interpretation should seem an explaining away of His words, we would observe that His injunctions against cursing are not stronger than those against swearing. Nay : they are not so strong. It is written, Swear not at all; it is nowhere written, Curse not at all. And yet by the general consent of the Church, the command against swearing is to be received in a modified sense. We are not to swear unnecessarily, profanely, lightly, thoughtlessly ; " but a man may swear when the Magistrate requireth, in a cause of faith and charity."

But granting that which we deny; granting that a curse cannot be pronounced without sin : we yet assert that an imprecation, thus pronounced, may bring misery on those against whom it is directed. For this is in complete analogy with the rest of GOD's dealings with mankind. Thou shalt do no murder, is the command. Yet if we disobey it, what then ? GOD will not interfere with a miracle to protect the life of an enemy. Speak every man the truth with his neighbour, is the injunction : yet GOD will often permit the success of a lie. Even perjury has frequently gone down to the grave unpunished.

It is therefore more than probable that, when an oppressed man, in the bitterness of his soul, prays that his oppressor may be destroyed, GOD will hear that prayer, even though it may not have been offered without sin. The man that is thus cursed meets but with his due, even should he that curses overstep his right.

Hence we conclude that the curse pronounced by the founders of Abbeys was in itself justifiable, in its effects likely to be terrible ; and that, even could it not have been pronounced without sin, its operation might still be effectual to the ruin of those on whom it was imprecated.

I.—4. It is likely, from the nature of the crime,

that temporal punishment would attach itself to Sacrilege.

It will be found, on a consideration of God's dealings with His creatures, that a certain analogy exists between crime and punishment. Not only is suffering proportioned to guilt, but the kind of each is similar. In a variety of instances, God's justice has shown itself to be strikingly retributive : and, as offenders have sinned, so have they been requited. Disobedience to parents is chastised by disobedience in children; drunkenness, and other sensual sins, which reduce a man to the level of a brute, are followed by the enfeeblement or deprivation of that intellect which raised him above the brutes : unbridled indulgence to the passions, by their acquiring an unbridled tyranny over the soul,—and the self-willed man becomes the madman. And such is the case in a thousand other instances.

The course of history reads us no other lesson. The builders of Babel sought to make themselves illustrious as an united company of fellow warriors ; and illustriously were they scattered over the face of the whole earth. Adonibezek, that had mutilated three score and ten kings, was himself mutilated by the unconscious Israelites. Abimelech, that slew sixty and nine of his brothers on the same stone, was himself slain by a piece of millstone, in the attack on Thebez. Lot's wife, who tarried in her flight, was eternally fixed to the spot, becoming a pillar of salt. Saul, that by the sword of Doeg slew four score and five persons, himself fell,—so says Hebrew tradition, —by the sword of Doeg. Hezekiah, that vain-gloriously exhibited his treasures to the ambassadors of the king of Babylon, was punished by the knowledge that the same treasures would one day adorn the palace at Babylon. And indeed the conclusion of the Canon of Scripture would seem to lead us to the same belief. "If any man shall *add* unto these things, God shall *add* unto him the plagues that are written in this book :—and if any man shall *take away* from the words of the book of this prophecy, GOD shall *take away* his part out of the Book of Life."

It is this retributive justice that, in profane history, approves itself so strongly to the mind of man. It was this that made the sufferings of Valerian and Galerius so terrible to ancient Rome: that made Europe shudder at the fate of Alexander VI.: that was renowned in the East in the captivity of Bajazet: that cast a deeper gloom round the death of lord Brooke. That catastrophe is based on more solid principles than mere poetical justice, where the king of Denmark mixes the poisoned cup for his son, and it is swallowed by his wife. The first exclamation of an untutored mind in reading, in the same play, the death of Laertes, would simply be,—How natural! And it needs a cold-blooded critic to discover with Dr. Johnson, that the change of weapons is a forced and unlikely expedient to terminate the tragedy.

This species of justice, then, is soonest comprehended, and most readily acknowledged by the least cultivated minds. A homely example shall prove this. Many will recollect how, when the miscreant Burke was paying the penalty of his crimes, and through the unskilfulness of the executioner the cord had slipped, so that instead of being strangled, he was suffocated; the vast multitude of spectators acknowledged,—brutally indeed, but acknowledged still,—that the hand of Providence was visible in his punishment, that, as he had done, so had GOD requited him.

It is to be believed, then, that if we know the distinguishing characteristics of any crime, we may be able, in a great degree, to guess at the probable nature of its punishment.

Now the first great mark that would suggest itself on a consideration of Sacrilege is this; it is,—so to speak,—a temporal crime. It has to do, for the most part, with material substances; with buildings, with lands, with ornaments, with stone, timber, and metal.

It lays waste that which is given to GOD by man as
a creature composed of matter and spirit; as the inhabitant of a material world, and unable to express
spiritual devotion without material adjuncts and as-
sistances.   It is for the most part a crime that could
not exist in a world of spirits.   For, when it is connected with persons, it still has respect to the body,
not to the soul.   Sacrilegious injury done to a Priest
affects merely his person : it cannot harm his spirit.
Sacrilegious injury done to a church affects the
material fabric alone : it cannot extend to the company of the Faithful that there assemble for worship.

We might hence conclude, even did we know
nothing further of the matter, that the punishment of
Sacrilege, while of course its heaviest part would be
reserved for another world, would also manifest itself
in this; and that in a material and personal character.
Spiritual injury, the deprivation of the means of
grace, is effected and preceded by means of material
injury.   Spiritual punishment will therefore, it is
probable, be preceded by temporal punishment.

Again,—the crime of Sacrilege, for the most part,
consists in robbery.   It is the robbing GOD.   For
though there have been bold blasphemers, who, for
the sake of profanity, have defiled GOD's House,
this is rather the act of a devil than of a man.   The
sacrilegious person, generally speaking, would be very
well content to avoid the guilt, if he could in any
other way secure his profit.   Esau did not give away
his birthright; he sold it for a mess of pottage.
Korah and his company sought rank and influence,
and could come at it by no other way than Sacrilege.
Jeroboam did not set up the calves out of an abstract
lust of idolatry, but to secure the allegiance of his
yet unconsolidated people.   Sacrilege, then, is, as
sir Henry Spelman begins by defining, " an invading, stealing, or purloining from GOD any sacred
thing, either belonging to the Majesty of His Person,
or appropriate to the celebration of His Divine
Service."

Whence we conclude that the punishment would

be the loss, by the offender, of those things for which he committed the crime; such as wealth, influence, or name. We may believe that the criminal would not be permitted to obtain the reputation, to thrive upon the gains, to build up the family for which he sinned. Just as Jeroboam, by the very sin to which he looked for the support of his kingdom and the establishment of his house, lost the one and destroyed the other. "This thing became sin unto the house of Jeroboam, even to cut it off." And as sacrilege exhibits itself under two phases, the one of utterly destroying, the other of merely impoverishing, consecrated things or places, so its effects will probably be twofold. In some cases all the offender's family or wealth will be destroyed by a sudden blow; in the other, the threatening addressed to Eli will be more strictly applicable, "The man of thine whom I shall not cut off . . . shall be to consume thine eyes, and to grieve thy heart."

Again, sacrilege is a crime that not only affects contemporaries, but leaves effects behind it which will injure unborn generations. A man sins for his children as well as for himself; they reap the advantage of his guilt; it is but just that they should also bear the punishment of it. The heathenish, and worse than heathenish state, of our manufacturing towns, of Birmingham, and Manchester, and Ashton-under-Line, lies in great measure at the door of Henry VIII. The cries of the famishing poor of our own day invoke vengeance against the Russells, the Seymours, the Audleys, the Clintons, the Dacres, of that. It is to them that we are indebted, in no small degree, for the moral and physical state of our labouring and manufacturing classes. There was wealth enough and to spare in the Church; she had willingness to assist up to her power, yea and beyond her power, the needy and the destitute.*

* In the Parish Chest of Lambeth is a very curious book, which shows the manner in which money was collected for relief of the poor after the dissolution of the Religious Houses, and when their

The rapacity of church-destroyers turned rectories into vicarages, and vicarages into perpetual curacies. The money laid out on their lordly mansions was wrung from the portion laid up for the artisan and day-labourer. The duke of Somerset's palace, in the Strand, has made a S. Giles's and a Saffron Hill; the earl of Bedford's erection at Woburn is dearly purchased by the churchless condition of S. Pancras. The traveller along the western road will wonder at the destitute condition of Brentford, and Turnham Green, and Hammersmith; till he remembers what Sion House was, and what it is.

From this we gather, that the punishment of Sacrilege may be expected to affect the descendants of the guilty person, as well as the offender himself. As the injury continues centuries after the deed of

tables no longer supplied the necessities of the indigent. It may be considered as the introduction of those rates so well known by the name of Poor-rates. It is on parchment and intituled, " A Register Booke of the Benivolence of the Parishoners for the Relief of the Pore, made in a°vj Regni *Edwardi*, vj^{tl}, et in ann.° Dom. MV^cLII. dez *Ambrose Willowes*." " A Register Booke gevyne by Master *Ambrose Wyllis*, gentylman, unto the Churche of *Lambethe*, wherein is declared the benyvolence of the Paryshoners of *Lambethe* affersaid, towards the releiffe of the poore inhabitors there which be not of poore (power) able to lyve wythoute the cheritye of the towne, as hereafter in this booke dothe appere, particularlye every man's name, and what his devosyon is to geve weklye towards the sustentacion of yher poore neybours according to the King's Highness proseydyngs; and also in another place of this Boke the distrebutynge wekelye of the same." The list that follows is :—

"My Lorde of *Canterbury's* Lordship.
"My Lorde of *Canterbury's* grace.
"My Lorde of *Wynchester.*
"My Lorde of *Suffecane.*
"Master Parson for half a year, 10s.
"My Lord of *Carlyll.*
"My Lady *Bridgewater* for a yere, 6s. 8d.

" On Sunday October 30 there was nothing distrybuted, because that Master *Wylles* did extend his charitye among the poore householders.

" On Sundaye the 6th of Auguste Master Parsone did geve his charitye to the poor people."

The sums given are in general very small, as appears by the

spoliation is at an end, so, it may be supposed, will
the retribution. How important a consideration this
is in our inquiry, we need not stay to point out.

We will mention but one more characteristic of
sacrilege. Until the Reformation, as well among
heathens as among Christian nations, it was a crime
of very uncommon occurrence. Men pointed it out
as something awfully singular; as a prodigy that
appeared from time to time, and for long intervals
was completely unknown. The very minuteness
with which historians have chronicled it proves its
rarity. They were not wont to describe, with such
particularity, other deeds of violence.

Hence it would seem to follow, that the punishment attached to sacrilege would then also be something startling,—something that should be talked

specimens, and payable by the week or by the quarter, and different
sums given in different years by the same persons. Besides these
there were collections at the Communions, in the Poor's box, and
collections at Christmas. To what extent this has since arisen will
appear by the following :—

"In 1749 the Poor Rates, Church Rates, Highways, and
Scavengers, were raised by a tax of six-pence in the pound. In
1764, of one shilling ; 1774, of two shillings, on a rental of
26,333l. which produced 2,362l. 200 persons then in the workhouse ; 1779, of two shillings ; 1780, the rental of 31,600l. ; 1783,
of two shillings and six-pence, produced 5.702l. the rental 35,147l.
In this year add, Rents of the Parish Estates, 968l. ; Penalties
received, 100l. ; Earnings by labour of about 280 Poor at 10s.,
140l. ; Gift of Mr. Hayes Fortee, 500l.—Total expended in 1783,
7,410l.

" One year's expence of the Parish, ending at Easter 1812, the
sums being put down at the nearest even hundred pounds, which
in some cases will be a little more, in some a little less, than the
actual amount, not making any material difference in the total,
was ;

" Food at the two workhouses, 8,400l. ;

" Cloathing, 900l. ;

" Fires, Candles, and Lamps, 700l. ;

" Lunatics and other Patients at Hospitals and Madhouses,
900l. ;

" Furniture and Repairs, 500l. ;

" Salaries, Wages, Commissions, and Gratuities, 1,500l. ;

" Weekly Payments to poor Persons out of the two Houses,
4,000l. ;

of,—something that should involve a visitation not according to the visitation of all men. And we may perhaps draw another, and not less important inference.

Following out the principle that we have laid down of an analogy between crime and punishment, we shall not only conclude that guilt of which the nature is uncommon will meet with retribution equally unusual; but that sin of a more usual kind will meet with a more ordinary (though perhaps not less formidable) reward. Sacrilege, at the Reformation, became one of the most ordinary of sins; after that time, then, we are to trace its fate in more ordinary punishments. We are not to look for signal visitations; deaths on the scaffold, like lord Seymour of Sudeley; nor by murder, as sir Francis Goodyere; nor by poison, as the earl of Essex; nor by the hand of a wife, like Thomas Arderne; any more than we are to expect that the earth will cleave asunder and swallow up the sinners, as it did of old time Korah and his company. But we may look for the fulfilment of the curse in the more usual method of childlessness, or a divided house, or an early death; we may see it in the consumptive tendency that will blot out a whole family no less surely than the pestilence or the earthquake. In the unnatural flush of the cheek, and the unnatural brightness of the eye, we may read the curse of Bolton, or Rievaulx, or Reading; in the forced exile of many that repair to warmer climates for a prolonged life, or an easier death, we may trace the vengeance due to that avarice by which so many Religious were driven forth on the world, houseless, friendless, and hopeless.

"Incidental expences, 2,100*l*.—
"Total about 20,000*l*. raised by a tax of 4s. in the pound."—Manning's Surrey, vol. iii., p. 463.

How great the rates for relief of the poor have grown to be in the present generation (they amounted to £8,296,230 expended in actual relief of the poor for England and Wales alone, in 1886) is known by experience: and the fact adds weight to the reflections made above.—[E.]

We conclude, then, that the punishment of Sacrilege would probably be temporal; that it would frequently consist in loss of property or good name; that it would attach itself to the descendants of the transgressor; and that while, in former ages, it would be signal and notorious, it may now be expected to manifest itself in more ordinary methods of retribution.

We thus end the first part of our argument. In it we have shown that, whether we consider the analogy of Scripture cases, as well in the New as in the Old Testament, both in the punishment that has befallen Sacrilege, and the reward promised to, and bestowed on, a special zeal for the maintenance of God's rights, and the honour of His temple; or the belief that has in all times, among all nations, under all religions, attached an especial curse to the violators of holy things; or the curse pronounced, in Christian countries, on the spoilers of Church property; a curse, imprecated by persons, on a subject, in a manner, which authorized the affixture of an anathema, and gave it power to be effectual; or, lastly, the very nature of the crime as taken in connection with the usual analogy that prevails between guilt and punishment; we have shown, we say, from all these considerations, the probability of an *à priori* belief that temporal punishment, and that not only involving the original criminal, but reaching to his descendants, would attach itself to the commission of Sacrilege.

II.—The argument, *de facto*, inductively.

1. It is certain, from the testimony of general history, that a temporal punishment has followed the commission of Sacrilege.

But, after all, it may be said, in a subject like this, an *à priori* argument can never be convincing. The theory must stand or fall by facts alone.

And we, on our side, are only too ready to appeal to facts. They constitute the great strength of our cause. Unbelievers may refute, or may imagine that they have refuted, what we have hitherto said : but, unless they can recast history, unless they can remodel God's past dealings with mankind, they cannot overthrow the assertion that Sacrilege and temporal ruin are (as a general rule) synonymous.

We appeal to Spelman's history, and to our own continuation. To anticipate here what he has said elsewhere, would be but to waste time and space. Were our argument arranged in the most logical manner, the history should be read here.

We will only add a few words on Sacrilege in France, which we have not elsewhere noticed.

During the wars of Religion between the Catholics and Protestants it was not committed so systematically as in England. It arose more from popular fury on both sides than from any law to legalize it. It was left for the great French Revolution to dissolve the Abbeys and to turn the Monks and Nuns starving into the open fields, as had been done more than two hundred years before in England. Still fearful Sacrilege was doubtless committed in the course of the civil wars which deluged France with blood. The Calvinists broke into churches and defaced them and robbed them, as if doing so were a pious act; the Catholics pillaged them to pay the troops they had raised against their adversaries. The profanation of churches by both parties, it is said by French writers, made gold and silver much more common than they had been; the holy vessels, shrines, images of saints, were melted down and coined into money. Extracts like the following from the Register of the Mint are but too common :—" May 29, 1590 : Received from the Treasurer Roland and the Monks of S. Denis, a crucifix of gold weighing 19 marks, 4 oz. 5 grains, which was melted down." Moreover, " June 16, 1590 ; received from the same a crown of gold weighing 10 marks, 10 oz. all but 2 grains, which was melted down." It would take too much of our space, even supposing it were practicable, to give individual instances of the Sacrilege of that time.   The impiety was general; was the punishment general too ?   At no period, perhaps, of the French history are there recorded so many fearful deaths of the great men of the country.   This is no new remark; a writer * who never dreamt that punishment followed Sacrilege, has noticed the fact. Let us review the fates of the kings and the principal nobles of France during the space of about a hundred years, namely, from the accession of Francis I. to the death of Henry IV., during which time no less than six monarchs reigned over the French, of which, be it remembered, the first alone occupied more than thirty years.

Francis I. devastated Italy and Germany in concert with the *Turks* to the great scandal of Christendom, and under the execration of the faithful.   He died of a shameful disease and left only one son, Henry II.

Henry II. was slain at a tourney by Montgomery; a lance running into his eye and killing him on the spot after a reign of twelve years.   He had four sons, of whom three wore the crown, and all died childless.

Francis II. reigned one year, and died of decline at the age of seventeen.

Charles IX. died of remorse, vomiting his own blood.

Henry III. was assassinated by Jacques Clement; his reign was the most miserable France had ever witnessed; he himself was despised by everyone, the most abject of creatures.

Henry IV. was assassinated by Francis Ravaillac; Jean Chatel attempted his life before.   His reign is accounted the most glorious France can boast of; his private life, however, was very bad; he divorced one wife, and was inconstant to the other.   His mistress, the famous Gabrielle d' Estrées, died at the house of the dean of S. Germain l' Auxerrois, which he had given her, in most fearful and ex-

* Saint Foix : Essais historiques sur Paris.

E

traordinary agonies, her mouth being drawn back to the hinder part of her neck, and she exclaiming, "Take me from this house." Jeanne d' Albret, mother of Henry IV., was poisoned.

Antoine de Bourbon, king of Navarre, father of Henry IV., was wounded at the siege of Rouen. His wound was dressed and doing well ; but he could not master his wicked passion for Mademoiselle du Rouët, and in his attempts upon her he caused the wound to break out afresh, and he died.

François comte d' Enghien was killed by a chest which fell on him at the castle of Roche Guyon, whilst he was at play with his companions.

Henri de Bourbon, marquis de Beaupreau, died of a fall from his horse, whilst out hunting.

Louis de Condé, brother of Antoine de Condé, commanded the Huguenots at the battle of Jarnac : before the battle began his leg was broken by a kick from a horse ; he fought, however, all day with it in that state, the bone sticking out through his boot. He was defeated and taken prisoner; when in a defenceless state he was murdered by Montesquieu, who shot him dead with a pistol. He left one son.

Henri de Condé, son of the above, was poisoned at S. Jean d' Angéli.

The marshal de S. André was murdered in cold blood by one Bobigni after the battle of Dreux.

Francis of Cleves was killed *accidentally* at the same battle (Dreux) by one who was his dearest friend.

Francis, duke of Guise, was assassinated by Jean Poltrot de Méré at the siege of Orleans.

Henri duke of Guise, his son, was murdered, by order of Henry III., by Loignac, almost in the king's presence. After he was dead Henry kicked his body about the room.

His brother, the cardinal de Guise, was murdered next day.

The cardinal de Lorraine, uncle of the two former, was poisoned by a monk at Avignon.

The cardinal de Chatillon was poisoned by his valet-de-chambre.

The admiral de Coligni was murdered on the night of the massacre of S. Bartholomew, and his body was trampled under foot by Henri de Guise.

The admiral André de Villars Brancas was taken prisoner by the Spaniards, and then stabbed by order of Contreras.

The duke de Joyeuse and his four brothers were courtiers of the time; the end of them all was most remarkable; they took an active part in the Religious wars. Anne duke de Joyeuse commanded at the battle of Coutras, where he was slain by one Bordeaux. Claude, his brother, was killed also at Coutras by Descentiers. George, their brother, was found dead in his bed the day before his intended marriage. Antony Scipio de Joyeuse drowned himself in the river Tarn, after the battle of Villemur. The fifth, Henry, a peer and marshal of France, turned capuchin monk and died as such : he headed the absurd procession called "des Battus;" his capuchin name was " Frère Ange."

II.—2. More particularly, it is certain from the testimony of English History, that Sacrilege is, generally speaking, followed by temporal punishment.

On this, as on the last branch of our subject, this is not the place to speak. For our proofs, we refer to the History : but more especially to our first and second Appendices, where we have traced the fate of all such original grantees of Abbey-lands as are in any way particularized, either in general or county histories, or as we have been able to discover by local inquiries.

We have already arranged, under different heads, the more usual misfortunes that have beset sacrilegious families. *Violent deaths:* such as the end of

William Rufus; the loss of prince William and the countess of Perche; the almost supernatural termination of the career of Mandeville, earl of Essex, and lord Brooke.   We will not here swell out the miserable list that our future pages will contain; the duke of Somerset, the two lord William Russells, sir John Arundel, sir Francis Goodyear, Leonard lord Grey, are some of the most striking examples. *Strange and unusual accidents*: such as the death of the late duke of Richmond, from the bite of a mad fox: the leprosy of Robert Bruce: the *morbus pedicularis* of the sacrilegious earl of Dorchester. Of the *rapid passing of the estates, great poverty*, and failure of male issue, it would be absurd to particularize instances.

But there is one observation which it is important to make.   Two of our most important heads, *the commission of detestable crimes*, and *unnatural hatred and domestic variance* are subjects on which it is almost impossible for us to enter.   The execution of lord Stourton for murder; that of lord Hatsbury [now spelt Heytesbury], that of Lodowick Grevill, the horrible history of the Darcies of Dambury, the tragedy of Arderne of Faversham, Brown of Lawson, and sir Walter Smyth of Stretton Baskerville, all murdered by their wives; the death, at Anglesey Abbey, of a son by the hand of his father—these things may now be safely related. But there are tales of crime, of deep, dark, diabolical crime—crime now, or within the last few years existing with which, even were we able to do so without legal danger, we would not pollute our pages.   We have been put into possession of a tale of such complicated incest, connected with the occupiers, for a long series of years, of a religious house in the West, as makes the blood run cold but to think of it.   As an instance of the more usual way in which crime is connected with Abbey-lands, we will mention the following, in the possessors of a house of Austin Canons.   A was the owner, who

living in adultery, had one illegitimate son, B.   B
has issue :—C, a son, who, living in adultery, has
two illegitimate daughters, one of whom is married
into a family afflicted with insanity :—D, a son, who
is blind and childless :—E, a daughter, who has
left her husband, and is living in adultery.

It is painful even to mention these things : but
without at least referring to them, our argument
would be betrayed by a false and over-sensitiveness.
In like manner, of domestic variance, more especially as displayed in divorce and disinheritance,
we have no right to speak.   Our readers will,
in the following pages, find ample proofs of our
assertion.

We will, however, as a *résumé* write down the
names of those noblemen who were the first
grantees of any Abbey-site, adding the fate of their
families.

Fitz Alan, baron *Arundel,* extinct in the male line ;
Touchet, baron *Audley,* extinct in the male line * ;
Bourchier,† earl of *Bath,* extinct ; *Russell,* earl of
Bedford, existing in the duke of Bedford ; *Blount,*
baron *Montjoy,* extinct; *Chandos,* baron *Chandos,*‡
believed to be extinct; *Clinton,* baron *Clinton,*
extinct in the direct male line; *Brooke,* baron *Cobham,*§ extinct; *Cromwell,* earl of *Essex,* extinct in
the male line ; *Clifford,*‖ earl of *Cumberland,* extinct ; *Darcy,* baron *Darcy,* extinct ; *Denney,* baron
Denney, extinct; *Grey,* marquis of *Dorset,* extinct ;
Dudley, baron *Lisle,* extinct; *Grey,* baron *Grey,*
extinct in the male line ; *Herbert,* earl of *Pembroke,*
existing in the present earl of Pembroke and Mont-

---

* This peerage became abeyant in 1872.

† Barony of Bourchier dormant in 1855.

‡ The present Duke of Buckingham and Chandos bears the
surname of Chandos.   But this was assumed by Royal licence in
1799.

§ The Viscounty and Barony of Cobham are still borne by the
Duke of Buckingham.

‖ Lewis Henry Hugh Clifford, 9th Baron Clifford, was created
in 1672.

gomery; *Seymour*, earl of *Hertford*, existing, after the total failure of the originally re-ennobled branch of the Seymours, in the present duke of Somerset; *Zouche*,* baron *St. John*, extinct in the male line; *Nevill*, baron *Latimer*, extinct in the male line; *Dudley*, earl of *Leicester*, extinct; *Stewart*, earl *Lennox*, merged in the Scotch crown, and extinct, with the Stuarts, in the male line; *Fitz Alan*, baron *Maltravers*,† extinct; *Brown*, viscount *Montagu*, extinct; *Howard*, duke of *Norfolk*, existing in the present duke of Norfolk; *Parr*, marquis of *Northampton*, extinct; *Percy*, duke of *Northumberland*, extinct in the male line; *Vere*, earl of *Oxford*, extinct; *Paulet*, baron *St. John*, existing in the present marquis of Winchester; *Herbert*, baron *Powis*, supposed to be extinct;‡ *Manners*, earl of *Rutland*, existing in the present duke of Rutland; *Sandys*, baron *Sandys of the Vine*, extinct in the male line; *Talbot*, earl of *Shrewsbury*, existing in the present earl; *Fitz William*, earl of *Southampton*, extinct; *Stafford*, baron *Stafford*, extinct; *Stanley*, baron *Strange*§, extinct in the male line; *Brandon*, duke of *Suffolk*, extinct; *Grey*, duke of *Suffolk*, extinct; *Ratcliffe*, earl of *Sussex*, extinct; *Talbot*, baron *Talbot*, extinct; *Windsor*, baron *Windsor*, extinct in the male line; *Somerset*, earl of *Worcester*, existing in the present duke of Beaufort.

Out of the forty-one noblemen who were thus enriched by the spoils of the Abbeys, eight only have, at the present time, representatives in the male line. And the families that do exist, have, as

* The baronies of Zouche and S. Maur have *twice* been in abeyance, in 1625 and 1828; and twice have been revived, both times in the female line. The family name of the present Lord Zouch is Curzon.

† The baronies of Fitz Alan and Maltravers are borne by the Duke of Norfolk.

‡ The ancestor of the present Baron and Earl of Powis (cr. 1804) assumed the surname and arms of Herbert by Royal licence in 1807.

§ The barony of Strange has devolved on the Duke of Athole (who sits as Earl Strange).—[E.]

we shall see, experienced, with scarcely an exception, fearful judgments.

One other observation we may here make, because we shall have no more convenient opportunity. Spelman, writing about 1630, says, "The whole body of the baronage is since the Dissolution much fallen from their ancient lustre, magnitude, and estimation. As the nobility spoiled GOD of His honour by parting those things from Him, and communicating them to lazy and vulgar persons ; so GOD to requite them hath taken the ancient honours of nobility, and communicated them to the meanest of the people: to shopkeepers, taverners, tailors, tradesmen, burghers, brewers, graziers." But what would the writer have said had he lived in our own time ? If he complained of the multitude of peers then, what would have been his astonishment now ? At the Act of Dissolution, forty-two temporal lords only voted in the Upper House : and these were by far the greater part of those then created. Now the peerage contains *five hundred and seventy!*

We purposely hurry over these considerations, because, though true in themselves, they may so easily be abused to evil. We would only desire to draw this moral:—" Them that honour Me, I will honour; but they that despise Me, shall be lightly esteemed."

III. It is certain, that families not implicated in Sacrilege do not meet with judgments, equal in number, nor equally dreadful in character, with those that are connected with it.

The two principal objections which are brought forward against our theory, are the following :—1. That the whole argument, however true in itself, has no practical connection with ourselves; because the destruction of the Abbeys was not a deed of Sacrilege ;—2. That the instances of misfortune and ruin which we have collected, prove nothing;

inasmuch as the same might be alleged against families in no way implicated in Sacrilege. The first of these, it will be observed, seeks to invalidate our argument *de jure*, but can have no influence on that *de facto*. The second addresses itself to our reasoning *de facto*, but cannot touch that *de jure*. We will apply ourselves first to the latter, reserving the former for a more fitting place.

Now, we would begin by observing that, on its plain face, the argument is unfair. We are not called on to prove a negative.—Not the slightest value ought to be attached to reasoning of this kind, when unsupported by facts. A mere assertion is quite sufficiently met by a mere assertion. We cannot refute that which is not stated. Let a list be made out in proof of the assertion, and we shall have something tangible to go upon. Till that be done, we simply deny that it can be done. So far as we are aware, it has been but once attempted; we refer to the conclusion of the younger Tanner's Preface to the *Notitia Monastica*. This we have quoted, and we may add, sufficiently refuted, in Chapter VIII.

But our opponents do not consider this; the greater force we allow to their argument, the greater strength we obtain for one of our own. Universal belief is, as we have already shown, a very strong proof of truth. But here we must make a distinction. Universal belief of a thing which is, or which appears, self-evident, is no confirmation of its existence at all. It is believed, simply because it is apparent. The two statements, or assertions, resolve themselves into one. But, the less self-evident a thing is, the more proof is to be obtained from its universal acceptation as true. An apparent impossibility, œcumenically believed, is an undoubted truth. *Certum est, quia impossibile*, is an axiom worthy of the Father that put it forth.

To take a familiar instance. Let us imagine a follower of Tycho Brahe disputing with one of

Copernicus. If the former argued, The sun must revolve round the earth, because the universal voice of mankind asserts that it does,—we should at once feel the argument to be perfectly valueless. It is true, we should reply—Mankind holds that belief; we know it, and we know the reason why. Its apparent truth is all its ground. When we assert it to be apparently true, we assert it also to be universally believed. Argue, if you will, from its apparent verity, but do not bring forward a consequence of that verity as a separate argument. On the other hand, were the disciple of Copernicus able to bring forward universal opinion on his side of the question, we should at once own the weight of that argument. The thing seems unlikely—and yet it is universally believed—how can that be? It must arise either from a tradition, handed down from the remotest ages, or from a continual impression effected on the human spirit—in either case, it is probably true. In like manner, it is à priori improbable that the earth was ever overwhelmed by a flood—yet that this was the case is affirmed by the popular credence of all nations. And this universal tradition is (most properly) used by those who have written on the credibility of the Mosaic writings.

To apply these remarks to our present subject. Our opponents assert, that the fate of families not guilty of Sacrilege is oftentimes as dreadful as that of those connected with it; i.e., that the punishment of Sacrilege, as Sacrilege, is not apparent. Let us allow that this statement is true. But popular belief, universal, œcumenical belief, belief without distinction of country, of age, of religion, asserts that the punishment of Sacrilege is distinguishable. If, to common eyes, it be not, this universal tradition must have a θεῖόν τι for its ground.

Again, it is surely an unworthy argument to say, Sacrilege is not punished, because persons who are

not implicated in it also suffer. It is as if a man
should say, Unbridled licence to the passions does
not lead to madness, because some lose their senses
who have set the strictest guard over their temper.
It is plain, that nothing which we assert is denied;
it is only endeavoured to add certain additional
statements which, if they were true, as they would
not remove the sin of Sacrilege, so neither do they
profess to disprove its danger.

At the same time, as this objection is, perhaps,
the commonest of any, and as it is generally considered to possess the greatest degree of weight, we
will meet it boldly. And we do so by asserting
that, statistically, the failure of male heirs in families
implicated in Sacrilege is much more frequent than
in those which are not so implicated, and further,
that church-lands change their possessors far more
frequently than those which have never been devoted
to GOD.

But, at the outset we are met by a great difficulty;
a difficulty which was far less in the time of Spelman than it is now. In the comparatively few
years which had then elapsed since the Dissolution,
it was easy to say what families were altogether
clear, and what involved in the guilt of abbey-
lands. Now, by purchase, by bequest, by exchange,
by marriage, the contamination has been communicated and recommunicated, till it is difficult to say
who is absolutely clear. And the case is still more
complicated with respect to lands. A manor, which
in itself was lay property, has often and often
come into a family otherwise tainted with Sacrilege.
For that other Sacrilege they suffered by extinction;
and so this uncontaminated manor passes to another
family. Yet statistically it must be reckoned as
innocently possessed. And therefore a statistic
account must, though valuable so far as it goes, be
very unfavourable to our argument, if compared
with the real truth.

Now, in Spelman's time, these statistics were not,

only far more true, but far more convincing. Sir Henry sat down, compass in hand. He described, taking a house near his own as a centre, a circle, the radius of which was twelve miles. In this he enclosed twenty-five abbey sites and twenty-seven gentlemen's parks. In the space of time that had elapsed between 1535 and 1616, that is, eighty years, he found that the latter had not changed families; whereas all the former (except two) had changed them " thrice at least, and some five or six times."

Nothing can be more convincing than this; and if the result of a similar inquiry would be less satisfactory at the present day, that is to be attributed to the impossibility of carrying it on with equal accuracy. We may add also another consideration. Doubtless the Sacrilege of the original grantees was far greater than that of those who, by purchase, have become possessed of abbey-lands—often, probably, in ignorance that they had been such. And the punishment therefore would be now proportionately less than it was in an age where no such ignorance nor thoughtlessness could exist.

We resolved, however, to inquire, if our theory were not, even now, capable of statistical proof; and we may assert—to say the least—that it has great statistical probability.

And firstly, with respect to the curse of childlessness :

Our first endeavour was to procure information as to the general proportion of barren to productive marriages. And here we found the difficulty far greater than we had expected. For, though it is well known that the average number of children produced by each marriage is, to speak approximately, 4.5, that fact brings us no nearer to a solution of our question. The volumes of the Statistical Society—the reports of the registrar-general—the principal medical works on marriage which the best libraries in England could furnish, were searched

with as little success.   Determined, if possible, to
obtain some more satisfactory result, we next in-
quired, by letter, of one or two of the most eminent
physicians, connected with lying-in hospitals,
whether any statistical accuracy on the subject were
attainable.   To those gentlemen we beg leave to
return our thanks for their courtesy in replying to
our inquiries.   "I regret to say," writes one, "that
I know of no work, in which you will be at all likely
to obtain any approximation to the truth.   The
difficulty of obtaining any statistical results is not to
be conceived by those who have no experience in
the management of our lying-in hospitals."

We were thus reduced to take the only statistical
proportion which (so far as we are aware) has been
published.   It is given as the result of a Continental inquiry.   In this, the proportion of non-
productive to productive marriages is stated at
24:478.

While we cannot lay much stress on the exact
numbers of this calculation, we have no doubt that,
substantially, it will be found to be correct.   Parish
priests will be the fairest judges, parish registers
(to one who is acquainted with the village) the best
tests, of its accuracy.   Had we been able to procure
a more satisfactory statistical account of the matter,
we should have entered into the subject more
largely; should we, at any future time, be furnished with more satisfactory premises, we shall
hope to use them.   At present we will only offer
one consideration deduced from these statistics.

If we make the inquiry in that quarter where we
can pursue it with the greatest accuracy, namely,
the Peerage of England, we shall be able to draw
some kind of comparison between tainted and un-
tainted houses.   Of the five hundred and seventy
peers who at this moment compose the Aristocacy,
about four hundred and seventy are more or less
implicated in Sacrilege.   Of these, sixty-six or
sixty-seven have no children.   And out of this

number we exclude those who have been so recently married as to render it extremely probable that, though at present childless, they may hereafter be surrounded with families.

We see, however, that assuming the statistical proportion that we gave above, unproductive marriages among those of the peerage who are, in any way, implicated in Sacrilege, exceed the usual average nearly as 3:1.

Let us add a practical illustration of what we have said. We give it in the words of Clement Spelman :—

"Reynerus * tells us, and upon good credit, that at the Dissolution, Henry the Eighth divided part of the Church spoils among two hundred and sixty gentlemen of families in one part of England, and at the same time Thomas duke of Norfolk rewards the service of twenty of his gentlemen with the grant of £40 a year out of his own inheritance ; and that, while not sixty of the king's donees had a son owning his father's estate, every one of the duke's hath a son of his own loins, flourishing in his father's inheritance ; and that he could have set

---

* Apostolatus Benedictinus; seu Disceptatio Historica de Antiquitate Benedictinorum in Anglia, p. 227. "Infausta laicis. bonorum cœnobialum possessio. Virum magnum et summa. familiarum Anglicarum, historiæque antiquæ notitia præditum citare testem possumus, quem coram aliquot viris intelligentibus, et nobilibus, religione Protestantibus, ipsum etiam professione protestantem narrantem audivimus, quo tempore Rex Henricus Octavus opima illa cœnobiorum latifundia, ducentis sexaginta et amplius nobilibus viris, vel gratis, vel permutatione facta distribuisset, etiam Thomam Norfolciæ ducem, viginti clientibus suis, qui ei diu fideliter liberaliterque serviissent, reditum perpetuum quadringentarum librarum sterlingarum ex æquo repartivisse : ex horum viginti clientium stirpe superesse adhuc hæredes singulorum, in ipsis hæreditatibus, quas a Duce patribusque suis acceperunt florentes ; ex toto autem eorum numero, qui cœnobiorum opibus fuerunt ditati, non superesse sexaginta familias, quæ in bonis. perseverant avitis ; omnes reliquas familias penitus eis rebus quas sic a Rege Henrico possederant, hodie excidisse. Idque sibi ita. notum dixit vir ille nobilissimus, ut si opus foret, singulos illos nobiles posset enumerare."

down their several names had conveniency required it."

The next question that arises is : In what degree does the guilt of Sacrilege shorten the time that each individual, and each family possesses the consecrated ground ?

Now it is clear that to distinguish the lands which never belonged to the Church, and have never been held by families implicated in Sacrilege from those in some measure connected with it, would require little short of Omniscience. We have endeavoured, however, to do what we might. We have collected with very considerable labour, a statement with respect to various Church-lands. 1. Of the number of years that they have been severed from the Church. 2. Of the number of possessors that have held them during that time. 3. Of the number of families that have possessed them during the same time. The instances we have given may, indeed, seem few ; but they are all that long search has enabled us to obtain. The succession of property is very seldom given in county histories, without any breaks ; and one break renders an account useless in this point of view.

Now, as everyone knows, the average length of one generation is measured by a space of thirty-three years. That is, thirty-three years elapse on an average from the death of the father to the death of the son. Which is the same thing as to say, that the average possession of an estate by an individual succeeding to its possession, is thirty-three years.

But another element is to be taken into consideration. A man may sell his estate ; and in this case no average can possibly be given or taken. But in all those instances where an estate has long remained in the same hands, there the most casual comparison will convince the inquirer how far short the average of possession falls of the given thirty-three years.

MANORS IN KENT—*Hundred of Scray.*

Lands not belonging to the Church.

Name.	Number of years.	Number of possessors.	Number of families.
Boughton	150	7	3
Butlers	500	23	7
Cheveney	500	22	5
Colkins	450	18	3
Dargate	450	22	6
Graveney.........	460	19	8
Marden	155	9	4
Nash	450	· 17	1
Rhodes Court...	450	20	7
Widehurst	590	21	8
	4155	178	52

Lands belonging to the Church.

Name.	Number of years.	Number of possessors.	Number of families.
Bokinfold	250	20	14
Combwell	250	12	5
Densted	150	17	8
Lambert's Land	260	15	9
Lovehurst	210	12 (?)	8
Monkton.........	250	13	6
Morehouse	250	13	4
Nagden	250	16	7
Newstead	240	12	7
Townland	115	12	8
	2225	142	76

In this instance, the average of individual possession in case of lay property is just twenty-three years and four months; in that of Church property, about fifteen years and eight months; in the former case the average possession by one family is just eighty years, and in the latter somewhat over twenty-nine. But many of the families who pos-

sessed property described above as lay, were guilty
of other Sacrilege; we will, therefore, take some
estates in the same hundred, and trace them down
to the Reformation, and therefore when the possessors were (in all probability) not implicated in
Sacrilege. We are not able to give the number
of individuals who have held them. In the manors
of Winchet Hill, Bedgebury, Twysden, Puttenden,
Glassenbury, Fleshinghurst, Hartridge, Course-
horne, Spilsill, Biddenham Place, we find the
aggregate of years 3545, that of families only
seventeen! So that we obtain, in this case, an
average of more than two hundred and eight years
for each family.

We will next go to the few instances we have
been able to collect in Hertfordshire. The examples
of lay property are taken in order from the second
volume of Clutterbuck's History of that county.

Lands belonging to the Church.

Name.	Number of years.	Number of possessors.	Number of families.
S. Amphibal ...	280	17	9
Cheshunt	280	20	15
Royston	270	7 (?)	4
Rowney	270	16	11
Ware	275	12	7
	1375	72	46

Lands not belonging to the Church.

Cheshunt	494	22	11
Andrewes	280	11	4
Essenden	274	10	2
Bedwell	144	10	3
Hertingfordbury	311	13	6
Gobions	650	25	5
Great Ayot......	210	6	3
	2363	97	34

Here we have an average, in case of Church property, of a little more than nineteen years for an individual, and nearly thirty for a family; in the case of lay property, of twenty-four and a half years for an individual, and nearly seventy for a family.

We shall, however, assume, (which we are amply able to prove, if the statement be denied,) that, since the Reformation, the average individual possession of a lay estate is more than twenty-three,— the average family possession more than seventy years. We purposely understate our own case.

Let us see how this agrees with the Church-lands of Essex, as traced from Morant's History.

Name.	Number of possessors.	Number of families.	Number of years.
Barking	6	4	78
Waltham	12	5	218
Earl's Colne	11	5	205
Tremhall	10	3	228
Colchester, S. John's	15	9	186
—— Crouched Friars	14	10	101
—— Grey Friars	13	9	224
Dunmow	12	5	228
S. Osyth	10	3	200
Hatfield Peverel	11	4	230
Wycke	11	5	220
Tackley	7	3	82
Walden	14	3	246
Cressing	16	3	228
Tiltey	10	2	225
Prittlewell	11	4	231
Bileigh	14	8	228
West Mersey	11	5	200
Blackburne	11	3	228
Tipten	17	12	237
	236	105	4023

Average possession of each individual $17\frac{11}{236}$.
„   „   of each family ... $38\frac{33}{105}$.

Let us try again the Church-lands in Warwick-shire from Dugdale's History. The computation of years,—to take the least advantage, is reckoned till 1656, the date of the publication of that work ;—though part of it was written as early as 1650.

Name.	Number of possessors.	Number of families.	Number of years.
Oldbury	10	7	121
Erdbury	8	4	128
Maxstoke...............	6	3	115
Abbat's Salford	6	4	109
Herdwick Priors......	9	4	113
Herberbury...........	6	4	64
Bishop's Itchington	7	4	107
Hodnell	6	3	117
Grandborough	6	3	103
Leek Wootton	7	4	107
Fletchamsted	6	3	117
Stonely	7	3	117
Shortley	12	9	113
Newland	5	2	98
Newnham Regis......	7	4	103
Monk's Kirby.........	7	5	110
Wilston	5	2	116
	120	68	1858

Giving an average of $15\frac{29}{60}$ years' possession for each individual, and $27\frac{11}{34}$ for each family.

We next turn to Abbey-sites and Manors in Kent generally, and employ Hasted's History of Kent.

Name.	Number of years.	Number of possessors.	Number of families.
Folkestone...........	255	15	6
Reculver	251	16	8
Minster Nunnery, afterwards be-longing to S. Augustine's ...	178	10	3
Minster	98	9	6

Malling	220	13	7
Lewisham	252	18	8
Leeds	238	19	10
Boxley	243	12	4
Feversham	250	16	9
Combwell	252	12	4
Newington	93	5	2
Davington	246	14	7
Mottenden	241	18	11
Wingham	237	7	1
Swingfield	239	9	3
Cobham	251	13	6
West Peckham	248	7	3
Wye	245	14	7
	4037	227	105

The average possession of each individual is, in this case, $17\frac{178}{227}$ years; that of each family, about $38\frac{47}{105}$ years.

In the seventy instances we have now quoted, individual possession averages at about seventeen, family at about thirty-five years,—instead of more than twenty-three for the former, and seventy for the latter.

IV.—The argument *de facto*, deductively.

By a consideration of the most remarkable and signal judgments which English history records, it will be found that they almost universally have occurred in sacrilegious families.

We have not yet noticed a species of argument, which, when urged *vivâ voce*, and tested by private experience, has sometimes been successful in convincing those who were proof against every other consideration. We would ask the reader to run over in his mind, whether in general history or within the limits of his local knowledge, the most remarkable and fearful judgments with which he is acquainted, and see whether they do not occur in families notoriously implicated with Sacrilege. It is clear that in an essay this argument is almost valueless, because it may be met with a scornful denial; but a man who is really in earnest will not so reject it. If, for example, we were called on to mention the most remarkable accidents that have, within the last ten years, occurred in the British Peerage, we should probably mention the deaths of lord William Russell, the earl of Darnley, and the earl of Morbury;—the first, killed by his servant; the second by his own hand, unintentionally; the third, shot by an assassin while walking in his demesnes at *Durrow Abbey;* and all sprung from families deeply implicated in Sacrilege. Look again at the late Indian actions; and reflect whether, in the most melancholy death among the conquerors, the curse of Tinterne did not make itself felt in the field of Moodkee. We are fully persuaded that this species of investigation will do more to convince, than a hundred pages of the most laboured argument.

V.—1. From the Confession of Enemies it is certain that a temporal curse attaches itself to Sacrilege.

We will now bring forward the testimonies of some, who, on account of the share they took in the Reformation, might have been supposed favourable to the appropriation of Church-lands to secular purposes. Bernard Gilpin, preaching at Greenwich before Edward VI.; bishop Ridley, in his letter to Cheke from Fulham, dated July 23, 1551; Latimer, in his sermon on Covetousness; Grindal, in his letter to Queen Elizabeth, 1580; Jewel, in his sermons on Haggai, i. 2, 3, 4,—all bear witness against the enormous sin of the times. "By it," says Luther, writing on Galatians vi. 6, "men seem to degenerate into beasts. Satan vehemently urges on this most horrid evil by the wicked magistrates in cities, and noblemen in the country, who seize the goods of churches. This is the devil's own masterplot to drive CHRIST'S religion out of the land. Will you know the calamities attendant upon such horrible ingratitude? Because an ungracious nature thinks it much to part with these carnal things, for the spiritual things of the ministry, therefore by a just judgment of GOD they shall forfeit and utterly lose both their own carnal things, and the spiritual things of the ministry too. However, GOD, for a while, delays His vengeance; yet in His due time, He will find you out."

So much,—leaving out some of his ribaldry,—for Luther. Let us now hear a less honest man than he —Calvin. His tract, addressed to the emperor Charles and the princes met at Spires, is designed to excuse the Sacrilege attributed to the Reformers. "To convert," he expressly says, "Church-revenues to other uses, is Sacrilege." "It is my grief," he adds, "and all good men lament with me, that the patrimony of CHRIST has not been employed only to that use to which only it was dedicated."

For a worthy companion to form a trio of witnesses, we will add John Knox. "We dare not," says he to the Privy Council in the first book of Discipline, "flatter your lordships; but for fear of the loss of your souls and ours, we desire to have back all the Church-lands of the Friars, and all other Mortifications restored back again unto the Church." And a fellow of Knox's,—one John Cragge, preaching at Lythe, in the year 1574,— lays down the same doctrine. And again, the General Assembly, in the year 1582, enjoined a general fast throughout the realm, "for appeasing GOD's wrath against the crying sin of Sacrilege."

We will add but one more testimony, and that of rather a curious kind. It is extracted from a poem, written 1575, and entitled "a memorial of two worthie Christians." Its author was a Presbyterian. Speaking in high praise of one Robert Campbell of Kingcancleugh, he says,—

The half tiends of hale Ochiltree
He did give o'er most willingly;
Quhilk his forbears had possest,
For Sacrilege he did detest.
The minister he put therein;
GOD grant that as he did begin,
So all the rest that do possess
The tiends of Scotland, more or less,
Most wrongously, would them restore,
As gude Robert has done before.
But no appearance can we see
That they will do it willingly,
For all the summoning has been
By GOD's heraudes these years fifteen;
Though I think they should fear to touch them,
Because the tiends did ne'er enrich them,
That has meld with them to this day,—
Yet no appearance is, I say,
That ever they shall with them *twin* (i.e., *part*)
Till GOD in Heaven Himself begin
With force whilk no man may withstand
To pluck them clean out of their land,
Whilk shall be to them wrack and wo,
Because they would not let them go,
For no forewarning He could send,
When they had time and space to mend;
Though now their Sacrilege seem sweet,
Their offspring shall have cause to greet,
When GOD shall call them for the wrong
Done to Him and His Church so long.

Those, then, who hold up to admiration such authors as the above, are bound to give all weight to their sentiments on this point. Sacrilege was one of the great crimes with which the Roman Church reproached those who had revolted from its obedience. The fact of the alienation of Church property could not, of course, be denied; but to justify it, had it been possible, would have answered the same end. But this it was not attempted to do. To bluster down the charge of Sacrilege was impossible even to Luther; to elude it, unhoped even by Calvin. They, at whatever risk, were constrained to confess that, the maintaining of which, is by their successors looked on as a part of the faith which they opposed. So it is that the continued perpetration of Sacrilege hardens men's hearts. Luther and Calvin had not centuries of GOD's vengeance on the possessors of Church property before their eyes—those of the present time have, and yet will not believe!

V.— 2. From the TESTIMONY of FRIENDS, it is certain that a temporal curse attaches itself to Sacrilege.

It would be easy to fill a volume from the works of the Fathers with their denunciations of the crime of Sacrilege. The writings of S. Jerome, S. Augustine, and S. Ambrose, are more especially filled with such. "A proposal," says the archbishop of Milan, "was made to me to deliver up at once the church plate. I made answer, that I was ready to give up anything that was my own, estate or house, gold or silver : but that I could not withdraw any property from GOD's Temple, nor surrender what was put into my hands to preserve and not to give up." "DE ECCLESIA," says S. Jerome, "QUI ALIQUID FURATUR, JUDÆ PRODITORI COMPARATUR." But such testimonies would add little force to our present argument : because they would tell the least with those who would otherwise be disposed to dispute our conclusions.

We will, therefore, string together a few passages from English writers, who have taken the same view of the subject as ourselves. And be it remembered, that to denounce Sacrilege two hundred years ago, required more courage than it does now : partly, because Abbey-lands were better known, and their lay-possessors more easily pointed out : partly, because in far more instances than at the present time these possessors had them by grant and not by purchase.

We find that even the time of the Dissolution itself did not want its witnesses against the crime then committed, notwithstanding the extreme danger which must necessarily have then arisen to anyone raising his voice against that which was committed by the great ones of the land. We regret that we have been unable to procure a sight of Feckenham's work above referred to, though we have searched the British Museum, the Bodleian, and all the Cambridge Libraries.

A blunt writer of that age (at the time of the Dissolution), calling himself Roderic Mors, but whose real name was Henry Brinklow, a merchant, of London, addressed both houses on the subject of the Dissolution. He acknowledged that much had been done amiss by the monks, and that the pretence of putting down abbeys was to amend this. " But," said he, " see now how much that was amiss is amended, for all the godly pretence. It is amended, even as the Devil amended his dame's leg (as it is in the proverb), when he should have set it aright he broke it quite in pieces. The Monks gave too little alms . . . but now, where £20 was given yearly to the poor in more than an hundred places in England, is not one meal's meat given ; this is a fair amendment ! " We may remark that Roderic Mors was no Romanist, for in the course of his speech he calls the Pope antichrist.*

In 1550, the reign of Edward VI., Lever, in a sermon preached on the 4th Sunday after Twelfth-tide, has the following :—" Seeing that impropriations being so evil that no man can allow them, be now employed unto the Universities, yea, and unto the yearly revenues of the King's Majesty that few dare speak against them, ye may see that some men, not only by the abuse of riches and authority, but also by the abuse of wisdom and policy, do much harm, and specially those by whose means this realm is now brought into such a case, that either learning in the University and necessary revenues belonging to the most high authority is like to decay, or else impropriations to be maintained, which both be so devilish and abominable, that if either of them come

---

* See White Kennet's history of Impropriations, p. 128.

to effect, it will cause the vengeance of GOD utterly
to destroy this realm."

Archbishop Whitgift, in the reign of Queen
Elizabeth, notwithstanding the flattery which it was
then the custom to lavish on that Sovereign, yet set
his face firmly, cost what it might, against the
sacrilegious designs of her favourite, the earl of
Leicester, and clearly pointed out the curse which
must come on the kingdom from such sins.

" I beseech your Majesty," said he, " to hear me
with patience, and to believe that yours and the
Church's safety are dearer to me than my life, but
my conscience dearer than both; and therefore give
me leave to do my duty, and tell you that Princes are
deputed nursing fathers of the Church and owe it a
protection; and therefore, GOD forbid that you should
be so much as passive in her ruin, when you may
prevent it; or that I should behold it without horror
and detestation; or should forbear to tell your
Majesty of the sin and danger. And though you and
myself are born in an age of frailties, when the
primitive piety and care of the Church's lands and
immunities are much decayed; yet, Madam, let me
beg that you will but first consider, and you will
believe there are such sins as profaneness and Sacrilege; for if there were not, they could not have names
in Holy Writ, and particularly in the New Testament.
And I beseech you to consider that, though our
Saviour said ' He judged no man;' and to testify it
would not judge nor divide the inheritance betwixt
the two brethren; nor would judge the woman taken
in adultery; yet in this point of the Church's rights,
He was so zealous, that He made Himself both the
accuser and the judge and the executioner to punish
these sins; witnessed, in that He Himself made the
whip to drive the profaners out of the temple : overthrew the tables of the money-changers and drove
them out of it. And consider, that it was S. Paul
that said to those Christians of his time that
were offended with idolatry, ' Thou that abhorrest

idols, dost thou commit Sacrilege?' supposing, I think, Sacrilege to be the greater sin. This may occasion your Majesty to consider that there is such a sin as Sacrilege, and to incline you to prevent the curse that will follow it. I beseech you also to consider, that Constantine, the first Christian Emperor, and Helena his mother, that King Edgar and Edward the Confessor, and, indeed, many others of your predecessors, and many private Christians have also given to GOD and His Church much land and many immunities, which they might have given to those of their own families and did not: but gave them as an absolute right and sacrifice to GOD. And with these immunities and lands they have entailed a curse upon the alienators of them. GOD prevent your Majesty from being liable to that curse!

"And to make you that are trusted with their preservation the better to understand the danger of it, I beseech you, forget not that, besides these curses, the Church's lands and power have been also endeavoured to be preserved as far as human reason and the law of this nation have been able to preserve them, by an immediate and most sacred obligation on the consciences of the Princes of this realm. For they that consult Magna Charta shall find, that as all your predecessors were at this coronation, so you also were sworn before all the nobility and bishops then present, and in the presence of GOD, and in His stead to him that anointed you, 'to maintain the Church lands and the rights belonging to it;' * and this testified openly at the holy altar, by laying your hands on the Bible then lying upon it. And not only Magna Charta, but many modern statutes have denounced a curse upon those that break Magna Charta. And now what account can be given for the breach of this oath at the last Great Day either by your Majesty or by me, if it be wilfully, or but negligently violated, I know not.

"And therefore, good Madam, let not the late·

* The first article of Magna Charta is " Que les Eglises de Engle-- terre seront franches et aient les droitures fianches et plenières."

lord's exceptions against the failings of some few clergymen prevail with you to punish posterity for the errors of this present age; let particular men suffer for their particular errors, but let GOD and His Church have their right. And though I pretend not to prophesy, yet, I beg posterity to take notice of what is already made visible in many families: that Church land added to an ancient inheritance hath proved like a moth fretting a garment and secretly consumed both; or like the eagle that stole the coal from the altar and thereby set her nest on fire, which consumed both her young eagles and herself that stole it. And though I shall forbear to speak reproachfully of your father, yet I beg you to take notice, that a part of the Church's right, added to the vast measure left him by his father, hath been conceived to bring an unavoidable consumption upon both, notwithstanding all his diligence to preserve it. And consider, that after the violation of those laws to which he had sworn in Magna Charta, GOD did so far deny him His restraining grace that he fell into greater sin than I am willing to mention.

" Madam, Religion is the foundation and cement of human societies; and when they that serve at GOD's altar shall be exposed to poverty, then Religion itself will be exposed to scorn, and become contemptible; as you may already observe in too many poor vicarages in this nation. And, therefore, as you are by a late act or acts entrusted with a great power to preserve or waste the Church's lands; yet dispose of them for JESU's sake as the donors intended: let neither falsehood nor flattery beguile you to do otherwise, and put a stop, I beseech you, to the approaching ruins of GOD's Church as you expect comfort at the last Great Day: *for Kings must be judged*. Pardon this affectionate plainness, my most dear Sovereign, and let me beg to be still continued in your favour, and the LORD continue you in His."*

Of William Cecil, lord Burleigh, we are told that

* See Walton's Lives. Zouch's edition, p. 243.

" he was a good friend to the Church, as then established by law : he used to advise his eldest son,
Thomas, never to bestow any great cost or to build
any great house on an impropriation, as fearing the
foundation might fail hereafter."*

If may well be imagined that a man like bishop
Andrewes was no favourer of the sin of Sacrilege.
And we are told accordingly by bishop Buckeridge,
in his sermon preached at Andrewes' funeral, that
he did much find fault and reprove three sins, too
common and reigning in this latter age. 1. Usury
was one. . . . 2. Another was Simony, for which
he endured many troubles. . . . 3. The third
and greatest was *Sacrilege*, which he did abhor as
one principal cause, among many, of the foreign and
civil wars in *Christendom* and invasion of the Turk.
Wherein even the reformed, and otherwise the true
professors and servants of CHRIST, because they took
GOD's portion and turned it to public profane uses,
or to private advancements, did suffer just chastisement and correction at GOD's hand ; and at home it
had been observed, and *he wished some man would
take pains to collect, how many families that were
raised by the spoils of the Church were now vanished,
and the place thereof knows them no more.* †

And when the fearful times of the great Rebellion
came on, and wicked men again laid their hands on
the Church and her property, faithful men were not
wanting to raise the note of alarm, then, as heretofore.   Amongst these, bishop Hacket stands the
foremost in his defence, before the House of Commons, of the Deans and Chapters of the Cathedrals.

" I will lead you," he says, " to the highest of all
considerations, to the honour of GOD.   The fabricks
that I speak of were erected to His glory, the lands
bequeathed to them were dedicated to His worship
and service ; and to that end I beseech you let them

* Life of Lord Burleigh in Fuller's Holy State.
† See Bishop Andrewes' Funeral Sermon by Bp. Buckeridge,
vol. v. of Andrewes' Sermons.   Oxford edition, p. 296.

continue for ever, and to the maintenance of such persons whom their liberality did expressly destine to be relieved by them. And withal, I must inform you, and I care not to conceal it from you, it is a *tremenda vox* which I shall bring forth, that they have debarred all alienation with many curses and imprecations. It is GOD's own sentence upon the censers which Core and his complices used in their schism with pretence to do GOD's service. (Numbers xvi. 38.) 'They offered them before the LORD, therefore they are hallowed.' This is not spoken after the way of a Levitical form and nicety, for the using of these censers was anti-Levitical: but it is an absolute theological rule out of the mouth of the LORD, That which is offered unto the LORD is hallowed. Again, Proverbs xx. 25, ' It is a snare to the man that devoureth that which is holy.' This is proverbial divinity, every man's notion and in every man's mouth, παροιμία ῥῆμα ἐν τοῖς οἴμοις λαλούμενον, theology preached in every street of the city and every highway of the field. Let me add that smart question of S. Paul, Rom. ii. 22, 'Thou that abhorrest idols, dost thou commit Sacrilege?' I have done, Mr. Speaker, if you will let me add this Epiphonema: Upon the ruins of the rewards of learning no structure can be raised but ignorance; and upon the chaos of ignorance no structure can be built but profaneness and confusion." *

To this may be added the following passage from an anonymous tract, published in London, 1641, entitled " A discourse of Sacrilege."

" Since then Religion is such a ground of happinesse, and riches and honours now such main props of Religion; justly hath Sacrilege or the diminution hereof beene ever accounted the highest, the boldest, and the damnablest sin in the world. Supplant Religion and we dissolve all the tyes betwixt GOD and men; we weigh anchor and fall to sea again, the sea of vulgar passions. Other mischiefs have their

* See Hacket's Life, by Plume, p. 25, prefixed to his " Century of Sermons."

limits, they hurt but one or other and there is an
end.   But this strikes at goodnesse itself, it sets the
world besides its hinges, and sweeps out peace from
off the earth.   GOD, the King, and all of us are
thereby damnified.   He hath a heart of iron, a
salvage and Cyclopike breast that can invade
Heaven and rob GOD, that can pull downe the prerogative of the King and his crown too, and spoyle
mankind of their safety.   Heathens themselves have
always had more reverence to things dedicated unto
their Gods; and to violate but the Religion of other
countryes though more vain than their owne, looked
so monstrous, that it was ever accounted inauspici-
ous, and the wrong done to a false deity carryed an
horror with it, and was usually revenged by the
true one.   Histories abound with such monuments,
and it was long ere this crime was known in Christendom. . . . Such profane ones as spoyle for the booty,
however they please themselves in their fury, will
one day finde a curse goe along with their prey,
which, like Achan's execrable thing will ruin themselves and their families.   They forfeit their confidence in a Providence and that comfort in their
brethren and their own breasts which should be their
life and stay in time of trouble.   They usually dye
forlorne of GOD and men, miserable, disconsolate
and detested : and yet have more to answer for in
the world to come."

The same year of the publishing of the above
quoted tract, 1641, lord Strafford laid down his life
for the Church.   When on the scaffold, " turning his
eyes unto his brother, sir George Wentworth, he
desired him to charge his son to fear GOD, to con-
tinne an obedient son of the Church of England and
not to meddle with Church livings, as that which
would prove a moth and canker to him in his estate.
The curse of GOD will follow all them that meddle
with such a thing as tends to the destruction of the
most apostolical Church upon earth." *

* Heylyn's Cyprianus Anglicanus, p. 451, and White Kennet's
History of Impropriations, p. 438.

"There is a parallel instance," says Kennet, "in the blessed instrument of restoring the King and the Church, George, Duke of Albemarle, who was a great detester of Sacrilege, and had often told the Bishop of Sarum with much joy and resolution, that he never had or would have in the compass of his estate any part that had ever been devoted to pious uses."

Bishop Jeremy Taylor says: "We know that when in Henry the Eighth or Edward the Sixth's days some great men pulled down churches and built palaces, and robbed religion of its just encouragements and advantages, the men that did it were sacrilegious; and we find also that GOD hath been punishing that great sin ever since; and hath displayed to so many generations of men, to three or four descents of children, that those men could not be esteemed happy in their great fortunes against whom GOD was so angry, that He would show His displeasure for a hundred years together."*

Heylyn's sentiments on the same subject are well known. He remarks on the strange fact, that "although an infinite mass of jewels, treasure of plate, and ready money, and an incredible improvement of revenue, had accrued to him [Henry VIII.], yet was he little or nothing the richer for it."

"*Noli me Tangere*" was written by Ephraim Udall, who calls himself "one that hath no relation for the present to, nor any expectation for the future from, the Bishops or Cathedrals, unless it be this, that the one would preach oftener in the other, and both of them govern and be governed better hereafter than heretofore." It may therefore be looked on as a "moderate" man's opinion on the subject in question. And though he talks as loudly as any one about "a purgation of the Church from superstitious Roman dregs," he also observes "that Henry VIII., in whose time the Statute of Dissolution was

* GOLDEN GROVE. Sermon X. between Whit-Sunday and Advent.

carried and the tithes alienated by statute, was met withall by GOD: for all his posterity, though they came respectively to the Crown, yet they were written childless, and he quickly, in them, turned out of the kingly possession; and the Crown transferred to a branch that sprang from his father Henry VII., under whose shadow we have had rest for many years, and have cause to pray that GOD would make that branch flourish." Alas, for the good man's augury of the future!

Again, he remarks very sensibly,—and when we remember the Irish Spoliation Act, we may add very seasonably for ourselves,—"Neither let any man think that this will take away the nature of sin from the alienation of Church-lands, that it is done by a national assembly of the states in Parliament, whose proceedings and sanctions must be by rule from GOD; otherwise, they become more out of measure sinful, than actions of the like quality in private men. The laws of the state are not therefore just, because enacted by the state, but when they agree with the common rules of justice that GOD hath given to every son of man. The truth is, many proud and foolish men do idolize a national assembly, as if it had not a superior rule, to which it ought to frame all its actions and decrees; but, like a kind of omnipotent creature, . . . it were a LORD GOD upon earth."

. . . "It will not, therefore, I say, take from Sacrilege the nature of sin, that it is committed by a national assembly, giving their sanction thereunto; but it will increase the evil, and make it a national sin, involving the Commonwealth therein. First in her nobility, as 'Make their nobles like Oreb and Zeb, yea, all their princes like Zebah and Salmana:' . . . and lap up the gentry, the citizens, the knights, the burgesses, the whole commons of England, yea, the whole nation in sin. For so saith GOD: 'Ye are cursed with a curse, for ye have robbed Me, even this whole nation;—and ye say, wherein?—'

for they would not believe it more than many of our people at this present. . . . Add unto all this, that it will make it the more sinful in that it shall be committed by law, which should be enacted for the prevention of sin, and not for the commission. *Shall the throne of iniquity have fellowship with Thee, that frameth mischief by a law?*

"The lands of cathedral churches are the bequests of men dead long ago, with fearful imprecations made against those that should alter their wills and testaments. Now the Apostle saith, If it be but a man's testament, no man altereth it. No man? Why, there be many men now set that way, and they pretend zeal in religion. . . . But you will say unto me, They may better be employed in some other use. . . . And I say unto you, If you fancy anything better, or know any other good work, either better in truth, or better in your own conceit and esteem, in GOD's Name, give something of your own to the maintenance thereof, permitting them that be dead to enjoy their own will and desire, in that, in which they put you to no charges.

"I could therefore wish, That all our gentry that would preserve their inheritances without ruin to their posterity, would beware they bring not any spoils of the Church into their houses, lest they be spoiled by them. . . . And to preserve them from this sin, That they would have a tablet hung up always in the dining-room, where they ordinarily take their repast, in which should be drawn an altar, with flesh and fire on it for a Sacrifice; with an eagle ready to take wing, having in her talons a piece of flesh, with a burning coal at it;—and higher than the altar, a tall tree, with an eagle's nest in it; and the heads of the young ones discovered above; and the nest flaming with a light fire about them, with this inscription over the altar, *Noli me tangere, ne te et tuos perdam.*"

Another treatise against Sacrilege, written by William Waller, some time rector of Chiswick, ap-

peared in the shape of a sermon, originally preached
at Paul's Cross, November 28, 1628.   This writer,
a most zealous Anti-Romanist, pursues more particularly the hypocrisy of such as, under zeal for
purging out "Popery," appropriated its riches to
themselves.   "There were," says he, "many such
earnest abhorrers of idols in the days of Henry
VIII., that they loved not to see gold, silver, jewels,
or any other ornament or rich thing in God's
Church.   But for fear, forsooth, of idolatry, they
carried all away to their own houses, and spoiled
God's Temples of their ornaments, and Christ's
Ministers of their due maintenance.   Yet S. Augustine resolves us to the contrary (and he, I hope,
was a learned and a concionable casuist).   He, I
say, condemns all keeping to one's own private use
anything out of idol-temples, groves of idols, when
they have lawful authority and commission to overthrow them, that all may know it was God's glory,
not your own gain, that set you to work against idols.
And he commands to dedicate whatsoever they take
from idols to some publick use of God's service, as
God did the gold of Jericho.   Our demolishers . . .
did directly contrary to this counsel of blessed
Augustine.   Insomuch that William Turner tells
how one Knight had in one shire in his hands ten
benefices, and another two-and-twenty."   And he
proceeds to show, how the best families have been
ruined by this fearful Sacrilege.

But the best reasoned of the works which the
seventeenth century produced against Sacrilege is
undoubtedly Dr. Basire's.   It was written during
the siege of Oxford, and published, it appears, by
the express command of King Charles the Martyr;
and reprinted, in an enlarged form, some years after
the Restoration.   From the text, Thou that abhorrest idols, dost thou commit Sacrilege?—he takes
occasion to draw a comparison between the perpetrators of that crime in the Apostles' and in our
own time.   He next argues, syllogistically, that what-

ever is of the same nature with idolatry and adultery, that must needs be a sin now under the Gospel, as much as under the Law; but that Sacrilege is of the same nature; therefore, etc. :—that it is a sin against GOD Himself; a sin fenced about by many and terrible curses; not to be justified by any colour of religion, nor palliated by reasons of policy, as either justice upon delinquents, publick peace, or state necessity; that the King, by his coronation-oath, is bound in honour as a man, in justice as a magistrate, in conscience as a Christian, to put down this offence; that Sacrilege is condemned equally by Divine, Civil, and Canon Law, and by the Common and Statute Laws of this realm.

We will quote one passage. Speaking of the excuses brought forward for alienation—"Good GOD!" says he, "how ill art Thou requited for endowing such men with reason, that abuse it thus! Sure such a spirit of delusion in the patrons of Sacrilege must needs be a just judgment of GOD, because they will not receive the Truth. It is a sin, and theft, and sacrilege, and all these to steal but a Chalice. Thanks yet for granting so much. And shall it be no sin at all to take away those lands, that should maintain the service or servants that must serve GOD with all these? To commit Sacrilege is a crime which alone is damnable *per se,* but to teach men so to do, that is the superlative of all wickedness. Sure such men do scarce believe there is a hell, or a Kingdom of Heaven."

After the Restoration and even after the Revolution, we find the following very characteristic but eloquent passage in Dr. South's sermons, published 1692. It is taken from a sermon preached at the consecration of a Church.

"A coal we know snatched from the altar once fired the nest of the eagle, the royal commanding bird, and so has sacrilege consumed the families of Princes, broken sceptres and destroyed Kingdoms.

"In I Kings xiv. 26, we find Shishak, King of

Egypt, spoiling and robbing Solomon's temple; and that we may know what became of him we must take notice that Josephus calls him Sisac, and tells us that Herodotus calls him Sesostris, and withal reports that immediately after his return from this very expedition, such disastrous calamities befel his family that he burnt two of his children himself; that his brethren conspired against him, and lastly, that his son who succeeded him was struck blind, yet not so blind in his understanding at least but that he saw the cause of all these mischiefs; and therefore to redeem his father's sacrilege gave more and richer things to temples than his father had stolen from them. . . . See the same sad effects of Sacrilege in the great Nebuchadnezzar: he plunders the temple of GOD and we find the fatal doom that afterwards befel him: he lost his Kingdom, and by a new unheard of judgment was driven from the society and converse of men to table with the beasts and graze with the oxen. . . . But now lest some should scoff at these instances, as being such as were under a different economy of Religion, in which GOD was more tender of the shell and ceremonious parts of His worship, and consequently not directly pertinent to ours; therefore to show that all profanation and invasion of things sacred, is an offence against the eternal law of nature, and not against any positive institution after a time to expire, we need not go many nations off nor many nations back to see the vengeance of GOD upon some families, raised upon the ruins of Churches and enriched with the spoils of Sacrilege, gilded with the name of Reformation. And, for the most part, so unhappy have been the purchasers of Church lands, that the world is not now to seek for an argument from long experience to convince it that, though in such purchases men have usually the cheapest pennyworth, yet they have not always the best bargains; for the holy thing has stuck fast to their sides like a fatal shaft, and the stone has cried out of the consecrated walls they

have lived within, for a judgment on the head of the
sacrilegious intruder; and Heaven has heard the
cry and made good the curse.   So that, when the
heir of a blasted family has risen up and promised
fair, and perhaps flourished for some time upon the
stock of excellent parts and great favour; yet at
length a cross event has certainly met and stopped
him in the career of his fortunes, so that he has ever
after withered and declined, and in the end come to
nothing or to that which is worse.   So certainly does
that which some call blind superstition, take aim
when it shoots a curse at the sacrilegious person.
But I shall not engage in the odious task of recount-
ing the families which this sin has blasted with a
curse only; I shall give one eminent instance in some
persons who had sacrilegiously procured the demo-
lishing of some places consecrated to holy uses.   And
for this (to show the world that Papists can commit
Sacrilege as freely as they can object it to Protestants), it shall be that great Cardinal and Minister of
State, Wolsey, who obtained leave of Pope Clement
the Seventh to demolish forty religious houses;
which he did by the service of five men, to whose conduct he committed the effecting of that business;
every one of which came to a sad and fatal end.   For
the Pope himself was ever after an unfortunate
prince, Rome being taken twice and sacked in his
reign, himself taken prisoner and at length dying a
miserable death.   Wolsey, as it is known, incurred a
præmunire, forfeited his estate, honour, and life,
which he ended (some say by poison but certainly) in
great calamity.   And for the five men employed by
him, two of them quarrelled, one of which was slain
and the other hanged for it; the third drowned himself in a well; the fourth, though rich, came at length
to beg his bread; and the fifth was miserably stabbed
to death in Ireland.   This was the tragical end of a
knot of sacrilegious persons from highest to lowest.
The consideration of which and the like passages one
would think should make men keep their fingers off

from the Church's patrimony, though not out of love
to the Church (which few men have), yet at least
out of love to themselves, which, I suppose, few want.
Nor is that instance in one of another religion to be
passed over of a Commander in the Parliament's
rebel army, who coming to rifle and deface the
Cathedral at Lichfield, solemnly, at the head of the
troops, begged of GOD to show some remarkable
token of His approbation or dislike of the work they
were going about.   Immediately after which he was,
looking out at a window, shot in the forehead by a
deaf and dumb man; and this was on S. Chad's day,
the name of which saint that Church bore, being
dedicated to GOD in memory of the same.   Where
we see that as he asked of GOD a sign, so GOD gave
him one, signing him in the forehead, and that with
such a mark as he is like to be known by to all
posterity.   There is nothing that the united voice
of all history proclaims so loud as the certain unfail-
ing curse that has pursued and overtaken Sacrilege.
Make a catalogue of all the prosperous sacrilegious
persons that have been from the beginning of the
world to this day, and I believe they will come
within a very narrow compass, and be repeated much
sooner than the alphabet.   Religion claims a great
interest in the world, even as great as its object—
GOD, and the souls of men.   And since GOD has
resolved not to alter the course of nature, and upon
the principles of nature, Religion will scarce be
supported without the encouragement of the ministers of it; Providence, where it loves a nation,
concerns itself to own and assert the interest of
religion by blasting the spoilers of religious persons
and places.   Many have gaped at the Church
revenues; but before they could swallow them, they
have had their mouths stopped in the churchyard."

We will end our "testimony of friends" by a
quotation from a sermon preached in 1782, before a
benefit society, and entitled, "The History of Collections for the Poor," by the Reverend W. Jones,

of Nayland.   He was a bright and a shining light in a dark place, and on this matter he speaks with his accustomed boldness, and forms a worthy link in the chain of English Divines who have touched on our subject, and the opinions of some of whom we have given in this part of our essay.   He speaks of the property conferred on the Church, out of which the poor before the Reformation were maintained ; he then speaks of the taking of this property by the laity, and shows that they did not comply with the conditions of the tenure.   He then proceeds as follows :—" Reason and law suggest to us, that they, who got the lands of the Church, took them with the encumbrance that was upon them. Out of those lands the poor had been maintained ; therefore they that took the lands should have taken the poor with them ; and they made a great show of doing it for a time, because that was the pretence with which they took them from the clergy ; but when the fish was taken, the net was laid aside.

" I need not inform you what state we are in at present, when the poor's rates are come to such an enormous height throughout the kingdom, that about the year 1700, they were computed at a million yearly : and from that time to this they have more than doubled ; so that there is more than twice as much paid to the poor, as is now paid to all the clergy of the kingdom.*   And in all this expence there is no charity, no devotion as formerly ; it is an involuntary payment forced from us by law and squeezed out of many, who are fitter to receive something for their own wants than to contribute to the wants of others.

" If there was a time when one-fourth of the tithes was found sufficient to maintain the parish poor, and the revenues of the national poor are now twice as great as the revenues of the Church, thence it follows, that where they had one poor man we have eight throughout that kingdom, i.e. 1,000 poor

* See Note on p. xlvi.

instead of 125. It may please GOD still to increase
the poor, till they swallow up the rich who devoured
them : for I think it requires no degree of superstition and credulity to see the hand of GOD in this
whole matter.

" Even heathens were persuaded that their gods
were the avengers of sacrilege; and if it is a certain
fact that the poor have increased as the Church hath
gone down, they who lessened the patrimony of the
Church brought upon us such an evil as might be
expected; indeed, such as seems to follow naturally
and necessarily; for, ' what a man soweth, that
shall he also reap ;' therefore he that soweth in
sacrilege must expect to reap in poverty. Even in
this parish there is a singular concurrence of circumstances : and if I speak of them, you all know
me too well to suspect I have any design in it, but
that of following the order of my subject ; which
required me to give you a brief and impartial history of collections for the poor, and the nature of
them in different ages. It is a fact known to us
all, that in this place no part of the property of the
parish is settled upon the service of the Church.
The rectorial tithes are in the possession of a lay
impropriator, who is a papist ; the vicarial are taken
by the minister of another parish; and the only
certain dependance of a minister is upon the
benefactions of a modern date from other quarters.
So stands the case with the Church. Now look at
the poor ; and you will find such a change as occurs
but in few parts of the kingdom; for the sum
expended annually upon the poor amounts, one
year with another, to three hundred and fifty
pounds; i.e. to more than one-fourth part of the
whole rents of the parish. Amongst the rest of our
national burthens, the single tax upon the land, a
new imposition, never thought of till within the
last hundred years, takes more from the landed
interest than would at the time it was, have been
sufficient to maintain all the poor in the kingdom,

and these two burthens were neither of them felt by the nation while the poor were maintained by the Church. So many ways has the Providence of GOD of showing us that He is stronger than we are; and how little they are like to gain in the end who mix Sacrilege with their policy and hope to enrich themselves by an act of impiety.

"We can only lament these things; we cannot correct them. We have no reason to think GOD will be reconciled to national sin without national restitution; and there is less chance of that every day. The work of sir Henry Spelman,* showing the manifest judgments of GOD upon the violation of Churches and the usurpation of Church lands, had its effect for a time in some instances, but it is now almost forgotten."

We may remark that the opinion of GOD's visiting the sins of the fathers upon their children, was one held by Jones in a very remarkable instance. He was descended from the notorious Colonel Jones, who married a sister of Oliver Cromwell, and was one of the regicides. W. Jones is, even as a lad, reported to have expressed his fears *that his family would never prosper* in the world for the iniquity of his forefather.†

---

* "See the work of sir Henry Spelman, 'De non Temerandis Ecclesiis,' 'a tract of the Right due unto Churches.' A work alarming in its subject and unanswerable in its argument; the author of it being equally skilled in law and divinity. W.J."

† Which presentiment was remarkably fulfilled. Mr. Jones's only child married — Walker, Esq., of Gestingthorp, Essex: the property once held by that family has dwindled away almost imperceptibly; and besides many other family misfortunes, one of the grand-daughters of Mr. Jones was married to the notorious Dr. Bailey.

III.

We will next proceed to consider some of the more usual objections that are brought forward against the theory. No one person ever did, or ever could make use of all,—for we have to deal with very different classes of opponents. We have to answer alike the Protestant and the Ultra-Montane, the mere establishment-man and the progressionist of the nineteenth century; and we must therefore address ourselves, as well as we can, to all.

Objection I.

THE SUPPRESSION OF ABBEYS WAS NOT SACRILEGE.

It has often been urged, by Protestant writers, that—however much it is to be lamented that the money wrung from the Dissolution of the Abbeys was not expended on works of charity and devotion, —the corruption of the whole system was such that to destroy it was doing God a service, and to dissipate its property among the principal reforming noblemen, and among some who called themselves Catholics,—for the purpose of rewarding the former, and of purchasing the silence of the latter, was only the necessary evil that accompanied a great good.

We hear much of the dissolute lives, and immoveable idleness of the Monks; of the guile by which money was wrung forth from dying men; of the threats of Purgatory employed to procure a more ample endowment; of the absurd ends to which some bequests were made; of families im-

poverished, that the Church might be aggrandized;
and then we are asked, Can it be Sacrilege to lay
hands on money thus obtained, thus employed?

There are two answers to this argument. The
first denies the assertion; the second, the consequence.

To enter into a discussion on the inestimable
benefits that the Monastic system bestowed on the
Church, on the poor, on art, on science, on literature,—to dwell on its innumerable offices of intercession, on its boundless hospitality, on the asylum
it offered to the unprotected, the refuge to the aged,
to contrast the monastery with the union, the lot of
the nun with that of the governess or apprentice,
the holiness of S. Albans as it was, with the god-
lessness, of Manchester as it is,—to prove that the
discipline of monasteries even when they fell was
singularly strict, the lives of their inmates extraordinarily pure,—to quote the testimony of their
adversaries in their favour,—to show that the Commissioners for the Dissolution, men fleshed in
iniquity, pleaded hard on behalf of some,—to ask
what now we have to supply their place,—what
training for Candidates for Holy Orders, what
asylum for aged Priests, what machinery for pour-
ing forth an army of preachers on a district assaulted
by infidelity or heresy, what schools of ecclesiastical
literature, what funds for its encouragement and
promotion, what places of retreat for those that are
overcharged with the business of this world,—to
inquire whether the parish doctor supplies the place
of the infirmarer, whether the tenant of the abbey
fared not better than he who is taxed to his utmost
by an absentee landlord, whether daily and nightly
devotion were not likely to bring down a greater
blessing than churches opened once or twice a week,
—all this, we say, we do not mean to consider. We
have carefully avoided all theological questions
hitherto, and we will not enter on them now. This
only we will say,—how false, how futile, how absurd

beyond all common absurdity are the stale Protestant figments concerning abbeys, we equally want
words and inclination to express.

But allowing all that has ever been written about
abbeys; assuming that Burnet is veracious, Fox
accurate, Bale reverent, Grindal honest; that
Henry VIII., out of mere desire for the purity of
the Church, dissolved the religious houses; that
Somerset, out of zeal for orthodoxy of doctrine,
built his palace in the Strand out of churches and a
bishop's palace; that sir Horatio·Palavicini, out of
his sincere love to Protestantism, embezzled the
Papal tax; allowing all this,—and as much more as
the advocates of the Dissolution can assert or
believe,—still, we say, it was an act of Sacrilege.
Our opponents on this question are fond of appeal-
ing "to the law and to the testimony," and to that
only. It shall be so. "Hast thou appealed unto
Cæsar? unto Cæsar thou shalt go."

The followers of Korah were guilty of the most
deliberate blasphemy against the Majesty of God
that heart can conceive. Unwarned by the death
of Nadab and Abihu for a similar though far less
heinous offence, they took every man his censer, put
strange fire therein, and boldly presented themselves
before the Lord. There came out a fire, and consumed them; and the question arose, what was to
be done with the censers. "They are hallowed,"
is the decision of God Himself: "the censers of
these sinners against their own souls, let them make
broad plates for a covering of the altar; for they
offered them before the Lord; therefore they are
hallowed."

Now, can anyone deny that the deed of foundation of our abbeys was, in the most solemn and
express manner possible, offered before the Lord?
Will anyone be bold enough to assert that this offering was made from a worse motive than that which
actuated Korah and his company? How, then,
can the inference be avoided? "They offered them

before the Lord; therefore they are hallowed." By offering, the Jewish rebels sinned against their own souls,—for offering, they were suddenly cut off,—but their oblations became holy. This is the great Scriptural Canon; and the inference is plain enough. An offering made to GOD by never so wicked a hand, and with never so blasphemous an intent, becomes, *ipso facto*, holy.

This law is so express, that if any other part of Scripture seems to contradict it, it is clearly owing to our misunderstanding only. The case of the Brazen Serpent is sometimes alleged on the other side. The Israelites, it seems, preserved this relic; and in process of time, regarded it as an object of worship, and offered incense to it. Hezekiah, indignant at such an abuse, broke it up; and called it Nehushtan, a mere "piece of brass." Now this case is in no way to the point. The serpent had never been dedicated to GOD—was in no sense holy—had nothing beyond its associations and antiquity to recommend it.

As little, moreover, can any argument be drawn from the dealings of the Jews towards the altars of false gods. Yet, at the same time, we never find even these made the subject of lucre. They were destroyed, and most righteously; but no man was enriched by them. If the house of Baal was broken down, it was "made a draught house" unto this day. If Josiah took away the chariots of the sun, he did not appropriate them to his own use; he burnt them with fire. The stratagem by which Jehu assembled the worshippers of Baal in the house of that god, though recorded, is recorded without comment; and appears as properly the subject of blame as of praise.

Another argument to the same effect has sometimes been put forward by the supporters of the Dissolution. It is said, that very much of this money was, in different ways, restored to the Church,—that, if abbeys were suppressed, colleges and schools were founded.

Of the extent of this restoration we will take a Protestant estimate. Dr. Willet, in his *Synopsis Papismi,* of which the fifth edition was published in 1634, estimates the money laid out on deeds of charity since the Reformation at £778,000. There is no doubt that this is overstated.

There is as little doubt that the yearly income of the abbeys was extremely understated. Speaking roughly, they were calculated at £141,000. In a hundred years then, by their means, to say nothing of interest, £14,100,000 would have accrued to the Church. But to this must be added the worth of the buildings themselves :—stone, lead, glass, shrines, precious metals, jewels, tapestry and work of various kinds, and the like. This is underrated at ten years' income; which would give £1,410,000. And we have still to estimate the ninety colleges, one hundred and ten hospitals, 2,374 chantries and free chapels dissolved at a later period ; as also the plate and furniture of parish churches, which was in great measure confiscated by Edward VI. Now, that we may be entirely under the mark, we will assume the revenue of the colleges and hospitals at £100 a year each ; that of the chantries at £5. We will not reckon the spoliation of cathedrals and parish churches at all, because we have no satisfactory accounts on which to go. Thus, then, we form a rough estimate.

In the first century after the Dissolution, there would have been devoted to GOD,—

From religious houses	£14,100,000
From colleges and hospitals	2,000,000
From chantries	1,187,000
Add, for materials, etc., of the abbeys	1,410,000
	£18,697,000

It is certain, that the materials of the chantries, etc., and the plate and ornaments of churches, would have raised this to more than twenty millions. And, of this sum, £778,000 *is said* to have been restored!

We must further notice, that the nominal value of the former sum taken at the time of Dr. Willet's estimates, would have been infinitely more than it is, on account of the rapidly increasing price of money.

We will only make one observation more. If we take the total revenue of religious houses, etc., at £150,000 a year,—if we suppose, with the greater part of modern historians, that land has increased tenfold in nominal value since the Dissolution—if we double this on account of the improved state of cultivation, and the easy rents at which Church-lands were then let, and this is almost ludicrously below the truth, we shall find that, again leaving interest out of the question, during the last century, the Church has been defrauded of *three hundred millions* of pounds. Will anyone pretend that this amount, too, has been restored in other ways?

OBJECTION II.

THE RULE OF PUNISHMENT IS NOT UNIVERSAL.

The assertion that there are exceptions to the rule we are laying down, would really be unworthy of notice, were it not that with some people it seems to have its weight. They are not content with the wonderful manner in which GOD's hand is stretched out to avenge Sacrilege, and will refuse to believe that it is lifted up at all, unless they may have a standing mark before their eyes. It is not enough that every year, and we ought to say every month, GOD does things with respect to perpetrators of Sacrilege and their posterity, " at which both the ears of everyone that revolts shall tingle." He must, if they are to believe, never act otherwise. As of old,—so now: " They thought not of His hand . . . how He had wrought His signs in Egypt and his wonders in the field of Zoan."

These sceptics require a deviation from the ordinary rules of Providence. Can they point to one of the usual dealings of GOD with man to which there are not great,—and indeed startling—exceptions? Long life is promised to the honourers of their parents;—are all, therefore, that are cut off in youth disobedient? The inheritance of the earth is promised to the weak—are the rich and great men of this world universally weak? " Them that honour Me I will honour,"—and yet to bear contempt and shame in this world is no certain sign of GOD's anger.

For, in truth, there is far more and far deeper truth in the proverb, that " the exception proves the rule," than is usually thought. It would seem to say, that where a rule is pretended to be absolutely universal, such pretence, *ipso facto*, proves it to be false : because such are not GOD's dealings with His creatures. It is founded, in that case, on a partial or imperfect deduction :—it is a one-sided view of the subject. Hence, if we pretend that the rule of the punishment of Sacrilege were absolutely universal, we should at once prove its hollowness. We willingly allow that there are exceptions;—nay, in more than one instance we have gone out of our way to call attention to them. How few they are, we have shown when writing " of families in which Church property has continued." But still they exist :—Lord Combermere's family—(where the very title reminds of Sacrilege)—is an instance. Lord Newborough's another, the more remarkable, because it seemed, no long time since, threatened with extinction in the male line. The Giffards of Brewood are another; and so (though in a less signal manner) are the Masters of Cirencester Abbey.

At the same time, these exceptions, we have also shown, are far less frequent than they are usually supposed to be, and every day is diminishing their number. Even since we took this work in hand, it is sensibly lessened. And how much more striking, in this respect, the proof now is, than it was in the days of sir Henry Spelman, the additions we have made to his history of the families of those peers who were present in the Parliament of Dissolution will amply show.

But in truth, no one that has ever studied the dealings of GOD with man, as such, could attach any importance to the objection of which we have been speaking. We leave it, and pass on to one of more moment.

OBJECTION III.

THE CHURCH IN FOREIGN COUNTRIES HAS ALLOWED THE ALIENATION OF CHURCH-LANDS.

But it is argued that, as the Church received the lands and wealth offered to GOD as His Vicegerent and Representative, so, as His Vicegerent and Representative, she may, if she please, surrender them—that, as matter of fact, she has at various times, and more especially as relates to Abbey lands in England, given them up—and that, if her reclaiming them perilled the souls of their lay owners, she would rather yield her claims to her earthly than endanger her heavenly treasure.

Let us see what decisions the mediæval Church has pronounced in this matter. The pseudo-decretals of Pope S. Pius I., of Pope S. Stephen, of Pope S. Lucius, the Council of Agde (A.D. 506), the Third of Toledo, the Second of Nicæa, the Decretals of Pope Symmachus, expressly, and in the strongest terms, forbid the alienation of Church-lands or Church goods.

On the other hand, the so-called eighth Œcumenical Council, in its sixteenth canon, allows the alienation of the holy vessels for the redemption of captives; S. Gregory acquits Demetrius and Valerianus of the money expended by their Church for the redemption of themselves and their bishop: the third Council of Orleans forbids Abbats, Presbyters, and other Ecclesiastics, to alienate Church

H

goods without the consent of the bishop: whence
it seems to follow, that with it they might do so: a
Council of Carthage ordains that the Presbyters
shall sell nothing belonging to the Church, without
the knowledge of the bishop; and, according to the
Canon Law, alienations appear to be valid, when
the consent of the clerks of the Church together
with that of the bishop is obtained.   To the same
point tend certain things allowed by the Church,
such as infeodation of Church-lands, modus of tithes,
exemptions, arbitrary consecrations, compositions,
and appropriations.

It is further argued, that the Church has, in
many cases, relinquished and alienated her property.
The suppression of the Canons Regular of the HOLY
GHOST at Venice, and of those of S. Gregory in
Alga, in the same city—where the revenues were
given to the Senate to defray the expense of defending Candia—are instances.   So, we believe, several
religious houses in Poland were, about the year
1685, dissolved by the Pope, and the revenues
applied to the Turkish wars; the prince of Condé
was allowed to possess the lands of the Berg de
DIEU, valued at £20,000 yearly revenue; two-thirds
of the revenues of S. Denys were given by the Pope
to the famous female seminary established by Louis
XIV., and at Liege, the prince was allowed by
Rome to enjoy the buildings and lands of the (Benedictine?) nunnery in that place.

It is also urged, that in the Treaty of Munster it
was agreed that Archbishopricks, Bishopricks, Pre-
latures, Abbacies, Bailiwicks, Provostships, and
Commendams, should be indifferently possessed by
Catholics or Augustans, as they had happened to
hold them on the first day of January, 1624; that
Collegiate churches, if possessed partly by Luthe-
rans, partly by Catholics, should still be so held,
and both offices be performed in them; and that
Maximilian, duke of Bavaria, and his son, with the
Pope's express consent, appropriated to themselves

the revenues of several abbeys. If it be replied
that Pope Innocent X., in his bull, *Zelo domus Dei*,
protested against this treaty, it may be answered
that he could not well, at the time, do less; and
that to the league between France and Spain, ten
years after that of Munster, in which Louis XIV.
calls himself a confederate for the preservation of
the treaty of Munster, Alexander VII. made no
objection.

It is further argued that the Concordats by which
the Church affairs of France, Spain, and Portugal
were settled, could never have been carried out but
by the cession on the part of the Roman see of
Abbey-lands; and, indeed, in the case of France,
of all Church-lands whatever. Nor is there wanting an example of the same kind in the Eastern
Church. The Holy Governing Synod acquiesced,
when Peter the (so-called) Great took all Abbey-
lands into his own hands, and substituted a yearly
government pension for an annual income.

These are the principal foreign examples that have
come to our knowledge. And before we proceed
to the consideration of Cardinal Pole and his
concordat with respect to our own abbey-lands we
will make a few observations.

In the first place, the Canons of the Primitive
Church cannot be considered as bearing on the
subject. There is a great difference between her
permitting her sons to yield, and her permitting her
enemies to take (far more to keep). All her constitutions on the question seem to resolve themselves into this:—that, whereas it is the undoubted
duty of priests (to say nothing of other Christians)
to defend the smallest portion of Divine Truth at
the expense, if need be, of their lives, they are not
bound thus to defend the earthly treasures that are
committed to their charge. In compassion, perhaps, to their weakness—perhaps out of pity to
their flocks, the Church exonerates them from the
obligation of following the example of S. Lawrence,

and dying for her wealth, which is the wealth of the poor.

Papal bulls, no doubt, go farther than this. We will assume (without, however, granting) that the Pope has the right of alienating consecrated property in the churches of his own communion. We may do this the more easily, because it is well known that the Roman see has always been the last to fall in with such a deed. So that where the Vatican has given way, the point would have been yielded but the sooner, did the right of yielding lie in a private bishop or in a provincial council. We would endeavour to meet, at once, two sets of objections, Ultra-Montane and Protestant. As to the former, one of the most able writers of the present day, among continental Ultra-Montanes, once observed to us, that he could not believe in the curse that followed Sacrilege, because where the Pope had legalized it, it ceased to be sinful. As to the latter, they would argue, that if the See of Rome could yield its right, much more might the Church of England.

Now we must draw a distinction. Sacrilege is followed by temporal suffering on two grounds :— 1. *Quoad* it is a sin that in its very nature must be thus followed; and 2. *Quoad* it has been exposed to a special curse by the Church. We have carefully distinguished these two grounds through the whole course of this essay, and only one of our arguments *à priori* was drawn from the latter. All Jewish and most heathen Sacrilege was free from the one, but yet implicated in the other.

Doubtless the Church can free from that curse with which it has itself bound. If (for we shall presently have to inquire whether the case be really so) the Church, speaking by the mouth, either of the Pope or of any other, has rescinded the curse it pronounced on church violators, they have no more to fear from its ill effects. But this does not, and cannot secure them from the other part of the consideration. It is merely an acquittal of the prisoner from the second count; it leaves him guilty of the first.

For it is surely a maxim which no Ultra-Montane will controvert, that the Pope, even acting *ex plenitudine potestatis*, has no power to absolve from unrepented sin (*i.e.* where it was known and is remembered). But if Sacrilege be sin, those members of the Church who persist in retaining their sacrilegions property when solemnly warned of their guilt, are living in unrepented sin. For to profess to be sorry for a sin which is still continued, and the advantages of which are continually enjoyed, is a mere mockery. Now those who, as now in France and Spain, hear Sacrilege condemned by the voice of their Church, and still enjoy its benefits, put themselves very nearly in their case. Let Rome, therefore, or whoever else, absolve them from the curse of the Church, it cannot, and it would not profess to, absolve them from the curse of God.

By way of corollary to this distinction of a double curse, we will say a few words on an attempted *reductio ad absurdum* of our whole argument.

It is sometimes said that, if the demolition of churches and other consecrated places is punished as we have asserted, a church once created, however much it might now conduce to reverence and the religious welfare of the neighbouring population that it should be pulled down, must remain till it falls to pieces, and the very site is forgotten. For example, it is urged, in Italy, where oftentimes the meanest villages have their twenty or thirty chapels, mean, miserable, lath-and-plaster structures, erected in honour of a saint whose worship is now supplanted by newer and more fashionable devotions, erections without a priest, or people, or altar, or revenue, doorless and windowless, the receptacles of filth, and the hiding place of irreverence: in this case what is to be done? Would it not clearly be for the advantage of religion and morality that these things should be removed? And is the remover, therefore, if he acts solely with a view to the promotion of GOD's honour, to be punished as a Sacrilegist?

We might remind the objector, that similar reasoning on the part of Uzzah did not exempt him from punishment: and undoubtedly it often happens that GOD must be left to vindicate His own honour in His own way. But, in such cases as those mentioned above, two conditions seem requisite to make the removal of a consecrated building safe. It must be done with a good intention; and it must be done with the Church's permission: one of these things will not avail without the other: it is to be presumed that where both are united, they will exempt from guilt.

OBJECTION IV.

It is urged that, at the Reconciliation of England to the Roman Church, one of the stipulations on the part of the Houses of Parliament was the alienation of Abbey-lands, by the Pope, to the then owners.

This is an objection on which we may dwell the more briefly, because it is not likely to have much weight with many of our readers. Such Protestant writers as Burnet deny that Rome did surrender the Abbey-lands, by any other than a construction of words which was intended to bind to nothing. And though this assertion is false, yet a consideration of Cardinal Pole's powers will prove, we think, thus much :—That in allowing the then church owners to retain their possessions, the Church pledged herself simply to this,—to the using no legal measures, at an earthly tribunal, to procure restitution of her own. She did not pretend to take the curse off those properties :—nay, she raised her voice in warning to the depredators. We shall content ourselves with a brief statement of the case; and shall quote from the work of Dr. Johnston, to which we have already referred.

The Act of Parliament for Reconciliation to Rome, after repealing all statutes against the Supremacy, proceeds to this effect:

"Finally, where certain acts and statutes have been made in the time of the late schism, concerning the lands and hereditaments of archbishoprics and bishoprics, the suppression and dissolution of monasteries, abbeys, priories, chantries, colleges, and all other the goods and chattels of religious houses, since the which time the right and dominion of certain lands and hereditaments, goods and chattels belonging to the same, be dispersed abroad, and come to the hands and possessions of divers and sundry persons, who by gift, purchase, exchange, and other means (according to the laws and statutes of the realm for the time being) have the same. For the avoiding of all scruples that might grow by any of the occasions aforesaid, or by any other ways or means whatsoever, it may please you r Majesties to be intercessors and mediators to the said most Reverend Father Cardinal Pole, that all such causes and quarrels, as by pretence of the said schism, or by any other occasion or means whatsoever, might be moved by the Pope's holiness, or by any other jurisdiction ecclesiastical, may be utterly removed and taken away; so as all persons, having sufficient conveyance of the said lands, and hereditaments, goods and chattels, may without scruple of conscience enjoy them, without impeachment or trouble, by pretence of any general council, canons, or ecclesiastical laws, and clear from all dangers of the censures of the Church."

The clergy in convocation set forth, " That they (viz., the clergy) were the præfects of the Church, and the care of souls was committed to them, and they were appointed defenders and curators of the goods, jurisdictions, and rights of the said churches by the disposition of the Holy Canons : therefore they ought with the remedies of law to recover to the ancient right of the Church, the goods, jurisdictions, and rights of the Church, spent, or lost in the late pernicious schism.

" Nevertheless, having had among themselves

mature counsel and deliberation, they do ingenuously
confess themselves best able to know how difficult,
and as it were impossible, the recovery of the goods
of the ecclesiastics would be, by reason of the manifest, and almost inextricable contracts and dispositions had upon them; and if those things should be
questioned, the quiet and tranquillity of the kingdom
would be greatly disturbed; and the unity of the
Catholic Church, which by the piety and authority
of their Majesties was introduced into the kingdom
with greatest difficulty, could obtain no due progress,
or finishing.

"Therefore, preferring the public quiet before
private commodities, and the health of so many
souls, redeemed with the precious Blood of CHRIST,
before earthly goods, not seeking their own profit,
but the things of JESUS CHRIST, they earnestly
request, and most humbly supplicate their Majesties,
in their names to communicate these things to the
Legate, and vouchsafe to intercede, that concerning
these ecclesiastical goods (in part, or in whole,
according to his pleasure, and the faculty and power
given him by the most holy Lord the Pope) he
would enlarge, or set at liberty, and relax the
detainers of those goods, preferring public good
before private; peace and tranquillity before dissolution and perturbation; and the health of souls
before earthly goods: they giving their assents to
whatever he should do, and that in the premises he
would not be strict or difficult."

The Cardinal's dispensation, after setting forth the
importance of preserving peace and unity, proceeds:

" And whereas the stability of either of them,
consists mostly in that no molestation be brought
upon the possessors of ecclesiastical goods, whereby
they may not retain them, which so many and such
grave testimonies cause us to believe; and the
intercession of your Majesties (who have so studi-
ously and holily laboured for restoring the unity
of the Church and the authority of the Apostolic
See) may have that authority with us that is fit, and

that the whole kingdom may know, and in truth
and reality experience, the motherly indulgence of
the Apostolic See towards it. Absolving, and
judging to be absolved, every one to whom these
writings may appertain, from all excommunications,
suspensions, interdicts, and other ecclesiastic
sentences, censures, and punishments, by law or
by man, upon any occasion, or cause whatsoever
pronounced (if for the causes aforesaid only they
be inflicted)." And so the Cardinal passes to the
particulars in the supplication : and lastly as to the
ecclesiastic goods, adds these words.

"And to whatever person of this kingdom, to
whose hands ecclesiastic goods, by whatever contract, either lucrative, or onerose they have come,
or they have held, or do hold them, and all the
fruits, tho' unduly received, of them, in the whole
he doth remit and release. Willing and decerning
that the possessors aforesaid of the said ecclesiastic
goods, moveable and immoveable, may not at
present, or for the future, by the dispositions of
general or provincial councils, or the decretal
epistles of Roman bishops, or any other ecclesiastic
censure be molested, disquieted, or disturbed in
the said goods, or the possession of them, nor that
any ecclesiastic censures, or punishments, be imposed or inflicted, for the detention, and non-
restitution of the same; and so by all kind of judges
and auditors, it ought to be adjudged and defined,
taking from them all kind of faculty, and authority
of judging otherwise, and decerning it to be null
and void, if anything happen to be attempted to the
contrary."

"Notwithstanding the foresaid defects or whatever apostolic special or general constitutions and
ordinances published in provincial and synodal
councils, to the contrary."

"Then follows the admonition, that tho' all the
moveable things of the Churches were indistinctly
released to those that possess them, *yet he would
admonish them, that having before their eyes the severity*

of the Divine judgment against Belshazzar, King of Babylon, who converted to prophane uses the holy vessels, not by him, but by his father taken from the temple; if they be extant they will restore them to their proper churches or to others. Then follows:—

"Exhorting also and by the bowels of the mercy of JESUS CHRIST vehemently intreating all those, to whom this matter appertains, that not being altogether unmindful of their Salvation, at least they will do this; that out of the ecclesiastical goods principally of those which were specially destined for the support of parsonages and vicarages, that in Cathedrals and other inferior Churches, now in being, it may be so provided for them that have the care of souls, that their pastors, parsons, and vicars may commodiously, and honestly, according to their quality and state be maintained, whereby they may laudably exercise the cure of souls, and support the incumbent burthens. This is dated at Lambeth the 9th of the Kalends of January, the 5th of Pope Julius the Third."

Now, without entering into the question whether Pope Paul IV. did not resume this grant, we are confident in maintaining that, even if we grant the Pope all the authority over Church-lands which he claimed in Cardinal Pole's dispensation, that act contains not a syllable to justify Church plunder *in foro conscientiæ*, nor to diminish the probability that a curse will follow those who acquired the estates or houses of Monasteries and other ecclesiastical bodies.

OBJECTION V.

IT IS ARGUED THAT THE PROSPERITY OF ENGLAND HAS NEVER BEEN GREATER THAN SINCE THE DISSOLUTION.

"Eighteen hundred years ago, the Eternal City was in the height of her glory. The spoils of all nations flowed into her; the known world wore her chains; the Thames and the Ganges, the Nile and the Orontes, were tributary to the Tiber; the invincible legions kept every province in awe: gold was plentiful as brass, silver as iron : to be a Roman citizen was the ambition of a life. The capital, from its rocky height, looked serenely down on the thousand temples of the gods; the sacrificial processions daily went forth ; numberless victims bled at the altars of Neptune and Mars; the Pontifex ascended the Capitol with the silent virgin; the Pantheon, and the Temple of Apollo of the Palatine, and the shrine of Diana of the Janiculum, and the glorious house of Victory, were redolent with Sabæan incense; the art of Greece, and the riches of Asia, and the wisdom of Egypt waited on the mistress of the world. With such glory had the ancestral deities of Rome encircled her children : they lived in their worship, they throve by their favour ; as long as they served them, they were invincible.

" But, in an evil hour, certain strangers came to the City. They were the meanest men in the lowest nation of the world. Jews they were, for the most part, but they had collected to themselves a train of followers, the scum and the offscouring of other nations : their rites were impious and barbarous, themselves atheists. They held midnight assemblies for their obscene ceremonies ; they drank the blood of infants, and they worshipped an ass's head. Their GOD was One That had been crucified under the Procurator of Judea, and Whose Body had been stolen from the grave where it had been laid. But, through the evil fortune of the empire, such doctrines as these spread widely, and were received greedily. There wanted not the fitting animadversion on the part of the Magistrates; and more than ten times the Augusti raised their swords against the ' execrable superstition.' But still it prospered. The altars of the great gods were deserted, their temples fell to ruins, their images were defiled, and in their stead, and often on their site, rose the edifices of a new religion, that scorned the ancient deities of the Quirites.

" But their anger slumbered not.   Thenceforth, Rome ceased to be invincible.   The Persians in the East encroached upon her dominions.   From the North, barbaric tribes of dissonant names and obscure tongues, poured down upon Italy.   The sceptre itself was removed to another city.   The huge universal empire was split into two parts. The Emperors of the West grew feebler and feebler, as the sect of the Nazarenes grew stronger and stronger, until, at length, under the rule of Augustulus, Rome herself was humbled under the hands of the barbarians, and the invincible city bowed her neck to her captors."

Now, had any Pagan author written in this strain, those, whose objection we are considering, would (for aught we see) have been bound to assert that his logic was no less true than his history. Rome Pagan was the mistress of the world : Rome Christian sank to a far different position.   In the same manner, England, before the Dissolution, ranked among the second-rate powers of Europe : since the Dissolution, it has gradually attained the pre-eminence among them.   The argument that would prove the Dissolution, in the latter case, to have been a good thing, proves, in the former, that Christianity itself was visited with GOD's displeasure.   A truer account would be, that the decay of Rome had commenced long before the rise of the Church, and that the foundation of England's greatness had been laid long before the Dissolution of the Abbeys.

It may further be observed, that GOD's dealings with nations have often been remarkably opposite to the system which our opponents would lay down. When the Faith was first preached in Japan, for instance, that empire was divided into a number of petty monarchies, rudely united under a kind of feudal head.   Those chieftains who embraced Christianity were almost without an exception

unfortunate ; and the difficulty and trial of the mis-
sionaries on this score, are only to be exceeded by
the calmness and resignation with which they sub-
mitted to them.

Another question, however, might most justly be
asked. *Has* England been so prosperous since the
Dissolution ?   Are wealth and conquests the only
criterion of a nation's happiness ?   If so, Macedonia,
under Alexander, and Babylon, under Nebuchadnezzar, and Asia, under Tamerlane, were more
prosperous than even England ever was. And how far
the future historian may not be able, when he sees
the effects of the present distracted state of our
manufacturing districts, and the working out of our
system of national debt, to give a very different
description of the commercial prosperity of England
from that which is usually now received, may be a
question worthy of consideration. At all events,
it must never be forgotten that Niebuhr, one of the
acutest judges of modern times, long since pronounced that England was sick of an incurable
disease, of that same gradual and unaccountable
and incurable decline, by which Rome perished.

At all events, two things are certain :—the first,
that, be the prosperity of England what, or as enduring as, it may, the fact in no respect weakens
our argument ; the second, that this same prosperity
must be much more distinctly proved than it has
been, or perhaps can be, before it is made a weapon
against the Truth we are asserting.

OBJECTION VI.

IT IS URGED THAT THE WHOLE INQUIRY IS
UNCHARITABLE.

The last objection which we shall notice, is one,
which, as indicating a reverent tone of mind, certainly deserves consideration.   Granting, it is said,
that Sacrilege has been, and is, in many instances,
followed by the express, and more than ordinary
chastisement of Providence, it is presumptuous in

man to decide what are, and what are not, judgments of GOD. We are not sent into the world to
be the judges of our fellow-men ; we have no right
to explore the secret things which do not belong
to us, and which are, perhaps, beyond the reach of
our faculties.—On the contrary, we find many
warnings in Scripture against such investigations.
" Judge not, that ye be not judged :" " Suppose ye
that these Galilæans were sinners above all the
Galilæans, because they suffered such things ? "—
" or those eighteen upon whom the Tower in Siloam
fell, and slew them, think ye that they were sinners
above all men that dwelt in Jerusalem ? "

I. To the Scriptural argument, we would reply
as follows.—A distinction must carefully be drawn
between the private characters of men, which we
have no right to judge, seeing that to their own
Master they stand or fall, and their public actions,
which certainly are fairly open to praise or blame ;
in other words, between intention and performance.
The punishments of the Israelites in the wilderness
happened unto them—so S. Paul expressly states—
for an admonition; to the extent that we should
not lust after evil things, as they also lusted. Here
then we have express authority for judging others,
to the end that we may avoid their sin and their
punishment. The death of Ananias and Sapphira,
for Sacrilege, was commented on by the Church of
Jerusalem ; and by that very method, produced a
beneficial effect on others. We do not pretend—we
most earnestly disclaim—the passing any judgment
on the private characters of those whose History
and Fate we are about to trace. Nothing forbids
us to hope that the most Sacrilegious of the ungodly
assembly that lifted up their hands against the
Abbeys, may find mercy in That Day; and we
believe that many of their successors were punished
in this world, to the end they might be delivered in
that which is to come. For so far are we from supposing that all of these men were sinners above their
fellow-countrymen, of that age, that, in some

instances, they are illustrious examples of piety. Among those that may be presumed to have suffered for Sacrilege are to be found King Charles the Martyr, Lord Falkland, Dr. Hammond, the Earl of Strafford. And, doubtless, of these it may be said that, though *they were punished in the sight of men,* yet was their hope full of immortality. On the other hand, it is not a little remarkable, that some of the most fearful acts of Sacrilege ever committed, have been suffered to go unpunished in this world ; and this remark applies more particularly to the French Revolution, the bold blasphemy of whose Sacrilege is unparalleled. The degree of guilt which each of the acquirers or possessors of Church-lands incurred, is a point into which we have as little inclination, as right, to inquire ; to point out the temporal misery to which Sacrilege is, by an almost universal law, exposed, can surely deserve no blame. We speak gently of the sinner—we seek to expose the sin; nay, by exposing the sin, we hope to preserve the sinner. For,

II. Fully persuaded as we are of the curse which attends the spoliation of Abbey and other Church-lands, is it not a work of mercy to call the attention of others to the same subject ? "The destruction of Korah," says Clement Spelman, "persuades more with the Israelites than the soft voice of Moses ; and such oratory may take thee ;—Hell hath frighted some to Heaven. View then the insuccess of sacrilegious persons in all ages—that will prevail with thee. For had Korah and his accomplices been visited after the visitation of other men, thou and I, nay perhaps the whole congregation of Israel, would have believed what they said as truth—it sounded so like reason—and approved what they did as pious—it looked so like religion ; but their end otherwise informed them, and better instructed us." Like the prince in the Tragedy —

We must be cruel only to be kind.

And what kindness greater than the opening the eyes to a danger, where the risk is so fearful—the prevention often so easy, always so possible?

III. We would ask, What is the use of the study of God's dealings with men? Is it not this?—Not only to adore His Wisdom, and to magnify His overruling Providence, but to derive, analogically, instruction and warning for ourselves? That, on the whole, innocence generally prospers, and wickedness is generally confounded, even in this world, is a great truth, and one which we can learn nowhere but in the pages of the historian. But then, to learn it at all, we must assume that such and such dealings of Providence are punishments for such and such crimes. If we are not to see and to confess God's Hand in the death of a Nero, a Galerius, an Alexander VI., a Cæsar Borgia, where is the use of reading History? But the common consent of mankind allows us to judge in these cases, and taxes us not with presumption for doing so. The licence which we claim is yielded here; why should it be refused elsewhere? If Lactantius acquired for himself no small reputation by writing on the Deaths of the Persecutors of the Church, why is Spelman to be refused praise for tracing the fate of its robbers? And is not the inquiry in strict accordance with Scripture? " Yea, with thine eyes shalt thou behold, and see the reward of the ungodly."—"The righteous shall rejoice when he seeth the vengeance : he shall wash his footsteps in the blood of the ungodly ; so that a man shall say, Verily there is a reward for the righteous : doubtless there is a God That judgeth the earth."—"When the wicked perish, thou shalt see it."—"The righteous also shall see this and fear, and shall laugh him to scorn : Lo! this is the man that took not God for his strength, but trusted unto the multitude of his riches."—"And your eyes shall see, and ye shall say :—The Lord will be magnified from the border of Israel."

IV. God's chastisements, it is agreed on all

hands, are inflicted for one or more of three ends :—
for the amelioration of the sufferer, for a warning
to others; or for the utter extermination of an
obstinate offender. Human punishments are
directed to one of the two former results; the last
is left entirely to the GOD to Whom vengeance
belongeth. Here, therefore, we may propose a
dilemma (and, so far as we see, a fatal dilemma)
for the consideration of those to whom we write.
To which head, we would demand, of the three, is
the punishment of Sacrilege to be referred ? To
either of the two former? But then it follows
immediately, that by the investigation of GOD's
dealings, in this respect, with man, their end will be
more fully answered, for till they are considered,
compared, contrasted, how can they be understood ?
In consequence, such inquiries as that on which we
have entered, are both useful and laudable : useful,
because they tend to save man from misery ; laudable, because they are calculated to glorify GOD's
marvellous justice, and ever-present Providence. To
deny this is, in its result, to affirm that the curse of
Sacrilege must be referred to the last of three heads
which we have mentioned—that is, that it takes effect
only for the utter perdition of those who are implicated in it; a conclusion from which we, no less
than our opponents, should shrink with horror.

V. It is allowed that such inquiries are not without their danger, and that danger of a two-fold kind.
It is to be feared that, for the sake of supporting an
hypothesis, facts may be strained, or at least
coloured ; and that the memory of the departed may
unintentionally be wronged, by imputing to them a
crime as the cause, which in reality was not the
cause of their misfortunes. The remedy against
this is easy. It is to place the reader, by numerous,
and accurate references, as nearly as possible in the
situation of the compilers. We give the facts ; we
give the place where those facts are to be found ;
those who have time and inclination can search for

themselves.   These things are not done in a corner.
There is no mystery in a collection of examples :
and as to sir Henry Spelman, his word is amply
sufficient to prove those of which no other proof
can be given.   One caution only we would hint at.
Any local or genealogical mistake into which we
may have fallen ; any result at which we may appear
inconclusively to have arrived, cannot affect our
other facts, and our other results.   The argument
is one of accumulation, not of induction.   Break
one link of a chain, the whole is ruined ; carry one
pebble from a heap of stones, their weight is
scarcely diminished.

The other danger to which we refer, is that of
rejoicing in sin : or (which is nearly as bad) in
punishment.   And there is undoubtedly a temptation to be pleased with the discovery of new facts
in accordance with a general rule ; with the quick
succession, for example, and extraordinary extinction of families under the curse.   Each example is
a new proof: and each new proof carries its own
weight.   But surely the reader is uncharitable if he
imagines that the temptation has not been resisted,
and that there are no counterbalancing advantages
in the inquiry; such as the delight of beholding
those instances of faith which has led a man to
restore His own to God; and the blessing which
has seemed almost visibly to descend on such acts
of restitution.

We have now noticed the principal objections
that have been brought before us; and it is more
than time to draw our inquiry to an end.

CONCLUSION.*

IF it be true, then, that on considering the analogy
of Scripture History, we find a temporal punishment,
from the days of Korah to those of Ananias, attach-
ing itself to the crime of Sacrilege : that this punish-

* We are indebted for some of the thoughts that follow, to an
article in the Christian Remembrancer for Aug. 1843, and to
Mr. Neale's *Ayton Priory.*

ment consisted, for the most part, in visitations
unlike the visitations of men, and pursued the
posterity as well as the person of the Sacrilegist;
that, in heathen countries, the same vengeance
followed the same guilt, and was recognized by
Pagan writers as supernatural; that popular
credence, in all ages and places, and under all
Creeds, has asserted the same thing; that natural
religion, the first principles of reason, and the
nature of the crime, conduce to a similar belief; if
it be true that our SAVIOUR CHRIST, Who came not
to judge the world, and who forgave the woman
taken in adultery, did nevertheless, in the case of
Sacrilege, Himself form the scourge, Himself drive
out the offenders; that this was done twice, at the
beginning and end of His Public Ministry, as if to
open and to close it; if it be true that the destruction of Abbeys, and the appropriation of Abbey-
lands, was Sacrilege of a most deep and damnable
character; that they were fenced about with
repeated and solemn curses, pronounced to a
lawful end, at a lawful time, by a lawful person;
that these curses had the deliberate sanction of the
Church, and would therefore be ratified by the Providence of GOD; if it be true that nevertheless bold
avaricious men, such as turned faith into faction,
braved these imprecations, laid hands on GOD'S
Houses, and reaped the fruit of His lands; that, at
that time, hundreds of His servants were driven
forth to die of want, and, from that time to this,
the poor, who are His, cry for vengeance on their
plunderers; that thousands of souls have perished,
because the Church wanted the physical means of
evangelizing them; that worse than heathen
darkness prevails in many districts in England,
because the Church is paralyzed through the
iniquity of her robbers; if it be true that time,
which confers a right to possessions illgotten from
man, gives none to those injuriously wrested from
GOD; that, on the contrary, retention is but adding

sin to sin, and each year's possession the heaping up
a treasure of iniquity and if, notwithstanding all
this, it be also true, that the successors of the first
spoilers still revel in their illgotten wealth, and
after three centuries of Sacrilege, still defraud GOD
of His own :—then we conclude that the probable
risk such men run, in robbing, not man, but GOD,
in insulting their Maker, Who is also the Maker of
the poor whom they defraud, in mocking their
Redeemer, Who is the Head of the Church that
they plunder, in contemning the HOLY GHOST, Who
is the author of the threatenings that they dis-
believe, that such a risk, we say, will be fearful
beyond the power of language to express.

But, since all arguments à *priori* must be, at the
best, uncertain, we proceed onwards, and assert,
that, if it be true that at the very commencement
of this Sacrilege, an evil fate seemed to hang over
those who were principally concerned in, or who
chiefly profited by it : that the chief actors perished
in the most miserable and unusual manners; that
of two hundred and sixty gentlemen who reaped
the largest profits from their iniquity, scarcely sixty
left an heir to their name and estate; that by the
scaffold, by murder, by unprecedented accidents,
in misery, in poverty, in crime, in contempt, the
majority of the Church spoilers ended their mortal
existence ; that men, at the time, avoided them as
accursed persons, or pointed them out as instances
of the terrible justice of GOD; that the same fate,
from that time to this, has followed the posterity of
the offenders; that of all families, theirs have been
the most miserable ; that of all fearful judgments,
by far the greater part have visited their descendants; if it be true that, at this very time, the
curse is powerful to their evil ; that to this very day,
fire and robbery, and sickness, in such households,
do their work; that male heirs fail; that jealousy
springs up between man and wife;—unnatural hatred
between parents and children; that a sickly season

carries off one, a violent death another; that speculations go wrong; that thief consumes, and moth destroys: that the curse evermore broods over its victims with its dry * and tearless eyes, crossing them in their best laid plans, entrapping them in an inextricable web, perplexing, and harassing, and impoverishing, and weakening, and ruining, and only leaving them, when the last heir is laid in the family vault; that no analogy of human justice, no appeal to human law, no reference to past tolerance of the Church, no allegations of supposed impossibilities,—can shield the offender;—that instances of God's hitherto forbearance, alleged by any that would thence deduce the innocence of their Sacrilege, prove only that their judgment now of a long time lingereth not, and their condemnation slumbereth not;—then, we say, the infatuation of such as retain these possessions, that wilfully shut their eyes to their dangers, that hazard family and prosperity, wife and children, body and soul, daring God to do His worst, and refusing to own that whom He blesseth is blessed, and whom He curseth cursed, is nothing short of judicial.

The days, it may be said, are passed, when chalices were used as carousing cups, horses watered in stone coffins, stoups used as sinks, beds covered with copes,—and that thought but a sorry house which could not boast some of such spoils. They are passed;—and the authors of such sin are passed, and have given account of their own works to God. But the spirit still continues in their successors. Even while we write, an instance is occurring in no remote part of the kingdom. In the valley of the Ouse, near Lewes, the daughter of the Conqueror founded a stately house of Cluniac brothers. And she endowed it with broad lands and goodly pastures, that in the present day might bring in a rental of £60,000 a year—and she willed

---

* ξηροῖς ἀκλαύστοις ὄμμασιν προσιζάνει. Sept. Adv. Thebas.

that hospitality should there be exercised, the poor
there fed, the sevenfold office of the Church there
chanted, and the LORD's death there set forth till
His coming again. A railway company is formed—
the line must run through the Abbey grounds,—
through the Abbey church,—must, we believe, cross
the very spot where the High Altar once stood.

The tomb of the Founder was violated, and many
of the pious brotherhood, that had hoped to rest
well till the end of all things, were rudely ejected
from their narrow dwelling-places—and without
respect to Christianity, without respect to humanity,
their bones were treated as the bones of an ass,
heaped up together here, kicked out of the way
there, made the subject of the scurrilous jest and
ribald evil—those very bones which (many of them,
at least) shall take to themselves at the Last Day
glorified bodies, and dwell among the Blessed.
Such a scene recalls the bold speech of the Con-
stantinopolitan Patriarch. Pressed by Justinian to
compose a form of Prayer on occasion of the pulling
down a church which stood in the way, we suppose,
of some "metropolitan improvements," the old man
long and strenuously refused. At length, wearied
out by the pertinacity of the emperor, " Say thus,"
he exclaimed, " Glory be to GOD, Who *suffereth* all
things, now and evermore."

You, for whom we write, are in some few, some
very few instances, the descendants,—in all, the successors,—of them that pulled down churches, that
forcibly banished the Holy Angels from GOD's
chosen dwelling-places, that spent upon rioting and
gluttony, upon the prodigal and the harlot, endow-
ments which ancient piety had consecrated ; that
visited with desolation the places where the Holy
Mysteries had been celebrated for centuries ; that
caused wild beasts of the field to lie there, and their
houses to be full of doleful creatures ; you share in
these sins, for you deny restitution ; you have, in
your own persons added to them ;—and you have

three additional centuries of legalized guilt to answer for. And can you deem so meanly of the Majesty of GOD, so unworthily of the power of the Church, can you think so little of the imprecations of the poor,— of the bitter heritage that the departed have bequeathed you, as not to tremble?

> An orphan's curse would drag to hell
> A spirit from on high ;
> But oh, more horrible than that
> Is the curse in a dead man's eye !

It is to you that the festering mass of corruption and guilt in our manufacturing districts is owing ; to you that draw your thousands from the revenues of the Church, and subscribe your annual guinea to some benevolent society ; that have defrauded the Church of hundreds of acres, and are chronicled as prodigies of benevolence if you resign one :—it is to you that, in great measure, the miserable destitution of the manufacturing districts is to be ascribed ; that we have ceased to feed CHRIST's poor, and have begun to cage them ; that we have pulled down almshouses, and erected gaols ; that so many souls are perishing, which, unless you kept back the money of the Church, would have entered into Paradise. And can you believe that this long series of wrongs—wrongs against GOD and against man, wrongs audaciously perpetrated at first, pertinaciously persevered in now, can go unpunished ? Has it ever done so ? Does it so now ? " Shall not GOD avenge His own ·elect, which cry day and night unto Him, though He bear along with them ? I tell you that He will avenge them speedily."

And you talk of the impossibility of restitution ! You confess that wrong has been done, you wish the Church had its rights, so it cost you nothing, you would be glad to see the poor possessed of their own, so you had not to refund it ! But as to restoration, that is out of the question. You cannot give up your London season—you cannot lay down your carriage—you could not do without your

hunters—you must have your box at the opera—
you will indulge in the thousands and thousands of
frivolous expenses to which you have been accustomed. Well, your choice is made; abide by it.
You will cling to these pleasures—take them ; and
with them take the judgments that the unappeased
curse of the Church is bringing upon you. And if
even these fail to open your eyes, there yet remains
one thing more. When you are giving in your
account to God, as one day you must give it in,
the blood of those whom, by defrauding God, you
have caused to perish, will be required at your
hands. You drew the tithes of such a parish ; you
were therefore its Ecclesiastical head : its people,
for whom you never took any care, if they are lost,
are lost by your means. God has spoken it, once
for all. "If thou dost not speak to warn the
wicked from his way, that wicked man shall die in
his iniquity, but his blood will I require at thy
hand." You possessed such an Abbey site,—you
kept up the ruin, and were praised as a man of
taste ; but the inhabitants of the neighbouring
hamlet had no access to the Sacraments, and one
after another went down to the grave without them.
And can you plead that you are guiltless of their
blood ?

It is a fearful thing to fall into the hands of the
Living God. And they that being often reproved,—
reproved from Scripture, by history, by natural
reason, by the heathens themselves, by examples of
all ages, by proof at the present time, still harden
their neck, shall doubtless suddenly be destroyed,
and that without remedy.

THE HISTORY OF SACRILEGE.

CHAPTER I.

SECTION I.

The Definition of Sacrilege, with the several kinds thereof, manifested out of Scripture; together with the punishments following thereon.

SACRILEGE is an invading, stealing, or purloining from God, any sacred thing, either belonging to the majesty of His person, or appropriate to the celebration of His divine service.

The etymology of the word implieth the description: for *sacrum* is a holy thing; and *legium à legendo*, is to steal, or pull away.

The definition divides itself apparently into two parts; namely, into Sacrilege committed immediately upon the Person of God, and Sacrilege done upon the things appropriate to His divine service.

That of the Person is, when the very Deity is invaded, profaned, or robbed of Its glory: of this kind was that sacrilege of Lucifer, that would " place his throne in the north, and ascend above the clouds, and be like the most Highest;"[1] *similis ero Altissimo.* Of this kind is all idolatry: and therefore when the Israelites worshipped Baal-peor that is, the God of the Midianites upon the hill

---

[1] Isai. xiv. 14.

Pegor, or Phagor, it is said in Jerome's translation (Numb. xxv. 18) to be *Sacrilegium Phagor*, the sacrilege committed upon Mount Phagor. So when the style of God is bestowed upon stocks or stones, or living creatures; or when man, in pride of Lucifer, will be called God, as Alexander, Caius Caligula, Domitian, Nero, and others.[a] In this high sin are blasphemers, sorcerers, witches, and enchanters : and as it maketh the greatest irruption into the glorious majesty of Almighty God, so it maketh also the greatest divorce betwixt God and man.

In this sin, above all others, was Satan most desirous to plunge our first parents, Adam and Eve ; that, as himself by it had fallen from all felicity, so he might draw them likewise into the same perdition : *You shall be* (saith he) *like God, knowing good and evil.* That divine faculty of knowing good and evil, tickled the itching humour of a weak woman ; and to be like God fired her wholly with ambition, and carried her and Adam into the highest kind of sacrilege, committing thereby robbery upon the Deity itself : for so it is censured, Philip. ii. 6, where it is declared, that to be *equal with God was no robbery in the second Adam*, implying by an antithesis, that it was a robbery (and so a sacrilege) in the first Adam ; who is also guilty in the other kind of sacrilege, by taking the forbidden fruit reserved from him, as the priest's portion ; for knowledge belongeth to the priest.

Thus the first man that was created fell into sacrilege several ways, and so did also the first man that was born of a woman. Cain bringeth an oblation to God, but sacrilegiously, either withholding the best of his fruits, and offering the worst, as some conceived, *rectè offert, sed non rectè dividit*, or doing it hypocritically, as the later expoundeth it : whichsoever it was (and like enough to be both ways) he robbed God of His honour and divine faculty of knowing all things ; he granted Him to be omnipotent, but not omniscient; he did not think Him to be καρδιογνώστης, to know the secret thoughts of a man's heart: upon which reason S. Ambrose chargeth him also with another sacrilege in answering God, that he could not tell what was become of his brother, when himself had murdered[2] him; with the crime of sacrilege (saith Ambrose), in that he durst lie to God's own face: a pattern to the sacrilege of Ananias and Sapphira in the Acts of the Apostles.

To my understanding Cain is yet chargeable with another grievous sacrilege, even the murder of his brother; for in it he destroyed the temple of God, and in that temple the very sacred image of God: *Do ye not know* (saith S. Paul) *that you are the temple of God, and that the Spirit of God dwelleth in you?*[3] And again positively, *Ye are the temple of the living God.*[4] This temple did Cain sacrilegiously destroy, and the Spirit of God which dwelled in it did he also sacrilegiously deface and expel; even that Holy Spirit [Which] was the very image of God, for *in the image of God created He him.*[5]

Thus it appeareth that Sacrilege was the first sin, the master-sin, and the common sin at the beginning of the world, committed in earth by man in corruption, committed in paradise by man in perfection, committed in heaven itself by the angels in glory; against God the Father by arrogating His power, against God the Son by comtemning His word, against God the Holy Ghost by profaning things sanctified, and against all of them in general by invading and violating the Deity.[(B)] Let us now see how God revenged Himself upon sinners in this kind, and by way of collation apply it to ourselves: for His wisdom, and power, and justice are the same perpetually.

---

[2] Crimine Sacrilegii, quod Deo credidit mentiendum. S. Ambros. de Paradiso, cap. xiv. tom. i. 129 M.
[3] 1 Cor. vi. 19.   [4] 2 Cor. vi. 16.   [5] Gen. i. 27.

SECTION II.

The Punishment of Sacrilege in Lucifer and the Angels, upon Adam, Eve, and Cain, and upon the Old World, by the Flood, and upon them that built the Tower of Babel, Nimrod, and others.

First, He punished them by disinheriting and casting them out of their original possession. Lucifer is cast out of heaven, Adam and Eve out of paradise, Cain (whose name signifies a possession) out of his native possession, to be a runagate upon earth: all of them deprived of the favour of God, and all of them subject to a perpetual curse. Lucifer to perpetual darkness, Adam to perpetual labour, and Cain to perpetual fear and instability: by perpetual, I mean during their lives; for at their death they all meet in eternal damnation. The life of Satan is till the day of judgment; so, though he liveth so long, he reigneth in labour and travail to work wickedness: there is his end, and then is the time of his further and eternal punishment; then shall he and all his angels be cast into everlasting fire.[6] There I leave both him and them hopeless of mercy, which notwithstanding is graciously extended to Adam and his posterity repenting, by the meritorious Passion of our Saviour, Who, to expiate the sacrilege committed by man, in aspiring to be like God, debased Himself, being God, to become a man; and as man would have left the earth, and have scaled the heaven, so He left the heaven, and came down into the earth, living here in subjection to man, when man himself would not be subject to God: therefore (*ut contraria contrariis curentur*) as the sacrilege was a capital sin, that contained in it many other special sins, pride, ambition, rebellion, hypocrisy, malice, robbery, and many other hellish impieties; so for a punctual satisfaction He made Himself a capital Sacrifice, that contained innumerable graces, humility, contempt of the world and of Himself,

[6] Matt. xxv. 41, 46.

obedience, sincerity, love, bounty, and all other celestial virtues.

The contemplation of this exorbitant mercy, which I leave to be sounded forth by the golden trumpets of the Church, hath led me a little forth of my course. I return to Adam and his posterity, and will go on with them safely, as I find them left in the hands of justice, and the dint of the curse. Adam in his children, and they in him, are all unhappy : his good son Abel is cruelly murdered, and by whom, but (to increase his grief) by his other son Cain ? who, according to the law of nature, ought to die for it, as himself confesseth,[7] and then was Adam destitute of them both. Yet so is he notwithstanding ; for his son Cain, the murderer, is a condemned person, a banished man, and a continual fugitive to save his life ; which nevertheless was at length casually taken from him by the hand of Lamech ; as S. Hierome (out of an author) reporteth :[8] "Thus two of Adam's sons died unnaturally ; and all the rest, except Seth, living wickedly, are not therefore mentioned in Holy Scriptures." Touching their worldly affairs, all was evil and out of course ; labour, and sweat, and sorrow vex their persons ; the beasts of the earth, and the fowls of the air, that formerly were subject to Adam, will rebel and become his enemies ; the earth, that formerly gave him sustenance of her own accord, will now yield nothing but by compulsion, and is besides unto him both false and refractory : he commits his corn unto it, and it renders him thistles and weeds ; he planteth his vineyard in it, and it bringeth him thorns and briars ; all the works of man are now in the sorrow of his hands.[9] The thoughts of his heart are only evil continually,[1] and the earth is corrupt before God, and full of cruelty.[2]

Thus the soul, the body, the mind, and the man-

[7] Gen. iv. 14.
[8] S. HIERONYM. Ep. xxxvi. ad S. Damasum, tom. i. 157.
[9] Gen. iii. 17-19.   [1] Gen. vi. 5.   [2] Ibid. ver. 11.

ners of men, the nature of beasts and fowls, and the condition of the earth itself, being wholly altered from the original constitution, and corrupted by the contagion of sacrilege, it pleased the justice of God to bring the flood upon the earth, to sweep away all the posterity of wicked Cain in the seventh generation; and not to spare any either of Adam's line, or of righteous Seth's generation [save Noah] and his family, as a type of the sacred portion appropriated to His worship, which those sinners of the old world had so much corrupted. Thus for sacrilege was the whole world destroyed; in that universal destruction was nothing saved but the tenth generation; that out of it, as from a better root, the new world might be produced and replenished.

But the coals of that old ambition (which, before the flood, being once fired by Satan in the hearts of our first parents, pricked them on in a desire to be like gods) came, by propagation of original sin, to be kindled again after the flood, in the proud builders of the tower of Babel, who by their miraculous work would also be like gods; and by giving themselves a name upon earth, live (as it were) eternally; and withal, provide so against the hand of God, as they would be no more in danger of drowning. *Go to* (say they), *let us build us a city and a tower, whose top may reach up unto heaven, that we may get us a name, lest we be scattered upon the whole earth.*[3] These were the giants spoken of by the ancients, that did *bellare cum diis:* they preferred their own glory before the honour of God, and that Calvin termeth " a sacrilegious insolence, that breaketh out against God himself, and like the giants assaults Him."[4] See the punishment: their sacrilegious interest is miraculously defeated by God's own immediate hand, their language confounded, their society

---

[3] Gen. xi. 4.

[4] " Sacrilegam audaciam quæ prorumpit contra Deum Ipsum, ut gigantum more cœlum oppugnet." CALVIN. Comm. in Gen. i. 60, col. 1, ad fin.

broken; they are cast out of their ancient habitation, and that which they most feared falleth upon them; to be scattered over all the face of the earth, and to be bereaved of their friends and kindred. For it is said, they understood not *labium proximi sui*, the language of their friends and neighbours, and were thereby compelled to leave them, as if they had been dead, and their family extinct, and to associate with those whom they did understand.

Besides this, as there fell a grievous curse upon the posterity of Adam and Cain for their sacrilege, so (the divines observe) did there also upon the whole posterity of their children, that is, upon the whole world. "The whole world at this day (saith Calvin) feeleth the evil of this curse of the confusion of languages;"[5] for by it the strongest bond of human society and concord is broken, the hearts of men alienated one from another, their means of commerce taken away, their manners changed, and their minds, thoughts, studies, and dispositions contrary for the most part, and repugnant.

Sacrilege being thus got up again, bringeth forth immediately the other branches of impiety: for Nimrod, the proud hunter, and chief builder of the tower of Babel, is not satisfied with being like a god, but is adored of his people as a god indeed, and at length so taken of all the Gentiles under the name of Saturn, or Saturnus Babylonicus. So, after him, is his son, Jupiter Belus, whom the Scripture calleth Bel, Baal, and likewise many other of their children and posterity, by whom the world in a short time becometh full of gods: and though they daily saw these their gods to grow old and feeble, and to die like men, and to rot and putrify like the basest creatures; yet such was their stupidity, that out of wood and metal they framed their images, and styling those blockish lumps by the names of gods, erected altars and temples to

[5] " Hodie mundus hanc calamitatem sustinet." CALVIN. Comm. in Gen. i. 61, col. 2.

them ; and honouring them with the rites of sacrifices and divine worship, belonging only to the true
living God, did thus bring the abomination of idolatry
over all the world.

How fearfully God punished this high kind of
sacrilege, appears abundantly in the book of Joshua
and other scriptures : all the kingdoms of Canaan,
where it first began to spread itself, were so universally devoured with fire and sword, as never any
under the sun were like unto them. Yea, when
there were strange gods in the house of Jacob, both
against his will, and perhaps without his knowledge,
yet the hand of God was so upon his house, as that
his daughter Dinah is ravished, his sons Simeon and
Levi commit a cruel murder on the Sichemites; Jacob
thereby liveth in grief and fear of his neighbours, his
wife Rachel dieth in childbed, and his son Reuben
committeth incest with his concubine Bilhah.[6]

What should I tell of the three thousand slain at
once, about the golden calf :[7] how for Solomon's
idolatry his issue lost the kingdom of Israel :[8] how
Israel itself was carried captive into Babylon :[9] how
Manasses is taken prisoner by the Assyrians,[1] his
son Amon slain by his servants,[2] his grandchild
Josias, a good king, yet also slain,[3] and his eldest
son, Jehoahaz, reigning after him, taken prisoner by
Pharaoh Nechoh, and dying in Egypt ; his second
son, Jehoiakim, succeeding, taken also prisoner by
Nebuchadnezzar ; Jerusalem spoiled, and he, his
princes, people, treasure, and golden vessels of the
temple, all carried to Babylon, and all for idolatry.[4]
For Jehoram's idolatry Jerusalem is taken, he with
his wives and treasure ; and all his sons, save the
youngest, slain ; and himself, after a long torment-
ing disease, hath his bowels fall out.[5] So Amaziah

[6] Gen. xxxiv. 2, 26, xxxv. 19, 22.   [7] Exod. xxxii. 28.
[8] 1 Kings xii. 20.   [9] 2 Kings xvii. 6.
[1] 2 Chron. xxxiii. 11.   [2] 2 Kings xxi. 23.
[3] 2 Kings xxiii. 29.   [4] 2 Kings xxiv. 2, xxv. 1.
[5] 2 Chron. xxi. 17, 18, 19.

seeth Jerusalem defaced, the temple spoiled, his treasure carried away, and himself a prisoner; and being restored, driven out by treason, and slain at last.[6]

I will wade no farther in this kind of sacrilege, which is never passed over in scripture but with some remarkable punishments: our country, I hope, doth not at this day know it.

SECTION III.

Of the other sorts of Sacrilege, commonly so called, as of Time, Persons, Function, Place, and other things Consecrated to the Worship of God. And first of Time, in profaning the Sabbath.

I COME now to the second part, which indeed is that which the schoolmen and canonists only call sacrilege, as though the former were of too high a nature to be expressed in this appellation: so exorbitant a sin, as that no name can properly comprehend it: θεομαχία, a warring against God, and θεοβλάβεια a direful violence upon Divine Majesty, a superlative sacrilege.

The other and common kind of sacrilege is (as was said, a violating, misusing, or a putting away of things consecrated or appropriated to divine service or worship of God: it hath many branches —time, persons, function, place: and materially. All (saith Thomas Aquinas) that pertains to irreverent treatment of holy things, pertains to the injury of GOD, and comes under the character of sacrilege.[7] This description of sacrilege may well enough be extended further than Aquinas did perhaps intend it, to the former or superlative kind.

Sacrilege of time is, when the sabbath or the Lord's day is abused or profaned: this God expressly

[6] 2 Chron. xxv. 14, 27.

[7] " Omne illud quod ad irreverentiam rerum sacrarum pertinet, a l injuriam Dei pertinet, et habet sacrilegii rationem." Secunda secundae, Qu. 99, Art. I.

K

punished in the stick-gatherer. Some canonists seem
not to reckon this under the common kind of sacrilege.[8] So that in all that followeth we shall run the
broken way of the schoolmen and canonists.

SECTION IV.

*Sacrilege of Persons, that is, Priests and Ministers conse-
crated to the service of God, and the punishment thereof.*

SACRILEGE against the person is, when priests or
ministers of God's divine service are either violated
or abused : *Fear the Lord, and honour His priests.*[9]
*For he beareth the iniquity of the congregation, to
make an atonement for them before the Lord.*[1] *For
the Levite is separate to the Lord, to minister unto
Him, to bless thee in His name :*[2] therefore when
Micah had got a Levite into his house, he rejoiced,
and said, *I know that the Lord will be good unto me,
seeing I have a Levite to my priest.*[3] *Touch not
Mine anointed, nor do My prophets no harm.*[4] Mine
anointed, that is, not My kings, nor My priests : and
*Beware that thou forsake not the Levite as long as
thou livest upon the earth.*[5] Beware, saith God, as
intimating danger and punishment to hang over
their head that offered otherwise : and what? not
for wronging the Levite (a thing too impious), but
for not loving and cherishing him all the days of
thy life. I must here note, as it cometh in my way,
the remarkable justice and piety of Pharaoh towards
his idol priests ; that when by reason of the famine
he had got and bought unto himself all the money,
cattle, lands, wealth, and persons of the Egyptians,
yet stretched he not forth his thoughts to the lands
or persons of his priests ; but, commiserating their
necessity, allowed them a [portion] at his own
charge, that they might both live and keep their

[8] Soto, de justitia et jure, lib. ii. qu. 4, fol. 50, 6.
[9] Ecclus. vii. 29, 31.   [1] Num. viii. 19.
[2] Deut. x. 8.   [3] Judg. xvii. 13.
[4] Ps. cv. 15.   [5] Deut. xii. 19.

lands.[6] Musculus hereupon infers, " How great a
sacrilege is it in our princes, that the good and lawful
ministers of holy things are thus neglected ? "[7] It is
to be noted, that as Micah expected a blessing from
God for entertaining an idolatrous Levite into his
house, so Pharaoh's piety towards his priests wanted
not a blessing from God upon his house, though
God hated both the idolaters and idolatry itself.

Let us see how sacrilege in this kind hath been
punished. The Benjamites of Gibeah wrong a
Levite villainously, in abusing his wife :[8] Gibeah
is therefore destroyed with fire and sword, above
twenty-six thousand valiant men of the Benjamites
slain, and the whole tribe almost wholly rased out
of Israel, with their cities and castles.[9]

Jeroboam, making golden calves, driveth the
priests of the Lord out of Israel, and makes himself
other priests, not of the tribe of Levi: for this he
is overthrown by Abijah, king of Judah, and five
hundred thousand of his men slain, his son taken
from him, and his posterity threatened to be swept
away like dung; and those of them that died in the
city, to be eaten of dogs, those in the fields, by the
fowls of the air.[1] Jeroboam also stretched but out
his hand against the prophet, to have him apprehended, and it is presently withered.[2]

Joash commanded Zacharias, son of Jehoiada the
priest, to be slain in the court of the Lord's house :
this done, he is overcome the next year following
by the Aramites ; all his princes are slain, his treasure and the spoil is sent to Damascus, himself left
afflicted with great diseases, and at last murdered
in his bed by his servants.[3]

---

[6] Gen. xlvii. 22.

[7] " Quantum sacrilegium est in nostris principibus, negligi legi-
timos probosque sacrorum ministros ? " [We can find no such
sentence in the Commentary of Musculus, but it is a fair abridge-
ment of his meaning. Comm. in Gen. p. 789.—Eds.]

[8] Judg. xix. 25.   [9] Judg. xxi. 3.

[1] 2 Chron. xiii. 9; 1 Kings xiv. 11.   [2] 1 Kings xiii. 4.

[3] 2 Chron. xxiv. 21, etc.

Zedekiah, king of Judah, casteth Jeremiah the prophet, first into prison, then for a season into the dungeon, and useth him harshly.[4] He, and those that counselled him to it, are overthrown by Nabuchodonosor, Jerusalem taken, his sons slain before his eyes, and then his eyes put out, and the people carried captive to Babylon: but Jeremiah himself is set at liberty, and well intreated by his enemies the Chaldeans.[5]

SECTION V.

Sacrilege of Function, by usurping the Priest's office; and the Punishment thereof.

SACRILEGE of function is, when those that are not called to the office of priesthood or ministry do usurp upon it. So Gideon made an ephod (that is, a pontifical ornament of the tabernacle), not at Shilo, but in his own city Ophra, whereby the Israelites fell to worship it: or, as others think, that he made all the things of the tabernacle, whereby the people were drawn to worship there, and not to go to Shilo, where the tabernacle was. This (saith the text) was the destruction of Gideon and his house; for his son Abimelech, rising against his brethren, slew seventy of them upon a stone, and them with a stone cast upon him by a woman, himself was first brained, and after, by his own commandment, thrust through by his page.[6]

Saul takes upon him to offer a burnt-offering to God in the absence of Samuel. The kingdom therefore is cut from his family,[7] and nothing after prospers with him, but he runneth into other sins, as that of sparing Agag and the cattle. He is overthrown by the Philistines, himself and three of his sons are slain by them,[8] Ishbosheth, a fourth son, by treachery,[9] and seven more are hanged for appeasing of the Gibeonites.[1]

---

[4] Jer. xxxii. 3, xxxvii. 21, xxxviii. 9.   [5] Jer. xxxix. 11, etc.
[6] Judg. viii. 27, ix. 53.   [7] 1 Sam. xiii. 14.
[8] 1 Sam. xxxi. 8.   [9] 2 Sam. iv. 6.   [1] 2 Sam. xxi. 6.

Uzza, being no Levite, stretched forth his hand and stayeth the ark from falling: it seemed a pious act, yet God presently struck him dead for it.[2]

Uzziah the king, in spite of the priests, goeth into the sanctuary, and would burn incense, which belonged only to the priest's office. This (saith the text) was his destruction, for he transgressed against the Lord; therefore, whilst he was yet but about it, having the incense in his hand to burn it, the leprosy presently rose in his forehead: so that he was not only constrained to haste himself presently out of the temple, but to live all his life after sequestered from the company of men; and, being dead, was not buried in the sepulchre of his fathers, but in the field there apart from them.[3]

Let those that have impropriations consider whether these cases concern not them; for, like Uzzah, they stretch out their hands to holy things (but would God it were to no worse intent), like Gideon they bring them into their own inheritance, and like Saul and Uzziah they take upon them the priest's office: for they are parsons of the parish, and ought to offer up prayers for the sins of the people.

SECTION VI.

Sacrilege of Holy Places, Churches, and Oratories consecrated to the honour and service of God: and the fearful punishments thereof showed by many examples.

SACRILEGE of the place is, when the temple or the house of God, or the soil that is consecrated to His honour, is either violated or profaned. When God was in the fiery bush at Horeb, the place about it was presently sanctified, so that Moses himself might neither come near the bush, nor stand aloof upon the holy ground with his shoes on, but in reverence of the place must be barefooted.[4] So

---

[2] 2 Sam. vi. 6, 7.   [3] 2 Chron. xxvi. 16, etc.

[4] Exod. iii. 5.

when God descended upon Mount Sinai, His Presence made the place round about it holy. He commanded therefore that marks should be set upon
the border, to distinguish it from the other ground;
and that if man or beast did but touch it, they should
be either stoned or thrust through with a dart.[5]

Thus afore the law : when the law was given, first
the tabernacle, and then the temple, were full of
sanctification, both by the Presence of God and by
the decree of His mouth, as appeareth abundantly
in scripture :[6] therefore grievous punishments were
always inflicted upon such as did violate them in
any thing. *If any man* (saith the Geneva translation) *destroy the temple of God, him shall God
destroy ; for the temple of God is holy.*[7] The Greek
is much more copious, and doth not restrain it to
them only that destroy the temple, but extendeth it
to all that either destroy or abuse it in any sort :
Εἴ τις τὸν ναὸν τοῦ Θεοῦ φθείρει, φθερεῖ τοῦτον ὁ Θεός· ὁ
γὰρ ναὸς τοῦ Θεοῦ ἅγιός ἐστιν, οἵτινές ἐστε ὑμεῖς. The
vulgar Latin doth well express it : *Si quis templum
Dei violaverit, disperdet eum Deus, etc.;* for the
word φθείρω is *corrumpo, vexo, calamitatem infero,
perdo, defloro, violo, vitio :* so that it contains as well
the lesser injuries done to the temple, as that great
and capital crime of destroying it : but because the
Apostle useth one word in both places, φθείρει and
φθερεῖ, they likewise in the [Geneva version] would
have one word in both places, [and fix] upon the
word *destroy,* which to my understanding is too
particular, and might have been better expressed
by a word of more general signification; as to say,
if any man spoil the temple of God, God shall spoil
him :. that is to say, if he spoil the temple, either by
destroying it, or defacing it, or violating it in any
course, as by robbing, stealing, or taking from it
any ornaments . . . goods, rights . . . means of
maintenance, or by abusing it in any manner what-

[5] Exod. xix. 21.
[6] Exod. xl. 34, 35; 1 Kings viii. 10, 11.   [7] 1 Cor. iii. 17

soever, God shall spoil him in one sort or other, as of his patrimony, lands, goods, liberty, pleasures, health, and life itself ; children, family, and posterity : and not so only, but by casting also upon him divers fearful visitations and misfortunes, more or less, as ιu His wisdom shall [seem fit.*] The word *destroy* is not properly said of any punishment that tendeth only to work amendment : and God doubtless often spoileth a man of the things he delighteth in, not to his whole destruction, but to awaken him to amendment.

Let us see in what manner God hath punished this kind of sacrilege among the Jews.

In the time of the law, though frequent examples are not to be expected, for that there was but one temple of God in both the kingdoms of Judah and [Israel], namely that of Jerusalem, built by Solomon, and for the most part p[iously] preserved in after ages. Another there was at Samaria, which [was] builded upon Mount Gerizim, like to that of Jerusalem, by license of Alexander the Great, and being afterward destroyed by Hyrcanus, king of Judah, gave occasion to the Samaritan woman to say unto Christ, *Our fathers worshipped in this mountain.*[8] A third also, for the dispersed Jews in Egypt, built by Onias, son of Onias the high-priest, in the time of Antiochus Epiphanes.[9] But these two, being against the commandment of God (Who would have no temple but at Jerusalem) I meddle not with, nor with the synagogues of the Jews, being many in every city, four hundred and eighty in Jerusalem, instituted for strangers, as the temple was for the citizens, and erected of later time without any mention of them in the Old Testament or books Apocryphal. Let us see, I say, examples of this kind.

---

* [The printed copy reads—*as in His wisdom shall soon* . . . which seems an error of the transcriber.—Eds.]

8 S. John iv. 20.

9 Joseph. Antiq. l. 12, c. 14. De Bello Judaico, c. 7.

Nadab and Abihu, sons of Aaron, polluted the tabernacle, by neglecting the sanctified fire of the altar, and offering incense by strange and common fire : they were therefore devoured by strange fire sent upon them by the Lord Himself.

Hophni and Phinehas, the sons of Eli, made a sacrilegious rapine upon the offering of the Lord, upon the fat, and upon the flesh, and upon the holy portion; polluting also the sanctified place with sacrilegious adultery.[1] God termeth this a dishonouring Himself, and saith, *Them that honour Me, I will honour ; and they that despise Me, shall be despised.*[2] Hereupon He threateneth, first, to cut off the arm of Eli's father's house (*i.e.*, the authority and honour of the priesthood) ; which was performed when Solomon cast out Abiathar [the great grandson of Eli] out of the priest's office, and bestowed it on Zadoc, being of another family :[3] secondly, that all of his family should die before they came to be old, which himself did partly see in his own sons: thirdly, that his sons Hophni and Phinehas should die both in one day : fourthly, that he should see his enemy possess his office, and that the remnant of his family should crouch and be suitors to him for relief and favour. All of which undoubtedly came to pass : and yet with all this was not the wrath of God appeased; but spreading itself into a further agony of indignation, fell not only upon the whole people of Israel, but also upon the holiest monuments of the glory of God. The word of the Lord became rare and precious : there was no manifest vision : the army of Israel is beaten by the Philistines, and about four thousand of them slain in one battle, and thirty thousand in another : the ark of God taken prisoner, and carried captive into the house of Dagon, the Philistines' idol: Hophni and Phinehas die : Eli falleth backward and breaketh his neck : the wife of Phinehas

---

[1] 1 Sam. ii. 12.   [2] Ibid. ii. 30.
[3] 1 Kings ii. 26, 27

falleth untimely into travail, and dieth with grief.[4] Fourscore and five priests of Eli's house are, at Saul's commandment, tyrannously slain all in one day. Nob, the city of the priests, with the men, women, children, sucklings, oxen, sheep, and asses, all destroyed.[5] And finally, to cut the priesthood for ever from the house of Eli, Solomon cast Abiathar out of it (being the fourth in succession after Eli), and brought in Zadoc of another family.[6] Oh, the dreadful justice of Almighty God! But such of old was the fruit of sacrilege; and such effects it still produceth.

Joash stoned Zachariah in the court of the temple. This double sacrilege of person and place was punished by the slaughter of his people, loss of his treasure, diseases of his body, and murder of his person, as we have already cleared in "Sacrilege of the Person."

So Uzziah, entering the sanctuary by force, and attempting the priest's office in burning incense, committed sacrilege of place and person [and] was punished as we have cleared.

Ahaz committeth idolatry, and spoileth the temple of the treasure and some other ornaments. He is first given into the hands of the Azarites or Assyrians; then Pekah, king of Israel, slayeth one hundred and twenty thousand of his soldiers, all in one day, and taking two hundred thousand women and children prisoners, took away also much spoil, which they brought to Samaria. The Edomites also beat him, and captivated his people; and the Philistines took and inhabited many of his cities. In this affliction he farther spoileth the temple of the vessels, and shutteth it up; and, dying an idolator and sacrilegious, is not buried in the sepulchre of his father, but apart in Jerusalem.[7]

Nabuohodonosor, otherwise called Nebuchadnezzar, spoileth the temple, carrieth thence all the treasure and holy vessels,[8] slayeth those that were

[4] 1 Sam. iv. 18, 19.   [5] Ibid. xxii. 18.   [6] 1 Chron. vi. 8.
[7] 2 Chron. xxviii., 27.   [8] 2 Kings xxiv. 13.

fled thither for safety; after by his servants burnt
it.[9] He is stricken with madness, cast out of his
kingdom, liveth among beasts, and, like a beast,
feedeth upon grass, till his hairs were grown like
eagles' feathers, and his nails like birds' claws.[1]
And in the days of his grandchild was his family
clean extinguished, and his great empire taken from
him by force, and given to the Persians.[2]

Antiochus Epiphanes, son of Antiochus the Great,
king of Syria, entereth into the sanctuary, and
taketh away the golden altar and the treasure of the
temple, even one thousand eight hundred talents.
Presently his posterity and glory altereth, his
captains are slain, his armies beaten, and all his
affairs were so unfortunate, that calling his friends
unto him [he] confesseth that he was fallen into
that adversity and flood of misery, for that evil he
had done at Jerusalem : " for I took " (saith he) " all
the vessels of gold and silver that were in it . . .
and I know that these troubles are come upon me
for the same cause; and behold I must die with
great sorrow in a strange land."[3] Thus in passions
of grief he ended his days.[4] Yet did not this end
his tragedy, for his son Antiochus Eupator was
deprived of his kingdom by his uncle Demetrius,
and put to death: and although Alexander Epiphanes, his other son, a brother of Antiochus
Eupator, recovered the kingdom, and slew Deme-
trins, and fortified himself by the marriage of
Cleopatra, daughter of Ptolemy, king of Egypt, to
his great happiness, as he thought, yet God turned
it to his own destruction; for Ptolemy took both
her and the kingdom from him, and gave them to
his enemy, Demetrius Nicanor; and whilst he fled
to save his life, to his friend Zabdiel the Arabian, he

---

[9] 2 Chron. xxxvi. 17.   [1] Dan. iv. 33.   [2] Dan. v. 31.

[3] He had a violent fall out of his chariot, and he was tormented
with an horrible disease; worms came out of his body, and his
flesh fell off for pain, and no man could endure his stink.—2 Macc.
ix. 7, 8, etc.

[4] 1 Macc. vi. 11, 12.

struck off his head, and sent it to Ptolemy :[5] notwithstanding this, his son Antiochus Theos, being
but a child, by the help of Tryphon, was restored
to his father's kingdom, and overthrew Demetrius
Nicanor,[6] who flying, is imprisoned by Arsaces, king
of Persia,[7] and after slain : so that Antiochus seemeth
now * secure, but the hand of God is still upon the
posterity of Antiochus Epiphanes the sacrilegist; for
even now doth Tryphon himself murder his grandchild Antiochus Theos,[8] and ending that line,
usurpeth the kingdom.[9]

Touching the sacrilegious attempt made by Antiochus and some of his soldiers upon the temple of
[Nanea] (or Diana, as Lyra taketh it), in Persia, and
the terrible destruction that fell immediately upon
them,[1] I pass it over, as not belonging to this place.

Heliodorus, the treasurer of king Seleucus, is sent
by his master to fetch the innumerable money that
was in the temple of Jerusalem, not belonging to
the provision of the sacrifices, but deposited there
in safety for widows and orphans. The high-priest
Onias declareth to him, that there was not above
four hundred talents of silver and two hundred of
gold ; and both he and the rest of the priests, and
the rest of the city, prayed instantly to God to
preserve the treasury ; notwithstanding Heliodorus
and his soldiers approach unto it, and presently
there appeared a terrible man on horseback, richly
barbed, between two young men of notable strength,
and the horse running fiercely upon him, struck
him on the breast with his forefoot, and the young
men scourged him continually with many sore stripes;
so that Heliodorus falling to the ground, and
covered with great darkness, was carried away in a
horse-litter, desperate of life, till by entreaty Onias
prayed for him, and thereupon the young men ap-

[5] 1 Macc. xi. 17.   [6] 1 Macc. xii. 55.   [7] Ibid. xiv. 2.
* [The printed copy, with a manifest error, reads *not.*—EDS.]
[8] Within thirty years after the sacrilege.
[9] 1 Macc. xiii. 31.   Read 2 Macc. ix. 7.   [1] 2 Macc. i. 16.

pearing again to Heliodorus, willed him to give Onias thanks, because God for his sake had spared his life. Seleucus after this would have sent another, but Heliodorus advising him to send his enemy he gave it over: *If thou hast an enemy or traitor send him thither, and thou shalt receive him well scourged: for in that place, no doubt, there is an especial power of God: for He that dwelleth in heaven hath His eye on that place, and defendeth it, and He beateth and destroyeth them that come to hurt it.*[2]

Lysimachus, a man of great power in Jerusalem, brother and deputy to Menelaus the high-priest, purloineth much of the golden vessels, and in the Geneva translation is termed a church robber. He falleth into hatred of his countrymen, the Jews, and having about three thousand for his guard, is notwithstanding, in a tumult of the people, oppressed with clubs, dust, and stones, and in that manner slain near unto the treasury, with some of his company, many others of them being wounded.[3]

Callisthenes, who had set fire upon the holy gates, flying after into a cottage, the same was also set on fire and he burned in it.[4]

Menelaus, having obtained by money the high-priesthood, stealeth certain of the golden vessels out of the temple, giving part away, and selling part unto the Tyrians and others: he is afterwards accused to Antiochus Eupator to have been the author of the evils in Judea, and for the sacrilege committed by him about the holy fire and ashes of the altar, he is put to death at Beræa, by an engine upon the top of an high tower, ordained for the punishment of sacrilege and other great offences, by overwhelming the offenders with ashes; and being dead, he must not be buried, for that he was a sacrilegist.[5] Let those clergymen that defraud their churches of their lands or goods consider this example.

Nicanor, governor of Judæa under Eupator

2 2 Macc. iii. 38, 39.   3 Ibid. iv. 39.
4 2 Macc. vi. 33.   5 Macc. xiii. 4.

(stretching forth his hand towards the temple), sweareth, that if Judas Maccabæus were not delivered unto him prisoner, he would make it a plain field, and break down the altar, and erect an [altar and a] temple to Bacchus. At the next encounter, Judas with a small power slayeth thirty-five thousand of Nicanor's army, and among them, unwittingly, Nicanor himself, whose head, and the hand with the shoulder that he had stretched forth against the temple, he caused to be cut off and carried to Jerusalem, and showed there to the priests and others; and cut out the tongue, and minced it, and cast it to the birds, and set the head on the castle.[6]

Thus, touching local sacrilege, I have gone through the canonical and apocryphal books of the Old Testament : before I enter into the New (which will be very short), I desire to remember one that happened in the meantime.

Pompey the Great, by help of Hyrcanus, taketh Jerusalem, and battering down a wall of the temple, maketh there a great slaughter, not only of the Jews, but of the priests themselves, that even then were at the sacrifices, and choosed rather to die than to intermit the same : and then entering with his soldiers into the sanctuary, did behold those sacred things which a profane eye never saw before ; the golden table, the candlestick, the sacrificing instruments, and what might tempt a wasteful general, two thousand talents of holy treasure, which Pompey notwithstanding, to the glory of his heathen piety, would never touch, but commanded that the ministers should cleanse the temple presently, and continue their daily sacrifices, making Hyrcanus now high-priest.[7] Hitherto all glory and fortune attended Pompey's servants ; three times he triumpheth, and is as well conqueror of the hearts of his nation, as of their persons, whom he subdued. Some in Plutarch (where his conquests are recited) compare them with Alexander the Great; but after

[6] 2 Macc. xiv. 33; xv. 27.   [7] JOSEPH. Antiq. lib. xiv. § 8.

this sacrilege (to my knowledge observe it) nothing doth prosper with him, but as conducing to his hurt: "Oh, would God he had died while his fortune was yet like Alexander's! for in the rest of his life his prosperities were hateful, and his miseries bitter." (c) He hasteth home into Italy to enjoy the pleasures of his family and country, where he findeth that his wife Mutia had played the harlot, and therefore divorceth her: that the senate one while slight and deride him, another while magnify him and use him for necessity, but always suspect him, in great opposition with the principal men: and when he had married Julia, the daughter of Cæsar, to be reconciled with him, she became abortive of her first child, and died of her second, and the child also, all in a short space. Then runneth the dissension between Cæsar and him, which groweth to arms on both sides; and when Cæsar at first had the advantage, yet he offereth Pompey conclusions of peace, which Pompey (ordained to destruction) refuseth; and having at last, by the confluence of senators and active men unto him, more than double the army of Cæsar, besides an invincible navy to secure him, he joineth battle with great hope and probability of victory near Pharsalia in Thessaly, but is overthrown, and flying to his great friend Ptolemy in Egypt, is there barbarously murdered at his landing, in the sight of his wife and son, his head struck off, and his body cast upon the shore. Plutarch, in his life, admiring whence this change of fortune should come, supposes it to be for misgoverning the commonwealth: I, by the precedent examples, impute it to his sacrilege, which after that manner wrought still upon his posterity to the extirpation of his family. For his son, Cneius Pompeius, overcome in Spain by Cæsar, is slain also in fight.[8] And his other son, Sextus Pompeius, driven out of Egypt into Asia, is there slain by the commandment of Antonius.[9]

[8] APPIAN. de Bell. Civil. ii. 105.   [9] Ibid. v. 144.

Marcus Crassus,[1] being the second time consul
with Pompey the Great, had now by lot the charge
of Syria; and marching with a mighty army against
the Parthians, he came to Jerusalem, and seeing the
treasure of the temple (which Pompey forbare
to meddle with), he took away two thousand talents
of money, and all the gold, amounting to eight
thousand; and besides this, the golden beam, weighing seven hundred and fifty pounds, whereon the
veils did hang. To say truth, the golden beam was
delivered to him by Eleazar the priest, as a ransom
for all the rest, Crassus swearing to take nothing
else: but having the one, he would not leave the
other. The beam he broke, and coined it into
money for payment of the soldiers.

The success was this. Many grievous tempests
of thunder and lightning opposed his army; a
violent wind brake the bridge he made for his
passage; his camp was twice stricken with lightning : and divers other such prodigious events are
noted by Plutarch. Joining battle with his enemy,
his dear son was first slain in his own sight, with the
flower of his cavalry, and then all the Roman army
slaughtered or discomfited. Himself, though Surenas
the general would have saved him, was also slain :
being dead, his head and his hand (that committed
the sacrilege), like Nicanor's in the Maccabees, were
stricken off, and, with other monuments of the
Roman glory, most contemptuously abused and
derided, in triumphs, plays, and public meetings.
It is noted to be one of the greatest overthrows that
ever the Romans had.[2]

Some report, that the Parthians, in derision of his
avarice, poured molten gold into his mouth; and say
also, that he slew himself, by thrusting his riding-

[1] This larger account of Crassus' sacrilege was found in a loose
paper, written with Sir Henry Spelman's own hand. [Note by
Jeremy Stephens.—In the present edition the shorter account is
omitted.—EDS.]

[2] JOSEPH. Antiq. lib. 14, cap. 13. PLUTARCH. in M. Crasso
PSEUDO-APPIAN. Bell. Parth. III. 65 [Ed. Schweigh.]

wand into his own brains through his eye. But, I take it, he that thus killed himself was Pub. Crassus Nucianus, brother to the grandfather of this M. Crassus, overthrown also in the Parthian wars by Aristonicus.

It is much to be admired, that none of the heathen Emperors of Rome, after Titus (many of them being notoriously wicked and prodigal), nor Gensericus and his Vandals, did not convert such goodly rich vessels of gold and silver, as those of the temple were, into ready money, for the maintenance of their great armies, and other public necessities of state; but that they should suffer them to be preserved without any loss or embezzling, for the space of five hundred years together. But the providence of God is very remarkable in preserving them, until they came to the great Christian Emperor Justinian, who disposed them to Christian churches, as is showed. (ᵖ)

The learned Mr. Fuller[3] thinks that it is unknown what became of these vessels after Titus carried them to Rome. But it appeareth he is mistaken in this; though not in his opinion, that the Holy and Holy of Holiest remained entire and untortured till all was destroyed at the captivity of Babylon; though the outward courts and chambers had been often plundered. And if this be true, as it is very probable, hence may we well consider and admire the wonderful providence of God, in defending the temple in the principal parts of it, for the benefit of His own worship and glory, though He suffered the outward to be plundered oftentimes, for the sins and wickedness of the people. Though at last, when God resolved to put an end to the Jews' state and religion, then He suffered the Temple to be burnt and destroyed utterly; never suffering it to be built again, though it were attempted divers times.

But yet the gold and silver vessels of the Temple (which were moveable things that might be carried

---

[3] Nic. Fuller, Misc. Sac. lib. iii. p. 438.

away to another country, and at one time or other might serve for some good use and purpose), God preserved in all the changes and transmigrations that happened, till He brought them at length to the hands of a religious and pious Emperor, who bestowed them upon Christian churches, even at Jerusalem, from whence they came.

Shortly after this our Saviour, Christ, cometh into the world; and though reproving it of all kinds of sins, He punisheth not one, save only sacrilege. He refuseth to be judge in parting the inheritance between the two brethren, and He would give no sentence against the woman taken in adultery; but in case of sacrilege, Himself makes the whip, Himself punisheth the offenders, Himself overthrows the money-tables, and drives out the profaners of the temple, with their sheep and their oxen; not suffering the innocent doves to remain, though all these were for sacrifices, and put in the court-yard.[4] Such was His zeal in this kind of sacrilege, that He refused not to be the accuser, the judge, and the executioner: and this not only once, but twice; [the first time] at the beginning of His ministry, recited by S. John, and the last near the conclusion thereof, mentioned by S. Matthew.

As for the sacrilege of Judas and Pilate, the one in robbing the sacred purse of our Saviour, the other of rifling the holy treasure of the temple; they are such petty things in respect of their unexpressible crimes about the death of our Saviour, as I dare not apply their punishment hither. But Judas hanged himself,[5] and throwing himself down headlong, burst asunder in the midst, and all his bowels gushed out.[6] Pilate, in the displeasure of Caius the Emperor about the money of the temple, is by him banished to Lyons, in France; and there, distracted with grief and misfortune, slayeth himself with his own hands.[7]

[4] S. John ii. 14 ; S. Matt. xxi. 12.
[5] S. Matt. xxvii. 5.　　[6] Acts i. 18.　　[7] EUSEB. l. ii. c. 7.

So Herod is deposed by Caius from his tetrarchy, and perpetually banished also to Lyons, with his wife Herodias, and dies miserably; their goods confiscate by Caius, and given to Agrippa.[8] Josephus also noteth, that within an hundred years all his progeny, except a very few of the multitude, were consumed and extinct.[9]

SECTION VII.

Sacrilege of Materials or Things; as of the Ark of God taken by the Philistines: of the Two Hundred Shekels of Silver, a Wedge of Gold, with the Babylonian Garment, stolen by Achan:[1] of the Money Concealed by Ananias and Sapphira:[2] with the fearful punishments that fell upon them all.

SACRILEGE of things and materials, I call that which is done upon things properly settled in holy places, or belonging unto them; of this sort seemeth the very Ark itself, whiles it travelled up and down, and remained not either at the tabernacle at Shiloh, or the temple at Jerusalem.

The citizens and borderers of Ashdod, overthrowing the children of Israel, took in battle the Ark of God; they use it with all reverence, and place it in their temple, by their god Dagon: but the next morning their god Dagon was fallen down on his face (as adoring the Ark), his head and hands were stricken off, and such a destruction and death was upon the people, that the very cry of the city went up to heaven, and those that were not slain were smitten with emerods,[3] besides a plague of mice that was upon them: consulting therefore with their priests, they not only send back the Ark with all honour, but with a sin-offering also of golden emerods and golden mice, to be a perpetual monument of their penance and punishment.[4]

---

[8] JOSEPH. Ant. lib. xviii. c. 7.   [9] Id. lib. xviii. c. 5.
[1] Josh. vii. 21.   [2] Acts v. 6.
[3] 1 Sam. v. 4.   [4] 1 Sam. vi. 4.

The Bethshemites (whilst the Ark was among the Philistines) presumed to look into it : God for this attempt slayeth of the people fifty thousand and seventy men. *And the people lamented, because the Lord had smitten many of the people with a great slaughter. And the men of Bethshemesh said, Who is able to stand before this holy Lord God? and to whom shall He go up from us?* [5] So for touching it with unsanctified hands (though to save it from falling) was Uzzah slain, as we said before in the *Sacrilege of Function.* [6]

Achan, in the destruction of Jericho, stealeth two hundred shekels of silver and a wedge of gold, from the rest of the gold and silver and metal, that by the commandment of God [7] was to be consecrated and brought into the treasury of the tabernacle, and did put it even with his own stuff, saith the text. [8] This offence of this one man brought a punishment in general upon the whole people : in the assault at Ai they are overthrown, and can no more stand before their enemies (as God himself tells them) till this sacrilege be punished and purged. [9] Therefore not only Achan himself, but his sons and his daughters, his oxen, his asses, his people, and his tent, and all that he had, were both stoned and burnt together. [1]

Of this sort is the sacrilege of spoiling God of His tithes and offerings, spoken of in Malachi iii. 8 ; where likewise the penalty is declared by God's own mouth, *Ye are cursed with a curse, even this whole nation.*

Of this sort also is the sacrilege of Ananias and Sapphira, in the Acts of the Apostles, whereof we shall speak anon.*

[For, that they were guilty of sacrilege it is plain, not only by the verdict of the holy fathers,

[5] 1 Sam. vi. 19.   [6] 2 Sam. vi. 7.   [7] Josh. vii. 21.
[8] ver. 11.   [9] Josh. vii. 12.   [1] Josh. vii. 24.

* [As Sir Henry Spelman never executed this intention, we have inserted the parallel passage from Dr. BASIRE's *Sacrilege Arraigned;* which we have mentioned in our Introductory Essay. —EDS.]

both Greek and Latin, as S. Chrysostom, S. Ambrose, S. Austin; but, to name no other writers, by a full jury of Protestants upon the place, amongst the rest Calvin,[2] and Beza, whose testimony[3] amounts to these five concessions—1. That there may still be a consecration of things under the Gospel; 2. That this consecration may be of lands; 3. That this consecration, because it was offered *Ecclesiæ*, to the Church, therefore it was construed to be offered *Domino* too, to the Lord, as Irenæus by-and-bye, *in Usus Dominicos*, so that the Lord is still a Party in this cause; 4. That this consecration is done *Spiritus Sancti impulsu*, and so Diodati[4] too upon the place, by the good motion of the Holy Ghost (so far are this kind of devotions from being unlawful or unacceptable), which good motion because they had not sincerely obeyed, therefore (saith that Italian doctor) they did abuse the Holy Ghost; 5, and lastly, they all agree, that to alienate this from a consecrated use is sacrilege. . . . And because this fact of Ananias was the first notorious act of sacrilege that ever was committed under the Gospel; therefore, lest any after them should presume upon their impunity, as they gave ill example to their generation, and to posterity to boot (it is Peter Martyr's note), themselves became a sad example to both; they were confounded body and soul. And that too with a sudden destruction, in an instant, the usual destiny of sacrilege; witness Belshazzar,[5] Athaliah, and so many more slain, ἐπ' αὐτοφώρῳ, as we say, in the very act of sacrilege. This is a history brimful of horror, in all the grievous circumstances of it: to see a man and his

[2] Erat sacrilega fraudatio, quia partem ex eo subducit, quod sacrum esse Deo profitebatur. Calv. ad locum. See the rest in Marlorati Ecclesiastiac Expos. ad locum.

[3] See at large Beza on Acts v. 2.

[4] Per mentire allo Spirito Santo : c. In quanto quella consecratione potera essere stata un movimento desso, à cui egli non havea sinceramente ubbidito. Diodati in ver. 3, cap. v.

[5] Dan. v. 30; 2 Kings xi. 16.

wife, children of the Church, auditors of the Apostles, professors of Christ's true religion outwardly, conformable to the apostolical discipline, benefactors to the Church, no apparent professed enemies or atheists, no persecutors or apostates, or notorious evil-livers (for anything we read of them). Ah! I tremble to think it, that such persons, so qualified, should yet be liable to so execrable an end, as (say some[6]) in a moment to be damned, body and soul (dying without repentance); should, as they were man and wife in the sin upon earth, be still man and wife in the torment of hell: and all this damnable rigour for grudging a few pence, or pounds at the most, to God and Holy Church. But *secret things belong unto the Lord our God;*[7] and *God's judgments are past finding out.*[8] Our best course therefore is, to adore them with admiration; to lay them to heart with fear and trembling, and to acknowledge with all humility, that God seeth not as man seeth. However sacrilege may be extenuated in the world's deceitful scales, yet, in the just balance of the sanctuary, you see the heavy doom of it weighs down to the bottom of hell.]

A multitude of examples there be of this kind, but for the most part they fall as well under the title of *local sacrilege*, as under this of *holy things:* I will therefore refer the reader to that which hath been already delivered, and will here close up the books of the Holy Scripture for matters done before the Passion of our Saviour.

NOTES.

(A) Of this kind of sacrilege Herod was guilty. "The people gave a shout, saying, It is the voice of a god and not of a man: and immediately the angel of the LORD smote him, because he gave not GOD the glory." Acts xii. 23. It has been long ago observed, that Captain Cook, immediately after allowing himself to receive divine honours from savages, perished miserably by the hands of those very savages.

[6] GOSTWICK'S Anatomy of Ananias' Sacrilege, chap. vi.
[7] Deut. xxix. 29   [8] Rom. xi. 33.

(B) It has been noticed, that the arrogating to things, the titles justly due to GOD alone, has often met with exemplary punishment ; for example, that ships named the *Invincible*, the *Thunderer*, etc., nay even those called by the less arrogant, though still haughty names of the *Swiftsure* and the *Victory*, have often been miserably destroyed.

(c) Cf. JUVENAL. x. 283.

> Provida Pompeio dederat Campania febres
> Optandas : sed multæ urbes, et publica vota
> Vicerunt.   Igitur Fortuna ipsius et Urbis
> Servatum victo caput abstulit.

(D) "Titus also did not convert them to any private use, but carried them to Rome, where they continued many years in the capitol, until Gensericus the Vandal sacked Rome, and from thence among other treasures carried them to Carthage, and there also they were preserved till Belisarius, the great general under Justinian the Emperor, conquered Carthage ; and among the riches and plunder that they won there, when Gelimer the fourth king, a successor after Gensericus, was taken, and other riches and great spoils, he took and recovered the holy vessels of the Temple, and brought them to Constantinople to the Emperor Justinian. When Justinian had them, he was informed by a Jew and some others, that they were the consecrated vessels of the Temple, and that they would not prosper in any man's custody ; and that for detaining of them formerly, Rome was conquered by Gensericus. When thus the vessels were brought to Constantinople, and presented to Justinian the Emperor, he greatly feared, and was very unwilling to convert them to any private use, or to his own treasury ; but upon advice sent them to Christian churches at Jerusalem, and so cleared himself of them, and would not be guilty of any suspicion of sacrilege."—JEREMY STEPHENS.

[The Editors have here omitted a section, inserted by Jeremy Stephens, and containing some just animadversions on the "omissions of the Presbyterians in their late annotations upon the Bible," as having lost their interest in the present day.]

CHAPTER II.

Sacrilege among Heathens before the Christian Era.

XERXES, having ten hundred thousand men in his land army, and as many, by estimation, in his navy, intendeth to make an absolute conquest of Greece; and spoiling all Phocis, leaveth a part of his army among the Dorians, commanding them to invade Delphi, and to fire the temple of Apollo, and to bring away the sacred riches of it. The soldiers, marching towards it, came to [the Temple of Athene of the Vestibule] a place not far from Delphi, where a wonderful tempest of rain and lightning suddenly came upon them, and rending down part of the mountains, overwhelmed many of the army, and so amazed the rest, that they fled away immediately in all the haste they could, fearing to be consumed by the god who, by this prodigious miracle, thus preserved his temple. In memory hereof a pillar was erected in the place, with an inscription to relate it.

But this seemed not a sufficient revenge for so horrible a design, accompanied with other acted sacrileges. Nothing, therefore, prospereth with Xerxes; [his invincible navy is overthrown at Salamis, where the Æacidæ and Dionysus were believed to fight on the side of the Greeks; he himself, who had set forth with splendour, pomp, and luxury from Persia, retreats in disorder, distress, and want to the Hellespont. Mardonius, whom he leaves behind as general, being also his son-in-law, is defeated with great slaughter and slain at Plateæ; on the same day, a mighty power of Persians is overthrown, not, as it was believed, without a supernatural omen of success to the Greeks before the battle began. Thus Xerxes ended his wars with inestimable loss, derision, and shame.] Vengeance notwithstanding still pursued him; so that after many years, Artabanus, the captain of his guard (aspiring to the kingdom though he obtained it not), murdered both him and his eldest son Darius.[1]

Himilco, a famous general of the Carthaginians, for their wars of Sicily, in the time of Dionysius the tyrant, prevailed very fortunately in all his enterprises, till that taking the suburbs of Achradina, he spoiled in it the temple of Ceres and Proserpina. This sacrilege (saith Diodorus) brought a just punishment upon him: for in the next encounter the Syracusans overthrew him. And being arrived in his camp, fears and tumults rise amongst his soldiers in the night time, and sudden alarms as if the enemy had been upon his trenches. Besides this, a grievous plague at last [broke out] in his army, accompanied with many fierce diseases that drove his men into frenzies and forgetfulness; so that running up and down the army, they flew upon every man they met with. And no physic could help them; for they were taken so suddenly, and with such violence, as they died within five or six days, no man daring to come near them for fear of the infection. Hereupon ensued all other calamities : their enemies assail them both by sea and land; they invade their forts and their trenches, fire their navy, and (to be short) make a general confusion of the whole army. An hundred and fifty thousand Carthaginians lie dead on the ground. Himilco himself, who lately possessed all the cities of Sicily (except Syracuse, which he also accounted as good as his own), flieth by night back into Carthage, and feareth now the losing of it. This great commander (saith Diodorus), that in his haughtiness placed his tent on the temple of Jupiter, and perverted the sacred oblations to his profane expenses, is thus driven to an

[1] Diodor. lib. xi. 55.

ignominious flight, choosing rather to live basely
and contemned at home, than to expiate his wicked
sacrilege by a deserved death. But he came to such
misery, that he went up and down the city in a most
loathsome habit, from temple to temple, confessing
and detesting his impiety; and imploring at length
some capital punishment for an atonement with the
gods, ended his life by the extremity of famine.[2]

Cambyses, the son of Cyrus the Great, being at
Thebes in Egypt, sent an army of fifty thousand
men to spoil the Ammonians, and to burn the temple
and oracle of Jupiter Ammon. Himself, with the
rest of his forces, marched against the Æthiopians;
but, ere ever he had gone the fifth part of his
journey, his victuals so failed him, that his men were
forced to eat their horses and cattle. And whilst,
like a man without reason, he still forced them to go
on, and to make shift with herbs and roots; coming
to a desert of sand, divers of them were constrained
to tithe themselves, and eat the tenth man; whereby
his voyage was overthrown, and he driven to return.
His other army, that went to spoil and fire the
oracle, after seven days' travel upon the sands, a
strong south wind raised the sands so violently upon
them, as they were all overwhelmed and drowned in
them.[3]

Cambyses, after this, in despite of the Egyptians,
wounded the sacred calf Apis (which they worshipped
for their god) with his sword upon the thigh; derided the image of the god Vulcan; and entering the
temple of the Cabiri, where none might come but
the priests, burnt the images of their gods. Presently, upon wounding Apis, he fell mad, and committed divers horrible facts; as he mounted upon
his horse his sword fell out of the scabbard, and
wounded him in the same part of the thigh wherein
he had wounded Apis, and thereon he died, having
reigned but seven years, and leaving no issue, male

[2] DIODOR. SICUL. Hist. lib. xiv. 63.   [3] HERODOTUS lib. iv.

or female, to succeed him in the great empire of his father Cyrus, wherein, for securing of himself and his posterity he had formerly murdered his brother Smerdis.[4]

A rich citizen of Egypt, longing to eat of a goodly peacock that was consecrate to Jupiter, hired one of the ministers to steal it; who going about to do it, was at the first interrupted by a serpent; and the second time the peacock (that had lived by report an hundred years) flew towards the temple, and resting a while in the midway, was after seen no more. The practice being discovered by a brabble between the parties about the hiring money, the minister was justly punished by the magistrate for his treachery; but the citizen, that longed to eat of the sacred fowl, swallowed the bone of another fowl, was choked therewith, and died a very painful death.[5]

Dionysius the elder rose by his own prowess from a private man to be king of Sicily; and in performing many brave exploits both in Italy and Greece, committed divers sacrileges upon the heathen gods, and defended them with jests. Having conquered Locris, he spoiled the temple of Proserpina, and sailing thence with a prosperous wind, " Lo 1 " (quoth he) " what a fortunate passage the gods give to sacrilegious persons."

Taking the golden mantle from Jupiter Olympius, he said it was too heavy for summer and too cold for winter, and gave him therefore one of cloth.

So from Æsculapius he took his beard of gold, saying it was not seemly that the son should have a beard, when his father Apollo himself had none at all.

With such conceits he robbed the temples of the golden tables, vessels, ornaments, and things of price dedicated to the gods. Whereupon ensued a change of his fortunes : for afterwards he was ordinarily overcome in all his battles, and growing into con-

[4] HEROD. lib. iv.   [5] ÆLIAN. de Animal. l. xi. c. 33.

tempt of his subjects, was murdered by them at last.[6] His son, named as himself, succeeds in the kingdom, and ordained as it were to extirpate the family of his father, put his brethren and their children to death. He groweth odious also to his subjects, and falling into civil war with them, is thrice overcome by them; and after various events, is at last driven out of his kingdom irrecoverably. He seeth the death of his sons, his daughter violently ravished, his wife (who was his sister) most villainously abused, and in fine, murdered with his children. His days he consumed in exile among his enemies; where he lived not only despised, but odious to all, consorted with the basest people, and in the vilest manner: and so ending his tragedy, gave Plutarch occasion to say, " That neither nature nor art did bring forth anything in that age so wonderful as his fortune."[7]

Antiochus, the great king of Syria, being overcome by the Romans, and put to a great tribute, not knowing how to pay it, thought that necessity might excuse his sacrilege; and therefore in the night spoils the temple of Belus. But the country people rising upon the alarm of it, slew both him and his whole army.[8]

Q. Fulvius Flaccus Pontifex spoiled the temple of Juno. One of his sons dies in the war of Illyricum; and the other lying desperately sick, himself between grief and fear falleth mad, and hangeth himself.

Divers that had spoiled the temple of Proserpina, at Locris, were by Q. Minutius sent fettered to Rome. The Romans sent them back again to the Locrians, to be punished at their pleasure: and caused the things taken out of the temple to be restored, with oblations besides for an atonement.[9]

Agathocles, surprising the Lipareans, imposeth a ransom of sixty talents of silver upon them: they

[6] Justin. lib. xx. 45.   [7] Just. lib. xxi. Plut. in Timoleon.
[8] Just. lib. xxxii. 2.   [9] Liv. xxxi. 13.

made as much toward payment of it as they could,
and desired delay for the rest, saying, that they had
never upon any necessity meddled with that which
was consecrated to the gods. Agathocles would
none of that answer, but enforced them to bring
him that money, it being dedicated part to Æolus
and part to Vulcan. Having it, he departed; but
in his return Æolus raised such a tempest, that
many thought him sufficiently revenged; and Vulcan
after burnt him alive.[1]

But that which we shall now deliver is most
remarkable, both for the excessive sacrilege and
punishment. And because the relation perhaps
shall not be unpleasing, I will presume to be a little
the longer in it. The general Senate (of the
chiefest part of Greece) called the Amphictyonic,
imposed a grievous fine upon the Phocæans, for that
they had taken a piece of the Cirrhæan territory,
being consecrate to Apollo, and had profaned it to
works of husbandry; adding further, that if the
fine were not paid to the use of Apollo, their territories should be consecrate unto him. The Phocæans, nettled with this decree, as not able to pay
the fine, and choosing rather to die than to have
their country proscribed; by the council of Philomelus they protest against the decree of the Amphictyones as most unjust, that for so small a piece
of ground so excessive a fine should be imposed;
and pretend that the patronage of the temple of
Delphi itself (where the famous oracle of Apollo
was) did of antiquity and right belong unto them:
and Philomelus undertaketh to recover it. Hereupon the Phocæans make him their general: he
presently draweth into his confederation the Lacedæmonians (whom the Amphictyones had bitten with
the like decree), and with an army on the sudden
invadeth and possesseth the temple of Delphi,
slaying such of the city as resisted him. The fame
hereof flew far and wide; and upon it divers cities

[1] Diodor. Sicul. lib. xx. 101.

of Greece undertake in their devotion a sacred war against the Phocæans and Philomelus.

First, they of Locris give them battle, and are overcome. Then the Bœotians prepare an army for their aid; but in the meantime Philomelus, the better to defend his possession of the temple, encloseth it with a wall; and though he had formerly published through Greece that he sought nothing but the patronage, yet, seeing many cities to join in force against him, he now falleth apparently upon spoiling of the temple for supporting of his war, taking from it an infinite wealth in precious vessels and oblations. Nor did the progress of his fortune suddenly teach him to repent it; for he prevailed still against the Locrians, Bœotians, Thessalians, and other their confederates, till the Bœotians at last overthrew his sacrilegious army, and slaying a great part thereof, drove himself to that necessity, that to avoid the tortures incident to his impiety, he threw himself headlong down a rock, and so miserably ended his wicked pageant.

Onomarchus (his partner in the sacrilege) succeedeth in his room of command and impiety; and after variety of fortune, his sacrilegious army is overthrown by King Philip of Macedon, and by his command the soldiers that were taken prisoners were drowned, and Onomarchus himself, as a sacrifice to his sacrilege, hanged.

Then Phayllus, the brother of Onomarchus, is chosen General; who, rotting by little and little whilst he lived, died at length in most grievous torture for his sacrilege.

After him succeeded Phalæcus, son of Onomarchus, who beyond all the former sacrilege (wherein some accounted that as much was taken as the whole treasure was worth that Alexander the Great brought out of Persia) added this, that hearing there was an infinite mass of gold and silver buried under the pavement of the temple, he, with Philon and other of his captains, began to break up the

pavement near the Tripos; but frighted suddenly
with an earthquake, durst proceed no further.
Shortly after, Philon is accused for purloining much
of the sacred money committed to his dispensation;
and being tortured nameth many of his consorts,
who, with him, are by the Phocæans themselves all
put to a terrible death. And the Bœotians, by the aid
of king Philip, put to flight divers troops of the
Phocæans, whereof five hundred fled for sanctuary
into a chapel of Apollo's, seeking protection under
him whose temple they had so violated. But the
fire they left in their own tents fired their cabins:
and then taking hold of straw that lay near the
chapel burnt it also, and in it them that were fled
into it. For the god (saith Diodorus) would give
them no protection, though they begged it upon
their knees.

Now after ten years this sacred war came to an
end. Phalæcus, not able to subsist against Philip
and the Bœotians, compoundeth with him for license
to depart, and to carry the soldiers he had about
him with him.

The Phocæans, without all means to resist, are, by
a new decree of the Amphictyons or grand council,
adjudged to have the walls of three* of their cities
beaten to the ground; to be excluded from the
temple of Apollo and the court of the Amphictyons
(that is, to be excommunicated and outlawed); to
keep no horses nor armour till they had satisfied
the money, sacrilegiously taken, back to the god;
that all the Phocæans that were fled, and all others
that had their hands in the sacrilege, should be duly
punished, and that every man might therefore pull
them out of any place; that the Grecians might
destroy all the cities of the Phocæans to the ground,
leaving them only villages of fifty houses apiece,
distant a furlong the one from the other, to inhabit;
that the Phocæans should retain their ground, but

* [Spelman probably wrote, or meant to write, *twenty-three;* the
real number was twenty-two.—ED.]

should pay a yearly tribute of sixty thousand talents to the god, till the sum mentioned in the registers of the temple at the beginning of the sacrilege were fully satisfied.

The Lacedæmonians also and Athenians, who aided the Phocæans, had their part (and justly) in the punishment. For all the Lacedæmonian soldiers that were at the spoil of the oracle were afterwards slain, and all others universally (saith Diodorus), not only the principal agents in the sacrilege, but even they that had no more than their finger in it, were prosecuted by the god with inexpiable punishment.

Nor did Phalæcus escape it, though he compounded with Philip, and lived long after. For his long life was no happiness unto him, but an extension of his torture, living perpetually in wandering up and down, perplexed with restless fears and variety of dangers; till at last, besieging Cydonia, and applying engines to batter it, lightning falling upon them consumed both them and him, and a great part of his army; yet others say that he was slain by one of his soldiers.[2]

The residue of his army, that escaped the fire, were by the exiled Eleans hired to serve against their countrymen of Elis; but the Arcadians joining with the Eleans, overthrew their exiles, and this their army of sacrilegious soldiers, and having slain many of them divided the rest (being about four thousand) between them. Which done, the Arcadians sold their part to be bondmen; but the Eleans, to expiate the spoil of Delphi, put all their part to the sword. Many also of the noblest cities of Greece (that had aided the Phocæans), being afterwards overcome by Antipater, lost both their authority and liberty. And besides all this, the wives of the prime men of Phocis that had made themselves jewels of the gold of Delphi were also punished by an immortal hand; for she that had

[2] DIODOR. lib. xvi.

got the chain offered by Helena became a common strumpet, and she that adorned herself with the attire of Eriphyle (taken thence) was burnt in her house by her eldest son, stricken mad, and firing the same.

These fearful punishments fell on them that were guilty of misusing sacred things : whereas, on the other part, Philip the king (that at this time had nothing but Macedon) by defending the cause of the temple and oracle, came after to be king of all Greece, and the greatest king of Europe.[3]

In the next age after this, Brennus the Gaul (or, as our chroniclers say, the Briton, for the eastern nations did of old account the Britons under the name of the Gauls, as they do at this day under [that of Franks]), raising a mighty army of Gauls, invaded Greece, and prospering there victoriously, came at length to Delphi, with an hundred and fifty thousand foot and fifty thousand horse; where his army, endeavouring to spoil the temple standing upon the hill Parnassus, was in scaling of it valiantly resisted by four thousand citizens. But suddenly an earthquake, tearing off a great part of the hill, threw it violently upon the Gauls, who being so dispersed, a tempest of hail and lightning followed that consumed them. Brennus, astonished at the miracle, and tormented at the wounds he had received, slew himself with his dagger.[4]

Another of the captains, with ten thousand of the soldiers that remained, made all the haste he could out of Greece; but their flight was little benefit unto them : for in the night they durst come in no houses, and in the day they wanted neither labour nor dangers. Abundance of rain, and frost, and snow, and hunger, and weariness, and the extreme want of sleep, consumed daily this miserable remnant: and the nations they passed through pursued them as vagabonds, to prey upon them. So that of that numerous army, which of late in the pride of

[3] Diodor. Sic. lib. xvi. [4] Just. xxiv.

their strength, despised and spoiled the gods, none was left to report their destruction.

Thus Justin affirmeth : but Strabo saith that divers of them returned to their country (being Toulouse in Provence), and that the plague there falling amongst them, the soothsayers told them they could not be delivered from it till they cast the gold and silver they had gotten by their sacrilege into the lake of Toulouse.

About two hundred and forty years after,* Q. Servilius Cæpio, the Roman consul, taking the city of Toulouse, took also this treasure (then being in the temple, as seemeth by Aulus Gellius[5]), and much increased by the citizens out of their private wealth, to make the gods more propitious unto them. The gold (saith Strabo) amounted to a hundred and ten minas, and the silver to one thousand pounds in weight. In truth (saith Strabo) this sacrilege w: s the destruction both of Cæpio himself and of lis army : and Gellius addeth, that whosoever touched any of that gold, perished by a miserable and torturing death. Hereupon came the proverb, which this day is so usual among scholars, *Aurum habet Tolosanum;* spoken (saith Erasmus) of him that is afflicted with great and fatal calamities, and endeth his life by some new and lamentable accident. See more in Strabo.

A soldier of Verus, the emperor, cutting by chance a golden cabinet (*arculam*) in the temple of Apollo at Babylon, there issued such a pestilent breath out of it, as infected both the Parthians, and all other parts of the world wheresoever they came, even to Rome.[6]

It were endless to sail in this stream, the heathen authors are so copious in it. But for a corollary to that hath been spoken, I desire to add a fable of Ovid's,[7] wherein he showeth what opinion the world

---

* [*I.e.* after the Sacred War ; not after the invasion of Brennus. —EDS.]

[5] AUL. GELL. iii. 9.   [6] JUL. CAPITOLIN. in Aug. Hist.

[7] Metam. viii. 780.

then had of sacrilege, and what fatalities it brought upon the offenders in it. Erysichthon, profaning the grove of Ceres, cutteth down her sacred oak, and contemning his superstition that offered to hinder it, cleaveth his head with a hatchet. Ceres striketh him with an unsatiable and perpetual hunger; nothing doth satisfy him, nothing fills him, nothing thrives with him; all his wealth is consumed on his belly: and when all is gone, then he is driven to dishonest shifts, and forbeareth no wickedness. He prostitutes his own daughter[8] to one for a horse, to another for a bird, to a third for an ox, to a fourth for a deer. And when this is also devoured his hunger at last compelleth him to tear his own flesh with his teeth, and by consuming himself in this horrible manner, to finish his days most miserably.

[SECTION II.

Sacrilege among Heathens after the Christian Era.]

DIOCLESIAN and Maximianus[9] having divided the empire between them, this enjoying the west, and the other the east, they united themselves again in raising the greatest persecution that ever was against the Christians, putting priests and people to death, seventeen thousand persons by sundry torments, in thirty days, confiscating their goods, burning the books of holy Scripture, razing and utterly subverting their churches, altars, and places of prayer and divine worship. Having continued in this fury about twelve years, they grew at last to be troubled in mind; and in one day, Maximianus at Milan, in the west, and Dioclesian at Nicomedia, in the east, of their own accord renounced the empire, and betook themselves to a private life: Dioclesian choosing Galerius for his successor, and Maximianus, Constantius[1] for his. But Maximian afterwards repenting,[2] endeavoured with his

---

[8] Her transmutation into these shapes is thus expounded.
[9] EUSEB. viii. I., seq.
[1] CARION, Chron. p. 194 (ed. 1580).   [2] OROSIUS, vii. 25.

son Maxentius to re-assume the government, and was therefore by the commandment of Constantine put to death ; and Dioclesian, after long discontentment, slew himself.   Yet for a further revenge of the horrible persecution and sacrilege, God sent a grievous plague and famine (as Eusebius reporteth)[3] over all the world.

Certain Arians (A.D. 356), by an edict of Constantius the emperor, attempt to expel Athanasius from the bishoprick of Alexandria : and in rifling the church, a young man laboureth to pull down the bishop's seat, when suddenly a piece thereof falling upon him, rent out his bowels, that he died the next day save one.   Another, bereaved of his sight and sense for the present, was carried forth, and recovering about a day after, remembered nothing of what he had done or suffered.   But these accidents stayed the rest from proceeding farther.[4]

Julianus (A.D. 362), president of the east part of the empire, and uncle to Julian the emperor (both apostates), with Felix the treasurer, and Elpidius, keeper of the privy purse, all persons of high dignity, come to Antioch, by commission from the emperor, to carry from thence the sacred vessels to the emperor's treasury.   They enter that goodly church, and Julian going to the holy Communion-table, defileth it ; and because Euzoius offered to hinder him, he gives him a box on the ear, saying, " That God regarded not the things of Christians." Felix also, beholding the magnificence of the sacred vessels (for Constantine and Constantius had caused them to be sumptuously made), "Lo," (quoth he) "in what state the son of Mary is served ! "   Presently the bowels of Julian rotted in his body, and the dung which formerly went downwards, now passeth upwards through his blasphemous mouth, and so ended his life.   Felix is stricken suddenly with a whip from heaven, casteth his blood day and night

---

[3] ix. 8.
[4] S. ATHANAS. ad Monach. 848 D. (ed. Paris, 1627).

from all parts of his body out at his mouth, and for want of blood so dieth presently.[5]

Chrysostom saith that Julian burst asunder in the midst; and Ammianus,[6] that Felix died suddenly (*profluvio sanguinis*) of a gushing out of blood.

What became of Elpidius, Theodoret doth not mention; but Nicephorus[7] reporteth that though the third blasphemer was not so suddenly punished, yet being at length apprehended amongst them that aspired to the government (*tyrannidem*), he was stripped of all he had, and suffering much misery in prison, died loathsomely, accounted as a cursed and detested person.[8]

A.D. 430. Divers bondmen of a great person, not enduring the severity of their master, fly into the church at Constantinople, and with their swords do keep the altar, refusing to depart from it, and do thereby hinder the Divine service divers days together: but having killed one of the clerks, and wounded another, they at last killed themselves.[9] This happened a little before the Council of Ephesus, where Nestorius was condemned, and was a *prœludium* to those evils, as it is said in Socrates, that then followed in the Church:

> Nam sæpè signa talia dari solent,
> Cùm sacra fœdum templa polluit scelus.

[5] THEOD. Eccl. Hist. lib. iii. cap. 11, 12.
[6] Lib. xxxiii.
[7] Lib. x. cap. 29.
[8] BARON. ann. 362, 110.
[9] SOCR. vii. 33. NICEPH. xiv. 34, 35. EVAG. i. 3, 45.

CHAPTER III.

Sacrilege among Christians.

IN the time of Childebertus, king of Paris, and son of Clodover the first, his brother Theodoricus besiegeth Montclere, the chief city of Avernia, which Childebertus, his brother, had taken from him. A knight then hearing that divers citizens had carried their goods into the church of S. Julian, leaveth the siege, and, with his followers, breaking open the doors, taketh all away. But God, the just Revenger of sacrilege, struck them all incontinently with madness;[1] where he admonisheth soldiers, by this example, to take heed of sacrilege; and thereupon addeth another example.

Sigivaldus (saith he), governor of the Avernians, found this to be true; for, puffed up with a desire of enlarging his patrimony and dominion, after he had wrung many things from the inhabitants, he took also from the church of S. Julian, the town of Bulgrate, which Tetradius had given unto it; and being presently stricken mad, recovered not his senses till he had left the town again unto them, and made a recompense for that he had taken.

A.D. 508. Some of the Burgundians, with a great power, besiege *Brivatensem Vicum*, the town of Brivat, killing many, and taking many prisoners, do also carry away *ministerium sacrosanctum*, the implements of the church. Passing over the river, as they were dividing the captives, one Hellidius coming from Vellavum [le Velay] suddenly upon them with his company, slew them all save four,

---

[1] GAGUINUS, Rer. Gallic. ANN. I. 5, 6.

the Burgundians are overthrown by the Franks and
Goths, and their country divided amongst their
enemies.[3]

A.D. 556. Whilst king Chramnus was at Auvergne,
five of his people brake by night into an oratory at
Issoire,* and stole from thence the ornaments of
the ministry, and flying into the territory of Orleans,
there divided them : shortly after four of them were
slain in tumults, and the fifth, having all the goods
in his house, as survivor, was stricken blind with
an humour of blood that fell upon his eyes : which
touching him with repentance, it pleased GOD to
have mercy on him : so that, recovering his sight,
he carried back the ornaments, and restored them.[4]

A.D. 570. Chilperic, king of Soissons in France,
who flourished anno 570, sent his son Theodebertus
with an army to waste Normandy, and the other
territories of his brother Sigebert. Theodebert, in
doing it, forbare not the Christians, but spoiled
them also. At last part of his army come to Lætra,
a monastery of S. Martin's; and twenty of them
(the rest refusing) entered into a bark, and passing
over the river, sacked the monastery, slew some of
the monks, and carried the prey into their bark.
Having lost their oars, they were constrained to use
their spears in rowing themselves back, and coming

[2] S. GREGOR. TURON. De Miracul. S. Julian. 7, 8.
[3] BARON. ann. 508, 33, 34.
* [Sir Henry Spelman translates incorrectly, "the oratory of
the house of Juaccn." . . . EDS.]
[4] S. GREGOR. TURON. de Glor. Mart. 66. BAR. 556, 42.

into the midst of the river the bark sunk, and they
falling down upon their spears were both slain and
drowned, one excepted, who had begged of them
not to do such great wickedness. The monks, recovering their goods from the water, buried the
bodies of them that were drowned. Theodebert
himself, and all his army, falling after into an
ambush laid for them by Sigebert, were also slain.[5]

A.D. 576. The leaders of king Guntheranus' army,
hearing that Gundebaldus, dislodging with his forces
from the side of the river Garonne, was gone to the
city Convenica [Comminges], they in pursuit having ·
swam over the river, and drowned some of their
horse, came with the rest to the church of S.
Vincent, which is near the borders of the city Agen ;
and finding that the inhabitants of that part had
carried all their wealth into the same church, as
supposing the sanctity of that place should preserve
it, they set the doors on fire, being fast locked, and
so consuming them, entered the church, and carried
away the substance of the inhabitants, and what
else belonged to the Divine service, which by the
work of God was presently punished : for the hands
of most of them were strangely burned, and made a
smoke, as things used to do that are set on fire ;
some were carried away by the devil. Many after
they were departed wound themselves with their
own weapons, and some of the rest straggling
abroad are slain by the inhabitants about Com-
minges.[6]

This author (as Sigebertus saith) was made Bishop
of Tours in the year 571, and is much honoured
generally for his life, gravity, and fidelity ; yet must
I note, that he hath delivered this story somewhat
differingly in another book,[7] though to the same
effect (memory in all men being sometime stronger,
sometime weaker). There he saith, that the soldiers

[5] Aimoin de Gest. Franc. iii. 12. Bar. 576, 1, 2, & 579, 13.
[6] S. Greg. Turon. Hist. vii. 7, c. 35.
[7] De Gloriâ Mart. lib. 1, c. 105.

could not of long time, and with much labour, make
the church doors take fire; and that at last they
were fain to use the help of hatchets, and to chop
them in pieces : that being entered, they took both
the things that were there, and slew all the people
that were fled thither for safety. That this was not
long unpunished, for some were rapt away by the
devil, some drowned in the river Garonne, many
lying in the cold got divers diseases in divers parts,
that vexed them grievously : for myself, saith he,
did see in the territory of Tours many of them that
were partners in this wickedness, grievously tormented, even to the loss of this present life, with
intolerable pains.[8]

Childeric,* the greatest man with Sigebert, king of
Austrasia, claimeth wrongfully a town from Franco,
bishop of Aix-en-Provence, pretending that it belonged to the public revenue, and judicially, before
the king and other judges, doth recover it with three
hundred crowns (*aureos*) damages. The bishop, in
great anguish of mind, goeth to the church, and falling down at the tomb of S. Metrias, patron of the
church, prayeth for vengeance, and threateneth the
saint, that there should be neither lights nor singing
in that church until he were revenged of his enemy,
and the things restored that were taken away from
it so wrongfully. And laying thorns upon the tomb,
he shut the church door, laying others there also
(for that was a type that the place was forsaken).
Presently hereupon Childeric, that had done this
wrong to the church, falleth sick of a fever, and
continueth so for a whole year, eating little and
drinking little, save water in the heat of his fit; but
perplexed in his mind, and sighing much, yet re-
lented not in that he had done. In the meantime
all the hair, both of his beard and head, came wholly
off, and all his head became bare and naked : then
he bethinks him of the wrong he had done to the
Church, and restoreth the town with six hundred

crowns, for the three hundred he had received, hoping so to recover his health, by the means of the saint, but died notwithstanding.[9] This happened in the time of king Sigebert, who was this year murdered by the practice of his brother's wife Frede-gundis.

A.D. 579. Ruecolenus, with a power of the Ceno-manians, wasteth all about the city Tours, so that the houses and hospital of the church were without hope of sustenance. He demandeth also of the churchmen there that they should deliver unto him some that had taken sanctuary in the church, and threateneth to fire all if they refused. S. Gregory of Tours, being then bishop there, and that writ this relation with his own hand, goeth to the church; and praying for aid (*Beati auxilia flagitamus*), a woman that had twelve years been contracted with the palsy was made straight: but Ruecolenus him-self being now come to the other side of the river, was presently stricken with the king's evil, and with the disease of king Herod; and the fiftieth day after died, all swollen of the dropsy. This S. Gregory himself (as I find) reporteth.[1]

A.D. 670. Certain servants or officers of Egbright, the third king of Kent after Ethelbert, had done great injury to a noble woman called Domneva (the mother of S. Mildred); in recompense whereof the king promised, upon his honour, to give her what-soever she would ask of him. She begged upon this so much ground of him to build an abbey on, as a tame deer (that she had nourished) would run over at a breath. The king had presently granted it, but that one of his council, named Timor, stand-ing by, blamed his inconsideration, that would upon the uncertain course of a deer depart with any part of so good a soil. But presently (saith the author, William Thorne, a monk of S. Augustin's) the

---

[9] S. GREG. TURON. De Glor. Confess. cap. lxxi. BARON. ann 579, 15.

[1] De Mirac. S. Mart. lib. ii. c. 27. BARON. 579, 18.

earth opened, and swallowed him up alive; in
memory whereof the place till his time was called
Timor's Leap. It may be the monk hath aggravated
the matter, and that Mr. Lambard justly doth
count it fabulous; but it seems some notable misfortune followed upon Timor, hindering, in this
manner, the propagation of religion in the beginning
of our church. Yet no learned man, I think,
doubteth but that in the first conversion of heathen
people, God was pleased to show some miracles
upon sacrilegious impediments. The story goes on,
that the king, moved with the event, granted
Domneva's petition; and that the hind being put
forth, ran the space of forty-eight plough-lands
before it ceased. In which precinct this lady, by
the king's help, builded the monastery for nuns,
called Minster Abbey, in Thanet.[2]

A.D. 684. Egfrid, king of Northumberland,
sendeth an army into Ireland under the conduct of
Bert;[3] and wasting miserably that harmless nation,
which then was friend to the English, spared neither
churches nor monasteries. The inhabitants resisted
as they could, but rested not to call upon God with
continual curses for revenge. And though those
[that curse*] cannot inherit the kingdom of God,
yet it is to be thought of those that are justly
cursed for their iniquity, that the vengeance of God
doth therefore fall the sooner upon them : for this
same king, this next year after, in a voyage against
the Picts, was drawn into straits, and both himself
and most of his army slain.

And in the eleventh year of king Ino (saith Huntingdon[4]) the Earl Berutus felt the curses of the
Irish people, whose church he had destroyed, as his
master had done before: for as king Egfrid, enter-

---

[2] LAMBARD, Itin. in Thanet. p. 99.
[3] BED. l. 4, c. xxvi. § 341. (Ed. Stevenson.)
* [Spelman evidently read, by mistake, *maledicti* for *maledici*
in V. Bede.]
[4] Lib. iv. p. 337 (ed. 1601).

ing into the land of the Picts, was there slain; so he, entering it also to revenge his master's death, was likewise slain by them.

Circ. A.D. 710. Osred, king of Northumberland, being but eight years old when he began to reign, and reigning but eleven years, even thus young broke the monasteries, and deflowered the nuns, with much other wickedness: for which the just hand of God being upon him, as Bonifacius, archbishop of Mentz, and other bishops, assembled after in a German council, do testify by their epistle to Æthelbald, he was murdered by his kinsmen, Kenred and Osrick, and his kingdom usurped by Osrick, contrary to Osred's meaning, who had decreed it to Ceolwulfe, brother of his father, as Beda reporteth,[5] who saith farther, that his whole reign abounded with so many crosses of fortune, that no man knew either what to write of them, or what end they would have.[6]

Circ. A.D. 712. Ceolred, king of the Mercians, or midland England, was guilty also of spoiling monasteries, and defiling of nuns; and was the first, with Osred before named, that, since the entrance of Austin, brake the privileges granted by the Saxon kings unto monasteries, and for these sins, saith Boniface and the other bishops in the said epistle, *Justo judicio Dei damnati de culmine regali hujus vitæ abjecti, et immaturâ et terribili morte præventi, etc.* For Ceolred (as those that were present did testify) being at a great feast among his earls, that evil spirit which before had moved him to do such wickedness, struck him there with madness, and in that case he died impenitently, the same year that Osred, his fellow in sacrilege, was murdered, viz., A.D. 716. It seemeth his line was also extinct.

Circ. A.D. 742. Ethelbald, the next successor of

---

[5] Lib. v. cap. 24.

[6] Epist. apud. MALMES. de Gest. Reg. lib. i. 80 (ed. Hardy). Sed fusiùs apud BARON. in A.D. 745, num. 5.

Ceolred in the kingdom of Mercia, succeeded him also in his wicked courses. He forbeareth lawful marriage, but liveth adulterously with the nuns, and breaking the privileges of churches and monasteries, taketh away also their substance, which gave the occasion that Boniface, archbishop of Mentz, and other German bishops, wrote the fore-mentioned epistle unto him, desiring him to mend his course, and the wrongs he had done, which like a good king he willingly did: and at a council holden at Clovesho, now called Cliff, in Kent, acknowledging his sin, did also by his charter restore what he had taken or broken, with an overplus, and founded the monastery of Crowland: yet so was the hand of God upon him, that in a war unwisely begun, he was treacherously slain by Bartred, *alias* Beornred, and the kingdom by him usurped.*

A.D. 725. Eudo, *alias* Oda, duke of Aquitaine, not able to resist Charles Martel, draweth an excessive army of Saracens out of Spain unto his aid. They being come into France, waste all places, and burn down the churches as far as to Poictiers. Charles Martel, assisted by the hand of God, encountereth them, and slayeth three hundred seventy-five thousand (others say three hundred eighty thousand) of them, together with their king Abderama, losing not above an hundred and fifty of his own men. Then Eudo himself, reconciled to Charles, spoileth the camp of the Saracens, and destroyeth the rest. But fighting again with Charles in Gascony, loseth both his dukedom of Aquitaine and his life: his sons also, Gaifer and Haimald, are overcome, and the Saracens wholly beaten out of France.[7]

A.D. 845. The Normans, under Ragenarius their

* [The Editors have here omitted a few paragraphs, inserted without sense in this place, and consisting of extracts from Celsus Veronensis, evidently intended to be worked into the History at more leisure.]

[7] SIGEBERT, 8. a. GUIL. DE NANGES. ibid.

captain, besides other sacrileges, spoil the church of S. German's, by Paris, and attempting to cut down some of the fir beams to repair their ships, three of them attempting it are dashed in pieces. Another, hewing a marble pillar with his sword to overthrow some part of the church, had his hand (like Jeroboam's) dried up, and the haft of his sword stuck so to it, as it parted not without the skin. Many were stricken with blindness, and, as it was commonly reported, some of their army died daily so thick of the bloody flux, as they feared that none of them should escape; whereas all the Christians that were amongst them were free from it. They hasted therefore into the country, but died there as fast, and infected others so grievously, as Horich their prince, fearing that both himself and the nobility and people should be consumed, commanded the rest of them to be beheaded; and though some fled upon it, yet it was thought they died of the disease.

Ragenarius their general, and author of all the evil, at his return bragged before Horich, in the presence of Kobbo, the ambassador of king Louis, and many others, what great things he had done at Paris; and said, that the dead there had more power than the living, and that an old man, whom they called German, most resisted him. Speaking thus, he began to tremble, and falling down, cried out that German was there, and did beat him with his staff. Being presently taken up and carried out, he continued three days in grievous pains: whereupon, repenting of what he had done, he commanded that his statue should be made of gold, and that Kobbo should carry it to the old man German, promising that if he recovered he would become a Christian: but his bowels passing from him as if he were burst in the midst, he so died. And, because he was not a Christian, his statue would not be received, though it were of gold.

Kobbo, the ambassador for Louis, king of Bavaria,

to the Normans, being yet Pagans, was an eye-witness of these things, and related them to Aimoinus, who living at the same time, and seeing much of it himself, did, by the commandment of king Charles, write a history of strange things then happening, which he entituled, *De Translatione et Miraculis S. Germani Episcopi*, whence this above mentioned is taken.[8]

A.D. 865.   The Danes with a great army destroy the monks and monastery of Bardney, kill the abbot and monks of Croyland, and burn their church, make the like havoc at Peterborough, and murder the nuns at Ely.   Shortly after, their whole army is overthrown in battle at Chippenham, by Ælfred, brother of king Æthelred, and Hubba their king, with five earls, and many thousands of their pagan nation slain.[9]   Huntingdon[1] saith there were nine earls slain this year.

A.D. 874.   Abdila, *alias* Agdila, a Saracen prince, coming with a great army out of Africa, besieged Salerne, and made the church of SS. Fortunatus and Caius, his lodging, placing his bed upon the altar, and abusing it with all filthiness: but it happened, that having gotten a maid, and going about to ravish her there, as she resisted and struggled with him, a piece of timber falling down from the top of the church, slew him in his wickedness, and hurt not the maid, which seemed apparently to be the very work of God; for that the timber fell not perpendicularly, but aslope.   He being thus extinct, the Saracens chose Abimelech, an eunuch, king in his stead.[2]

Circ. A.D. 880.   Leofstane, a noble Saxon, and of great authority, in the heat of his youth entered the place where S. Edmund, the king and glorious martyr of our East Angles, was entombed ; and causing the tomb or coffin to be opened, made the body to be

---

[8] BARON. A.D 845, num. 22, et seq.   [9] STOW, p. 101.
[1] Lib. v. 349.
[2] BARON. A.D. 874, num. 2, Cod. MS.

showed forth to the beholders, many labouring to hinder it. But in that instant, whilst he stood looking on it, he was struck with madness; which his father, a religious man, hearing, gave thanks unto the martyr for it, and casting off his son, suffered him to live in great penury, wherein afterward, by the hand of God, he was consumed with worms, and so ended his life.

The same author, Jornalensis, in the same place telleth also, that divers lewd persons robbing in the night-time the church where his tomb was, were all taken, and by the judgment of Theodore, the archbishop of Canterbury in those days, hanged together. But addeth, that the archbishop repented the deed all the days of his life afterward, remembering the speech of the prophet, saying, *Eos qui ducuntur ad mortem eruere non cesses.* And that hereupon he put himself to great penance, and calling the people of the diocese together, persuaded them to fast and pray for him three whole days, that it might please God to turn the wrath of his Divine indignation from him for doing this deed.

Circ. A.D. 888. In the reign of Charles the Fat (who began 886, and died 891) there happened a strange accident, memorable in France, as well by common fame as by writing to the later times, that the monks of Cluni, going forth in their habit to meet the Earl of Matiscon,* he not only slew them, but with torture and cruelty, and in that manner raged continually against the church. It fortuned, therefore, that he being one day at a feast with many of the nobility, an unknown person coming to the door required to speak with him; and the earl going out was never seen after. Some write that he was carried away, fearfully crying, through the air, with a black horse (*pullo equo*).[3]

[A.D. 925. Burchardus,† a German leader, coming

[3] PARADINUS de antiquo Statu Burgundiæ, p. 62 (ed. 1542).
* Mâçon [E.]
† [Vit. S. Guiborat. in BOLLAND. Act. Sanct. Mai. i. p. 289, col. 1, B.—EDS.]

to the monastery of S. Gall, is offered a chalice and a paten, they of the church thus thinking to secure his favour. He, although warned that the ornaments of the altar were none of his, took them notwithstanding. But shortly afterwards, being in his wars in Italy, and his horse falling with him into a pit, he perisheth miserably.]

Circ. A.D. 964. Nicephorus, emperor of Constantinople, had marvellous success in all his affairs, and in a short time obtained so many and so famous victories against the Saracens, as are scarcely to be believed : he falleth then to spoiling of churches and sacred houses, taking from them that which usually was given unto them, and pretended that the bishops consumed the money that was given to the use of the poor, whilst the soldiers lived in want and poverty. After he had thus laid his hands upon the goods of the church, he not only wasted all his own goods, but overwhelmed with evils, found the hand of God to be against him, and to pursue him with revenge, as the Greek historians are of opinion : for by-and-bye his army is beaten in Calabria, an innumerable multitude of his people slain, many with their noses cut off are sent back to Constantinople ; the citizens there murmur, mutiny, and rebel, his wife conspireth with them, and, by the hands of John Zimisces, one of his army, do murder him, and make the same John emperor in his room.[4]

A.D. 974. Upon the rebellion of the Welshmen, king Edgar, entering with an army into the country of Glamorgan, some of his soldiers, among other spoil, took away the bell of S. Ellutus, and hanged it about a horse's neck. It then chanced, as the report was, that king Edgar sleeping in the afternoon, there appeared one unto him, and smote him on the breast with a spear. By reason of which vision he caused all things that had been taken away to be restored again. But were there any such vision or no, it is said he died within nine days;

[4] BARON. A.D. 964, num. 34; 968, num. 3, 4, 5.

and the truth is, that he died indeed at his age of thirty-seven years, when he had reigned sixteen years and two months.[5]

This king Edgar was buried at Glastonbury; and when Ayleward, the abbot there, had unworthily digged open his grave, he (the abbot) fell mad, and going out of church brake his neck and died.[6]

A.D. 1054. Griffith, the valiant and victorious king of North Wales,[7] in aid of Algar, earl of Chester, whom king Edward the Confessor had expelled and banished, invadeth Herefordshire, putteth to flight Radulf, earl thereof, and son of Goda, the Confessor's sister, with his whole army, and taking the city of Hereford, fired the cathedral church, slew Leogar (the bishop) and seven of the canons that defended it, burnt also the monastery built by bishop Æthelstane, carried away the spoil thereof, and of the city, with slaughter of the citizens, fully restored Algar the earl both now and a second time. Upon this king Edward sent Harold against him; who, upon his second voyage into North Wales, burnt his palace and ships. After this, Griffith raising an army for revenge, and going to meet Harold, was by his own people traitorously murdered, and his head brought to Harold.

Circ. A.D. 1068. Alfgarus, stalhere (that is, constable of the army) to Edward the Confessor,[8] invaded the town of Estre, otherwise called Plassie, and pulling it from the monastery of Ely, converted it to his own use. The abbot and monks there besought him by all fair means to restore it, but prevailing not, they proceeded to denounce daily curses and imprecations against him, and at last (although he were so great a person in the kingdom) to excommunicate him. Hereupon the king reproving him sharply, and the people shunning his com-

---

[5] HOVEDEN, s. a. DCCCCLXXIV.

[6] [The Editors have here omitted a repetition, in other words, of the last paragraph.]

[7] HOVED. in A.D. 1055.　　　　　[8] HOLINSH. p. 866.

pany, he at last sought to be reconciled to the
church, and for obtaining thereof granted by his
deed, and ratified by his oath, that the town after
his decease should again return to the monastery :
yet (after the death of Edward the Confessor, and
Harold the usurper) he was by the Conqueror cast
into prison, and there, among others in fetters of
iron, ended his life.

A.D. 1078.   Jordan, prince of Capua, hearing that
the bishop of Rosella had brought and laid up a
good sum of money in the monastery of Monte-
Cassino, in Italy, sent his soldiers, and by force
took it out of the treasury of the church; but was
shortly after stricken blind.[9]   Upon this Gregory
the Seventh calleth a council, and maketh a canon
against sacrilege; and writing to Jordan, reproveth
him for this and other offences, admonishing him to
amend them.[1]   The prince, touched with remorse,
granteth in recompense, the next year after, to the
monastery of Cassino, divers great territories and
privileges, with a penalty of £5,000 of gold upon
the violators thereof.[2]

SECTION II.

RICHARD, Robert, and Anesgot, sons of William
Sorenge, in the time of William, duke of Normandy,
wasting the country about Say, invaded the church
of S. Gervase, lodging their soldiers there, and
making it a stable for their horses.   God deferred
not the revenge : for Richard escaping, on a night,
out of a cottage where he was beset with his
enemies, a boor, whom he had fettered a little
before, lit upon him, and with an hatchet clave his
head asunder.   Robert, having taken a prey about
Soucer, was pursued by the peasants and slain.
Anesgot, entering and sacking of Cambray, was
struck in the head with a dart, thrown downward
on him, and so died.   Lo, (saith Gemeticensis) we

9 LEO. MARSIC. lib. iii. cap. 45.
1 BARON. A.D. 1078, 24.   2 LEO. MARSIC. lib. iii. cap. 46.

have here seen that truly performed which we have
heard : *If any man shall violate the temple of God,
God shall destroy him.*[3] And admonishing such as
spoil churches to look about them, and not to soothe
themselves in their sin, for that God often deferreth
the punishment, he concludeth with these verses of
another man's :[4]

> *Vos male gaudetis quia tandem suscipietis*
> *Nequitiæ fructum, tenebras, incendia, luctum :*
> *Nam pius indultor, justusque tamen Deus ultor*
> *Quæ Sua sunt munit, quæ sunt hostilia punit.*
> Dear bought, for thou must one day undergo
> The price of this, hell, darkness, fire, and woe :
> God's threats are sure, though mercy be among them,
> He guards His rights, and pays them home that wrong them.

William the Conqueror, in making the forest of
Ytene, commonly called the New Forest, is reported
to have destroyed twenty-six towns, with as many
parish churches, and to have banished both men
and religion for thirty miles in length, to make
room for his deer. He had ruined also some other
churches in France upon occasion of war; and in
Lent-time, in the fourth year of his reign, he rifled
all the monasteries of England of the gold and silver
which was laid up there by the richer of the people
to be protected by the sanctity of the places from
spoil and rapine ; and of that also which belonged
to the monasteries themselves, not sparing either
the chalices or shrines. But He That in the like
attempt met with Heliodorus, met with him also
grievously, both in his person and posterity.

Touching his person, as God raised Absalom
against David, so raised He Robert, duke of Normandy, against his father the Conqueror, and fought
a battle with him by the castle of Gerborie in France,
where the Conqueror himself was unhorsed, his son
William wounded, and many of their family slain.
Hereupon the Conqueror (as casting oil into the fire

---

[3] 1 Cor. iii. 17.

[4] GUL. GEMETIC. de Ducum Normannorum Gestis, lib. vi. cap.
13, 14.

of God's wrath that was kindled to consume his own family) cursed his son Robert, which to his dying day wrought fearfully upon him, as shall by-and-bye appear. But to proceed with the Conqueror himself: it is very remarkable, that being so great and renowned a king, he was no sooner dead, but his corpse was forsaken of his children, brethren, friends, servants, and followers, and wickedly left (saith Stow) as a barbarous person, not one of his knights being found to take care of his exequies: so that a country knight, out of charity, was moved to take care thereof, and conveying the corpse to Caen in Normandy, the abbat and monks of S. Stephen's there, with the rest of the clergy and laity of the town, met it reverently; but in conducting it to the church, a terrible fire broke out of a house, and spreading suddenly over a great part of the town, the whole company was dispersed, and only the monks left to end the office begun. The funeral, notwithstanding, proceeded afterwards in great solemnity, the bishops and abbats of Normandy attending it: but when the mass was done, and that the bishop of Evreux, at the end of his sermon, had desired all that were present to pray for the dead prince, and charitably to forgive him if he had offended any of them; one Anselm Fitz-Arthur, rising up, said aloud, "The ground whereon ye stand was the floor of my father's house, and the man for whom ye make intercession took it violently from him while he was duke of Normandy, and founded this house upon it: I now therefore claim my own, and forbid him that took it away by violence to be covered with my earth, or to be buried in my inheritance." The bishops and nobility hearing this, and understanding it to be true by the testimony of others, presently compounded with the party in fair manner, giving him sixty shillings in hand for the place of burial, and promising a just satisfaction for the rest; for which he received afterwards £100 in silver by consent of Henry, the Conqueror's son. This blur being thus wiped away, they proceeded to put the corpse into the tomb or coffin prepared by the mason, whereupon another followed very loathsome; for it being too short and straight, as they strove violently to thrust the corpse into it, the fat belly, not being bowelled, burst in pieces, and vapoured forth so horrible a savour, as the smoke of frankincense and other aromatics, ascending plentifully from the censers, prevailed not to suppress it, but both priest and company were driven tumultuously to dispatch the business, and get them gone. Thus much of the disasters touching the person of the Conqueror. To which may be added, that his very death proceeded from a violent accident happening unto him in the sacking of Meaux, where the heat and heaviness of his armour, and the extreme clamour upon his soldiers, wrought, as was reported, a dissolution of his entrails (*à ruina intestinorum ejus liquefacta,* saith Gemeticensis), for though he lived a while after, yet he languished till his death. But note by the way, that he who had in his life time destroyed so many churches and burying-places, being dead, although he were so great a king, yet he wanted the office of his children, friends, and servants, to carry him to church or to take care of his burial: that being carried thither by others, the very fire wherewith he had devoured certain churches, interrupted his passage: that being come to the church, he that had put so many by their places of burial, was now put by his own: and lastly, that when the place of his burial was obtained for money, it happened (fatally) that it was too straight to receive him, as though the earth of the church (which he had so grievously injured) were unwilling to open her mouth to entertain him. But after all difficulties, did he not rest quiet at last? Reason would he should; for the grave is *asylum requiei,* the sanctuary of rest, and he did enjoy it for many ages: yet the bishop of Bayeux, in the year 1542, opened his tomb, and brought to light his epitaph hidden in it, graven upon a gilded plate of brass.   But in the year 1562, certain French soldiers, with some English, that under the conduct of De Chastillon took the city of Caen, and fell to spoiling of churches there, did barbarously break down and deface the monument of this great king, and (as though the *malus genius* of the churches, which himself had destroyed, still pursued him with revenge) did take out his bones and cast them away.[5]   What befel these soldiers that thus rifled churches, appeareth not; obscurity and oblivion do conceal them.   But the lamentable end of De Chastillon himself, that suffered this outrage, is very notorious in the massacre of Paris.

To come to his posterity: his sons were four, all of them, at times, in war amongst themselves. Robert, the eldest, deprived of his birth-right, the crown of England; first by his brother William, then by his brother Henry, who also took from him his duchy of Normandy, put out his eyes, and kept him cruelly in prison till the day of his death.   His only son Richard, hunting in the New Forest, was slain in the life of his father, by an arrow shot casually, as Florentius Wigornensis reporteth. Others name him Henry, and say he was hanged there, like Absalom, by the hair of the head.   Be it one or both, the death was violent, and in the New Forest.   But this Robert died without issue, nothing prospering with him (as Stow noteth) after his father cursed him.

Richard, second son of the Conqueror, duke of Beorne (as Stow saith) died also in the same forest, in the fifteenth year of his father, upon a pernicious blast that happened on him; but Gulielmus Gemeticensis[6] saith, with a blow of a tree.

William Rufus, the third son, was contaminate as well with his own as his father's sacrilege; for he

[5]   VERSTEGAN, Restitution, p. 189 (ed. 1643).
[6]   Lib. ii. c. 9.

would part with no bishoprick that came into his
hands without money for it, by reason whereof he
had lying upon his hand (for want of chapmen)
thirteen bishopricks at the time of his death. He
was also slain in the same forest, an. 1100, with an
arrow (out of the quiver of God) shot casually by
Sir Walter Tyrrell; and, as Florentius reporteth, in
the very selfsame place, where a church did stand
till the Conqueror destroyed it. He also died without issue.[7]

Henry, the fourth son, being king Henry I.,
abstained (as I imagine) hunting in the New Forest,
but God met with him in another corner; for having
but two sons, William legitimate and Richard
natural, they were, in the twenty-first year of his
reign, both drowned, with other of the nobility,
coming out of France; and himself dying afterward
without issue male, in the year 1135, gave a period
to this Norman family. Here I must observe (as
elsewhere I have done) that about the very same
point of time, viz., sixty-eight years, wherein God
cut off the issue of Nebuchadnezzar, and gave his
kingdom to another nation after he had invaded the
holy things of the Temple; about the very same
point of time, I say, after the Conqueror had made
this spoil of churches, did God cut off his issue male,
and gave his kingdom to another nation, not of
Normandy but Blois.

A.D. 1061, 1070. Ursus, abbat, was made sheriff
of Worcester by William the Conqueror; and building a castle in Worcester, near the monastery, cut a
part of the churchyard into the dike of his castle,
which Aldred, the archbishop of York, seeing, said
to him, "Hightest thou Urse: have thou God's
curse, unless thou takest down this castle, and
know assuredly that thy posterity shall not long
inherit this ground of S. Mary's." He foretold
(saith Malmsbury) that which I saw performed; for
not long after his son Roger, possessing his father's

[7] GEMETICENSIS, lib. vii. cap. 9.

inheritance, was banished by king Henry I. for **put-ting** an officer of the king's to death in an headlong fury.[8] And his sheriffwick went to Beaumont, who married his sister.

A.D. 1098. Hugh, earl of Shrewsbury, with Hugh, earl of Chester, was sent by William Rufus to assail the Welchmen in Anglesea, which they performed with great cruelty, not sparing the churches. For the earl of Shrewsbury made a dog-kennel of the church of S. Fridank,* laying his hounds in it for the night-time, but in the morning he found them mad. But it chanced that Magnus, king of Norway, came in the meantime to take also the same island, and encountering the earl of Shrewsbury at sea, shot him in the eye, where only he was unarmed, and the earl thereupon falling out of the ship into the sea, was both slain and drowned, and died without issue.[9]

Circ. A.D. 1100. Geoffrey, the sixteenth abbat of S. Alban's, living whilst he was young a secular man, and teaching at Dunstable, did there, about the beginning of king Henry I., make a play of S. Catharine, called Miracula; and for acting of it, did borrow of the sexton of S. Alban's, divers copes that belonged to the choir of S. Alban's for the service of God, and having used them profanely in his play, both the house wherein they were, and the copes themselves, were the next night casually burnt. Geoffrey, for great grief, hereupon gave over the world, and by way of a propitiatory sacrifice, offered up himself a monk in S. Alban's where afterward, in the year 1119, viz., 19 or 20 of Henry I., he was made abbat.[1]

A.D. 1157. Madoc ap Meredith, prince of Powis, spoiling two churches in Anglesea, and part of the isle, was, with all his men, slain in the return.[2]

Sherborne in Dorsetshire was made an episcopal see in the year 704 or 705. And as the use of the

[8] MALMS. de Gest. Pont. p. 271.   [9] HOV. in ann. 1098.
[1] Lib. MS. de Abbatibus Sti Albani.   [2] STOW, p. 217.
* ? S. Fridian. [E.]

time was, with many curses (no doubt) against him
or them that should violate it, or should get or
procure it to be alienated from that bishoprick. S.
Osmund (who flourished 270 years after) fortified
those curses, as is reported, with divers other bitter
imprecations. It continued peaceably in the possession of the bishops till the time of king Stephen :
then Roger, bishop of that see (translated by his
predecessor to Salisbury), building three sumptuous
castles, one at Sherborne, another at Devizes, and
the third at Malmesbury; the king supposing they
might turn to his prejudice, sent for the bishop, and
took and imprisoned him, with some others of his
coat; and calling a council of the peers and baronage, obtained a statute to this effect :[3] that all towns
of defence, castles, and munitions through England,
wherein secular business was wont to be exercised,
should be the king's and his barons'; and that the
churchmen, and namely the bishops, as divine dogs,
should not cease to bark for the defence and safety
of their sheep, and to take diligent heed that the
invisible wolf, that malignant enemy, worry not
or scatter the Lord's flock. Thus the king obtained
these castles that he thirsted after, with the bishop's
person and treasure beside. And being summoned
hereupon to a synod at Winchester, by his brother
Henry, bishop there, and legate of the pope ; he
sent Aubrey de Vere, earl of Guisne and chamberlain
of England, a man of excellent speech, and singularly
well learned in the law (whom some report to be
made chief-justice of England after the said Roger),
him I say did the king send to the synod as his
attorney or sergeant-at-law, to defend his cause,
which he did with so great art and dexterity, that
nothing was therein determined. But mark the issue;
ere a twelvemonth came to an end, the earl Aubrey
de Vere was slain in London.[4] The king himself
within another twelvemonth taken prisoner, and
being delivered upon an exchange for the earl of

[3] Contin. Florent. in an. 1161.   [4] FLORILEG. in ann. 1140.

Gloucester, spoileth divers churches by his Flemish soldiers, and buildeth the nunnery of Wilton into a castle; where the town is fired about his ears, his men slain, his sewer, plate, and other things taken, and himself driven to escape by a shameful flight. He continueth his wars with unprofitable success; falleth at discord with his barons, and is driven to make peace with duke Henry, his adversary. His son Eustace displeased therewith, applieth himself to spoil Cambridgeshire and those parts, falleth upon the lands of the abbey of Bury, and carrieth the corn to his castles; and sitting down to dinner, as he put the first morsel in his mouth, he fell mad, and died miserably.[5]

In the end he stated the crown upon the duke Henry, being compelled thereto; and dying, had no lawful issue male to propagate his family, his sons of that sort being taken away in his lifetime.

Having spoken of those curses, set of old like bulwarks about the castle of Sherborne to defend it against sacrilegious assailants, and of the operation they had in those ancient days, it falleth very fitly in my way to show also in what manner they have uttered their venom since that time of old; for, though poison tempered by an apothecary, with over-long keeping will lose its strength; yet the poison that lurketh in the veins of curses lawfully imposed, is neither wasted nor weakened by antiquity, but oftentimes breaketh forth as violently after many ages, as if they were but of late denounced: like the implicit curse that devoured the seven sons of Saul, for breaking the covenant with the Gibeonites, made above five hundred years before their time.

See therefore a farther collection touching this matter.*

[5] MAT. PAR. ann. 1152. STOW, ann. 1153.
* [We have here inserted, instead of Spelman's Collection, that from PECK's *Desiderata Curiosa*, vol. i. pp. 518-520, as fuller and more satisfactory.—EDS.]

[OF THE STRANGE CURSE BELONGING TO SHERBORNE CASTLE.

S. Osmond . . : died bishop of Sarum. And by the said Osmond's gift, the lands of Sherborne continued in the possession of his successors, the bishops of Sarum, until the reign of king Stephen.

Roger Niger, or Roger the Rich, being the next bishop, took part with Maud, the empress, against the king; whom the king, in respect of his power and wealth, much feared and earnestly prosecuted. The bishop, flying to his castle of the Devizes, was there straightly besieged; which castle was as manfully defended, and could not be persuaded to yield, until the king commanded a pair of gallows to be set up at the castle gate, and the bishop's nephew (whom the bishop entirely loved, being then a prisoner with the king) to be brought forth, and threatened to execute him, unless the bishop would yield up the castle: which lamentable object so prevailed, that to save his kinsman's life he yielded himself, his castle, and his wealth, being forty thousand marks in ready coin, to the king's pleasure, who took from him, not only the castle, but the castle and barony of Sherborne also.

But it fell out that, whereas before the king had prosperous success in the war, now his enemy Maud, the empress (being his prisoner in Wallingford castle, and all her confederates disheartened), his prosperity forsaking him, escaped out of prison in a great snow, Henry Fitz-Empresse came with a great power out of Anjou, the Earl of Gloucester was freed, his own brother (the bishop of Winchester) forsook him; and he, hopeless of power to oppose his enemies, was forced to yield to these ignoble conditions, viz., to adopt Henry for his heir to the crown (which for his life only he is to enjoy; having yet a son of his own, who was endowed with parts sufficient to manage a kingdom). Not long after his son Eustace, for grief (as some suspect, by poison) ended his days;

and the king himself but a short time enjoyed this peace so dearly bought.

King Stephen being dead, these lands came into the hands of some of the Montagues (after earls of Sarum), who, whilst they held the same, under-went many disasters. For one or other of them fell by misfortune, as by the hands of justice, one be-headed, another slain, the father of one of them (teaching his son and heir to ride and run at tilt) [the said son] was by the hands of his own father slain, to the father's unspeakable grief. And finally, all the males of them [became] extinct, and the earldom received an end in their name. So ill was their success.

After this, Robert Wyvill, bishop of Sarum, in the time of king Edward III., brought a writ of right against William Montague, then earl of Sarum, for these lands so wrongfully detained; for which right a trial was to be had by battle. The day of the combat being come, and the champions of the earl and bishop being ready before the judges, armed with their coats of leather, and bastoones in their hands of equal length, it pleased the king (when those lands had been above two hundred years out of the hands of the bishops) to take up the matter; who caused the earl to yield up the lands for two thousand marks, given by the bishop to the earl. And in memory of this noble enterprise, this bishop Robert lieth buried in Sarum church, with a castle over his head, and, by his side, the portraiture of a champion armed.

Since which time these lands continued in the church until the duke of Somerset's time, in the reign of king Edward VI., when the duke, being hunting in the park of Sherborne, he was sent for presently unto the king (to whom he was protector) and, at his coming up to London, was forthwith committed unto the tower, and shortly after lost his head.

After whose death, John Capon, bishop of Sarum,

exhibited his bill of complaint unto the high Court of Chancery, against sir John Horsley, to whom these lands were given by king Edward; the bishop pretending that he had conveyed the same to the duke upon menaces and threats, and for fear of his life. And, upon this bill, these lands were decreed again to the bishop, he paying to sir John Horsley two thousand marks.

Since which time these lands remained to the bishop of Sarum until the time of sir Walter Raleigh, who unfortunately lost them, and at last his head also.

Upon his attainder they came, by the king's gift, to prince Henry; who died not long after the possession thereof.

After prince Henry's death, the earl of Somerset (Carr) did possess them. Finally he lost them, and many other great fortunes.[6]

To conclude the consideration of this curse. The manor of Sherborne and the castle are now in the possession of the earl of Bristol.[7]]

Circ. A.D. 1142. Geoffrey Mandeville, earl of Essex, being called, among other of the nobility, to a council at S. Alban's, he was there, by the king, in revenge of a former injury, unduly taken at S. Alban's, prisoned, and could have no liberty till he had delivered the tower of London, and the castles of Walden and Plessy; being thus spoiled of his holds, he turned his fury upon the abbey of Ramsey, it being a place of security, and invading it by force, drove out the monks, and placed his soldiers in their room, and fortified the church instead

---

[6] In May 1616, he was tried and condemned to die for the hand he had in poisoning Sir Thomas Overbury, but pardoned.

[7] John, the youngest son of Sir George Digby, of Sherborne; and created earl of Bristol, Sept. 15 (20 Ja. I.), 1622. He died Jan. 16, 1650, at Paris, and was there buried in the common burial-place of the Huguenots.—George, his son and heir, by Anne, daughter to Francis, earl of Bedford, had two sons, viz., John (who succeeded him in his honour) and Francis (slain in the Dutch war, May 28, 1672), but neither of them left any male heirs; and so the honour became extinct.—*Britannia ant. et nova*, vol. I. p. 567, b.

of his castle. The abbat and monks betook them to
their arms, and with all the force they could, shot
their curses and imprecations against him and his
complices; thus prepared to his destruction, he
besieged the castle of Burwell, where a peasant
shooting him lightly in the head with an arrow,
contemning the wound, he died of it, in excommunication, leaving three sons inheritors of that malediction, but of no lands[8] of their father, the king
having seized them.[9]

Arnulph, his eldest son, who still maintained the
church of Ramsey as a castle, was taken prisoner by
king Stephen, stripped of all his inheritance,
banished, and died without issue.[1]

Geoffrey Mandeville, second son, was restored by
king Henry II., and married Eustachia, the king's
kinswoman, but had no issue by her.

William Mandeville, the third son, succeeded his
brother, and was twice married, but died without
issue. Thus the name and issue of this sacrilegious
earl were all extinct, and the inheritance carried to
Geoffrey Fitz-Peter, another family, by the marriage
of Beatrix Say, his sister's grandchild.

Now we have related the fortune of the earl Mandeville and his children, we must not omit what
Nubrigensis reporteth, touching two of his captains,
the one of his horsemen, the other of his footmen,
both of them cruel executioners of his impiety.
The first had his brains dashed out by a fall from
his horse; and the other (whose name was Rayner),
the chief burner and breaker into churches, being
passing over sea with his wife, they were both of
them turned out of the ship into a boat, and so left
to fortune, were there drowned. More of the story
you may see in Nubrigensis, lib. i. c. 2.

[8] Cat. Com. Essex.
[9] Stow, an. 9, Steph. MATTH. WESTM. ann. 1143, HEN. HUNTING.
Hist. lib. viii. p. 393.
[1] Hov. in ann. 1144; Catal. Com. Essex, p. 177; MAT. PAR.
ann. 1143.

About the same time, Robert Marmion, a man of great power, in like manner invaded the church of Coventry, and turning out the monks, placed his soldiers in their room; then going to battle against the earl of Chester, he showed himself in a bravery before both the armies; and having forgotten privy trenches, which himself had made to entrap his enemies, or hinder their approach, he fell (as he pranced up and down before the monastery) into one of them, and breaking his thigh bone, could not get out; which a peasant of his enemies perceiving, ran to him and cut off his head.[2]

A.D. 1179. William Albemarle (whom I certainly take to be William le Gros, earl of Albemarle, that died 25 Henry II.), by the former examples, thrust the regular priests out of the church of Belingcon (?) and fortified it with his soldiers. But by example also of their grievous punishment, it pleased God to touch him with repentance, so that to expiate his sin, he did many noble works of charity, both in relieving the poor abundantly, and in erecting of two (if no more) worthy monasteries, that of Melsa, in the year 1150, and the other of Thorneton, where he was buried in peace. Yet God delighted rather in obedience than sacrifice, cut off the line of his family, and transposed his inheritance by his only daughter Hawis (who was thrice married) to three several families: but in the two first it stuck not at all, and but two descents in the last of them.[3]

King Henry II., in the year 1170 and the sixteenth of his reign, being in Normandy, and hearing that Thomas of Becket, archbishop of Canterbury, after a peace lately made between them, carried things so imperiously in England, as there was no living under him; growing into an extreme passion, used (as they say) these words: " In what a

[2] NUB. lib. i. c. 12; MAT. WEST. an. 1143; HUNTING. lib. viii. p. 393; MAT. PAR. 1143.

[3] NUB. l. 1, c. 12; HOV an. 1179.

miserable state am I, that I cannot be quiet in
my own kingdom for one only priest! Is there no
man that will rid me of this trouble?" Hereupon
(or upon what other motives, God knoweth) four
barbarous knights, sir Hugh Morvill, sir William
Tracy, Sir Richard Brittain, and sir Reynold
Fitz-Urse, hasting into England, slew the archbishop, at evensong, in his cathedral church, at the
very altar, embruing it with his blood and brains,
committing at once this horrible murder and triple
sacrilege : first, in respect of the person ; secondly,
of the place ; and thirdly, of the time and business
then in hand. Yet vengeance seized not presently
on their bodies, but tormented their souls upon the
rack of desperation; so that neither trusting themselves one with another, nor the solitary woods, nor
the mantle of night, they fled into several countries,
where they all within four years after (as it is
reported) died miserable fugitives, saith the story.

Touching their issue, I find that Fitz-Urse fled
into Ireland, and I heard there that the wild Irish,
and rebellious family of M'Mahunde, in the north
parts, is of that lineage. The family of another of
them is, at this day, prosecuted with a fable (if it be
so) that continueth the memory of this impiety ; for
in Gloucestershire, it is yet reported that wheresoever any of them travelleth, the wind is commonly
in their faces.

The quadripartite history, called Quadrilogus,
printed at Paris, A.D. 1495, saith, the murderers,
after this horrible fact, rode that night to a manor
of the archbishop's, named there (corruptly) Suman-
tingues, forty miles (leucas) distant from Canterbury ;[4] and that being men of great possessions, active
soldiers, and in the strength of their age, yet now
they became like men beside themselves, stupid,
amazed, and distracted, repenting entirely of what
they had done, and for penance took their way to
the Holy Land. But sir William Tracy being come

[4] Lib. iii. c. 20.

to the city of Cosenza in Calabria, and lingering
there, fell into an horrible disease; so that the parts
of his body rotted whilst he lived, and his flesh
being dissolved by the putrefaction, himself did, by
piecemeal, pull it off, and cast it away, leaving the
sinews and bones apparent. In this misery this
wretched murderer (as it was testified by the bishop
of that city, who was then his confessor) ended his
days, but very penitently. His other complices
lived not long after, for all the four murderers were
taken away within three years after the fact committed.

SECTION III.

A.D. 1199. It appeareth by a MS. copy of Matthew
Paris, which I have (wanting much of that which is
published, and having much which the published
wanteth), that king Richard I. had spoiled some
church of the chalice and treasure; and that it
was thereupon conceived that the revengeful hand
of God pursued him to his death. First, by tickling
his covetous mind with the report of a hidden
treasure found by one Vidomer, a viscount of Bretagne, in France, which he (the king) claimed to
belong to him by his prerogative: and then in
stirring him to raise war against the viscount for it,
and to besiege him in the castle and town of Chalus,
in the country of Limousin, whither the viscount was
fled and had carried the treasure, as it were, to
train the king to that fatal place, importing the
name of a chalice. But here it so fell out, that the
king being repelled in his assault, and surveying the
ground for undermining the town walls, one Peter
Basil struck him in the left arm, or about the
shoulder, with a quarrel from a cross-bow, out of
the castle. The king, little regarding his wound,
pursued the siege, so as within twelve days he took
the town, and found little treasure in it. But his
wound, in the meantime, festering, deprived him of
his life (April 9) in the tenth year of his reign, being

o

about forty-four years old. Hereupon a satirist of that time wrote this tart distichon, related in the MS.[5]

> *Christe, Tui chalicis prædo fit præda Chalucis :*
> *Ære brevi rejicis qui tulit æra crucis.*
>
> He that did prey upon Thy chalices,
> Is now a prey unto the Chaluces ;
> And thou, O Christ, rejectest him as dross,
> That robb'd Thee of the treasure of Thy cross.

* Giraldus Cambrensis, a good author, reporteth that one Hur, chaplain to William de Bruce (a great lord in Wales in the time of king John), of his chapel of S. Nicholas, in the castle of Aberhodni, did dream in a night that one bid him tell his lord (that had taken away the land given in alms to that chapel, and presumed to detain it) that *Hoc aufert fiscus quod non accipit Christus ; dabis impio militi quod non vis dare sacerdoti.* The king's exchequer shall take that from thee that thou wilt not suffer Christ to enjoy ; and the impious soldier, that which thou wilt not permit unto the priest. The words are S. Austin's, spoken against them that invade tithes and church rights : and that which is there threatened against them, saith Giraldus, happened most certainly in a very short time to this with-holder. For we have seen (saith he) in our own days, and found certainly by undoubted verity, that princes (and great men) usurpers of ecclesiastical possessions, and chiefly by name king Henry II., reigning in our time, and tainted above others with this vice, a little leaven corrupting the whole lump, and new evils falling thereby daily upon them, have consumed all their whole treasure, giving that unto the hired soldiers which they ought to have given unto the priest.

He mentioneth not what it was particularly that happened to Bruce, but commiserating him as a sin-

---

[5] MATT. PAR.

* [We have here omitted a few paragraphs relating to king Edward I., which are repeated, in their proper place, further on.— EDS.]

gular good man, runneth out into a long commendation both of him and his wife.   The rest, therefore, of this tragedy I must supply out of Matthew
Paris, who in A.D. 1209 reporteth thus, that king
John, doubting the fidelity of his nobles, sent a
troop of soldiers to require of them their sons, or
nephews, or near kinsmen for hostages.   Coming to
William Bruce's and demanding his sons, the lady
Maud his wife, in the humour of a woman, prevent-
ing her husband, said, " I will deliver no sons of
mine to your king John, for that he beastly murdered his nephew Arthur, whom he ought to have
preserved honourably."   Her husband reproved her,
and offered to submit himself to the trial of his peers
if he had offended the king; but that would not
serve.   The king understanding it, sent his soldiers
in all haste, as privily as he could to apprehend
William de Bruce and his whole family; but he
having intelligence of it, fled with his wife, children,
and kinsmen, into Ireland ; whither the king coming
afterwards besieged his wife, and his son William
with his wife, in a munition in Meath, and having
taken them, they privily escaped to the island of
May, where being again recovered and brought
unto him, he now bound them surely, and sent them
to Windsor castle, and there by his commandment
they all died miserably famished.   William himself,
the father, escaping into France, died also shortly
after, and was buried at Paris; leaving all, according to S. Austin's words, to the king's extortioners.
What reax king John kept among churches, is
generally well known ; yet I find not that either he
destroyed or profaned any of them, otherwise than
by rifling of their wealth, and persecuting the
clergy as his enemies.   To say truth, they were
not his friends.   But the last riot that he committed among them was in Suffolk and Norfolk, as
he brought his army that way to waste the lands
of the barons his enemies, and to pass by the
town of Lynn (which stood faithful to him

when the most of England had forsaken him) into the north parts. Having lodged there to his great content, and taking his journey, *spoliis onustus opimis.* over the washes, when he came upon the sands of Wellstream, a great part of his sacrilegious army, with the spoils he had taken, and his treasure, plate, jewels, horses, and carriages were all drowned : so that it was judged (saith the history) to be a punishment by God, that the spoil which had been gotten and taken out of churches, should perish and be lost by such means, together with the spoilers. Stow reporteth, " that the earth opened in the midst of the waves, on the marshes, and the whirlpit of the deep so swallowed up both men and horses, that none escaped to bring king John tidings ;" for he with his army, going before, escaped (more happily than Pharaoh) but very narrowly with his life, especially if it were any happiness to live in that miserable condition he was now brought to, having lost his treasure and fortunes at the very time where above all other he had most need of them as flying from his enemy, Lewis, the dauphin of France, called in by his subjects to take the crown, and possessing peaceably the city and tower of London, the cities of Canterbury and Winchester, with all the castles of Kent, except Dover, which could not hold out; and all the barons, in a manner, with the citizens of London and Winchester, having sworn him fealty and done him homage ; as also the king of Scots for the lands he held of the king of England, who likewise had subdued all Northumberland, except Barnard Castle, to him. If after all this, I say, it were any happiness to live, yet enjoyed he that miserable happiness but a very short time; for whether by poison given him at Swineshed abbey, as the common report is, or by a surfeit taken with eating peaches, accompanied with an intolerable grief for his losses, as others deliver it; he died about five or six days after at Newark castle, and wanting all civil lamentation, was presently so spoiled by his servants, who fled every man his way, as they left nothing worth the carriage to cover his dead carcase.

Discite, O reges, sacratæ parcere turbæ

Circ. A.D. 1220. Robert Fitz-Walter (so great a baron in the time of king John, that Matthew Paris saith of him, *Cui vix aliquis comes in Anglia tum temporis potuit comparari*), was a grievous enemy to the monastery of S. Alban; and persecuting it with many injuries, did among others besiege the priory of Binham in Norfolk (a cell of S. Alban's) as if it were a castle, and constrained the monks there to extreme famine; for that John, the abbat of S. Alban's, had removed Thomas, the prior of Binham, and put another in his room, without the assent of the said Robert, who was patron of the priory, and a singular friend of Thomas. The complaint hereof being brought to the king, he presently sent forces to remove and apprehend the besiegers; but they having notice thereof, departed. Matthew Paris[6] wondereth at the revengeful wrath of God, which thereupon fell on Robert Fitz-Walter: " From that time " (saith he) " he never wanted manifest pursuit of enemies, or the afflictions of infirmities. All that he had is confiscate; and during the life of king John he lived in exile and vagrant, suffering great adversities and misfortunes. And though king Henry III. granted peace to all, yet did he never recover fully his favour, but died dishonourable and infamous."

A.D. 1224. Falcasius de Brent, a valiant and powerful baron, that on the part of king John grievously afflicted the barons his adversaries, and all England beside, pulled down the church of S. Paul at Bedford, to have the stones and materials thereof for the building and fortifying his castle of Bedford. He fell afterward in the . . . year of Henry III., to be fined before the justices itinerant at Dunstable £100 apiece for thirty

<hr>

[6] MATTH. PARIS, vit. MS. Johan. Abbat. S. Albani xxi.

forcible entries and disseisins made by him upon
divers men; in all at £3,000. Upon this he
attempted, by his brethren and followers, to have
taken the justices sitting in court, and to imprison
them in his castle at Bedford. But they all, save
Henry de Braybrock, escaped; him they imprisoned;
and his wife complaining thereon to the king and
parliament then sitting at Northampton, they all set
all other business apart, and with all the power
they could make, went and besieged the castle;
which was to the utmost admirably defended against
them, and to the extreme loss of the assailants. Yet
by raising a wooden tower close by it, which they
call Malvisine, it was at length taken, the justice
delivered, twenty-four hanged, and the brethren
[of Falcasius]; himself being escaped, lost all his
possessions, and whatsoever else he had. But for
the great service he had done king John, his life,
upon his submission, was pardoned, and he banished;
yet vengeance still pursued him, for he died by
poison.

I must not forget a memorable relation, which
Matthew Paris further maketh touching this matter.
The abbess of Helnestene [Elstow] hearing that
Falcasius had pulled down S. Paul's church to build
his castle, caused the sword which was in the hand
of the image of S. Paul to be taken out of it, and
would not suffer it to be restored till now that he
had so worthily revenged himself. Whereupon one
writ thus:

> *Perdidit in mense Falco tam fervidus ense*
> *Omnia sub sævo quicquid quæsivit ab ævo.*[7]

> The fierce Sir Falco ere one month was run
> Lost all the wealth that in his life he won.

A.D. 1245. William, earl of Pembroke, surnamed
the great Earl Marshal, tutor of King Henry III.,
took by force of war two manors belonging to the
church and bishoprick of Fernes in Ireland. The
bishop, a godly man, required restitution; and

[7] MATT. PAR. A.D. 1224.

failing of it, excommunicated the earl, who little regarded it. The earl so dieth; the bishop cometh into England, and reneweth his suit to earl William his son and heir, obtaining to have the king his mediator, but prevailed not; for earl William and his brethren answered that their father did the bishop no wrong, having gotten the manors by right of war. The bishop, in the agony of his spirit, reneweth the curse against their father and them, and said that the Lord had cast it grievously upon earl William, as is written in the Psalm: *In a generation his name shall be put out, and his sons shall be vagabonds*, as touching the blessing promised by the Lord of increase and multiply.

Earl William, the father, at the time of his death and burial (which was in the New Temple at London, March 14, 1219, and 4 Hen. III.), left five sons and as many daughters.

Earl William, the eldest son, first married Alice the daughter and heir of Baldwin, earl of Albemarle, etc. After, Eleanor, daughter of king John, and died without issue, April 6, 1231, 15 Hen. III.

Earl Richard, the second brother, succeeded; he married the lady Gervasia, and was slain in Ireland, 18 Hen. III., leaving no issue.

Earl Gilbert, the third brother, succeeded; he married Margaret, daughter of William, king of Scots, and was killed by his own horse at a tournament at Hertford, 25 Hen. III., 1241, leaving no issue.

Earl Walter, the fourth brother, succeeded; he married Margaret, daughter and co-heir of Robert lord Quiney, and died at London, Dec. 6, 1245, 30 Hen. III. (or as others report, Nov. 24), and was buried at Tinterne, leaving no issue.

Earl Anselm, the youngest, was, at the death of his brother Walter, dean of Salisbury, but admitted to be earl of Pembroke and marshal; and in haste married Maud, the daughter of Humphrey de Bohun, earl of Hereford, that he yet at last might propagate the most noble family. But *non est consilium contra*

Dominum; for he died within eighteen or twenty-four days after his brother, before he was actually possessed of his county.

Thus, according to the malediction of the bishop, the name of those great earls marshal was utterly extinct; all the five brethren being married and dying childless within fifteen years.[8]

SECTION IV.

KING EDWARD I., in the zeal of his religion (his father yet living), took the Cross upon him and went to assist the Christians in the wars of Jerusalem. The pope, in recompense of his charges, granted unto him in the second year of his reign (he being returned) the tenth part of all ecclesiastical benefices of the kingdom for one year, and the like to his brother Edmond for another. But afterwards the king, forgetting his old devotion, in the eleventh year of his reign seized all the treasure of the tenths collected for that purpose and laid up in divers places of the kingdom, and breaking open the locks caused it to be brought unto him, and employed it to his own use.[9]

This taste of things separate to God drew him on to a further appetite. In the twenty-third year of his reign he took into his hands all the priories[1] aliens throughout the kingdom; committing them (as Charles Martel of old had done in France) to officers under him, and allowing every monk eighteenpence a week, retained the rest for the charge of his war, as he did also the pensions going out of those houses to the greater monasteries beyond the seas. Yet obtained he further, in the same parliament, of the clergy and religious persons a subsidy of half their goods, to the value of £100,000, whereof the abbey of Bury paid £655 0s. 11d.[2]

---

[8] MATT. PAR. A.D. 1219 et 1245.
[9] STOW [A.D. 1283].
[1] There were at that time about one hundred and ten.
[2] STOW [A.D. 1295].

King Edward I. being in great want, by his sub-
duing Scotland, about the end of the twenty-third
year of his reign, caused all the monasteries of
England to be searched, and the money found in
them to be brought to London.   Shortly after, in
the twenty-fourth year of his reign, at a parliament
at S. Edmundsbury, he required a subsidy, which
the laity granted.   But the clergy (pretending that
pope Boniface at the same time had forbidden, upon
pain of excommunication,[3] that either secular princes
should impose tallages upon the churchmen, or that
churchmen should pay any), they refused to supply
the king's necessity; and having day to advise better
on the matter till the next parliament at London
shortly after, they persisted in the same mind.
Whereupon the king put them out of his protection;
so that being robbed and spoiled by lewd persons
without remedy, to redeem the king's favour, the
archbishop of York and many of the bishops laid
down a fifth part of all their goods in their churches;
and some by other courses satisfied the king's
desire, and so recovered his protection.   But all the
monasteries within the province of Canterbury were
seized into the king's hands, and wardens appointed
in them to minister to the monks and religious
persons therein only what must be had of necessity,
taking all other moneys and surplusage to the king's
use.   So that the abbats and priors were glad to
follow the court, and to repair their error with the
fourth part of their goods.   The archbishop of
Canterbury after all this, fearing the pope's excommunication, continued in his refusal, lost all he had,
was forsaken of his servants, forbidden to be received either in any monastery or without, and
rested in the house of a poor man, only with one
priest and one clerk.   How these courses were
censured *in foro cœli* is not in me to judge, nor will
I pry into the ark of God's secrets.   But see what
followeth in the story.

[3] [In the famous bull *Clericis laicos.*—EDS.]

King Edward having with great triumph subdued Scotland, and taken the king prisoner, did at this present peaceably enjoy that kingdom, and governed it by his own officers. But ere three months came to an end, William Wallace began such a rebellion there as put all in hazard; and in fine it was so revived by Robert le Bruce, the king's natural subject, that at length he overthrew the king's armies, slew and beat out his officers, and without all recovery gained the kingdom to himself and his posterity. King Edward attempting the recovery, died at the entrance of Scotland. His son Edward II., pursuing his father's intent with one of the greatest armies that ever was raised by the English, was miserably beaten and put to flight, hardly escaping in his own person. All his life after full of tumult; not only his nobles but his very wife, his enemy; abandoned of his subjects, turned out of his kingdom, imprisoned, and traitorously murdered. In all which, the curse which his father upon his death-bed laid upon him, if he should break the precepts he gave him, had no doubt a co-operation; for he observed none of them.

Touching the pulling of lands from the church, all have not always been of one mind. For though the makers of the statute of mortmain did truly think that the clergy had so disproportionable a share by way of excess in the lands of the kingdom; yet, when in 17 Edward II. it came to the point that the order of the Templars for their wickedness was overthrown, the parliament then (wherein many of those, no doubt, that made the statute of mortmain were present) would not give the lands and possessions of the Templars to the king or the lords of whom they were holden, but ordained that they should go to the order of the hospital of S. John of Jerusalem, then lately[4] erected for the defence of Christendom and the Christian religion.

A.D. 1315. Edward le Bruce, brother to Robert.

[4] [This is, of course, a palpable inaccuracy.—EDS.]

le Bruce king of Scots, invaded the north parts of
Ireland with six thousand men; and accompanied
with many great persons of the nobility, conquered
the earldom of Ulster, gave the English many overthrows, and prevailed so victoriously, that he caused
himself to be crowned king of Ireland. His soldiers,
in the meantime, burn churches and abbeys with
the people whom they found in the same, sparing
neither man, woman, nor child : and most wickedly
entering into other churches, spoiled and defaced the
same of all such tombs, monuments, plate, copes,
and other ornaments, as they found there. He thus
prevailing, and the Irish much revolting to him, the
archbishop of Armagh blesseth and encourageth the
English army against him. Whereupon they joined
battle, overthrew the whole power of the Scots, slew
two thousand of their men, and amongst them, this
their king Edward le Bruce himself.

SECTION V.

KING EDWARD III., to begin his wars with France,
in A.D. 1337, taketh all the treasure that was laid up
in the churches throughout England for the defence
of the Holy Land.[5] And whereas there were anciently
in England many cells and houses of religion (one
hundred and ten were counted, and more) belonging
to greater monasteries beyond the seas, fraught with
aliens and strangers, especially Frenchmen, and those
of the orders of Cluni and Citeaux; king Edward
III., at his entry into his French wars, A.D. 1337,
reg. 12 (partly fearing that they might hold intelligence with his enemies, but seeking chiefly to have
their wealth toward the payment of his soldiers),
confiscated their goods and possessions, letting their
priories and lands to farm for rent, and selling some
of them right out to others of his subjects. Yet, like
a noble and religious prince, touched with remorse
when the wars were ended, viz. A.D. 1361, reg. 35,
he granted them all (save those few that he had put

[5] SPEED, p. 190.

away) back again unto them by his letters-patent
as freely as they had formerly enjoyed them.   And
divers of those that were purchased by his subjects,
were by them new founded and given back to
religious uses.   This act of the king was a precedent
of singular piety; yet was it but a lame offering, not
an holocaust.   He gave back the possessions, but he
retained the profits, which he had taken for twenty-
three years.[6]

King John (whom they so much condemn) did
more than this, if he had done it as willingly : he
restored the lands with the damages.   But let not
this good king want the charitable commendation
due unto his piety ; though having dipped his hands
in this [sacrilege], we be driven, by the course of our
argument, to observe what after befel to him and his
offspring.   There be some things, saith [the wise man],
are sweet in the mouth, but bitter in the belly; pleasant at the beginning, but woeful in the end.   If these
priories and their churches were of that nature, the
sequel verifies the proverb.   The middle part of the
king's life was most fortunate and victorious, yea,
all the while that these things were in his hands;
even as if God had blessed him ; as He did Obed-
Edom[7] whilst the ark was in his house ; and had
the king then died, he had been a most glorious
pattern of earthly felicity.   But the wheel turned,
and his oriental fortunes became occidental.   The
peace he had concluded with France for the solace
of his age, brake out again into an unfortunate war.
Many of his subjects there rebel; Gascony in effect
is lost.   Afflictions at home fall upon him in sequence:
his son Lionel, duke of Clarence, dieth without issue
male, and when he had greatest need of his renowned
son the Prince of Wales (miracle of chivalry, and
the anchor of his kingdom), him even then did God
take from him : his court and nobles discontented
and in faction : himself and all things much mis-
governed by his son the duke of Lancaster and

others of that part; who by the parliament are therefore removed from him, and by him recalled, notwithstanding, to the grief of all the kingdom. Thus he dieth, leaving his unwieldy sceptres to the feeble arms of a child of eleven years old, king Richard II., whose lamentable history, for the honour of kings, is best unspoken of. But so unfortunate he was among his other calamities, that he was not only deposed by his unnatural subjects, but imprisoned and murdered, dying without issue, and leaving an usurper possessor of his kingdoms; which kindled such fuel of dissension, as consumed almost all the royal line and ancient nobility of the kingdom, by the civil war between the houses of York and Lancaster.

To return to the restitution made by king Edward III. of the priories alien. An historian termeth it, " A rare example of a just king; " it being seldom seen that princes let go any thing whereon they have once fastened. But this king having made a door in this manner into the freedom and possession[s] of the church, all the power he had, either ordinarily or by prerogative, could not now so shut it up, but that this precedent would for ever after be a key to open it at the pleasure of posterity; which was well seen not long after. For in the Parliament, 9 Ric. II., the knights and burgesses, with some of the nobility, being in a great rage (as John Stow saith) against the clergy, for that William Courteney the archbishop would not suffer them to be charged in subsidy by the laity, exhibited a petition to the king, that the temporalities might be taken from them, saying, that they were grown to such pride, that it was charity and alms to take them from them, to compel them thereby to be more meek and humble. And so near the parliament men thought themselves the point of their desire, that one promised himself thus much of this monastery, another so much of another monastery. And I heard (saith Thomas Walsingham) one of the knights deeply swear, that of the abbey of S. Alban's, he would have a thousand marks by the year of the temporalities. But the king, hearing the inordinate crying out on the one side, and the just defence on the other, denied his consent, and commanded the bill to be cancelled.[8]

[A.D. 1374. Laurence, earl of Pembroke (temp. Edw. III.), took money by force from several religious houses and secular priests; he in a more especial manner injured the cathedral of S. Etheldreda at Ely. On S. Etheldreda's day (46 Edw. III.), he was taken prisoner at Rochelle, with many of his friends, by a Spanish fleet; and after four years' miserable imprisonment was believed to be poisoned, and died on S. Etheldreda's day (50 Edw. III.).][9]

SECTION VI.

A.D. 1379. Two valiant esquires, John Shakel and Robert Hauley, having taken the earl of Dene prisoner at the battle of Nazers* in Spain, and received his son hostage for performing conditions between them, the duke of Lancaster in the king's name, and the king himself by the duke's procurement, demanded their hostage; and for that they would not deliver him they were committed to the tower, from whence they escaped and took sanctuary at Westminster. This highly offended the duke of Lancaster, who thought that the having the earl's son might be some help to his enterprise for the kingdom of Castile. Whereupon sir Ralph Ferreis† and sir Alan Boxhull constable of the tower, consulting with the lord Latimer, the duke's friend, resolved to fetch them back into the tower, and on Aug. 11, 1378, with certain of the king's servants and other armed men (about fifty in all) entered S. Peter's church, and the parties being then hearing of mass, they laid hands upon Shakel, drew him forth of it, and sent him to the tower. But Hauley, standing upon his

[8] STOW, s.a. 1385   [9] DUGDALE'S Warwickshire, p. 742.
* Najara, ad. 1367.—[E.]   † ? Ferrers.

ᴠlefence, they murdered him in the choir before the stall of the abbat, together with a monk that besought them to forbear him in that place.

The archbishop of Canterbury, with five of his suffragans, openly pronounced sir Ralph Ferreis and sir Alan Boxhull, and all that were present with them at this murder, accursed, and all them likewise that were aiding or counselling to it; the king, the queen, and the duke of Lancaster, nominately excepted. The excommunication for long after was denounced every Sunday, Wednesday, and Friday in Paul's church by the bishop of London. And though the duke was excepted in it, yet did it trouble him very sore for his friends; it being commonly said, that they had done what was done by his commandment. He causeth therefore the bishop to be required by letters from the king to come to a council holden at Windsor, but the bishop would neither come nor stay the curse. Whereupon the duke said, that the bishop's froward dealings were not to be borne with; and that if the king would command him, he would gladly **go** to London and fetch the disobedient prelate in despite of those ribaulds (so he termed them) the Londoners.[1]

My method ties me to relate what followed. Yet I dare not suggest this wicked sacrilege to be any cause thereof. For God's judgments are secret; and no author doth so apply them.

The king himself seems excusable by reason of his tender age, if the omission of justice upon the offenders in his riper years lay not against him. His other errors were many, as those also of his grandfather, which perhaps were visited upon him. God left him to follow evil counsels, he lost the hearts of his subjects, was bereaved of his kingdom, thrown into prison, and there miserably murdered, leaving no issue to prosecute his murderers.

The duke of Lancaster's issue male, as well those

---

[1] HOLINSHED, p. 421, col. 2.

born in lawful wedlock as legitimate by Act of Parliament, in the third or fourth generation were all extinct. And though the eldest line obtained the crown, yet was it pulled again from them by the sword: king Henry VI. being also deprived of it, cast into prison, and himself and son murdered most unmercifully, as in *lege talionis* for [the murder] of Richard II.

A.D. 1379, 3 Ric. II. Sir John Arundel, brother to the earl of Arundel, with many noble knights and esquires and other soldiers, were sent to aid the duke of Bretagne. Lying at Portsmouth for a wind, he went to a nunnery thereby, and entreated the governess that he might lodge his soldiers in her monastery. She, foreseeing the danger, besought him on her knees not to desire it. Her prayers availed not; he turned in his soldiers. They quickly fell to rapine, brake into the chambers of the nuns, and by report deflowered many of them and many other virgins that were among them for education, spoiling also the country about. Upon the day they went to ship, they took a bride as she came from church, and many widows, wives, and maids, out of the monastery, to do them villainy on ship-board; and a chalice off the altar from the priest, having ended his mass. Sir John Arundel having heard much complaint, regarded it not; but sir Thomas Piercy, sir Hugh Calverley, and others (before they departed) made proclamation, that those to whom their soldiers had done wrong, should come and have recompense; which they performed. The people therefore prayed for them and their company, but cursed bitterly sir John Arundel and his soldiers; which was much aggravated by the priest that lost the chalice: for he, drawing other priests unto him, pursued them to the sea-side; and there after the manner of their devotion cursed them with bell, book, and candle; and throwing a light[ed] taper into the sea, wished that they might be so extinguished.

Not many hours after, there arose a storm, which the master of sir John's ship (one Robert Rust of Blakeney) mistrusted by some sore tokens, and persuaded him to have staid till it were passed; but sir John would not. This grew so violent, as all presently despaired of life. First, they threw out what they might to lighten the ship. When that served not, the soldiers with the same arms where-with before they had amorously embraced the women, with the same now they tyrannously threw them overboard (sixty in number, as was reported), and yet continued in the jaws of death for divers days together. Tossed thus with fears, they at last espied an island on the coast of Ireland. Sir John being glad thereof, furiously compelled the mariners to make for it; though they importunately (for fear of rocks) desired to have kept the deep. Thrusting therefore between it and the main, and finding nothing but horrible rocks, their fear was multi-plied, and their ship now began to take water also. Yet at last they perceived where with difficulty they might climb up into the island; and therefore run-ning the ship on ground (that being broken they might escape by the pieces of it), they got so near the island, that Robert Rust the master leaped to the sands, and many others following him. Then sir John Arundel leaped also; and being on the sands he stood as out of danger, shaking the water off him that he had taken in the ship, when as the place, being a quicksand, began suddenly to swallow him up; which the master, Robert Rust, perceiving, stepped to him, and striving to help him out, a billow coming upon them washed them both into the sea, where thus they ended their lives. N. Musard, a most valiant esquire of sir John's, being also leaped on the sands, and having hold of a piece of the ship, was washed back and dashed in pieces against the rocks: so also was one Derrick, another esquire, sir Thomas Banaster, sir N. Trompington, sir Thomas de Dale, being leaped on the sands, and

P

hindered by striving to outrun one another, the billows fetched them also back into the deep. Some escaping to the island all wet, and finding no houses there, it being the 16th of December, died for cold. The rest with running and wrestling saved their lives, but in great penury, from Thursday till Sunday at noon. Then the storm being ended, the Irish, by boats, fetched them to their houses and relieved them. It is said, that sir John Arundel lost in this storm (besides his life) fifty-two suits of very rich apparel, much princely stuff, with his great horse and other horses and things of price, to the value of ten thousand marks; twenty-five other ships which followed him with men, horses, and other provision, all perishing with him.

Touching the residue not guilty of this outrage and sacrilege, sir Thomas Piercy, sir Hugh Calverley, sir William Elmham, and the rest of the army, they were far and near dispersed on the seas with the same dangers; but it pleased God to preserve them. Yet as soon as the storm was ended, a new misfortune fell upon sir Thomas Piercy; for being weak and weather-beaten with all his company, a Spanish man-of-war now setteth upon him singled from the rest of the navy, and drives him to bestir himself as he could; which he did so happily, as at last he took the Spaniard, and bringing him home, brought also the occasion of double joy, one for his safety, the other for his victory. And then pawning that ship for £100, he presently furnished himself forth again, and with as great joy arrived safely at Brest (whereof he was one of the captains with sir Hugh Calverley), and thus supplied that charge also very fortunately.

Sir Hugh Calverley also, and sir William Elmham, with the rest of those ships, returned safely into [their] parts, and by the great mercy of God lost not either man, horse, nor any other thing, in all this so furious a tempest. All this is much largerly related by Thomas Walsingham in A.D. 1379.

A.D. 1380. Though the attempts of rebels and traitors be usually suppressed by the power of the prince; yet that notorious rebel Wat Tyler and his confederates prevailed so against king Richard II., that neither his (the king's) authority, nor the power of the kingdom could resist them ; insomuch as they became lords of the city and tower of London, and had the king himself so far in their disposition, as they got him to come and go, to do and forbear when and what they required : but after they had spoiled and burnt the monastery of S. John's of Jerusalem, be-headed the archbishop of Canterbury, and done some other acts of sacrilege, their fortune quickly changed ; and their captain Wat Tyler being in the greatest height of his glory (with his army behind him to do what he commanded, and the king fearfully before him, not able to resist), was upon the sudden woun-ded and surprised by the mayor of London, his prosperous success overturned, and both he and they (whom an army could not erst subdue) are now by the act of a single man utterly broken and discomfited, and justly brought to their deserved execution.[2]

---

[2] HOLINSHED and STOW in 4 Rich II.

CHAPTER IV.

The attempt and project upon the lands of the clergy in the time of Henry IV. disappointed [and of other Sacrileges until the Reformation.]

BY that time king Henry IV. was come to the crown, the clergy of England had passed the meridian of their greatness, and were onward in their declination. For the people now left to admire them, as before they had done, and by little and little to fall off from them in every place, being most distracted, though not wholly led away, by the prime* lectures, sermons, and pamphlets, of them that laboured for an alteration in religion. The commons also of parliament, which usually do breathe the spirit of the people, not only envied their greatness, but thought it against reason, that those whom the laity had raised, fed and fatted by their alms and liberality, should use such rigorous jurisdiction (so they accounted it) over their patrons and founders; and against religion also, that they who had devoted themselves to spiritual contemplation, should be so much entangled with secular affairs; but above all, that they who laboured not in the commonwealth, nor were the hundredth part of the people, should possess as great a portion almost of the kingdom, as the whole body of the laity. For an estimate hereof had been taken anciently by the knight's fees of the kingdom, which in Edward the First's time were found to be sixty-seven thousand, and that twenty-eight thousand of them were in the clergy's hands. So that they had gotten well

* [So in the printed copies, though there is probably some mistake.—EDS.]

towards one half of the knight's fees of the kingdom, and had not the statutes of Mortmain come in their way, they were like enough in a short time to have had the better part.   Yet did not the statutes otherwise hinder them, but that with the king's license they daily obtained great accessions, and might by the time of king Henry IV. be thought probably enough to have half the kingdom amongst them, if not more, considering that out of that part, which remained to the laity, they had, after a manner, a tenth part by way of tithe, and besides that, an inestimable revenue by way of altarage, offerings, oblations, obventions, mortuaries, church duties, gifts, legacies, etc.

The parliament therefore, 6 Hen. IV. (called the Laymen's Parliament, that all lawyers were shut out of it), casting a malevolent eye hereon, did not seek by a moderate course a reformation, but, as may be observed in other cases, to cure a great excess by an extreme defect, and, at one blow, to take from the clergy all their temporalities.

This was propounded to the king by sir John Cheiney their speaker, who in former time had been himself a deacon, and lapping then some of the milk of the Church found it so sweet, as he now would eat of the breasts that gave it.   He enforced this proposition with all the rhetoric and power he had, and tickled so the ears of the king, that if the archbishop of Canterbury had not that day stood, like Moses, in the gap, the evils that succeeded might even then have fallen upon the clergy.*   But the archbishop declaring, that the Commons sought thereby their own enriching, knowing well that they should be sharers in this royal prey, assured the king, that as he and his predecessors (Edward III. and Richard II.) had by the counsel of the Commons confiscated the goods and lands of the cells or monasteries, that the Frenchmen and Nor-

* [See the very curious scene described by Stow, s. a. 1404. Eds.]

mans did possess in England, being worth many thousands of gold, and was not that day the richer thereby half a mark; so if he should now (which God forbid) fulfil their wicked desire, he should not be one farthing the richer the next year following. This demonstrative and prophetical speech pronounced with great vehemency by the archbishop, it so wrought upon the heart of the king, that he professed, he would leave the Church in better state than he found it, rather than in worse. And thus that hideous cloud of confusion, which hung over the head of the clergy, vapoured suddenly at this time into nothing. Yet did it lay the train that [in] Henry V. did make a sore eruption, and in Henry VIIIth's time blew up all the monasteries. The event of which project of the speaker's, his lineal heir sir Thomas Cheiney, Lord Warden of the Cinque Ports, did then behold, and shortly felt the wrathful hand of God upon his family; whether for this or any other sin I dare not judge.

But being reputed to be the greatest man of possessions in the whole kingdom, insomuch as Queen Elizabeth on a time said merrily unto him, that they two (meaning herself and him) were the two best marriages in England, which afterward appeared to be true, in that his heir was said to sue his livery at three thousand one hundred, never done by any other, yet was this huge estate all wasted on a sudden.

Yet when the Commons did desire to have the lands of the clergy, they did not design, nor wish that they should be otherwise employed, than for public benefit of the whole kingdom, and that all men should be freed thereby from payment of subsidies or taxes to maintain soldiers for the defence of the kingdom. For they suggested that the value of the lands would be sufficient maintenance for a standing army, and all great officers and commanders to conduct and manage the same, for the safety of the public; as that they would maintain one hundred and fifty lords, one thousand five hundred knights, six thousand esquires, and one hundred hospitals for maimed soldiers. Thus they projected many good uses to be performed, not to enrich private men, nor to sell them for small sums of money, which would quickly be wasted : but to be a perpetual standing maintenance for an army and all public necessities.

A.D. 1414. Priories alien, not being conventual, with their possessions, except the college of Fotheringhay, were by the Parliament given to king Henry V. and his heirs, and he suppressed them to the number of * one hundred and ninety and more :[3] but gave some of them to the college of Fotheringhay. King Edward IV. gave them afterward to the two colleges of the kings in Cambridge and Eton: yet Henry V. died young, his son Henry VI., after many passions of fortune, was twice deprived of his kingdom, and at last cruelly murdered ; and prince Edward, his grandchild, son of Henry VI., cruelly also slain by the servants of king Edward IV.

A.D. 1447.[4] Humphrey, duke of Gloucester, coming to the Parliament at S. Edmundsbury, and lodging there, in a place (as Leland saith) sacred to our Saviour; he was, by the lord John Beaumont, then high constable of England, the duke of Buckingham, the duke of Somerset, and others, arrested of high treason, suggested ; and being kept in ward in the same place, was, the night following (viz. February 24), cruelly murdered by De la Pole, duke of Suffolk. Some judged him to have been strangled, some to have a hot spit thrust into his bowels, some to be smothered between two featherbeds. But all indifferent persons (saith Hall) might well understand that he died some violent death.

* [The number cannot now clearly be ascertained ; some reckon it at about 110, Spelman's own computation further back : but the highest estimate probably falls short of the truth.—EDS.]

[3] STOW, s. a.   [4] HOLINSH. STOW, s. a.

Being found dead in his bed, his body was showed
to the lords and commons, as though he had died of
a palsy or imposthume, which others do publish.[5]

But it falleth out, that this lord John viscount
Beaumont, and the duke of Buckingham, were both
slain in the battle of Northampton, 38 Henry VI. :
the duke of Somerset taken prisoner at the battle of
Hexham [Levels], A.D. 1462, and there beheaded.
The duke of Suffolk being banished the land, was in
passing the seas surprised by a ship of the duke of
Exeter's, and brought back to Dover road; where,
in a cock-boat, at the commandment of the captain,
his head was stricken off, and both head and body
left on the shore.[6]

[A.D. 1491. King John II. of Portugal, marrying
his only son Alfonso to Isabel of Castile, celebrateth
the wedding with great pomp and ceremonial at
Evora. And forasmuch as the press of knights and
noblemen could not be contained in the city, he laid
hands on a monastery hard by, and drave forth the
monks : not without the malediction of some, that
God's curse should therefore alight on him in his
son, which threat he at that time regarded so much
as to send for absolution from the pope. But mark
what followed. The king himself, drinking of a
poisoned fountain, narrowly escaped with his life :
his son (for whom that injustice was committed)
persuaded by his father, against his will, to bathe
with him in the Tagus, is there slain by his horse;
and in him the house of Aviz, in its direct line,
cometh to an end.] *

A.D 1527. Cardinal Wolsey, intending to build a
college at Oxford, and another at Ipswich, obtained
licence of pope Clement VII., to suppress about
forty monasteries. In execution whereof he used
principally five persons, whereof one was slain by
another of these his companions; that other was
hanged for it; a third drowned himself in a well; the

---

[5] STOW, s. a. 1447.   [6] HOLINSH. p. 627.
    * [LEMOS. Hist. de Portugal, s. a. 1491.—EDS.]

fourth, being well known to be worth £200 [no small sum] in those days, became in three years' time so poor, that he begged to his death; Dr. Allen, the fifth, being made a bishop in Ireland, was there cruelly maimed. The cardinal, that obtained the licence, fell most grievously into the king's displeasure, lost all he had, was fain to be relieved by his followers, and died miserably, not without the suspicion of poisoning himself. The pope that granted the licence was beaten out of his city of Rome, saw it sacked by the duke of Bourbon's army, and himself then besieged in the castle of S. Angelo, whither he fled, escaping narrowly with his life, taken prisoner, scorned, ransomed, and at last poisoned as some reported. But these five were not the only actors of this business. For Mr. Fox saith, "That the doing hereof was committed to the charge of Thomas Cromwell; in the execution whereof he showed himself very forward and industrious. In such sort, that in handling thereof he procured to himself much grudge with divers of the superstitious sort, and some also of noble calling about the king, etc." Well, as he had his part in the one, let him take it also in the other: for he lost all he had, and his head to boot; as after shall appear in the progress of these his actions.

[We have here omitted a long note, apparently by Jeremy Stephens, on the subject of knight's fees, and drawing a comparison between the sacrilege of Henry VIII. and that of the Puritans in the Great Rebellion.—Eds.]

CHAPTER V.*

*Of the great sacrilege and spoil of Church-lands done by
Henry VIII. His promise to bestow and employ the lands
to the advancement of learning, religion, and relief of the
poor. The preamble of the Statute 27 Henry VIII., which
is omitted in the printed book. The neglect of his promise
and of the statute. The great increase of lands, and
revenues that came to the Crown by the dissolution, quadruple to the Crown-lands. The misfortunes which happened
to the king and posterity : and to agents under him, as
the lord Cromwell and others, to the Crown, and the whole
kingdom, and to the new owners of the monasteries. A
view of the Parliaments that passed the Acts of the 27 and
31 Henry VIII., and of the lords that voted in them, and
what happened to them and their families. The names of
the lords in the Parliament of 27 Henry VIII. omitted in
the record, but those of the 31 Henry VIII. are remaining.
The names of the Lords Spiritual in those Parliaments,
and the spoil and great loss of libraries and books. The
names of the Lords Temporal in those Parliaments with
the misfortunes in their families and their great honour
and dignity abated. What happened to the Crown itself :
and the loss of Crown-lands. What happened to the kingdom generally, and the great injury done to the poor of all
sorts. The mischief of the tenure of knight's service in
capite, which by Act is to be reserved upon all Abbey-lands
that pass from the Crown. The ancient original of wardship from the Goths, and Vandals, and Lombards ; the
abuse of it amongst us. The prediction of Egelred, an
old hermit. The unfortunate calamities of the Palsgrave
and other princes of Germany, by invading the patrimony
and revenues of the Church. King John's letter to the
University of Oxford about impropriations.*

* [From the commencement of this chapter down to p. 101, l.
9, we have followed the original MS., which varies considerably
from the printed copies. In the enumeration, etc., of Abbeys, we
follow NASMITH'S TANNER, as undoubtedly under, rather than
overrating the sacrilege.—EDS.]

SECTION I.

I AM now come out of the rivers into the ocean of
iniquity and sacrilege, where whole thousands of
churches and chapels dedicated to the service of God
in the same manner that the rest are which remain
to us at this day, together with the monasteries and
other houses of religion and intended piety, were,
by king Henry VIII., in a tempest of indignation
against the clergy of that time mingled with insa-
tiable avarice, sacked and razed as by an enemy.
It is true the Parliament did give them to him, but
so unwillingly (as I have heard), that when the Bill
had stuck long in the lower house, and could get no
passage, he commanded the Commons to attend him
in the forenoon in his gallery, where he let them
wait till late in the afternoon, and then coming out
of his chamber, walking a turn or two amongst them,
and looking angrily on them, first on the one side,
then on the other, at last, I hear (saith he) that my
Bill will not pass; but I will have it pass, or I will
have some of your heads : and without other rhetoric or persuasion returned to his chamber.
Enough was said, the Bill passed. and all was
given him as he desired.

First, in the twenty-seventh year of his reign, all
monasteries, etc., not having £200 per annum in
revenue; then in anno 31, all the rest through the
kingdom; in anno 32, cap. 24, the hospitals and hospital churches of S. John's of Jerusalem, in England,
and Ireland, with their lands and appurtenances;
and in anno 37, cap. 4, all colleges, free chapels,
chantries, hospitals, fraternities, guilds, and stipendiary priests, made to have continuance for ever,
being contributary to the payment of first-fruits,
tenths, etc. : what should have been next, God
knows, bishopricks I suppose, and cathedral
churches, which had been long assailed in the
time of Richard II., Henry IV., and Henry V.
But the next year was the time of his account to

Almighty God, to which, as it is said, he passed in great penitency for his sins. It is to be observed that though the Parliament did give all these to the king, yet did they not ordain them to be demolished or employed in any irreligious uses, leaving it more to the conscience and piety of the king, who in a speech to the parliament promised to perform the trust, wherein he said, " I cannot a little rejoice, when I consider the perfect trust and confidence which you have put in me, in my good doings and just proceedings; for you, without my desire and request, have committed to my order and disposition, all chantries, colleges, and hospitals, and other places specified in a certain Act, firmly trusting that I will order them to the glory of God and the profit of the commonwealth. Surely if I, contrary to your expectation, should suffer the ministers of the church to decay, or learning (which is so great a jewel) to be minished, or the poor and miserable to be unrelieved, you might well say that I, being put in such a special trust as I am in this case, were no trusty friend to you, nor charitable to my emne-christen, neither a lover of the public wealth, nor yet one that feared God, to Whom account must be rendered of all our doings ; doubt not, I pray you, but your expectation shall be served more godly and goodly than you will wish or desire, as hereafter you shall plainly perceive."

So that the king hereby doth not only confess the trust committed to him by the parliament in the same manner that the Act assigns it, viz., to be for the glory of God, and the profit of the common-wealth ; but he descendeth also into the particulari-ties of the trust, as namely, for the maintenance of the ministers, and the advancement of learning, and provision for the poor.

So likewise in the statute of 27 Henry VIII., c. 28, the preamble doth expressly ordain that the lands, houses, and revenues should be converted to better uses, as appears fully in the preamble, which

because it is omitted in the printed edition of the
. statutes shall here follow out of the record. For as
much as manifest sins, etc.[1]

But notwithstanding these fair pretences and projects little was performed: for desolation presently
followed this dissolution; the axe and the mattock
ruined almost all the chief and most magnificent
ornaments of the kingdom, viz., three hundred and
seventy-four of the lesser monasteries, one hundred
and eighty-six of the greater sort, ninety colleges,
one hundred and ten religious hospitals, two thousand three hundred and seventy-four chantries and
free chapels. All these religious houses, churches,
colleges, and hospitals, being about three thousand
five hundred little and great in the whole, did
amount to an inestimable sum, especially if their
rents be accounted as they are now improved in these
days. Among this multitude it is needless to speak
of the great church of S. Mary in Boulogne, which
upon the taking of that town in A.D. 1544, he caused
to be pulled down, and a mount to be raised in the
place thereof for planting of ordnance to annoy the
besieged.

I will not be so bold as to father that which
followed upon this that preceded, but the analogy
of my discourse, and the course of [this] history, do
lead me to relate what happened after this, (1) to
the king himself, (2) to his children and posterity,
(3) to them that were agents in the business, (4) to
the crown itself, (5) to the whole kingdom generally,
(6) to private owners of these monasteries particularly.

First, then, touching the king himself. The
revenue that came to him in ten years' space was
more, if I mistake it not, than quadruple that of the
crown-lands, besides a magazine of treasure raised
out of the money, plate, jewels, ornaments, and
implements of churches, monasteries, and houses,

---

[1] [This statute having since been frequently published, the
Editors have followed the printed copies in omitting it.]

with their goods, state, and cattle, first-fruits, and
tenths, given by the parliament in the 27th of his
reign : together with a subsidy, tenth and fifteenth,
from the laity at the same time. To which I may
add the incomparable wealth of cardinal Wolsey, a
little before confiscated also to the king, and a large
sum raised by knighthood in the 25th of this reign.

A man may justly wonder how such an ocean of
wealth should come to be exhausted in so short
a time of peace : but God's blessing, as it seemeth,
was not upon it; for within four years after he had
received all this, and had ruined and sacked three
hundred and seventy-four of the monasteries, and
brought their substance to his treasury, besides all
the goodly revenues of his crown, he was drawn so
dry, that the Parliament in the 31st was constrained
by his importunity to supply his wants with the
residue of all the monasteries of the kingdom, one
hundred and eighty-six great ones, and illustrious
with all their wealth and prince-like possessions.
Yet even then was not this king so sufficiently
furnished for building of a few block-houses for
defence of the coast, but the next year after, he
must have another subsidy of four-fifteens to bear
out his charges. And (lest it should be too little)
all the houses, lands, and goods of the knights of
S. John at Jerusalem, both in England and Ireland.

Had not Ireland come thus in my way I had forgotten it : but to increase the floods of this sea, all
the monasteries of Ireland likewise flowed into it by
Act of Parliament the next year following, being the
33rd of his reign, to the number on^ and other of
[about seven hundred].

But as the Red Sea by the miraculous hand of God
was once dried up, so was this sea of wealth by the
wasteful hand of this prince immediately so dried up,
as the very next year, in the 34th of his reign, the Parliament was drawn again to grant him a great subsidy, for in the statute book it is so styled : and this
not serving his turn, he was yet driven not only

to enhance his gold and silver money in the 36th, but against the honour of a prince to coin base money; and when all this served not his turn, in the very same year to exact a benevolence of his subjects to their grievous discontent. Perceiving therefore that nothing could fill the gulf of his effusion, and that there was now a just cause of great expense, by reason of his wars at Boulogne and in France, they granted him in the 37th year two subsidies at once, and four-fifteens; and for a corollary all the colleges, free chapels, chantries, hospitals, etc., before-mentioned, in number two thousand three hundred and seventy-four, upon confidence that he should dispose them (as he promised solemnly in the Parliament) to the glory of GOD, Who in truth (for ought that I can hear) had little part thereof.

The next year was his fatal period; otherwise it was much to be feared that deans and chapters, if not bishopricks (which had been long levelled at), had been his next design, for he took a very good essay of them, by exchanging lands with them, before the dissolution, giving them racked lands and small things for goodly manors and lordships, and also impropriations for their solid patrimony in finable lands; like the exchange that Diomedes made with Glaucus, much thereby increasing his own revenues; as he took seventy-two from York, besides other lands, tenements, advowsons, patronages, etc., in the 37th of his reign, which are mentioned particularly in the Statute 37 Henry VIII., cap. 16. He took also thirty and above, as I remember, in the 27th year, from the bishop of Norwich, to whom he left not (that I can learn) one foot of the goodly possessions of his church, save the palace at Norwich; and how many I know not, in the 37th year also, from the bishop of London.

I speak not of his prodigal hand in the blood of his subjects, which, no doubt, much alienated the hearts of them from him. But GOD in these eleven years' space visited him with five or six rebellions. One in Lincolnshire; one in Somersetshire, and four in Yorkshire. And though rebellions and insurrections are not to be defended, yet they discover unto us what the displeasure and dislike was of the common people for spoiling the revenues of the Church; whereby they were great losers, the clergy being merciful landlords and bountiful benefactors to all men by their great hospitality and works of charity.

Thus much touching his own fortunes, accompanying the wealth and treasure gotten by him, as we have declared, by confiscating the monasteries; wherein the prophetic speech that the archbishop of Canterbury used in the Parliament 6 Henry IV. seemeth performed, that the king should not be one farthing the richer the next year following.

SECTION II.

What happened to the King's children and posterity.

TOUCHING his children and posterity, after the time that he entered into these courses, he had two sons and three daughters, whereof one of each kind died infants : the other three succeeding in the crown without posterity. His base son the duke of Richmond died also without issue; and as the issue of Nabuchodonosor was extinct, and his kingdom given to another nation the sixty-eighth year after he had rifled the Temple of Jerusalem, and taken away the holy vessels ; so, about the same period that king Henry VIII. began to sack the monasteries, with their churches, and things dedicated to God, was his whole issue extinct, male and female, base and legitimate, and his kingdom transferred to another nation ; and therein to another royal family (which is now his majesty's singular happiness) that had no hand in the like depredation of the monasteries and churches of that kingdom, there committed by the tumultuous, if not rebellious subjects. Contrary as it seems to the good liking of our late sovereign king

James, who (as is reported) said, that if he had found the monasteries standing, he would not have pulled them down; not meaning to continue them in their superstitious uses, but to employ them, as Korah's censers, to some godly purposes. Wherein most piously he declared himself both in restoring (as I hear) some bishopricks and divers appropriations in Scotland, and also by moving the universities of England to do the like.* So his grandfather king James the Fourth of Scotland, when he was solicited by sir Ralph Sadler, then ambassador from king Henry, to augment his estate by taking into his hands the abbeys: James refused, saying, What need I take them into mine hands, when I may have anything I require of them? And if there be abuses in them I will reform them, for there be a great many good. Which was a wise answer, and if king Henry had done the like here, he might have had an immense and ample revenue out of the monasteries and old bishopricks, while they enjoyed their lands (being a third part of the kingdom, as appears by doomsday-book) by way of first-fruits, tenths, pensions, and corrodies yearly; that he should never have needed at any time to ask one subsidy of his subjects. To return where we left off, having spoken of the extinguishment of the issue of king Henry, whereof the immortally renowned princess Queen Elizabeth was the golden period. Let us cast our eyes upon the principal agents and contrivers of this business.

But before we do this, we, who are able to take a more extended view of the subject, will pursue the history of the crown itself.†

The "immortally renowned Princess Queen Elizabeth," herself deeply guilty of sacrilege by forced exchanges of bishops' lands, the murderess of a

---

* [Spelman inserts this letter as a note; we have not thought it necessary to reprint it.—EDS.]

† [We have here inserted a continuation of Spelman's view of the calamities that happened to the crown; for which this seemed the best place.—EDS.]

crowned head, and the destroyer of the best families
of her nobility, was succeeded by James I.   Of his
children, Henry Robert, Margaret, Mary, and
Sophia, died in early youth, and Elizabeth's life
was one of constant calamities and danger.

Of the misfortunes of king Charles the Martyr we
need not speak.

King Charles II. lived a stipendiary of the French
crown, was in constant fear of plots, had a court
that was the hot-bed of vice, was cut off in the
midst of his sins, and died childless.

King James II. lost his crown, and though he left
issue, they never regained their possessions.   Ten
of his children died in early youth.   The other son
of Charles, the duke of Gloucester, died young, just
after the Restoration.

William was engaged in constant wars, was hated
by his subjects, lived in continual fear and danger,
was actually (it is said) on the point of resigning his
crown, died a violent death, and left no children.

Queen Anne was the very sport of contending
factions, was compelled to regard her own brother
as a traitor, and had nineteen children, who all died
young.

George I., one of the worst princes that ever filled
the English throne, was the persecutor and gaoler of
his innocent wife, was involved in deadly hatred with
his son (whom it was, in his presence, proposed to
send to the plantations), in constant fear of rebellion, and deservedly hated.

George II. was all but dethroned in the rising of
1745 ; saw the national debt increase to a fearful
extent; and died suddenly, by an unusual and
awful disease.   Of his children, Frederick lived
in enmity with his father, and died before him.
William was surnamed *the butcher :* the unfortunate
attachment of Elizabeth broke her heart.   Mary
was brutally treated by her husband, the prince of
Hesse.   Louisa, Queen of Denmark, was also most
unhappy as a wife.

George III. was involved, with but few intervals, for fifty-five years in a sanguinary war; was in great peril from the anarchical spirit of the times; and when peace was restored, the mind of this good king was in no condition to enjoy it.

He left seven surviving sons. 1, George IV., who had issue one daughter, the Princess Charlotte, whose melancholy death is yet fresh in our memory: to his unhappy separation from Queen Caroline we need only to allude. 2, The Duke of York; married, but died without surviving issue. 3, The Duke of Clarence who succeeded as William IV.; married, but died without surviving legitimate issue. 4, The Duke of Kent; died without male issue. 5, The Duke of Cumberland, now king of Hanover; who has issue one son, blind. 6, The Duke of Cambridge, who has issue a son and two daughters. 7, The Duke of Sussex, who died without surviving legitimate issue.

So that, in the third generation from George III., but two princes and three princesses exist.

[We may remark that, whereas Queen Victoria's children are descended by five female ancestors from Henry VII. (Margaret, Mary Queen of Scots, Elizabeth of Bohemia, Sophia, and their own royal mother), Henry VIII. was descended by but *two* female ancestors from William the Conqueror (the empress Maud and Margaret of Richmond).]

SECTION III.

What happened to the principal agents.

THE lord Cromwell was conceived to be the principal mover and prosecutor thereof, both before and in the Parliament of 27 and 31 Hen. VIII.: and for his good service (*impenso et impendendo*) upon the 18th of April before the beginning of the Parliament of 31, which was on the last of the month, he was created earl of Essex, and his son Gregory made lord Cromwell, yet ere the year was past, from the end of the Parliament of 31, he fell wholly into the king's displeasure, and in July, 32 he was attainted and beheaded, professing at his death that he had been seduced, and died a catholick. His son Gregory, lord Cromwell, being, as I said, made a baron in the lifetime of his father, and invested with divers great possessions of the Church, supported that new risen family from utter ruin ; but his grandchild, Edward lord Cromwell, wasting the whole inheritance, sold the head of his barony Oakham in Rutlandshire, and exchanging some of the rest (all that remained) with the earl of Devonshire for Lecale in Ireland, left himself as little land in England, as his great-grandfather left to the monasteries, and was I think the first and only peer of the realm not having any land within it : by the feudal law his barony I doubt (if it had been feudal) had likewise gone; but by the mercy of God, a noble gentleman now holds the style of it, and long may he. [His grandson, 7th baron, died without issue male: his daughter, baroness Cromwell in her own right, married Edward Southwell; and the title lay dormant in the family of Southwell baron de Clifford. That barony fell into abeyance in 1832 ; in 1833 that abeyance was terminated in favour of the present baroness de Clifford, in whom the barony of Cromwell is supposed to be vested.] *

Having sailed thus far in this ocean, we will advance yet further (if it please God to give us a favourable passage), and take a view of the Parliament themselves, that put the wreckful sword in the king's hands. The chief whereof was (as we have said before) that of the 27th year of his reign, touching smaller houses, and that of the 31st, touching the greater. I have sought the office of the clerk of the upper house of Parliament, to see what lords were present at the passing of the Acts of Dissolution; but so ill have they been kept, as

* Cf. BANKS' Dormant and Extinct Peerage, II. 129, with DEBRETT's Peerage.

that the names of 27 [Henry VIII.] were not then
to be found : and further since I have not searched
for them. The other of 31 [Henry VIII.] I did
find, and doubt not but the most of them were the
same which also sat in the Parliament of 27, though
some of them of 27 were either dead or not present
in 31. Those that were present at the passing of
the Bill of 31, I have hereunder mentioned in such
order as I therein did find them ; and will, as faithfully as I can attain unto the knowledge of them,
relate what after hath befallen themselves and their
posterity.

SECTION IV.

*The names of the Lords Spiritual who were present in
the Parliament upon Friday, the 23rd of May, 31
Henry VIII., being the fifteenth day of the Parliament,
when the Bill for assuring the Monasteries, etc., to the
King was passed.*

1. THE lord Cromwell, vicegerent for the king in
the spiritualities (and having place thereby both
in the Parliament and Convocation-house above the
archbishops), was beheaded the 28th of July in the
next year, being the 32nd of the king ; confessing
at his death publicly, that he had been seduced, but
died a Papist.

2. The archbishop of Canterbury, Thomas Cranmer, D.D., was burnt in the castle ditch at Oxford,
March 21, 1556, 3 Mary.

3. The archbishop of York, Dr. Edward Lee,
died September 13, 1544, 36 Hen. VIII.

4. The bishop of London, John Stokesley, died
within four months after, viz., September 3, 1539.

5. The bishop of Durham, Cuthbert Tonstal, was
imprisoned in the Tower all king Edward's time for
religion, and deprived of his bishoprick, and the
same *inter alia sacrilegia non pauca* (saith Godwin)
dissolved and given to the king by Parliament 7
Edw. VI. ; but the king being immediately taken
away, queen Mary restored both it and him, anno 1,

and queen Elizabeth again deprived him, and committed him to the archbishop of Canterbury, where he died in July, 1559.

6. The bishop of Winchester, Stephen Gardiner, was committed to the Tower, June 30, 1548, in Edward the Sixth's time; for that he had not declared in his sermon the day before at Paul's cross, certain opinions appointed to him by the council. Two years after, because he approved not the Reformation, he was deprived of his bishoprick, and kept in prison all king Edward's days, but restored by queen Mary. He died of the gout, November 12, 1555, being the third of her reign.

7. The bishop of Exeter, John Voisey (alias Horman), had the education of the king's daughter, the lady Mary, and discontented with the Reformation, aliened the lands of the bishoprick to courtiers, or made long leases of them, at little rent, leaving scarcely seven or eight manors of twenty-two, and them also of the least, and leased or laden with pensions. *Nefandum sacrilegium*, saith Godwin. Being suspected of the rebellion of Devonshire about the change of religion, he was put from his bishoprick, but restored by queen Mary, and died March 3, 1555.

8. The bishop of Lincoln, John Longland, the king's confessor, died 1547, 1 Edw. VI.

9. The bishop of Bath and Wells, John Clerk, carried and commended in an oration to the cardinals the king's book against Luther with much commendation; but being afterwards sent in embassage to the duke of Cleve, to show the reason why the king renounced his marriage with the lady Ann, the duke's sister; for the reward of his unwelcome message, was poisoned (as they said) in Germany, and returning with much ado, died in England in February, 1540-1, *i.e.*, 32 Henry VIII.

10. The bishop of Ely, Thomas Goodrich, continned from and in 26 Henry VIII., till 1 May, 1 Mary.

11. The bishop of Bangor, John Salcot (alias Capon), abbot of Hyde, was consecrated April 19 next before this Parliament, and translated to Salisbury in August following, where it seems he continued till queen Mary's time.

12. The bishop of Salisbury, Nicholas Shaxton, being consecrated 27 Henry VIII., was put out July, 1539, i.e., 31 Henry VIII., together with Latimer, and for the same cause, but recanted.

13. The bishop of Worcester, Hugh Latimer, made 27 Henry VIII., renounced his bishoprick in July 31 of the king, and was burnt with Dr. Ridley at Oxon, October 16, 1555.

14. The bishop of Rochester, Nicholas Heath, made April 14, before this Parliament in 31 Henry VIII., and about four years after translated to Worcester, was deposed by Edward VI., but made archbishop of York, 1 Mary, afterwards, also chancellor of England.

15. The bishop of Chichester, Richard Sampson, made June 5, 1536, and 28 Henry VIII. was translated to Lichfield 12th May, 1543. To flatter the king he wrote an Apology for his supremacy; yet in the year of this parliament 31, he was committed to the Tower for relieving such as were imprisoned for denying it. But it seems his Apology was written after this commitment to recover favour: about 2 Edw. VI. he declared himself for the Pope, whom he had written against, and so after divers turnings and returnings, he died March 2, 1554.

16. The bishop of Norwich, William Rugg, alias Repps, made 1536, 28 Henry VIII., and died 1550, about 4 or 5 Edw. VI.

17. The bishop of S. David's, William Barlow, was translated hither from S. Asaph, in April 1536, 28 Henry VIII., and by king Edward after to Bath and Wells, fled into Germany in queen Mary's time, and 2 Eliz. was made bishop of Chichester.

18. The bishop of S. Asaph, Robert Parfew, alias Werbington or Warton, was made July 2, 28 Henry

VIII., where having sat eighteen years, and, *nequis-simo sacrilegio*, sold and spoiled the lands of the bishoprick by long leases, he was by queen Mary, anno 1, translated to Hereford, where he sat almost till her death.

19. The bishop of Llandaff, Robert Holgate, March 25, 1537, 28 Hen. VIII., and in the 36th of his reign translated to the archbishoprick of York, and by queen Mary, at her entrance, committed to the Tower, where within half a year he was deprived.

20. The bishop of Carlisle, Robert Aldrich, was elected July 18, 1537, 29 Hen. VIII., and died March 5, 1555.

Concerning the bishops it doth not appear how they gave their voices; but it may well be supposed that divers of them were against a total suppression : and seeing in other Acts it is recorded, after that when a Bill was granted with an unanimous consent of all parties, none dissenting, that then it was passed *nemine dissentiente;* yet it is not so recorded upon this, but although many might dissent, and that publicly, yet there was a major part of temporal lords present, and so carried it by voices. It is testified of bishop Latimer, that he much desired that two or three abbeys of the greater sort might be preserved in every shire for pious and charitable uses; which was a wise and godly motion, and perhaps the occasion that the king did convert some, in part, to good purposes. Yet the desolation was so universal, that John Bale doth much lament the loss and spoil of books and libraries in his Epistle upon Leland's Journal, Leland being employed by the king to survey and preserve the choicest books in their libraries. If there had been in every shire of England (saith Bale) but one solemn library to the preservation of those noble works, and preferment of good learning in our posterity, it had been yet somewhat; but to destroy all without consideration, it is, and will be unto England for ever, a most horrible infamy amongst the grave seniors of other nations. Adding further, that they who got and purchased the religious houses at the dissolution of them, took the libraries as part of the bargain and booty—reserving of those library books, some to serve their jakes, some to scour their candlesticks, and some to rub their boots, some they sold to the grocers and soap-sellers, and some they sent over sea to the book-binders; not in small numbers, but at times whole shipfuls, to the wondering of foreign nations. And after he also addeth, " I know a merchantman, which all this time shall be nameless, that bought the contents of two noble libraries for forty shillings each, a shame it is to be spoken: this stuff hath he occasioned instead of grey paper by the space of more than these ten years, and yet he hath enough for many years to come: a prodigious example is this, and to be abhorred of all men who love their nation as they should do." And well he might exclaim, " a pro--d.gious example," it being a most wicked and detestable injury to religion and learning; yet thus are men often transported with passion in the heat of reformation and fiery zeal without wisdom.

SECTION V.

The Temporal Lords present in Parliament, May 23, 31 Hen. VIII.

1. THOMAS lord Audley of Walden, Lord Chan--cellor, died without issue-male, April 30, 1544, 3⅚ Henry VIII. Margaret, his sole daughter and heir, being first married to Henry Dudley, son of John duke of Northumberland, slain at S. Quintins, without issue, anno 1557. After, a second wife to Thomas duke of Norfolk, who was beheaded in July 1572. By him she had issue, Thomas, created by king James lord Howard of Walden, and after, earl of Suffolk, and made Lord Treasurer, but put out of his place and fined in the Star-Chamber, *termino*

. . . *anno* . . . for miscarriage thereof [married[1] to Elizabeth Knevit, a woman infamous for her rapacious disposition], and grievously afflicted by the wicked and odious practices of his daughter Frances, first married to the earl of Essex, then divorced and married to the earl of Somerset; and they both attainted and adjudged to death for the murder of sir Thomas Overbury.

2. The duke of Norfolk at that time, viz. in both parliaments of 31 and 27, was Thomas Howard (the third duke of that renowned family), who suffering the spite of fortune, was, upon the 12th of December, in the 28th of the king, committed to the Tower, with his magnanimous son and heir-apparent, Henry earl of Surrey. His son being first arraigned and attainted, the king, lying on his death-bed, caused him to be beheaded January 19, and deceasing himself on the 28th of the same month, left the sorrowful duke in prison, where he remained, as I take it, till queen Mary set him at liberty to go against Wyat; and being nothing fortunate in that employment, the earl of Pembroke was put in his room, and had the glory of the service.

Thomas Howard, son of Henry earl of Surrey beheaded, and grandchild of the last duke, was restored by queen Mary, and made the 4th duke of Norfolk; but affecting marriage with the queen of Scots, was heretofore attainted, and beheaded in June, 1572.

Philip, his eldest son, was in right of his mother, and by conveyance of the castle and honour of Arundel unto him, earl of Arundel, and after restored in blood, 23rd of Elizabeth; yet by fate of his noble family, after long imprisonment and attainder, died in the Tower; [but] his most honourable son, after restitution to his earldom and other dignities, [had] a reinvesting of the great office of Earl Marshal of England; and now, by

[1] BANKS' Dormant, etc., Peerage, II. 279.

God's blessing and his own singular wisdom, hath gotten the upper hand of fortune, and is likely to leave it to a temperate and virtuous son [as in fact he did; and from him the present family of Norfolk is descended].

3. The duke of Suffolk, both in this parliament and in that of 27, was Charles Brandon; and though he was not present at the passing of the Bill, yet being a principal parliament-man, the king's brother by marriage, and his minion in affection, it is very credible that he was a very great advancer of the business. [See therefore Appendix II. under the name.]

4. The marquis of Dorset, in this parliament of 31 Henry VIII., was Henry Grey, that married Frances, the eldest daughter of Charles Brandon, duke of Suffolk, by the queen of France, king Henry's sister; he had issue by her a son and three daughters. His son Henry, lord Harrington, died before him without issue. The lady Jane, eldest daughter, as we said before, was married to the lord Guilford Dudley, and together with her husband was beheaded. Catherine, his second daughter, was married to lord Herbert, and divorced. . . . Mary, the third daughter, was married to Martin Keyes, a groom porter, and their father himself was also beheaded.

5. The earl of Oxon was John Vere, the fifteenth of that name, whose grandchild, Edward earl of Oxon, not only utterly wasted the great and most ancient inheritance of that earldom, but defaced also the castles and houses thereof, and left a son by his second wife named Henry, the eighteenth earl of that noble family. The same Henry died without issue; and [the direct] male line thus failing, the office of Great Chamberlain of England, which had ever since Henry the First's time gone in this family, was now, by the lady Mary, sister of this Edward, being married to the lord Willoughby of Eresby, by judgment of the upper house of Parlia-

ment, anno . . . transposed to her son and heir,
the now earl of Lindsey. [The title is considered
to have expired in Aubrey de Vere, twentieth earl,
1702.]

6. The earl of Southampton was William Fitz-
William, who being Lord Privy Seal and Admiral
of England, was created earl of Southampton at
Hampton Court anno 29 Henry VIII. He married
Mabel, daughter of Henry lord Clifford, of West-
moreland, and sister and heir of Henry the first earl
of Cumberland, but died without issue, anno 34
Henry VIII.

7. The earl of Arundel was William Fitz-Alan,
who died 35 Henry VIII. He had a son, and by
two wives four daughters, which died without issue.
His son, Henry Fitz-Alan, succeeded in the earldom,
a man of great dignities. He was twice married;
by Catherine, his first wife, he had issue, Henry,
who being married, died without issue in the life
of his father, anno 1556. And so ended the noble
family and male line of these earls of Arundel.
But he had also by that wife two daughters and
heirs, whereof Jane, the eldest, was married to the
lord Lumley, who had issue by her, Thomas,
Charles, and Mary, who died all without issue.
Mary, his second daughter and co-heir, was married
to Thomas Howard, the last duke of Norfolk, and
by her the earldom, castles, and honours of Arundel
were transported to Philip Howard her son, and so
to her grandchild, Thomas earl of Arundel, and
Earl Marshal of England, now living, in whose line
God hold them.

8. The earl of Shrewsbury was Francis Talbot,
who, by his first wife Mary, daughter of Thomas
lord Dacres, of Gilsland, had issue—George his
eldest son, the sixth earl of Shrewsbury; and
Thomas, who died at Sheffield without issue.

Earl George had two wives and four sons, besides
three daughters, by his first wife; no issue by his
second.

Francis, lord Talbot, his eldest son, was married, but died without issue.

Gilbert, his second son, was the seventh earl of that family, married and had issue two sons, John and George; but both of them died in their infancy without other issue-male of their father, whose heirs therefore were three daughters.

Edward, third son of George, was the eighth earl; he married, but died without issue, Feb. 2, 1617.

Henry, fourth son, married and died without issue-male.   Thus was all the issue-male of Francis, earl of Shrewsbury, one of the peers of the upper house at the passing of the Act aforesaid, utterly extinct, and the earldom translated to another family of that name, the Talbots of Grafton, descending from John Talbot, the second earl of Shrewsbury (who died anno 39 Henry VI.) by his third son, sir Gilbert Talbot, captain of Calais.

9. The earl of Essex, Henry Bourchier, that was a peer of parliament at the Act of Dissolution in 27 Henry VIII., broke his neck by a fall from a horse about ten weeks before this parliament, viz., on the 12th of March, in 31 Henry VIII.; and having no issue-male, the king gave his earldom to Thomas lord Cromwell, who, in his bipartite dignity, sat among the ecclesiastical peers, and first of the rank as the king's vicegerent in *spiritualibus*; and here among the lay-peers, as in his own right a temporal earl; and temporal indeed, for not long after he was turned out of all his offices, attainted and beheaded, as we have formerly showed.   He brought in the bill the third time, and it was expedited the 23rd of May; but within two months following, viz., 29th July, himself was attainted in the same parliament, and condemned, so that vengeance fell speedily upon him.

10. The earl of Derby was Edward lord Stanley, a peer of the realm both in this and in 27 of the king.   He had divers sons and daughters; his eldest son Henry was earl after him, and left two sons

Ferdinando and William. Ferdinando succeeded in the earldom, and died without issue-male, 1594, leaving three daughters and heirs, who shared so deep in the patrimony of this goodly earldom as they not only pulled the feathers from the wings of it (whereby in times past it hath been so powerful) but the wings from the very body. [William became sixth earl; he was succeeded by James, seventh earl, beheaded after the battle of Worcester, 1651, and the descendants of Edward Stanley became extinct 1735.]

11. The earl of Worcester was Henry Somerset, lord Herbert, a peer also in 27. This honourable family seems more fortunate than any of the precedent; for their lineal descent remains entire and without blemish, having at this day many noble branches. Yet was not the issue of earl Henry free from the hand of God; for his third son, Thomas Somerset, died in the Tower of London; Francis, his fourth and youngest son, was slain at Mussellborough-field; and his son-in-law, the earl of Northumberland, who married his daughter, the lady Anne, was beheaded at York, 1572. [From this family the present duke of Beaufort is descended.]

12. The earl of Rutland was Thomas Manners, both in this parliament and the 27th. He had five sons and six daughters, and died in 35 Hen. VIII. His eldest son Henry was earl after him, and had issue Edward, the third earl of that family, who had only a daughter and heir, and died without issue-male.

John, brother of Edward, was the fourth earl. He had three sons, Edward, who died an infant, Roger, and Francis.

Roger succeeded, and was the fifth earl. He had only one daughter, his sole heir, married to sir Philip Sidney (slain at Zutphen), and died without issue-male.

Francis, after his brother Roger, was the sixth earl. He was twice married : by his first wife he had issue only the lady Catharine, married to the duke of Buckingham, who was murdered by Felton ; and two sons by his second wife—Henry, lord Rosse, and Francis, lord Rosse of Homelake, who died both young without issue.

13. The earl of Cumberland, both in 27 and 31 Henry VIII., was Henry Clifford, who died 34 of the king. He had issue, Henry the second earl of Cumberland, who had issue George the third earl, a valiant soldier, successful in his enterprises. He had issue two sons, Francis, lord Clifford, and Robert, who died young, and a daughter, the lady Anne, married to Richard Sackville, earl of Dorset, who died, as did also this earl of Cumberland, without issue-male.

Francis, brother of George, was the fourth earl, who had issue, Henry lord Clifford [afterwards fifth earl of Cumberland, in whom the title became extinct, 1643.]

14. The earl of Sussex was Robert Ratcliff, created 8th December, 21 Henry VIII. He had three wives and more sons, besides daughters, and died Nov. 28, 1541, 34 Henry VIII. His son and heir, Henry earl of Sussex, had five sons, whereof Egremont, his son by the second wife, was attainted of treason [and flying the kingdom, was put to death by duke John of Austria, for attempting[2] to murder him]. Thomas, the third earl, son and heir of Henry, had two wives, but died without issue. [The family became extinct, 1641.]

15. The earl of Huntingdon was George, lord Hastings, created 21 Henry VIII. He had issue, Francis, the second earl, and sir Edward Hastings, whom queen Mary made baron of Loughborough, who died without issue ; and Henry and William, besides three daughters. Francis, the second earl, had issue, Henry, the third earl, who died without issue, and four other sons, whereof William died without issue. Sir George Hastings, brother of

[2] BANKS, III. 697.

Francis, succeeded in the earldom, and left many male branches [which, though very numerous at the end of the seventeenth century, are now totally extinct; the present earl being descended from a brother of George, fourth earl], whereof Henry, the issue of his eldest son, Francis, was the fifth earl, and had issue Ferdinando.

16. The earl of Hertford was Edward Seymour, created anno 29 Henry VIII.; made duke of Somerset, etc., by Edward VI. He was committed to the Tower in the third year of the king for divers great offences, but then obtained a pardon; and being arraigned of treason and felony, 1° Decemb. 5 Regis, was quit for the treason, and condemned for the felony, and therefore beheaded the 22nd of July following. He had two sons by his first wife, who died without issue.

Edward, his third son, or eldest by his second wife, the lady Anne, daughter of John Stanhope, Esq., succeeded in all his father's honours for a short time, namely, from the death of his father, June 22, 5 Edward VI., to the end of the next session of parliament, which was the 25th April following. But the honours being entailed upon him, and therefore not forfeited for his father's attainder for felony; misfortune and the malice of his adversaries yet so wrought upon him, as in this session they were all taken from him by parliament with most of his inheritance, which gracious queen Elizabeth commiserating, restored him to the earldom of Hertford and barony of Seymour. To let pass his other offspring, his grandchild Edward, the third earl of Hertford, fell into king James's displeasure by marrying the lady Arabella Stuart, for which both of them were committed to the Tower.

17. The earl of Bridgewater was Henry lord Daubeney, created 20th July, 30 Henry VIII. He died without issue anno Edward VI., and so his name, family, and dignity was extinct. This earl of Bridgewater was reduced to that extremity that he

had not a servant to wait on him in his last sickness, nor means to buy fire or candles, or to bury him, but what was done for him in charity by his sister Cecily, married to John Bourchier, the first of that name, earl of Bath.

A Catalogue of the Barons present in Parliament.

1. AUDLEY. Then John Touchet, lord Audley, who had issue George Touchet, lord Audley, who had issue Henry Touchet, lord Audley, who had issue George Touchet, lord Audley, and earl of Castlehaven [who had issue Mervynn, second earl of Castlehaven, who was convicted[3] of assisting in a rape on his own wife, and of another enormous crime, and] attainted and beheaded, and the Barony of Audley being in fee extinguished [though afterwards regranted].

2. ZOUCHE, was John lord Zouche, who had issue Richard lord Zouche, who had issue [George lord Zouche, who had issue Edward lord Zouche.] lord St. Maur and Cantelupe, of Harringworth in Northamptonshire, who sold his ancient inheritance, died without issue-male, and his barony extinct, 1625. His first wife proving disloyal, she was divorced from him, that he regarded not the two daughters which he had, whom therefore he suffered to marry far below his degree and honour, as himself saith in his will upon record. The eldest being married to sir William Tate, in Northamptonshire, the other to [Thomas Leighton] in Worcestershire. "[The family of Zouche, once so numerous, seems now almost entirely extinct,[4] unless the Rev. Dr. Zouche, prebendary of Durham, the ingenious editor of Walton's Lives, be a remaining branch.]"*

3. DELAWARE. Thomas West lord Delaware, son of Thomas lord Delaware, that died 16 Hen. VIII., married Elizabeth, daughter and co-heir of John Bonville, died without issue. William West, son of

---

[3] BANKS, II. 20 [4] Ibid. II. 625.
* See p. liv.

George West, brother of Thomas lord Delaware, being of the age of eighteen years, 1 Edw. VI., was disabled by parliament to succeed his uncle, as conceived to have imagined his death, and 2 or 3 of Philip and Mary was attainted of treason by commission in London : restored in blood as heir to sir George his father about 3 or 5 Eliz., and created a new baron Delaware in 8, and had issue Thomas Delaware, father or grandfather of him now living.

4. MORLEY. Henry Parker, made lord Morley in right of Alice his mother, daughter and heir of William Lovell. Lord Morley died 27th November, 4 Mary, had issue Henry, who died in the life of his father, leaving issue Henry lord Morley, who died at Paris 1578. [He] had issue Edward lord Morley, who died April 1618, and [he] had issue William lord Morley, [who in right of his mother became lord Monteagle 1605], and died 1622 : and he had issue Henry lord Morley and Monteagle now living, [who[5] had issue an only son Thomas, in whom the male line became extinct, and the title fell into abeyance].

5. DACRES. Thomas Fines lord Dacres of the south, being in company with certain gentlemen hunting in Nicholas Pelham's Park, there committed a riot and murder of [one] Bransrigg. He was hanged at Tyburn on S. Peter's day, 33 Hen. VIII. He had issue Thomas lord Dacres, who died within age, and Gregory lord Dacres, who died without issue[6] 1594, and his family became extinct. Margery, his sister and heir, was married to Sampson Leonard, who had issue Henry lord Dacres, who had issue Richard lord Dacres, father of [Francis], now lord Dacres, a child. [He had issue Thomas, who dissipated the estate; and on his death the title fell into abeyance.]

6. DACRES of Gilsland. William died 1563, had issue Thomas lord Dacres, Leonard, Edward, Francis. George lord Dacres, son of Thomas lord

---

⁵ BANKS, II. 363.   ⁶ Ibid. 138.

Dacres, being but seven years old, and granted ward to the duke of Norfolk, broke his neck by a fall from a vaulting-horse at Charter-house, anno . . . Eliz., and his barony and family extinct, he dying without issue male.

7. COBHAM. George Brook lord Cobham (son of Thomas lord Cobham, who died 1529) died 1558; had issue William lord Cobham. He died 1597, and five other sons, which William had issue, Henry Brook lord Cobham. [See Appendix II. under that name.]

8. MALTRAVERS. Henry Fitz-Alan, son of William Fitz-Alan, the 10th earl of Arundel, which William died 35 Hen. VIII., was, in the life of his father, lord Maltravers, and baron of parliament, and after the death of his father the last earl of Arundel of that name.

9. FERRERS. Walter lord Devereux, lord Ferrers of Chartley, son of John Devereux lord Ferrers, was created viscount Hereford 1 Edw. VI.; had issue Richard, who died in the life of his father, and had issue Walter Devereux earl of Essex, suspected to be poisoned, and [he] had issue Robert Devereux earl of Essex, attainted and executed 1601, and Walter Devereux slain at the siege of Roan. Earl Robert had issue Robert, restored 1 James [the notorious rebel; and on his death in 1646, without surviving issue, the family became extinct].

10. POWIS. Edward Grey of Northumberland, lord Powis, son of John Grey lord Powis, married Anne the base daughter of Charles Brandon duke of Suffolk, and died without issue, and his family extinct.

11. CLINTON. Edward lord Clinton, whose father died 9 Hen. VIII., was made earl of Lincoln 14 Eliz., and died 27 Eliz., and had issue Henry earl of Lincoln, who had issue Thomas earl of Lincoln, father of Theophilus now earl [from whom the present duke of Newcastle is descended].

12. SCROOPE. John lord Scroope, of Bolton, son

of Henry lord Scroope, of Bolton, which John in
Henry the Eighth's time married the daughter of
the earl of Cumberland, had issue Henry lord
Scroope, who died 1592, and had issue Thomas lord
Scroope, who died 1609, who had issue Emmanuel
lord Scroope, earl of Sunderland, that died without
lawful issue, and both barony and earldom became
extinct.

13. WILLIAM STURTON had issue Charles lord
Sturton, who for murdering Mr. Argyle and his son
was hanged at Salisbury on the 6th of March, 1565.
He had issue John lord Sturton, who died without
heirs male, and Edward now lord Sturton [from
whom the present lord Stourton is descended].

14. LATIMER. John Nevil lord Latimer lived 23
Hen. VIII., and had issue John Nevil lord Latimer,
who died 1577, 19 Eliz., without issue male, and his
family and barony became extinct notwithstanding
his four daughters [among whose descendants this
barony is still in abeyance].

15. MONTJOY. - [See Appendix II. under the name.]

16. LUMLEY. John lord Lumley married Jane
the eldest daughter and co-heir of Henry Fitz-Alan,
the last earl of Arundel of that name, and had by
her Charles, Thomas, and Mary, who died all [young.
His second wife was Charlotte, daughter of John
lord Darcy, of Chichester, whose father was deeply
involved in sacrilege : but by her he had no child],
so his line was extinct.

17. MONTEGLE. Sir Edward Stanley, created lord
Montegle 6 Hen. VIII., had issue Thomas Stanley
lord Montegle, who married Mary, daughter of
Charles Brandon duke of Suffolk, and had issue
William Stanley lord Montegle, who died without
issue male, and his barony thus extinct.

18. WINDSOR. Andrew Windsor, made 21 Hen.
VIII. and died 33, and had issue William lord Windsor, died 1558, who had issue Edward lord Windsor,
who died 1575, who had Frederick lord Windsor,
who died Sept. 28 Eliz., and Henry lord Windsor,

who died 1605, who had issue Thomas now lord
Windsor, yet without issue [and died so in 1642].
    19. WENTWORTH.   Thomas lord Wentworth, made
21 Hen. VIII., had issue Thomas lord Wentworth,
who died 1590, who had issue William Wentworth,
who died 1582, S. P.,* and Henry lord Wentworth,
who died 1593, who had issue Thomas lord Wentworth, created earl of Cleveland 1 Charles, and had
issue Thomas his son and heir apparent [in whom
the earldom became extinct : but the barony is in
abeyance in the family of Noel baron Wentworth].
    20. BURROUGH.   Thomas lord Burrough had issue
William, who had issue Henry eldest son, slain by sir
Thomas Holcroft near Kingston, 1578, and Thomas
lord Burrough, deputy of Ireland, and sir John
Burrough, slain by sir John Gilbert, 1594.   Thomas
lord Burrough had issue Robert lord Burrough, who
died a child without issue 1601, and the barony
extinct.   The first Thomas had issue besides Edward
and William sir Thomas Burrough, who died S. P.,
and Henry father of Nicholas, who had issue sir
John Burrough (*ut creditur*) slain at Rees.†
    21. BRAY (sir Edmund) made baron 21 Hen. VIII.
and had issue John lord Bray, who died without
issue, and so the barony and line became extinct;
but he had six sisters.   [The abeyance was terminated in 1839 in favour of Sarah Otway Cave.]
    22. WALTER HUNGERFORD, made baron of Hatsbury
28 Hen. VIII., was beheaded for a [detestable crime].
    23. ST. JOHN.   William Paulet was created lord
St. John of Basing 30 Hen. VIII., and made earl of
Wiltshire 3 Edw. VI., and 5 Edw. VI. marquis of
Winchester, who had issue John marquis, who had
issue William marquis, who had issue William marquis, father of William lord St. John, who died S. P.
and of John now marquis.   [From William, fourth
marquis, the present marquis is descended.]

* Without issue (*sinc prole*).—[E.]
† [This account is extremely different from that of modern
peerages.—EDS.]

24. Sir John Russell.   [See below.]
25. William Parr.   [See Appendix II.]
Leonard lord Gray, lord-lieutenant of Ireland,
holdeth a parliament in Ireland on the 1st of May
28 Hen. VIII. at Dublin, wherein he passeth an act
for the suppressing of abbeys.[7] In the 32nd of the
king he is called home and sent to the Tower, and on
the 25th of June 33 Hen., he was to be arraigned
in the King's Bench at Westminster, and to be tried
by a jury of knights : being no lord of parliament, but
confessing the indictment, he had his judgment, and
was beheaded at Tower-hill the third day following;
a man of singular valour, that had formerly served
his prince and country most honourably in France
and Ireland.[8]

Now I labour in observing the particulars, seeing
the whole body of the baronage is since that fallen
so much from their ancient lustre, magnitude, and
estimation.   I that about fifty years ago did behold
with what great respect, observance, and distance
principal men of countries applied themselves to
some of the meanest barons, and so with what fami-
liarity inferior gentlemen often do accost many of
these of our times, cannot but wonder either at the
declination of the one or at the arrogance of the other.
But I remember what an eminent divine once said in
a sermon : he compared honour among dignities to
gold, the heaviest and most precious metal ; but gold
(said he) may be beaten so thin as the very breath
will blow it away ; so honour may be dispersed so
popularly, that the reputation of it will be preter-
mitted.

To say what I observe herein, as the nobility
spoiled God of His honour by pulling those things
from Him, and communicating them to lazy and
vulgar persons ; so God, to requite them, hath taken
the ancient honours of nobility, and communicated
them to the meanest of the people, to shopkeepers,
taverners, tailors, tradesmen, burghers, brewers, and

[7] *Chron. of Ireland*, p. 100.   [8] Stow, 32 and 33 Hen. VIII.

graziers : and it may be supposed that as Constantine the Great, seeing the inconvenience of the multitude of *Comites* of his time, distinguished them, as Eusebius reporteth,[9] into three degrees, making the latter far inferior to the former; so may it one day come to pass among these of our times; and it shall not want some precedent of our own to the like purpose.[1]

SECTION VI.

What hath happened to the Crown itself.

IT now remaineth to show how the lands themselves, thus pulled from the Church, have thriven with the crown, and in the hands of the king, his heirs and successors : truly no otherwise than the archbishop I spake of so long since foretold. For they have melted and dropt away from the crown like snow : yet herein that snow leaves moisture to enrich the ground, but those nothing save dry and fruitless coffers ; for now they are all gone in a manner, and little to speak of remaining for them to the treasury. For my own part I think the crown the happier that they are gone, but very unhappy in their manner of going : for as Samson going out of Gaza[2] carried with him the gates, the bars and posts of the city, leaving it thereby exposed to enemies weak and undefenced ; so those lands going from the crown have carried away with them the very crown-lands themselves, which were in former times the glorious gates of regal magnificence, the present and ready bars of security at all necessities, and like immoveable posts or Hercules' pillars in all the transmigrations of crown and kingdom, had to our time (one thousand years and upward) remained fixed and amortised to the sceptre. These, I say, are in effect all gone since the dissolution : the new piece hath rent away the old garment, and the title of *terra regis* which in Doomsday book was generally the target in every county, is now a blank I fear in most of them.

<hr>

[9] *De Vitâ Const.* l. IV. c. i.
[1] Vide *Glossarium*, in voc. *Comes*, p. 109.   [2] Judges xvi. 3.

But his majesty hath a great fee-farm reserved out of the greatest part of both of them—£40,000 a-year, they say, out of the crown-lands, and £60,000 out of the church-lands. I confess it makes a goodly sound, yet is it but froth in respect of the solid land, which is deemed to be more than ten times, if not twenty times as much; and this being but *succus redditus*, a sick and languishing rent, will grow daily, as our rents of assess have already done, to be of less worth as the price of lands and commodities increase and rise higher. But I hear there is . . . thousand pounds a-year of the crown-lands gone without any reservation at all, and above . . . thousand likewise of the church-lands: and to tell the truth, which myself do well know, a great proportion of the fee-farm rents themselves are likewise aliened already. But *mihi Cynthius aurem vellit*, I must launch no further. [It is well known that the crown-lands were given up for an allowance in the reign of George III., when the sovereign thus became the stipendiary of the people.]

In what light king Charles viewed abbey-lands, we may learn from his celebrated vow, at a time when all hope of regaining his kingdom seemed at an end:

" I do here promise and solemnly vow, in the presence, and for the service of Almighty God, that if it shall please the Divine Majesty, of His infinite goodness, to restore me to my just, kingly rights, and to re-establish me in my throne, I will wholly give back to His Church all those impropriations which are now held by the Crown; and what lands soever I do now, or should enjoy, which have been taken away either from any episcopal see, or any cathedral or collegiate church, from any abbey, or other religious house. I likewise promise for hereafter to hold them from the Church, under such reasonable fines and rents as shall be set down by some conscientious persons, whom I propose to choose, with all uprightness of heart, to direct me in this particular. And 1 humbly beseech God to accept of this my vow, and to bless me in the design I have now in hand, through Jesus Christ our Lord. Amen.

" CHARLES R.
" *Oxford, April* 13, 1646."
" This is a true copy of the King's vow, which was preserved thirteen years under ground by me.   " GILBERT SHELDON.
" *August* 21, 1660."

SECTION VII.

What happened to the whole Kingdom generally.

WHAT the whole body of the kingdom hath suffered, since these acts of confiscation of the monasteries and their churches, is very remarkable. Let the monks and friars shift as they deserve, the good, if you will, and the bad together,—my purpose is not to defend their iniquities : the thing I lament is, that the wheat perished with the darnel, things of good and pious institution with those that abused and perverted them ; by reason whereof the service of God was not only grievously wounded, and bleedeth at this day, but infinite works of charity, whereby the poor were universally relieved through the kingdom, were utterly cut off and extinguished; many thousand masterless servants turned loose into the world, and many thousand of poor people, which were constantly fed, clad, and nourished by the monasteries, now like young ravens seek their meat from God. Every monastery, according to their ability, had an ambery, great or little, for the daily relief of the poor about them : every principal monastery an hospital commonly for travellers, and an infirmary (which we now call a spital) for the sick and diseased persons, with officers and attendants to take care of them. Gentlemen and others having children without means of maintenance, had them here brought up and provided for, which course in some countries, and namely in Pomerania, as I hear, is still observed, though monks and friars be abandoned. These and such other miseries falling upon the meaner sort of people, drove them into so many rebellions, as we speak of, and rung such loud peals in the king's ears, that on his death-bed he gave back the spital of S. Bartholomew's in Smithfield, lately valued (saith Stow) at 308*l*. 6*s*. 7*d*., and the church of the Gray-Friars, valued at 32*l*. 19*s*. 7*d*., with other churches, and five hundred marks a-year added to it, to be united and called Christ Church

founded by king Henry VIII., and to be hospitals
for relieving the poor; the bishop of Rochester
declaring his bounty at Paul's Cross on the 3rd of
January, and on the 25th day following the king
died, viz., the 28th Jan.   This touching the poor.

SECTION VIII.

*What happened to private Owners of the Monasteries
particularly.*

I TURN now to the richer sort, and shall not need
to speak of the clergy, whose irreparable misery
Piers Plowman foresaw so many ages before, saying
that a king should come that should give the abbat
of Abingdon such a blow as incurable should be the
wound thereof.   Their misery and wreck is so notorious as it needs no pen to decipher it; nor will I
speak of the loss that the laymen our grandfathers.
had by this means, in their right of founders and
patronage, mean-tenures,* rent-services, pensions,
corrodies, and many other duties and privileges,
whereof some were saved by the statutes, yet by
little and little all in effect worn out and gone.
Those, I say, I speak not of, for that they are wounds.
grown up and forgotten; but of one instead of all,.
that immortal and incurable wound, which every
day bleedeth more than other, given to us and our
posterity by the infinite number of tenures by knight's
service *in capite,* either newly created upon granting
out of these monasteries and lands, or daily raised
by double *Ignoramus* in every town almost of the
kingdom.   For as the abbeys had lands commonly
scattered abroad in every of them, in some greater
or lesser quantity, according to the ability of their
benefactors, so the leprosy of this tenure comes
thereby as generally to be scattered through the
kingdom.   And whereas before that time very few
did hold on that manner besides the nobility and
principal gentlemen that were owners of great.

* Mesne.

lordships and possessions, which from time to time descended entirely to their heirs, and were not broken out into small parcels amongst inferior tenants and mean purchasers; now, by reason that those abbey lands are minced into such infinite numbers of little quillets, and thereby privily sown (like the tares in the parable) almost in every man's inheritance, very few (not having their tenure certain from the king by patent) can assure themselves to be free from this calamity. The truth is, that originally none held *in capite* but peers of the realm, who were therefore called the king's barons, and such as by this their tenure (as appears by the council of Clarendon, 10 Hen. II.) had the privilege to sit in the king's house, and to hear and to judge all causes brought before the king, and to be of his great council. And though afterwards the manner of them were neglected, yet king John was tied by his great charter to call them all to parliament, where the knights of the shires in that respect have their place at this day.

I am too prone, you see, to run out of my way into this discourse; but, to hold me nearer to my centre, I cannot but admire what moved the parliament, in 27 Hen. VIII. c. 27, to enact that a tenure *in capite* by knight's service should be reserved to the king upon their granting out of their abbeys and their lands, as though it were some singular benefit to the commonwealth. It may be they conceived that, according to the project of the parliament at Leicester in 2 Hen. V., the king should thereby have a perpetual means to support a standing army, or to have it ready whensoever need required, and so ease the subject of all military contribution. O how far was that great school of wisdom deceived! or what hath that art of theirs produced other than as if some scholars had bound their masters for to whip them soundly? And I suppose they have had their fill of it long ere this time.

But these tenures, by being by this means multi-

plied in such excessive manner, the king's former
officers, that before could span their business with
their hand, could not now fathom this with both
their arms. The greater harvest must have greater
barns and more labourers; and, therefore, in 32 Hen.
VIII. c. 46, and 33 Hen. VIII. c. 22 and 39, the
Court now called of wards and liveries, with the
orders, officers, and ministers thereto belonging,
was erected. What is thereby fallen upon the subject I need not relate; heavy experience makes it
generally known and generally felt; one while by
wardship and marriage, another while by suing
out livery by pardons of alienation, concealments,
intrusions, respite of homage, and other calamities
accompanying this tenure, almost innumerable, consuming the fruit of the wards' lands for many ages,
and (as sometimes I have seen) for many ages the
grandfathers', fathers', and sons' inheritance militant
together in this court; the mother equally lamenting
the death of her husband and the captivity of her
child, the confiscation of his lands for the third part of
his age, and the ransom of his person before he can
enter into the world; the family oftentimes so ruined
and impoverished, as if at last it recover, yet it
stands tottering and lame for a long time after.
Marriage is honourable and instituted by God in
paradise; do you think that a man by the word of
God may be compelled to pay for a license to marry?
I doubt the schoolmen would not so determine it;
nor did any civil or moral nation of old admit it;
the custom rose from the barbarous Goths and Lon-
gobards, and yet I confess not without reason, as
the genius of their nation did then lead them, and
by their example all others where they conquered.
It was an impious manner of those times to hold
malice and enmity one family against another, and
against their friends and alliances from one generation to another. Our ancestors called it *deadly feude*,
the feudist *feudum;* and Tacitus, in his time, noteth
it of Germans, saying, *inimicitias mutuo ponunt*

et suscipiunt. It was therefore of urgent necessity that the lord should be well assured that his tenant married not unto any family that might be either in feud with him, or in alliance with them that were; and to prevent that danger (as appears by the charter of Hen. I. c. 4) the lord would have him bound not to marry without his consent, for which in the beginning the tenant gave his lord some small matter as *munus honorarium;* but from thence it grew afterwards to *nundinaria gratissima.* And as bondmen used to pay to their lords chiefage for their marriage, so the tenant by knight's service, which in the feudal law is called *feudum nobile,* is likewise subject to this brand of servitude, and more grievously in some respect. But I reverence the law I live under and [which] hath been so long received and practised: all I aim at is only to show, in the course of my argument, the evils that have either fallen newly upon us, or been increased since the confiscation of the churches and church patrimony; which, if it be not offensive, I may say doth seem to be foretold eight hundred years since by one Egelredus, an hermit, who assigned three causes of those evils, viz., " 1st, Effusion of blood; 2dly, drunkenness; and 3dly, contempt of the House of God : " telling us farther, " that we should know the time of the fulfilling this prophecy, by the various fashions and mutability of apparel that should be in use, the very ear-mark of the age we live in."

How this contempt of the House of God worketh upon the sacrilegious instruments thereof, is to be seen in the particulars before recited, to which, if I should run higher into former ages, or further from home in other countries, I might tire you with thousands of examples. But, for a conclusion, mark this by the way; that as England hath not been faulty alone in this kind of transgression, so other nations offending in like manner, have likewise tasted of the same corrections, or others like them.

Scotland, after the rasing of their monasteries,

hath had the royal throne removed from them, and placed in another kingdom.

The Low-Countries, harassed with a continued war of sixty years and more.

The Palsgrave, beaten out of his own dominions, and living now with his royal wife and children in lamentable exile : to which may be added, as concurring with the usual infelicity of meddling with church-lands, that the Palsgrave, having obtained the crown of Bohemia, and seizing the ecclesiastical livings there for the maintenance of his wars (as the report goes), he was presently cast out both of that kingdom and of his other inheritance.

Having mentioned this unfortunate prince, I must add also another accident that befel him in this kind. The state of the Low-Countries, while he lived in exile among them, gave unto him as a place of recreation the abbey of Regutian, near Utrecht, where intending a sumptuous building, he drew out thereof such materials of stone and timber as might be useful to his new designs, and making a storehouse of the abbey-church, laid them up there to be in readiness. It chanced that the truly noble lord Craven, returning out of Italy (where my son was very happily fallen into his company), he went to this place to visit the prince, whom they called the king of Bohemia. My son seeing what the king was about, and how he had profaned the church by making it a storehouse, said to my lord Craven, "that he feared it might be ominous to the king:" my lord answered, "I will tell him what you say;" and turning to the king, said, "This gentleman fears this that your majesty doth will not be prosperous to you :" the king answered, "that was but a conceit," and so passed it over. But mark what followed upon it. The king, within a few months after, passing in a bark with the prince his eldest son over the Delf of Haarlem, his boat was casually stemmed and overturned by a barge that met him in the night; and though he himself with great difficulty was saved, yet that hopeful prince, his son, had not that woeful happiness to be drowned right out; but after he was ·drenched in the water, and gotten upon the mast of the bark wherein they perished, he was there most miserably starved with cold, and frozen to death: and the father himself, while he lamented the death of his son, was, by an unusual death of princes, taken away by the plague; laying thus the first stone of his unfortunate building like that of the walls of Jericho, in the death of his eldest son, and prevented in the rest by his own death. God's judgments are His secrets: I only tell concurrences.

The other German princes persecuted with the sword, and spoiled of their liberties.

CHAPTER VI.

The particulars of divers Monasteries in Norfolk, whereof the late Owners, since the Dissolution, are extinct, or decayed, or overthrown by misfortunes and grievous accidents.

ABOUT the year (I suppose) 1615 or 1616, I described with a pair of compasses, in the map of Norfolk, a circle of twelve miles, the semi-diameter according to the scale thereof placing the centre not far from Rougham, the chief seat of the Yelvertons: within this circle and the borders of it, I enclosed the mansion-houses of about twenty-four families of gentlemen, and the site of as many monasteries, all standing together at the time of the Dissolution; and I then noted that the gentlemen's seats continued at that day in their own families and names. But the monasteries had flung out their owners with their names and families (all of them save two) thrice at least, and some of them four or five or six times, not only by fail of issue, or ordinary sale, but very often by grievous accidents and misfortunes. I observe yet further, that though the seats of these monasteries were in the fattest and choicest places of all that part of the country (for our ancestors offered, like Abel, the best unto God), yet it hath not happened that any of them, to my knowledge, or any other in all this country, hath been the permanent habitation of any family of note, but, like desolate places, left to farmers and husbandmen, no man almost adventuring to build or dwell upon them, for dread of infelicity that pursueth them. Let me here report what hath been related to me from the mouth of sir Clement Edmonds, lately a clerk of his majesty's

Council, that did take his knowledge from the council-books, viz., that in the beginning of queen Mary's reign, the parliament was not willing to restore popery and the supremacy to the Pope, unless they might be suffered to retain the lands which were lately taken from the monasteries. This resolution was signified to Rome; whereto the Pope gave answer, that for the lands belonging to religious houses he would dispense for detaining of them; but for the situation of the houses, churches, and such consecrated ground, there could be no alienation thereof to profane uses: whereupon those that enjoyed them did not inhabit or build upon the houses, but forsook them for many years, till [in] the time of queen Elizabeth a great plague happening, the poor people betook themselves into the remainder of the houses; and finding many good rooms, began to settle there, till at length they were put out by them to whom the grant of the leases and lands were made.[1] We see hereby how fearful they were long after the Dissolution to meddle with places consecrated to God (though perverted to superstitious uses), when as yet they had no experience what the success would be: let them, therefore, that shall read this our collection following, consider of it as they shall see cause. I urge nothing, as not meddling with the secret judgments of Almighty God, but relate *rem gestam* only as I have privately gotten notice of it, and observed living in these parts almost all my life, and endeavouring faithfully to understand the truth: yet no doubt many things have been mistaken by those who related them unto me; and therefore I desire that wheresoever it so falleth out, my credit may not be engaged for it.

The collection of divers ancient gentlemen's families in Norfolk, all standing and continuing in their names and heirs, with the possessors of religious houses since the Dissolution; most part

[1] Mr. Stephen's Treat., 27th Feb., 1629.

whereof are cast out and changed often in few
years, besides many strange misfortunes and
grievous accidents happening to them, their
children, and heirs.

Monasteries.			*Gentlemen's Families.*
At Lynn . . {	1	1	Bedingfield at Oxburgh.
	2	2	Spelman at Narburgh.
	3	3	Yelverton at Rougham.
Crabhouse. .	4	4	Townsend at Raneham.
Wormgay . .	5	5	Fermor at Barsham.
Blackborough	6	6	Bolleyne at Blickling.
West Deerham	7	7	Calthorpe at Cokesford.
Pentney . .	8	8	L'Estrange at Hunstanton.
Westacre . .	9	9	Sherbourn at Sherbourn.
Castleacre . .	10	10	Walpool at Houghton.
Marham . .	11	11	Mordaunt at Massingham.
Shouldham .	12	12	Cobbs at Sandringham.
Wendling . .	13	13	Thursby at Wichen.
Walsingham .	14	14	Cocket at Brunsthorp.
[Brinton?] .	15	15	Astley at Melton.
Binham. . .	16	16	Gourney at Barsham.
Burnham . .	17	17	Cherville at S. Mary's Wigenhale.
Peterston . .	18	18	Gawsell at Watlington.
Cokesford . .	19	19	Pigot at Framlingham.
Flitcham . .	20	20	Grey at Martham.
Hempton . .	21	21	Woodhouse at Kimberley.
Creak . . .	22	22	Methwold at Langford.
Carbroke . .	23	23	Jermy at Streston.
Thomeston .	24	24	Bachcroft at Bexwell.
Attleburgh .	25	25	Pratt at Riston.

Lynn Monasteries.

1. Friars Carmelites, *alias* White-Friars, in South-
lane.

2. Friars Minorites, *alias* Grey-Friars.

3. Friars Preachers, *alias* Black-Friars.

4. Augustine-Friars.

5. A Cell or College of Priests, belonging to
Norwich.

The four first were purchased of Henry VIII. by John Eyre, Esq., one of the king's auditors or receivers, a great receiver of monasteries, and amongst others of that of S. Edmondsbury; he married Margaret, daughter of sir Thomas Blenerhasset, widow of sir John Spelman, eldest son of sir John Spelman, and died without issue.

He, in his lifetime, conveyed the four first monasteries to a priest, from whom the corporation of Lynn purchased the Carmelites and Minorites; and being thus entered into things consecrated to God, purchased also the impropriation of the church of S. Margaret's there; and defacing the church of S. James, perverted it to be a town-house for the manufacture of stuffs, laces, and tradesmen's commodities, whereby they thought greatly to enrich their corporation and themselves. Great projects and good stocks, with a contribution from some country gentlemen, were raised for this purpose, two several times of my knowledge; but the success was that it came to nought, and all the money employed about new building and transforming the church hath only increased desolation: for so it hath stood during the whole time almost of my memory, till they lately attempted, by the undertaking of Mr. F. Gurney and some artisans from London, to revive the enterprise of their predecessors; but speeding no better than they did, have now again, with loss of their money and expectation, left it to future ruin: thus, in this particular, hath been the success of their corporation. For other matters, I will only note what I have observed touching them in the general: when I was young, they flourished extraordinarily with shipping trading, plenty of merchandise, native and foreign; some men of very great worth, as Killingtree, Grave, Clayburne, Vilet, Lendall; many of good note, as Grant, Overend, Hoe, Baker, Waters, and many more of later time: but all of them, with their male posterity, are in effect extinct and gone; and as at this day they have little ship-

ping or trade otherwise than to the black Indies, as
they call it (that is, Newcastle for coal), so there is
not a man amongst them of any estimation for his
wealth, or of any note (that I can hear of), descended
from any that was an alderman there in the beginning of queen Elizabeth.

The Friars Preachers came from Mr. Eyre [to a
priest, who conveyed[2] it to] Thomas Waters, who
had issue Edward Waters, and a daughter married
to George Baker.   Edward died without issue-male,
leaving a daughter Elizabeth, who was first married
to Nicholas Killingtree, then divorced, and married to
Edward Bacon, who had no issue by her; after to
sir John Bowles, of Lincolnshire.

Sir John Bowles and she sold this Friar [Friary]
to Nicholas Killingtree, who left it to his son, William
Killingtree, and he sold it to Henry Barkenham,
a miller, who sold it to Mr. John Rivett, now living.
[Blomefield traces the descent no further.]

The Augustine Friars came from Eyre [to a priest,[3]
who sold it] to one Shavington, a bastard, who died
without issue, and by his will gave it to one Waters
(other than the former), and to the heirs of his
body.   This Waters died without issue, whereupon
the Augustine Friars was to revert to his [Shaving-
ton's] heir; but having none, because he was a
bastard, great suit ensued about it.

But John Ditefield, being then in possession of it,
left it by descent (as it seemeth), to his son John
Ditefield, who gave it in marriage with Thomasin,
his sister, to Christopher Pickering, brother of the
then lord-keeper; and he then recovered it in
chancery, and sold it to John Lease.

John Lease, pulling down the buildings, selleth
first the stones, and then dividing the ground into
divers garden-rooms, sold the same to divers persons.

·The Cell of Priests was near the Guild-hall, and
the Prior's house was somewhat remote from it, by
S. Margaret's church.

[2] [BLOMEFIELD'S Norfolk, IV. 615.]   [3] [Ibid. IV. 616.]

The College was sometime Mr. Houghton's, after Parker's, then Ball's, lately Sendall's, and now Hargott's: all of them, save Hargott, are extinct and gone; and Mr. Hargott is on the declining hand: the site of the Prior's house was lately consecrated, and annexed to S. Margaret's churchyard for a burying-place.

Shouldham-Abbey.—Sir Francis Gaudy, of the justices of the King's Bench, was owner of it: he married . . . the daughter and heir of Christopher Coningsby, lord of the manor of Wallington; and having this manor and other lands in right of his wife, induced her to acknowledge a fine thereof; which done, she became a distracted woman, and continued so to the day of her death, and was to him for many years a perpetual affliction.

He had by her his only daughter and heir, Elizabeth, married to sir William Hatton, who died without issue-male, leaving also a daughter and heir; who being brought up with her grandfather, the judge, was secretly married, against his will, to sir Robert Rich, now earl of Warwick.

The judge shortly after being made Chief-Justice of the Common-Pleas (at a dear rate as was reported), was suddenly stricken with an apoplexy, or double palsy, and so, to his great loss, died without issue-male, ere he had continued in his place one whole Michaelmas term; and having made his appropriate parish-church a hay-house or a dog-kennel, his dead corpse being brought from London unto Walling, could for many days find no place of burial: but in the meantime growing very offensive by the contagious and ill savours that issued through the chinks of lead, not well soldered, he was at last carried to a poor church of a little village thereby, called Runcton, and buried there without any ceremony; lieth yet uncovered (if the visitors have not reformed it) with so small a matter as a few paving-stones. [No stone[4] nor memorial was ever

4 [BLOMEFIELD, IV. 147.]

there erected for him; and were it not for the above account, the place of his burial would be unknown.]

Sir Robert Rich, now earl of Warwick, succeeded in the inheritance (by his wife) of this abbey, with the impropriation, and his great possessions, amounting by estimation to £5000 a-year; and hath already sold the greatest part of them, together with this abbey and impropriation, unto the family of Mr. Nicholas Hare, the judge's neighbour, and chiefest adversary.

For among divers other goodly manors that sir John Hare hath purchased of him, or his feoffees, he hath also bought this abbey of Shouldham, and the impropriation there, with the manor belonging to the abbey, valued together at £600 yearly rent. [His son, Robert, survived[5] his father scarcely a year, having not long before lost his only son, Robert, a youth of great promise, who married Frances, daughter of Thomas Cromwell, and died of the evil two months afterwards. The next earl was Charles, son of the Robert above mentioned by Spelman, whose only son died in his lifetime, s. p.; and, on his own death, this miserable family came to an end.]

Binham Abbey.—Binham Priory, a cell of S. Alban's, was granted by king Henry VIII. to sir Thomas Paston; he left it to Mr. Edward Paston, his son and heir, who living above eighty years, continued the possession of it till . . . Caroli R.; and having buried [Thomas Paston], his son and heir apparent, left it then unto his grandchild, Mr. — Paston, the third owner of it, and thereby now in the wardship to the king. Mr. Edward Paston, many years since, was desirous to build a mansion-house upon or near the priory; and attempting for that purpose to clear some of that ground, a piece of wall fell upon a workman, and slew him: perplexed with this accident in the beginning of this business, he gave it wholly

[5] [See BANKS, III. 734.]

over, and would by no means, all his life after, be persuaded to re-attempt it, but built his mansion-house, a very fair one, at Appleton.

Castle-Acre Abbey.—Sir Thomas Cecil, earl of Exeter, was owner of it, and of the impropriate parsonage here : he had issue sir William Cecil, earl of Exeter, who married Elizabeth, the daughter and heir of Edward earl of Rutland, and had issue by her (dying as I take it in child-bed) his only son, William lord Rosse.

This William lord Rosse married Anne, the daughter of sir Thomas Lake; and they living together in extreme discord, many infamous actions issued thereupon ; and finally, a great suit in the Star-Chamber, to the high dishonour of themselves and their parents. In this affliction the lord Rosse dieth without issue, and the eldest male-line of his grandfather's house is extinguished.

Sir Richard Cecil was second son of sir Thomas Cecil, earl of Exeter, and had issue David, who married Elizabeth, the daughter of John earl of Bridgewater, and is now in expectation to be earl of Exeter [as he afterwards was, and died 1643].

His third son was sir Edward Cecil, knight; his fourth and fifth, Thomas Cecil and Christopher, drowned in Germany.

Sir Thomas, the grandfather, earl of Exeter, made a lease of this monastery and impropriation to one Paine (as I take it), by whose widow the same came in marriage to Mr. Humfrey Guibon, Sheriff of Norfolk anno 38 Elizabeth, whose grandchild and heir, Thomas Guibon, consumed his whole inheritance ; and lying long in the Fleet, either died there a prisoner, or shortly after.

Sir Edward Coke, Lord Chief-Justice, married for his second wife the lady Elizabeth Hatton, one of the daughters of the said earl Thomas, and afterwards bought the castle of Acre, with this monastery and impropriation, of his brother-in-law, earl William, son of earl Thomas; since which time he hath felt abundantly the change of fortune, as we shall partly touch in Flitcham Abbey.

West-Acre Abbey.—This also belonged to sir Thomas Cecil, of whom we have now spoken. He sold both it and the impropriation of West-Acre to sir Horatio Pallavicini, an Italian, that, before his coming into England had dipt his fingers very deep in the treasure of the church.

Being in his youth in the Low-Countries (as his son Edward affirmed to me), he there secretly married a very mean woman, and by her had issue him this Edward, but durst never discover it to his father as long as they lived together. His father being dead, he came into England, and here married a second wife, by whom he had issue his son Toby; and for his wife's sake disinherited him his eldest son Edward, and conferred all his lands, with the abbey and impropriation of West-Acre, to Toby and his heirs.

Edward, after the death of his father, grows into contention with his brother Toby; and in a petition to king James accuseth both his father and his brother for deceiving, the one, of queen Elizabeth, the other, of king James, of a multitude of thousand pounds, the examination whereof was by his majesty referred unto me, among others; and the two brethren then agreeing among themselves, the reference was no further prosecuted. But Mr. Toby Pallavicini consuming his whole estate, sold the abbey and impropriation to Alderman Barcham, and yet lieth in the Fleet for debt, if not lately at liberty.

Blackborough and Wrongey [or Wormegay] Abbeys. These were by [Edward VI.] granted and annexed to the see and bishoprick of Norwich, where Edmund Scambler being made bishop, 27 Eliz., and doing as much as well he might to impoverish the church, made a lease of most of the manors and lands thereof, and amongst them of these two abbeys, to queen Elizabeth for twenty-nine years, at the lowest rent he might, which bishop Goodwin, in like cases, termeth sacrilege.

Queen Elizabeth assigneth this lease to sir Thomas [Heneage]; he leaveth it to his lady, after the countess of Southampton; she selleth her term in these abbeys, with the manors and lands belonging to them, to one Fisher, a skinner in London, by the procurement of Wrenham her servant.

Fisher entereth and enjoyeth them as undoubtedly his own; leaseth them for twenty-one years to Harpley at a great increased rent. Wrenham dieth without contradicting anything: his son, John Wrenham, pretending that Fisher had the grand lease but in trust for his father (who never paid penny for it), exhibits one bill in chancery against Fisher, another against his son, sir Edward Fisher, as having it from his father, a third against Harpley, the under-leaser. The lord-chancellor, Egerton, by an order declareth Harpley's lease to be good, who thereupon enjoyed it quietly and dieth. His executrix selleth it to sir Henry Spelman; Wrenham exhibiteth a bill against sir Henry. The suits proceed to a hearing betwixt Wrenham and the Fishers. The lord-chancellor decreeth against the Fishers, and all claiming under them. The lord-chancellor, Egerton, gives over his place, and sir Francis Bacon placed in his room. He reverseth his decree, and decreeth it back again to sir Edward Fisher; and by another decree giveth also sir Henry Spelman's lease unto him, without calling or hearing sir Henry. Wrenham complaineth in a petition to king James, and taxeth the lord-chancellor, Bacon, of corruption and injustice. The king himself peruseth all the proceedings, and approveth the lord Bacon's decree; Wrenham is censured for his scandal in the Star-Chamber to lose his ears on the pillory, etc.

A Parliament followeth, in . . . Jacobi: both Wrenham and sir Henry Spelman severally complain there. It is found that the lord-chancellor

Bacon had for these decrees of sir Edward Fisher a suit of hangings of eight score pounds. The lord-chancellor, for this and other such crimes, is deposed.

The bishop of Lincoln is set in his room; the suits are again in agitation before him between Wrenham and Fisher: and sir Henry Spelman, by a petition to the king, obtaineth a review of the proceedings against him, upon which a recompense is given him by decree against sir Edward Fisher.

The bishop of Lincoln is removed by king Charles, and the lord Coventry made lord-keeper, by whom the other differences are at last compounded, and the grand lease divided into many parcels.

Wrenham, that raised this tempest, besides his misfortune in the Star-Chamber, is never the richer by it, but liveth a projector.

Sir Edward Fisher, after the expense of £8,000 (as Bodon his servant protesteth) in the suit, is consumed, and not to be seen of every man.

Sir Henry Spelman, a great loser, and not beholden to fortune, yet happy in this, that he is out of the briars; but especially that hereby he first discerned the infelicity of meddling with consecrated places.

Sir Thomas Heneage died without issue-male, and his family extinct; Mr. James Scambler, out of whose bowels his father the bishop, hoped to raise a family of note, hath to this day no issue at all.

Walsingham Abbey.

Dedicated to S. Mary; Canons regular; valued at £446 14s. 4d.

One [Thomas] Sydney, governor of the spital there, as was commonly reported when I was a scholar at Walsingham, was by the townsmen employed to have bought the site of the abbey to the use of the town, but obtained and kept it to himself. He had issue Thomas, and a daughter, mother to Robin Angust, the foot-post of Walsingham.

Thomas, by the advancement of sir Francis Walsingham, brother to his wife, grew to great wealth, was customer of Lynn; and about a miscarriage of that place, was long harrowed in law by Mr. Farmer of Barsham, and died leaving two sons.

Thomas, the eldest, having the abbey, etc., married, and died without issue-male.

Sir Henry succeeded to the abbey, etc., married, and died without issue.

His lady, a virtuous woman, now hath it for life; the remainder being given for namesake by sir Henry to Robert Sydney, the second son of the earl of Leicester.

Walsingham Priory.

(Not mentioned in the Tax.)

One Mr. Jenner was owner of it, and had issue, Thomas, Francis, and Bartholomew.

Francis, a lawyer of Gray's Inn, married into Kent, and was drowned in going thither by boat.

Thomas, the eldest, had the priory, and three or four sons and a daughter: one of his sons (or as some say two) went up and down a-begging. His eldest he disinherited, settling his estate upon his younger son John, being my servant, who died in his father's life.

Then he gave his whole estate to his daughter, married to Bernard Utbarr, and a daughter of hers, his grandchild, with a particular sum of money to maintain suit against his son and heir, if he claimed anything after his death. Being dead, his son entered and got possession of the priory; but in fine, with some little composition, was wrested out by Utbarr: and now Utbarr's daughter coming to age, it is to be sold by her. [It was bought by one Bond, whose descendants[6] held it in 1715.]

Hempton Abbey, alias *Fakenham.*

Dedicated to S. Mary and S. Stephen; Black Canons, val. £39 9s.

[6] [BLOMEFIELD, v. 840.]

youngest poorly married; the middle, to Mr. Barney's son of Gunton, who, disinherited by his father, was slain by Thomas Betts, his wife's uncle of the half-blood, at a marriage at Litcham.

Nicholas Farmer, younger brother of Thomas, was attainted and pardoned* for coining; and after taking a boat to fly from the serjeants, was drowned in the Thames.

William, second son of Thomas, a right honest gentleman, still hath the impropriation; and having been married about eighteen years, hath only a daughter.

Mr. Richard Benson bought the abbey and manor of Pudding Norton of Mr. Thomas Farmer; con·sumed all, and went into Wales.

Mr. Gosveld bought the abbey of Mr. Benson, and left it to his wife in jointure.

Mr. Henry Gosveld of Ireland, his son and heir, sold the reversion to sir Thomas Holland, and goeth into Ireland.

Mr. Nicholas Timperley bought it of sir Thomas Holland.

Massingham Abbey.

(Not in the Tax.)

It was sir Thomas Gresham's, who died (as was said) suddenly in his kitchen, without issue-male.

His daughter and heir was married to sir William Read, who had this abbey.

[* So in MS.—Eds.]

Sir Thomas Read, his eldest son, married Mildred, daughter of sir Thomas Cecil, after earl of Exeter, and died without issue.

Sir Francis Read, his second son, an unthrift, lived much in the gaol, if he died not there.

The daughter of sir William was married to sir Michael Stanhope, who died without issue-male.

Jane, the eldest daughter of sir Michael, married to sir William Whitpel, is out of her wits, and sir William her husband in sore danger of his life about the slaughter of six or seven men tumultuously killed at——.

Elizabeth, the younger of his daughters and heirs, married to the lord Barkley, is out of her wits also.

Flitcham Abbey.

Sir Thomas Hollis had it, and was (by report) at dinner taken out of it in execution for debt by the sheriff, and his goods sold, whereof my father bought some. Much suit there was about it between one Payne and him, or his heir; but the matter being at length referred to the duke of Norfolk, he bought both their titles.

So the duke had it, and was attainted and beheaded, and it then came to the crown.

King James gave it in fee-farm to my lord of Suffolk, who was fined in the Star-Chamber and put out of the treasurership, and suffered much affliction by the attainder of the lady Frances, countess of Somerset, his daughter, and of her husband the earl.

My lord Coke bought it of the earl of Suffolk, and bought out the fee-farm from king James. He was put out of the place of Chief-justice of the King's Bench; fell into great displeasure of the king; and hath been laden with afflictions proceeding chiefly from his own wife, who liveth from him in separation.

His eldest son, sir Robert, having been married many years, hath yet no issue.

His daughter, the lady viscountess Purbeck, the fable of the time, and her husband a lunatick. [See Appendix II.]

Wendling.

Wendling abbey differed from all the rest of this circuit; for it was not dissolved by the statute or by the Act of Hen. VIII., but before that time by Cardinal Wolsey; and was one of the forty small monasteries that Pope Clement VII. gave him license to suppress [as we have already shown].

The Cardinal did grant it to his college at Christchurch in Oxon; and to whom they first leased it I do not yet find, but Mr. Thomas Hogan, of Bradenham, that was sheriff of Norfolk . . . Eliz., died in his sheriffship, and not long after him his son, Mr. Henry Hogan, leaving his son and heir very young; who, attaining near to his full age, and falling sick, acknowledged a fine upon his death-bed to the use of his mother, the lady Cæsar that now is, and his half-sisters; and dying without reversing it, did by that means cut off his heirs at common law, and was the last of his father's house in that inheritance; this begat great suits in the Star-Chamber, chancery, and parliament itself.

The lease is since come to Mr. Hamon.

Nor did the colleges, for which these monasteries were suppressed by the Cardinal, and which he meant to make so glorious, come to good effect; for that of Ipswich was pulled down, and the other of Christchurch was never finished, as also neither that of King's College in Cambridge, rising out of the ruins of the priory's aliens.

Coxford Abbey, alias *East Rudham Abbey.*

Coxford abbey, after the Dissolution, came to the duke of Norfolk, who was beheaded 2nd June, 1572, 14 Eliz.

The queen then granted it to Edward earl of Oxon, who wasted all his patrimony.

THE HISTORY AND FATE OF SACRILEGE.

Sir Roger Townsend then bought it, who had issue sir John Townsend and sir Robert Townsend. Sir Robert died without issue; sir John had issue sir Roger the baronet, and Stanhope and Ann, married to John Spelman; he falling into a quarrel with sir Matthew Brown of Betchworth castle, in Surrey, each of them slew other in a duel, 1 Jac. Stanhope Townsend wounded mortally by . . . in a duel in the Low-Countries came into England and died at London.

Sir Roger, the baronet, intending to build a goodly house at Rainham, and to fetch stone for the same from Coxford abbey, by advice of sir Nathaniel Bacon, his grandfather, began to demolish the church there, which till then was standing; and beginning with the steeple, the first stone (as it is said) in the fall brake a man's leg, which somewhat amazed them; yet contemning such advertisement, they proceeded in the work, and overthrowing the steeple it fell upon a house by, and breaking it down slew in it one Mr. Seller, that lay lame in it of a broken leg, gotten at football, others having saved themselves by fright and flight.

Sir Roger having digged the cellaring of his new house, and raised the walls with some of the abbey stone breast-high, the wall reft from the corner stones, though it was clear above ground; which being reported to me by my servant, Richard Tedcastle, I viewed them with mine own eyes, and found it so. Sir Roger, utterly dismayed with these occurrents, gave over his begun foundation, and digging a new wholly out of the ground, about twenty yards more forward toward the north, hath there finished a stately house, using none of the abbey stone about it, but employed the same in building a parsonage-house for the minister of that town, and about the walls of the churchyard, etc.

Himself also showed me that as his first foundation reft in sunder, so the new bridge which he had made of the same stone at the foot of the hill, which

ascendeth to his house, settled down with a belly as
if it would fall.

But if there be any offences or ominous consequences depending upon such possessions, he hath
very nobly and piously endeavoured to expiate it;
for he hath given back to the church three or four
appropriations.

Burnham Priory.

It was sometime in the Southwells of S. Faith's,
whose family is either extinct or gone out of the
county. It was afterwards Francis Cobbes', gent.,
who likewise is gone; then sir Charles Cornwallis,
knight, wasted, and by him sold to Alderman
Soame, who left the same to John Soame, Esq., his
second son deceased.

Peterston.

About the latter years of queen Elizabeth it was
Richard Manser's, gent., who had much suit and
quarrel with Firmine Gray about a lease of it, and
died without issue, disposing it by a will (as was
reported) to one Roger Manser, his brother; but
they were both nipt of it by —— Armiger, of
Creake, who married Richard Manser's sister, and
left it to William Armiger, his son and heir, who
sold it to my lord Coke, to secure the title.

Carbrocke.

A monastery of Hospitallers of S. John of Jerusalem.

Sir Richard Southwell, knight (a great agent in
spoiling the abbeys), was owner of it: he married
Thomasin, the daughter of sir Roger Darcy, of
Danbury, and living long together, had no issue by
her; but in the meantime, he had by Mary Darcy,
daughter of Thomas Darcy, also of Danbury,
Richard Southwell of S. Faith's, and Thomas
Southwell of Moreton, Mary and Dorothy, all born
in adultery, and Katherine, married to Thomas
Audley, of Beerchurch in Essex, cousin and heir-

male to the lord Audley (born, as it seems, after the death of Thomasin his wife), by the said Mary, who then and before was by sir Richard married to one —— Leech, a swallowman of Norwich, that had been his servant; and now his lady dying, he took this Mary from Leech her husband, and married her himself, alleging that she could not be Leech's wife, for that he had another former wife then living: hereupon a great suit ensued in the high Commission court, where sir Richard prevailed, and enjoyed her with shame enough.

Sir Richard dieth without other issue than by this Mary, leaving the abbey of S. Faith's to his base-born son Richard, and Moreton to his base son Thomas.

His son Richard marries Bridget, daughter of sir Roger Copley, knight, and had issue by her, Richard, Thomas, and Robert. This last Richard married the daughter of sir Thomas Cornwallis; and having issue by her, sir Thomas Southwell, and two or three other sons, dieth in the lifetime of his father, who for his second wife marrieth his maid, the daughter of one Styles, parson of Ellingham, and by her had issue sir Henry Southwell, Dunsanny Southwell, now owner of Moreton, and some daughters, whereof Ann was * —— in London. And this Richard, the father, having wasted his estate, and sold the abbey of S. Faith's to the lord Chief-Justice Hobart, died a prisoner in the Fleet.

Thomas Southwell, the other base son of sir Richard, dieth without issue; having given by his will the manor of Moreton to his sister Audley for life, the remainder to Thomas, her younger son. Sir Thomas Southwell, nephew of the testator, seeketh to overthrow the will, and to have the manor as heir at common law to Thomas the testator: hereupon the heir of Leech strikes in against them both, labouring with sir Thomas to falsify the will against Mrs. Audley, and excluding

* [So in the MS.—EDS.]

T

sir Thomas, by alleging bastardy against him in Richard his father, for that Mary Darcy, the mother of this Richard, was wife to the father of this Leech when Richard and Thomas the testator were born.

This brought all the filthiness aforementioned to be raked over again; and when all were notoriously defamed by it, they all sit down without any recompense.

Thomas Audley, that was in remainder, died without issue in the life of his mother, whereby Moreton came to his brother, sir Henry Audley.

Anthony Southwell and —— Southwell, brothers of sir Thomas, were in the robbery of Mrs. Grave, and fled into Ireland.

Sir Henry Southwell married the daughter of lord Hor* in Ireland, without issue.

After the death of sir Richard Southwell, his nephew, sir Robert, succeeded in the great inheritance and the hospital of Carbrook. He married the daughter of the earl of Nottingham, and died in the flower of his age, leaving his son, the now sir Thomas, an infant, who about his full age had a base daughter by Dr. Corbett's maid; and marrying her privily, liveth now in dislike of her, and keepeth the daughter of one Eden in a poorhouse at Notton, and hath consumed the greatest part of his estate.

His sister, Mrs. Elizabeth Southwell, liveth at Florence, in adultery with sir Robert Dudley, having another wife before he married her, and both of them still living.

Marham.

Sir Nicholas Hare, knight, and John Hare, citizen and mercer of London, 3rd July, anno 38 Hen. VIII. purchased [it] of the king.

Sir Nicholas Hare married the daughter and heir

* [The name is illegible in the MS. In the printed copy it is Hor; but there is no title in the peerage resembling this.—EDS.]

of Bassingbourn, and had issue, Michael that died without issue, Robert that died without issue, and Richard that died without issue; and his inheritance went away to his two daughters, the one married to Rouse, the other to Timperley. See more of this sir Nicholas in the Speaker of Parliament, anno 31 Hen. VIII., where he prophesied this ruin of his family.

John Hare, the citizen, had issue Nicholas the lawyer, that died without issue, Ralph that died without issue, Edmund, lunatic, at a lodge in Enfield Chase, Hugh that died without issue, Richard, Rowland and John that had issue, and Thomas, of Orford, that married and died without issue.

Richard, the elder [who slew — Blackwell, and obtained a pardon with £1,200], married Elizabeth, daughter of . . . and had issue sir Ralph Hare knight of the Bath; and he married . . . the daughter of Alderman Hambden [and Richard, who was lunatick,* and died in the King's Bench, and Margaret, married to Lewis Cocking]. John, son of John and brother to Richard, was clerk of the Court of Wards, and had issue Nicholas, who was lunatick, and died without issue, and Hugh, now lord Coleraine in Ireland. [Family extinct 1749.]

Sir Ralph Hare, to expiate this sin of his family, gave the parsonage impropriate of Marham, worth £100 yearly, to S. John's college in Cambridge, anno 1623,† and died, leaving one only child, sir John Hare, who married sir Thomas Coventry, the now lord-keeper's daughter, and hath by her, she not being . . . years old . . . sons and daughters, with hope of a numerous posterity. God bless them. [They had eleven children, of whom nine lived to be married.]

* [This sentence is omitted in the printed copy.—EDS.]
† [This money was, by sir John Hare's direction, in the first instance expended in the erection of S. John's Library.—EDS.]

Crab House.

I have yet gotten little intelligence of this abbey;
but I hear that it was not long since John Wright's
of Wigen Hall in Marshland, and that he had two
sons, whereof . . . his eldest son consumed his
estate, and sold the abbey with the greatest part of
the land, and died without issue-male.

It came after to Mr. William Guybon, of Watling-
ton, and is now in the hands of his son and heir.

Bromill Abbey.

Sir Thomas Woodhouse of Wapham, 38 Hen.
VIII., purchased Bromill abbey of the king: he
died without issue, and sir Henry Woodhouse, his
nephew, succeeded, who utterly consumed his whole
estate; and selling the abbey to John Smith, Esq.,
suits arose thereupon, which lasted many years, till
the death of sir Henry, in November, 1624.

Mr. Smith hath only daughters and no son, so
that the abbey is not like to continue in his name.[7]

Dereham Abbey.

Thomas Dereham, in 33 Hen. VIII., bought it of
the king: shortly after he was fetched out of it to
the Tower, about the treason of his brother Francis
Dereham, who was executed.

Thomas at length was delivered out of prison:
he had issue Thomas, Robert, John, and Baldwin,
and a daughter.

Thomas married . . . and died without issue-
male; Robert and John died without issue.

Baldwin, a decayed merchant of London, had issue
four sons, Thomas, Doctor of Divinity, John, and
Martha a daughter *non compos mentis.*

Thomas succeeded his uncle in the inheritance,
and is now knighted, having issue Thomas.

Thomas, eldest son of sir Thomas, married . . .
daughter of . . . Scot, Esq., of . . . in Kent:
she fell lunatick in childbed, upon the death of her

[7] Ex inform. ipsius Joh. Smith, 11º. *Nov.* 1624.

son . . . 1623, and so continueth, having yet only a daughter.

Thetford.

Hitherto I have kept myself within my circle : let us see, for our further satisfaction, whether the like fortune haunted the monasteries without it. We will begin with Thetford.

The monastery of the Black Nuns of S. Gregory in Thetford, being the Benedictines, was the duke of Norfolk's, whose misfortunes are here before in other places too often mentioned.

He sold the same to sir Richard Fulmerston, knight, who died without issue-male, leaving it to his daughter, and her married to sir Edward Clark, knight.

Sir Edward Clark had two sons by her, and a son by his second wife.

Sir Edward Clark, knight, of S. Michael, the eldest son, spent most of his life in one prison or other ; had issue a son, sir Henry Clark, baronet, that died without issue-male in the life of his father ; who consuming his whole inheritance, sold the chief seat of his baronetcy, Blickling, to the lord Chief-Justice of the Common Pleas, sir Henry Hobart ; and this monastery, upon exchange and money, to Mr. Godsalve, for Buckingham Ferry, which he . . .

Mr. Godsalve put over the monastery, among other lands, to Mr. John Smith and Owen Shepheard ; and having consumed all his estate, went beyond sea.

Mr. Smith and Mr. Shepheard had a long and chargeable suit about Mr. Godsalve's estate, and sold the monastery to sir William Campion, who now hath it, but with suit and trouble.

Sir Edward Clark the elder's second son Francis died without issue. This great and eminent family is wholly extinct, as those also of Fulmerston's, Godsalve's, and Smith's ; for Smith hath no issue-male.

I must here note that sir Edward Clark the elder
was one of the greatest hunters, by way of conceal-
ment, after church goods and lands that was in his
time; and that sewing these unfortunate pieces of
new-gotten cloth into the garment of his old inheritance, the new hath not only rent away the old
garment, but the family itself to which it served.

Pentney Priory.

Pentney Priory was purchased of the king, anno
37 Hen. VIII., by Thomas Mildmay the auditor,
whose son, sir Thomas, sold it to Francis Windham,
one of the justices of the King's Bench. He entailed
it first upon his own issue, then to his brothers,
Roger and Thomas the doctor; after to his sister
Coningsby, and after that to Edmund, and Edmund's
natural brothers : all which dying without issue, it
came to Thomas Windham, Esq., son of sir Henry
Windham, who, in anno 1622, sold it to sir Richard
Ballache, knight, and he, in anno 1631, to Judge
Richardson.

The abbey of S. Radegund, in Kent, by Dover,
is now sir Thomas Edolph's, knight, who did lately
build a fair house upon the site of the monastery,
and it hath fallen down three times : his two brothers
lunatics.[8]

S. Lawrence abbey, by Canterbury, now in the
hands of — Edolph, lunatic, whose grandfather was
also lunatic; his grandfather first purchased the
abbey.[*]

Hales abbey. [See the next chapter.]

.S. Osyth. [See under *Lord Darcy*, Appendix II.]

Travelling through Cambridgeshire, and passing
through a town there called Anglesey, I saw certain
ruinous walls, which seemed to have been some
monastery : hereupon I asked one of the town, if it
had not been an abbey. He answered me, yes : I

---

[8] Ex relat. D. Meares quam duxit uxorem Edw. Pegton, Bart.

[*] [Sir H. Spelman here reinserts an account of Sherborne.—
EDS.]

THE HISTORY AND FATE OF SACRILEGE.

demanded of him whose it was : he said one Mr. Foulke's. I asked him further, how long he had had it : he said his father, a Londoner, bought it. Then I desired to know of him what children he had : the man answered me, none ; saying further, that he had a son, who displeasing him once as he was grafting, he threw his grafting knife at his son, and therewith killed kim.

Passing also another time through Suffolk, I fell in company of a gentlemanlike man, who by way of discourse [said] there had been in the parts where we then were about twenty justices of the peace when he was young, and that at the present time there were not above three. He named also divers of the families decayed, some in estate, others for want of issue-male, and some by misfortune. I having a jealous eye upon it, asked if they were not settled upon church-land : he answered me, yes ; as sir Michael Stanhope, at Oxford abbey, sir Anthony Wingfield, at Letheringham abbey ; both which died, one without issue, the other without issue-male : Sir Anthony Playford, at Playford [?] abbey ; Mr. Brown, at Lawson [?] abbey, where he was murdered by his wife, she burnt, and her man hanged ; Mr. Ford, at Butley abbey, who disinherited his eldest son, etc.; saying further, that that part was church-land belonging to the abbey of S. Edmundsbury, and called it S. Ethelred's Liberty.*

Sacrilege Touching Bells.

When I was a child (I speak of about threescore years since), I heard much talk of the pulling down of bells in every part of my country, the county of Norfolk, then common in memory ; and the sum of the speech usually was, that in sending them over sea, some were drowned in one haven, some in another, as at Lynn, Wells, or Yarmouth. I dare

* Sept. 30, 1619.

not venture upon particulars; for that I then hearing it as a child, regarded it as a child. But the
truth of it was lately discovered by God Himself;
for that in the year . . . He sending such a dead
neap (as they call it) as no man living was known
to have seen the like, the sea fell so far back from
the land at Hunstanton, that the people going
much further to gather oysters than they had done
at any time before, they there found a bell with the
mouth upward, sunk into the ground to the very
brim. They carried the news thereof to sir Hamon
L'Estrange, lord of the town, and of wreck and
sea-rights there, who shortly after sought to have
weighed up and gained the bell; but the sea never
since going so far back, they hitherto could not
find the place again. This relation I received from
sir Hamon L'Estrange himself, being my brother-
in-law.

Such other reports I have often in times past
heard, touching some other parts of that kingdom;
but (as I said) I then regarded them not, and will
not therefore now speak anything of them.

At the end of queen Mary's days (Calais being
taken), sir Hugh Paulet pulled down the bells of
the churches of Jersey; and sending them to S.
Malo's, in Bretagne, fourteen of them were drowned
at the entrance of that harbour. Whereupon it is
a bye-word at this day in these parts, when any
strong east-wind bloweth there, to say, "The bells
of Jersey now ring."[9]

[In the reign of king Henry VIII. there was a
clockier or bell-house adjoining to S. Paul's church
in London, with four very great bells in it, called
Jesus bells. Sir Miles Partridge, a courtier, once
played at dice with the king for these bells, staking
£100 against them, and won them, and then melted
and sold them to a very great gain. But in the
fifth year of king Edward VI. this gamester had
worse fortune when he lost his life, being executed

[9] Ex relatione M. Bandinell Decani ibidem.

on the Tower-hill, for matters concerning the duke of Somerset.*

In the year of our Lord 1541, Arthur Bulkley, bishop of Bangor, sacrilegiously sold the five fair bells belonging to his cathedral, and went to the sea-side to see them shipped away; but at that instant was stricken blind, and so continued to the day of his death. (Bp. Godwin, in vit. ejus, fol. 650.) A sad peal at parting, and a judgment of blindness not unlike that wherewith Alcimus the high-priest was stricken, for offering some sacrilegious violence to the Temple. (Jos. Ant. xii. 10, p. 6.)†]

More to this purpose may appear in the discourse next following; which lying now at my hand, I thought good to insert, not only for coherence of the matter, but also to show the opinion, piety, and tenderness herein, of the greatest father and magistrate of our Church (under the king) at that time living.

Dining yesterday[1] at Lambeth with my lord of Canterbury,‡ his grace falling casually into a discourse of Spanish matters, and the wealth of their churches, said, "that he had heard that the very lamps of Spain were worth half the treasure of that kingdom." And calling to him Mr. —— Barkley, of ——, who had been a great traveller, and long in Spain, demanded his opinion herein. Mr. Barkley answered, that he thought it to be true, and gave a reason; for that everybody, for their delivery from any notable danger, either of sickness or otherwise, used to present a saint, by way of gratuity, with a lamp to burn before it, and commonly of silver; so that before some one saint there were four or five thousand lamps. His grace suggested S. James of Compostella: and Mr.

* [Stow's Survey in Faringdon Ward, fol. 357.]
† [Staveley's Hist. of Churches, p. 234.]
[1] Nov. 13, 1632.
‡ [Dr. Abbot : the story is more valuable, as related by one who was in heart a Puritan.—Eds.]

Barkley affirmed it of S. James; but added, that
the bells in Spain, and in other places, of France
and Italy, were few and small, yet holden to be
very powerful for driving away the devils and evil
spirits. I upon this recited, out of Gregorius
Turonensis, the History of Lupus, bishop of
Soissons, who, by sudden ringing of bells, drave
away the pagan army of Normans besieging that
city, having never heard of a bell before. Much
being then said of the nature and office of bells, his
grace esteemed the bells of England comparatively
with the lamps of Spain; and condemning the pulling
of them down, complained of the deformity they had
thereby brought upon the churches of Scotland;
saying, that at his being there, and lodging first at
Dunbar, he went to see the church; which being
shown unto him by a crumpt unseemly person, the
minister thereof, he asked him how many bells they
had there: the minister answered, None. His
grace thinking that somewhat strange, demanded
how it chanced. The minister thinking that question as strange, replied, It was one of the reformed churches. From then his grace went to
Edinburgh, where he found accordingly no bell in
all the city, save one only in the church of S.
Andrew. And inquiring what became of all the
rest, it was told him that they were shipped to be
carried into the Low-Countries, but were drowned
in Leith haven. I said that it was reported that
queen Elizabeth, hearing that sir John Shelton, for
want of other prey, had brought a bell from the
sacking of Cadiz, was highly offended at it, and said,
" By God's death, she would make him carry it
thither again." I might have added, that that
peerless princess was so far against defacing the
monuments in churches, and the pulling down of
bells and lead from them, as in the second year of
her reign she caused many proclamations not only
to be printed, but signed them also with her own
hand, and sent them in that manner (the more to

manifest her zeal and restrain the sacrilege) about into the counties. But because I had spoken of sending the bell back again, his grace then requited me with this relation.

A gentleman (quoth he) of great descent, richly married, and of fair estate (yet not naming him), showed me on a time a piece of unicorn's horn (sea unicorn), as much as the cover of a great salt-cellar, which was then standing upon the table before dinner, was about at the bottom; the piece of unicorn's horn having a crucifix graven upon it, and a gap in one of the quarters, where part had been cut or scraped away for curing infirmities. I desired to know of him where he had it, but he refused to tell it me; till after some pressure he discovered to me, that, in his travels beyond the seas, he came to a nunnery, where the nuns, in courtesy, showing him the relics of their house, he whilst they heeded him not, slipt this into his pocket, and brought it away. His grace reproving him for it, told him *it was Sacrilege;* and that although it was superstitiously used, yet it was dedicated unto God, advising him to use some means for sending it back again, saying that the nuns no doubt suffered great displeasure from their abbess upon the missing of it. The gentleman notwithstanding (quoth his grace) refused my counsel; but I observed (said he) that he never prospered after, and at length, having consumed his estate, died childless.

It came not then to my mind upon the sudden; but I might very truly have added the like of sir John Shelton, that having married the daughter of Henry lord Cromwell, he died very little or nothing worth, and without any issue (as I take it), but certainly without any issue-male to continue his family.

(Subscribed) HENRY SPELMAN.
I Jeremy Stephens being then present, do testify the truth of this relation.

Having made mention of Cadiz and queen Elizabeth, I will add further what was lately told me by a knight of worth (who was himself in the voyage) much conducing to the honour of that renowned princess, and to the scope also of this our discourse. It is said, that when she set forth her expedition for Cadiz, or other Spanish towns, she gave particular and strait instructions that in no case any violence should be offered to any church or consecrated thing. This notwithstanding, sir Conyers Clifford, upon the taking of Cadiz, fired and burnt the cathedral church there; and sir Charles Blunt (in the return from thence) the cathedral church of Faro, in Portugal. It followed, that sir Conyers Clifford never after prospered in anything, and was at last slain by the natives in Ireland, leaving no son to continue his nominal line; and that sir Charles Blunt, about two years after the fact, was drowned at sea, in passing for Ireland.[2]

[2] Ex relat. Will. Slingsby. Mil. 22 Nov. 1634.

CHAPTER VII

THE following particulars respecting the history and fate of Sacrilege have been collected in many quarters, and with no little trouble. Some will be found more, some less remarkable; but all, it is thought, will be, in their place, appropriate. No order has been observed in their arrangement; partly on account of its almost impossibility in such a list, partly because no great utility was likely to arise from it.

We begin with one of the most remarkable series of judgment on sacrilege, namely, the fate of the Stuarts.

Robert the Bruce slew sir John the Red Comyn before the high altar at the Minorite church of Dumfries. For this his sacrilegious deed, he and his posterity were fearfully punished. Robert himself, some time before his death, was afflicted with *leprosy*, of which at last he died. He had vowed a pilgrimage to the Holy Land to expiate his wickedness; but not being able to go there, he made his friend Douglas promise to carry his heart thither. Douglas, however, was defeated in Spain by the Saracens; and the heart, as if not worthy of being taken to the Holy Land, was carried back to Scotland. Robert Bruce was only fifty-four when he died. He was succeeded by his son, David II. David was an exile in France for some time, and afterwards taken prisoner by the English at the battle of Neville's Cross, and kept in prison eleven years. He was twice married, but died childless, being divorced from his second wife. With him the male line of Bruce failed.

He was succeeded by Robert II., son of Marjory,
daughter of Robert the Bruce, and Walter Stuart.
Robert Stuart was nearly *blind*, and lived in much
obscurity and retirement. He was succeeded by
Robert III. his son, who was *lamed* from a kick of a
horse. He was father of the duke of Rothsay, who
was starved to death by his uncle, Albany. James,
his second son, was taken prisoner by the English
on his way to France; and Robert III. died broken-
hearted.

James I. was captive in England eighteen years.
He was murdered by his own subjects.

James II., his son, succeeded him. He was constantly at war with his subjects, especially the family
of Douglas. He was killed by the bursting of a
cannon at Roxburgh.

He was succeeded by James III., his son, who
was a very weak man, a coward, and miser; he was
defeated by his subjects, the Homes and Hepburns,
at Stirling; and riding from the battle, was thrown
from his horse, which took fright at a pitcher in
which a woman was drawing water at a brook. He
was much hurt, and being taken up was laid on a
bed : a pretended priest came to confess him, and
stabbed him dead : he was only thirty-six.

James IV., though a child, had joined in the rebellion against his father, whom he succeeded. He
was slain at Flodden Field. His body was not buried,
since he died excommunicate; it was taken to Shene,.
in Surrey, where it remained till the Reformation,
when the monastery was dissolved; after that it lay
tossing about like lumber. Stowe saw it flung into
a work-room amongst old rubbish many years afterwards. Some workmen cut off the head, and one
Launcelot Young, glazier to queen Elizabeth, carried
it home, and kept it for some time; at last it was
buried in the charnel-house in S. Michael's, Wood-
street.

James V. succeeded his father at the age of two
years. He died of a broken heart, aged thirty-one

years, after the rout at Solway. His two sons died before him : the unfortunate Mary was born as he was dying.

" 'Tis a wonder" (says sir Simon Degge, in a letter appended to the first edition of Erdeswicke's History of Staffordshire, but omitted in the second and third, and dated Feb. 22, 1662) " that in sixty years (it being no more since Mr. Erdeswicke wrote this tract), one half, I believe, of the lands in Staffordshire have changed their owners; not so much, as of old they were wont, by marriage, as by purchase. And if it were not that I should tire out your patience, I could give you my conjecture of the reason; but I know the freedom of your disposition so well, that I hope you will pardon this boldness.

" The first reason I conceive to be, for that our ancient gentry were so guilty of Henry the VIIIth's sacrilegious robbing the church, that so mingled church-lands with their ancient inheritances; and 'tis no wonder to see the eagle's nest on fire that steals flesh from the altar for her young ones. This very subject would take up a large volume : and besides your own observations of Sherburn, with your patience I will give you a little taste of the success these lands have had in Staffordshire; for Abbey Hilton, etc., that was given in exchange to sir Edward Ashton, was with much more sold by his son; and where this issue will stay, God knows. You know how near to an end it hath brought that family; and as I told Mr. Hugh Sneyd, I feared it was a worm in his estate, for it was travelling apace. Dieulacres was given to the Bagnals, which, like a mushroom, rose on a sudden, and vanished as soon in the first generation. Anthony Rudyard has the Seyte,* and, as I take it, he is issueless. Jolley has Leeke, and some other things : how long it will stay there, God knows. Calwich is next in order, bought

* [Q. The Leyes ?—EDS.]

by sir Richard Fleetwood's grandfather: how unhappily it prospered with the grandson, you have seen; and the children of that family have been unfortunate.

" Roucester was granted to Thomas * Trentham, whose son Francis, soon after, so settled it, that he nor any of his sons could alienate it, which, if any of them had had power to have done, it had been gone ; and now it is got into a strange family, where it is believed it will not stay half another age.

" Croxden is next, which one of the Fuljambs had, and died a beggar in a barn, after he had sold it to sergeant Harris, who had a hopeful son, who died soon after the purchase, by which it came into a strange family.

" Tutbury was old Mr. Cavendish's, the common bull of Derbyshire and Staffordshire, yet died issueless : that still continues in his name; so doth Burton ; but the son of him that purchased it from the crown was attainted of treason. The father of this lord Paget repurchased it at £700 a-year rent ; and this has much wasted his estate, no body knows how.

" Canwell, you know, has changed its master twice in our time. But to come back to Trentham, there have been two successive owners, who are both like to die issueless. How Stone hath prospered, both in the Colliers' and Cromptons' hands, you have and will see.

" Blythebury hath sped no better : sir Thomas has staid longest; but the present owner most unfortunate.

" To conclude. It is my observation that the owners become bankrupts and sell, or else die without issue-male, whereby their memories perish. I wish no better success to the sacrilegious purchasers of this age ; and sure the same God That has been thus just in His own cause, neither slumbereth nor sleepeth, but will send the same vengeance after

* [Tanner says Richard.—Eds.]

it; for lands once given *Deo et Sanctœ Ecclesiœ*, I know no human power that can justly alien."

We will next take some instances from Surrey, relying for authority on Manning's History of that county.

I. WAVERLEY Abbey was a Cistercian house, valued at the Dissolution at £196 annual income.

Its possessors were, 1. 1537, the earl of Southampton, who died childless, 1543. 2. Sir Antony Brown, died 1548. 3. Sir Antony Brown, his son, died 1592. 4. Sir Antony Brown, his son; who sold it to, 5. — Coldham; who left it to, 6. John Coldham, whose heir, 7. Richard Coldham, died 1639; leaving it to, 8. Richard Coldham. It passed through, 9. (?) to, 10. William Aislabee (ruined in the South-sea bubble), who died 1725. 11. His executors sold it to, 12. — Child, who left it to, 13. Charles Child, who sold it in 1747 to, 14. T. O. Hunter; succeeded in 1770 by, 15. C. O. Hunter; who sold it, 1771, to, 16. Sir Robert Rich; who left it to, 17. Sir Charles Rich; who dying without heirs-male, it passed by a daughter to, 18. the Rev. C. Bostock, who sold it, 1796, to, 19. John Poulett Thomson.*

In these two hundred and fifty years, we find nineteen possessors and eight families.

[This abbey was dissolved by the Act of 27 *Henry VIII*. On the 20th July in the following year (1537), sir *William Fitz Williams*, at that time Knight of the Garter and treasurer of the king's household (soon after created earl of *Southampton*, and appointed Privy Seal), had a grant of the site of "the late house or abbey of the Blessed *Mary* of *Waverley*," with the church, churchyard, messuages, and lands thereto belonging, as well within the circuit of the said abbey as without, and the manors

* See more on this gentleman's history at the end of our notices of Surrey. We have corrected Manning's account from private information.

W

of *Waverley, Wanborowe, Markweke,* and *Monken-hoke,* in *Surrey,* to the said abbey belonging; also the rectories of *Waverley* and *Wanborowe,* in *Surrey,* and of *Netham, Sawroton,* and *Roviat,* co. *Southampton,* the manor of *Dokynfeld,* in *Surrey,* and *Southampton,* and the manor of *Shaw,* in *Berks,* to the said abbey belonging; and all mills, etc., and all advowsons, etc., in *Waverley, Stokedaborne, Donfeld (Dunsfold), Shallesford, Alford, Wytteley,* and *Zele (Seale), Southwerk, Godalmyne, Wokynge, Worplesdon, Farnham, Elsted, Puttenham, Peperharowe, Frynsham,* in *Surrey,* and in other places in the other counties, the whole being of the annual value of £188 14s. 11d., and no more. The rent reserved for the whole was £23 12s. 10½d. The grant extends to all corn and grain, chattels, lead, bells, etc.

He settled this with other estates (see *Send* and *Wanborough*) on himself and lady *Mabel,* his wife, and the heirs of their bodies, with remainder to his half-brother, sir *Antony Brown (i.e.,* son of *Lucy,* daughter and co-heir of *John Nevil,* marquis of *Montacute,* by sir *Antony Brown,* her second husband), and died without issue 14th October, 34 Henry VIII., 1543. From sir *Antony Brown* it descended to his son *Antony,* created viscount *Montacute,* who died, seised hereof, 19th October, 1592, leaving *Antony,* his grandson, his next heir. Its subsequent history is given in the preceding note.—[E.]

II. CHERTSEY Abbey. A Benedictine house, valued at £744.

The Abbey-house was granted, in 1610, by the crown, to,

1. Dr. John Hammond, who left it to his son, 2. the celebrated, but much persecuted Dr. Henry Hammond: it passed through, 3. (query, whom?) to, 4. Sir R. Carew; from him to, 5. — Orby; from him to, 6. Sir C. Orby, who sold it to, 7. Sir Nicholas Wayte, son of the regicide. From 8. his co-heirs, it was bought by, 9. — Hinde, a brewer; who left it to, 10. his son; who sold it to, 11. H.

Barwell; he left it to his son, 12. — Barwell; who left it to, 13. — Fisher, his natural son, a private soldier; who sold it in 1809, to, 14. a stockbroker, who pulled it down.[1]

In these two hundred years there were fourteen possessors and nine families.

[1] A visitor in recent times thus describes the site :—

" I went with eager steps to view the Abbey, [or] rather the site of the Abbey ; for so total a dissolution I scarcely ever saw ; so inveterate a rage against even the least appearance of it, as if they meant to defeat even the inherent sanctity of the ground. Of that noble and splendid pile, which took up four acres of ground, and looked like a town, nothing remains ; scarcely a little of the outward wall of the *precinctus*.

" The gardener carried me through a court on the right-hand side of the house, where, at the entrance of the kitchen-garden, stood the Church of the Abbey; I doubt not, splendid enough. The west front and tower-steeple was by the door and outward wall, looking toward the town and entrance to the Abbey. The east end reached up to an artificial mount along the garden wall. That mount and all the terraces of the pleasure-garden on the back-front of the house, are entirely made up of the sacred *rudera* and rubbish of continual devastations.

" Human bones of the abbots, monks, and great personages, who were buried in great numbers in the church and cloisters, which lay on the south side of the church, were spread thick all over the garden, which takes up the whole church and cloisters ; so that one may pick up handfuls of bits of bones at a time every-where among the garden stuff. Foundations of the religious building have been dug up, carved stones, slender pillars of Sussex marble, monumental stones, effigies, crosses, inscriptions, every-where, even beyond the terraces of the pleasure-garden.

" The domains of the Abbey extend all along upon the side of the river for a long way, being a very fine meadow. They made a cut at the upper end of it, which, taking in the water of the river, when it approaches the abbey, gains a fall sufficient for a water-mill for the use of the abbey and of the town. Here is a very large orchard, with many and long canals or fish-ponds, which, together with the great moat around the abbey, and deriving its water from the river, was well-stocked with fish.

" I left the ruins of this place, which had been consecrated to religion ever since the year 666, with a sigh for the loss of so much national magnificence and national history. Dreadful was that storm which spared not, at least, the churches, libraries, painted glass, monuments, manuscripts, that spared not a little out of the abundant spoil to support them for the public honour and emolument."—" Brayley's Surrey," Vol. II., p. 183.—[E.]

[III. Westminster Abbey (Manor of Battersea).
After the suppression of monasteries this manoꞁ
remained vested in the crown until Elizabeth, in thc
eighth year of her reign, granted it on a lease foꞁ
twenty-one years to (1) Henry Rᴜyden; and in 159ᵑ
(2) Joan, the o ꞁy daughter of Henry Royden, hac
another lease for a similar term. Subject to this
lease the manor, in 1610, was assigned towards the
maintenance of (3) Henry, Prince of Wales; and
after his decease it was appropriated in the same
manner to his brother, prince Charles (4), who,
about two years after his accession to the throne,
granted it (anno 162ꞏꞏ in fee, to (5) Oliver, lᴜꞏd St.
John, and ꝟꞏꞏcount Grandison of Limeriꞏk, in Ireland. On his decease without issue in 1630 the
title became extinct, but that of Grandison des'
cended to his grand-nephew (6), William Villiers,
father of the notorious duchess of Cleveland. The
Battersea estate also came into the hands of Villiers,
who granted it to his cousin (7), sir John St. John,
bart., who died in 1648. Oliver, the eldest son oꞁ
that gentleman, having died before him, this manor
devolved on his grandson (8), John St. John, a
minor; on whose decease, withᴜꞏⁱt issue, the baronetcy and family ertate became vested (after four of
his uncles who died successively childless) in (9) sir
Walter St. John, his uncle. He died on the 3rd of
July, 1708, at the age of eighty-seven, and was succeeded by his son (10) Henry, who, long previously,
viz., in 1684, had pleaded guilty of the murder of sir
Wm. Estcourt, bart., in a sudden quarrel. No
pardon is enrolled, but it is stated that the king
granted him a reprieve for a long term of years;
and in the Rolls Chapel is a restitution of his estates
(Pat. 36, Charles II.), for which it would seem, and
the reprieve conjoined, he had to pay £16,0ᴄ0, one-
hꞏꞏⁱ of which, Burnet says, "the king converted to
his own use, and bestowed the remainder on two
ladies then high in favour." On his decease iꞁ 1742
ɦis titles descended to (11) John St. John, his eldest

surviving son. By his first wife Henry, viscount St. John, had only one son (12), Henry, who was born at Battersea in October, 1678. In 1710 he became secretary of state to queen Anne, by whom, in 1713, he was created baron St. John of Lidiard Tregoze, and viscount Bolingbroke. He was attainted of treason, for intriguing with the partisans of the Pretender on the accession of George I., and having fled to France, he entered into the service of the chevalier de St. George, which, after a time, he relinquished; and in 1723, having been restored in blood, he returned to England. In 1725 an act of parliament was passed to annul the attainder so far as to enable him to inherit the family estate; in consequence of which, on the decease of his father, he became possessed of the Battersea property, and held it until his death in 1751. He was twice married, but had no issue by either of his consorts; and Battersea, with his other estates as well as his titles, descended to his nephew (13) Frederick (the son of his half-brother John, viscount St. John), by whom this manorial property was sold, in pursuance of an act of parliament obtained in 1762, to the trustees of John (14), earl Spencer, to whose descendant, the present and third earl Spencer, it now belongs. In 196 years eighteen possessors. "Brayley's Surrey," Vol. III., p. 444.]—[E.]

IV. MERTON Priory, an Augustinian house. Value £1039.

Granted 1586, to

1. Gregory Lovel. 2. Nicholas Zouch, and Thomas Ware, who sold it, 1601, to, 3. Charles earl of Nottingham; he conveyed it, 1604, to, 4. John Spilman; and he, 1606, to, 5. Sir Thomas Cornwallis; and he, 1613, to, 6. Thomas Merbury; he to, 7. Sir Edward Bellingham, in trust for, 8. Sir Francis Clarke, who conveyed it, 1624, to, 9. Rowland Wilson; who left it to, 10. Samuel Wilson; who sold it to, 11. Ellis Crispe; who conveyed it, 1668, to, 12. Thomas Pepys; who left it to, 13. Olivia

Pepys; by whose marriage it came to, 14. Edward
Smith; who sold it, 1696, to, 15. Susanna St.
John; and she, 1701, to, 16. William Hubbald;
from whom it passed to, 17. his creditor; who
sold it to, 18. William Ashurst, in trust for, 19.
Sir William Phippard; who, dying 1723, left it to,
20. his sons as tenants in common; ɑ d they all
dyi.g without issue, it came by marriage to R. F.
'Jansfield, about 1780.

In two hundred years we have twenty-one possessors and eighteen famil'es; the estate only twice
descending from father to son.

[MERTON Priory (Manor of Dunsfold).
The manor ɑi Dunsfold, which before the Reformation belonged to Merton priory, was granted by
Henry VIII. to (1) Charles Brandon, duke of
Suffolk; who sold it to (2) Thomas, lord Cromwell,
for £403 6s. 8d. On his attainder in 1541 it reverted to the (3) Crown. Queen Elizabeth, in 1564,
granted it to her favourite (4), Robert Dudley, afterwards earl of Leicester; of whom it was purchased
by (5) sir Wm. Cecil; and in the next year, 7th of
Elizabeth, conveyed by him to (6) John Swift, Esq.
He sold it to (7) Thomas Smith, Esq.; who held
his first court here 1569; and whose descendant
(8), George Smith, in 1661, transferred it to (9) sir
Alan Brodrick, ancestor of George Alan Brodrick,
5th viscount Midleton, its present owner.—" Brayley's Surrey," Vol. III., p. 491.].—[E.]

[MERTON Priory. (Kingswood and Ewell Manors.)
After the dissolution of this priory, in 1538, the
manor of Kingswood liberty reverted to the crown,
and, together with the capital manor of Ewell, was
annexed to the honour of Hamp'on Court. Queen
Elizabeth, by letters patent dated January 31st,
1563, granted it, with the mansion-house, etc., to
William, lord Howard of Effingham, lord chamberlain of the royal household, the lady Margaret, his
wife, and their heirs-male. That nobleman died
1572-3; but lady Margaret Howard survived until

May, 1581, when the estate came into the possession of her son Charles, lord Effingham, who was lord high-admiral of England in 1588, when the country was threatened by the Spanish Armada; and for his important services on that occasion, and at the capture of Cadiz, in 1596, he was rewarded with the title of earl of Nottingham. His death took place 1624. The eldest son of this peer having died before him, leaving no male issue, this manor, as well as his titles and his other entailed estates, devolved on his son Charles; who died without issue 1642, and was succeeded by his half-brother, Charles Howard, jun.; who also died childless, in 1681; when the title of earl of Nottingham became extinct. On the decease of the second consort of the second lord Nottingham, February 11th, 1650-1, the manor of Kingswood, which she had left in dower, is supposed to have come into the possession of sir John Heydon. That gentleman was the son of William Heydon, a military officer, who lost his life in the expedition to the Isle of Rhé, in 1627; and in consideration of his services his son, in 1630, obtained a grant, under letters patent, of the reversion of the fee-simple of this manor to trustees for his benefit. It seems probable that sir John Heydon had sold his reversionary interest in this manorial estate, for Mr. Manning says he "continned so short a time in possession that his name does not appear upon the rolls."

Sir Thomas Bludworth, knt., alderman of London, held a court-leet and court-baron here, as lord of the manor, 1660. He died in 1682; and was succeeded by his son, Charles Bludworth, Esq.; who held the manor till 1701. Thomas Harris, Esq., was the next proprietor; and held his first court 1708. His son, Thomas Harris, was lord of the manor in 1730; and from him it passed to his nephew, John Hughes; whose father, Isaac Hughes, Esq., held a court in the name of his son, then an infant, 1746.

The manorial estate was sold by Mr. Hughes, in
1791, to William Jolliffe; who, dying in 1802, left
it to his son, Hilton Jolliffe : since which it has
been purchased by Thomas Alcock, Esq., its present
owner.—" Brayley," IV., 270.] Sixteen possessors
in 256 years.—[E.]

[MERTON Priory (Manor of Shelwood).

After the suppression of the priory, Henry the
Eighth, in 1539-40, granted Shelwood, with other
lands in this parish, to sir Thomas Nevil for his life;
with remainder to sir Robert Southwell, knt., and
his wife, Margaret, the daughter of Nevil. After
the decease of sir Thomas, in 1547, Southwell and
his wife conveyed this manor, with Charlewood and
other estates, to Henry Lechford, Esq., in whose
family they remained until November, 1634; when
sir Richard Lechford, knt., transferred all his landed
property in Surrey to sir Garret Kemp., knt., and
John Caryl, Esq., by whom, in 1649, Shelwood was
alienated in trust for Edward Alston, M.D., who
obtained full possession in 1653.   In the following
year, sir Ambrose Browne, knt., of Betchworth
Castle, was owner; and his three sons, sir George
Browne, Ambrose, and John, succeeded each other
in this property; which, however, had been separated from the demesne lands under the provision
of an act of parliament obtained in the 13th of
Queen Anne, 1714.   All the brothers died without
issue; respectively, in the years 1685, 1729, and
1736.   John, the last survivor, devised this manor
to his nephew, Thos. Jordan, of Gatwick, who died
(unmarried) in 1750 ; leaving two sisters and co-
heiresses.   Three years afterwards the manors of
Shelwood and Buckland were, on a petition, allotted
to Mrs. Elizabeth Beaumont; whose grandson,
Thomas, sold Shelwood to Charles, duke of Norfolk,
in 1806.—" Brayley," IV., 281.] Sixteen possessors
at least, probably several more, in 258 years.—[E.]

V. SHENE Priory, a Carthusian house. Value
£962.

THE HISTORY AN FATE OF SACRILEGE.

Grantad 1540, to,

1. Edward earl of Hertford, afterwards d 1·· of Somerset, beheaded for high treason. 2. Henry duke of Suffolk, of whom we have already spoken. Refornded 1557. Redissolved 1559. 3. Perceval Gunston. 4. Sir T. Gorges. 5. James duke of Lennox. 6. Philip viscount Lisle, who sold it, 1663, to, 7. John lord Bellasyse. 8. Robert Rowarth, etc., in trust for, 9. Sir William Temple.

In one hundred and for·y years, nine possessors, and nine families ; the estate never descending from father to son.

VI. Boddileys, Southwark, which belonged to the hospital of S. Thomas of Canterbury.

In the first thirty-six years after its lay appropriation, there were ten possessors and nine families ! (See Manning's History, III. 500.)

VII. Hambledon Manor, which belonged to the see of Canterbury.

1. Thomas lord Cromwell, beheaded. 2. Queen Catharine Parr. 3. Cardinal Pole. 4. Sir C. Hatton. 5. Sir T. Cecil. 6. Sir E. Cecil; married twice but had no son. 7. Earl of Holland, beheaded. 8. Adam Baynes, 1650. 9. General Lambert. 10. The Crown. 11. George earl of Bristol. 12. Thomas duke of Leeds. 13. Earl of Abingdon, 1711, died without heirs-male. 14. Sir T. Janssen, a South Sea director ; this estate, with others, seized in 1720, by act of parliament, for the relief of those ruined by the South Sea bubble. 15. Sarah duchess of Marlborou·· . 16. John Spencer. 17. George John earl Spencer, died 1834.

In two hundred and forty-three years, we have seventeen possessors and fourteen families; the estate only twice descending from the father to son.

VIII. The Friery, Guildford.

Granted 1620, to,

1. John earl of Annandale. 2. James, his son, who sold it to, 3. James earl of Dirleton, who gave it to his daughter, 4. Elizabeth duchess of

Hamilton, at whose death, 1659, it passed to, 5.
Thomas Dalmahoy, her second husband, who sold
it to, 6. Elizabeth Colwall; she left it to, 7.
Arnold Colwall, and he to, 8. Daniel Colwall, who
conveyed it to, 9. T. Gibson, etc., who sold it in
1721 to, 10. J. Russell, etc., when it was sold in
moieties.

Ten possessors in a hundred years; six families.

We have traced above (p. 169) the manor of
Waverley down to John Poulett Thomson, esq.
From a private source, we are enabled to trace to
our own time that gentleman's history. " He pos--
sessed," says our informant, " Waverley for nearly
forty years, and nothing remarkable occurred that
I know of, if we except the dreadful death of his
sister, Mrs. Bonar, who, with her husband, was
murdered in the night by a confidential servant at
Camden-house, Chiselhurst. This was about the
year 1812 or 1813. Mrs. Thomson also died at
Paris. A son-in-law, Mr. William Baring, who had
married one of the younger daughters, was drowned
in going to his yacht off Lulworth Castle, Dorsetshire, where he resided; and the youngest daughter,.
who had married baron Biel, of Lubeck, died in
childbed. About the year 1831, Waverley was
sold to the present owner, — Nicholson, esq., and
the very day after the deeds were completed and
the money paid, the dwelling-house was, through
the carelessness of the workmen, burnt to the
ground.

" Of the three sons of Mr. Thomson, the eldest,
Andrew Henry, married for his first wife, Sophia,.
daughter of George Holmes Sumner, esq., of Hatch-
lands, Surrey, by whom he had two sons and one
daughter. In the year 1832, the youngest son,.
Henry, went to sea and perished with the ship and
every soul on board. The following year his mother
died, and soon after the remaining son, Andrew
John, after nine years of great suffering. In 1836,.

Mr. Andrew Poulett Thomson married a second
time, which event was shortly followed by the
death of two of his sisters, one in childbed. In
April, 1839, while rowing in the Thames, the boat
approached too near to a weir, went over and
upset. Of the party, consisting of Mr. and Mrs.
Thomson and a young friend, only Mrs. Thomson
was saved. The November following she gave
birth to a posthumous child, a son, who died at the
end of five months; and the same year the daughter and only remaining child, being married to T.
M. Weguelin, esq., died a fortnight after the birth
of her second child, in a most sudden and awful
manner, being apparently perfectly well within ten
minutes of her death. The second son, George
Poulett Thomson, married the daughter and heiress
of George Scrope, of Castle-combe, Wilts, esq., took
her name, and is childless. The third son, Charles
Poulett Thomson, was appointed governor of
Canada in 1839, and soon after created baron
Sydenham. He was on the point of returning to
England on account of his health in 1841, when his
horse, in riding, fell with him and fractured his leg
in two places, which occasioned his death a fortnight after. He was never married. Mr. Thomson,
the father, died himself in 1838, leaving a widow
his second wife, by whom he had one daughter.
She and her mother are all that remain of the name,
and the family may be said to be extinct."

[Dureford Abbey.

This moiety of the manor of *Compton* is the same
that was then, and is now called *Westborough*, or
Westbury, and remained in the Abbey of *Dureford*
till its dissolution; after which, *viz.*, 33 *Henry VIII.*,
it was granted to *William Fitz Williams*, earl of
Southampton, Lord Privy Seal, and 26 April, 35
Henry VIII., to *Edward Elrington* and *Humphrey
Metcalf*, his deputies in that office, in trust to sell
the same; and of them it was purchased in 37 *Henry
VIII.* by sir *Christopher More*, knight, of *Loseley;*

from whom it descended, with other estates, by a
female heir, to the family of *Molyneux*, whereof
James More Molyneux, esq., is the present representative (1811).—" Manning's Surrey," Vol. II., p.
3.—[E.]

[CROYDON Rectory and Manor.
21 July, 3 *Edward VI.*, 1550.   The rectory and
church of *Croydon* with the manors of *North Tadworth*
and *Southmerfield* and the rectory and advowson
of *Banstead*, were granted (1) to *Thomas Walsingham*,
son and heir of sir *Edmund Walsingham*, of *Chiselhurst*, and *Robert Moys*.   In 1659 we find that sir
Thomas Walsingham conveyed the manor to (2)
James Walsingham.

A (3) *James Walsingham*, by will dated 16 August,
1727, devised the manor and rectory of *Croydon* to
his sister (4) dame *Elizabeth Osborne* for her life, but
did not dispose of it after her decease.   He died 22
October, 1728, without issue, leaving three co-heirs,
viz. :—1. dame *Elizabeth Osborne* ;   2. *Anthony*
viscount *Mountague* ; 3. *Annabella Villers*.

*   *   *   *   *

19 January, 1733, lady *Osborne* by will devised
her third part of the estate to (5) *Henry Boyle* the
younger, second son of the hon. *Henry Boyle*, he
taking the name of *Walsingham*, and to his heirs-
male ; remainder to *Richard Boyle*, eldest son of
Henry the father ; remainder to her kinswoman the
wife of *Henry* the father.

In 1736 (6) *Henry Villers* conveyed his one-third
to (7) *William Taylor*, esq., a trustee for viscount
Mountague, who thus became owner of two-thirds.

In 1742 an act was passed for vesting the real
estates of the said *James Walsingham* in *Essex*,
Norfolk, and *Cambridgeshire*, and lady *Osborne's* third
of *Croydon* on (8) *John Howell*, and *George Wilson*,
in trust to sell.   *Anthony* viscount *Mountague* died
23 April, 1767, leaving (9) *Anthony Joseph*, his only
son and heir.   *Henry Boyle Walsingham* died, leaving

only one son *Henry*, who died an infant without issue; (10) *Charles Boyle Walsingham* succeeded, and dying also without issue, (11) *Robert Boyle Walsingham*, only remaining younger son of *Henry* earl of *Shannon*, inherited, and in 1770 sold to (12) *Anthony Joseph* viscount *Mountague*, who thus became possessed of the whole.

He died 9 April, 1787, leaving only two children, *viz.*—(13) *George Samuel*, and one daughter *Elizabeth Mary*, who married *William Stephen Poyntz*, esq. This nobleman by his will dated 26 August, 1784, devised his estates to trustees to sell such parts as they shall find necessary for fulfilling the purposes of his will, and subject thereto to his only son *George Samuel*, who inherited his title. In 1788 the trustees sold to (14) sir *Peter Burrell*, bart., now lord *Gwydir*, the tythes of his farm called *Ham-farm*, and of several other lands, and sold other parts to other landowners. What remained unsold they conveyed to viscount *George*, who sold further parts, and in 1793 conveyed the manor with the east or middle chancel of the church to (15) *Robert Harris*, esq., who died in September, 1807, and the trustees in his will have since sold the same to (16) *Alexander Caldcleugh*, esq., the present owner. This young nobleman going on his travels lost his life in October, 1793, attempting to pass in a boat down the great fall of the *Rhine* at *Schaffhausen*. What remained of the tythes has since been sold to different persons. "Manning's Surrey," Vol. II., p. 539.] Sixteen possessors, of nine different families, in two hundred and fifty-nine years.—[E.]

[NEWARK Priory. (Manor of Send.)

This manor had been given to *Newark Priory*, and belonged to that house in 1359. After the dissolution it was granted, by the name of *The Manor of Send and Jury* (with the manor of *East Clandon*, etc.) by patent 1 July 36 *Henry VIII.*, 1544, to sir *Anthony Brown*, with the rectory impropriate and advowson of the vicarage, a farm called *The Chapelry of Ruppeley*,

the site, farm, and hereditaments in the manor of
Sende called *Send Barnes,* late parcel of the said
monastery, to hold to sir *Anthony Brown,* and his
heirs in socage, paying to the Crown a rent of
£7 6s. 6d., to the curate of *Ripley* £6 *per annum,* to
repair bridges in *Send* and *Ripley* £8 6s. 8d. *per
annum,* and to *Thomas Rayle,* the bailiff, 40s. *per
annum* fo · his life.   Sir *Anthony* died 6 May, 1548,
leaving *Anthony* his son and heir, who was created
viscount *Montacute,* and died 19 October, 1592,
leaving *Anthony* his grandson and heir.   The latter
died 23 October, 1629, and was succeeded by his son
Francis.

In the reign of queen *Anne* an act was passed,
stating that *Francis* viscount *Montacute,* on May
26, *Charles II.,* 1674, conveyed *inter alia,* the
manors of *Ripley* and *Send,* and the rectory
of *Send, Newark Priory,* and other lands in *Send,*
to *John Caryll, William Roper,* and *William
Yalden,* and their heirs, upon trust for payment
of debts, and as to the remainder, for the
viscount himself.   The viscount died in 1682, and
was succeeded by his son *Francis;* and Mr. *Caryll*
having survived *Roper* and *Yalden,* in 1688, the
viscount and *Caryll* joined in conveying the estates
to new trustees, *viz. :*—the said *John Caryll,* the hon.
Henry Arundell, and *Richard Caryll,* for payments
of debts, and after payment, in trust for the viscount
and his heirs-male, remainder to *Henry Brown,* his
brother, and his heirs-male, remainder to the heirs-
male, of *Anthony* the first viscount (great-great-
grandfather of this *Francis*).   *Richard Caryll* died,
leaving *Henry Arundell* and *John Caryll* surviving.
John Caryll fled into *France,* and was attainted of
high treason and outlawed.   By this means his
moiety became vested in the Crown; but the queen
consented that it should be divested out of the
crown, and subjected to the trusts of the last deed.
An act was accordingly passed, and the whole was
vested in *Henry Arundell* and his heirs.

This estate was sold to the family of *Onslow*, and has passed with the *Clandon* estate to the present earl (1811). "Manning's Surrey," Vol. III., p. 108.]—[E.]

[HOLY CROSS Priory, Reigate.

On the dissolution of this priory by the act of 27 *Henry VIII.*, this rectory [let by the Prior at £17 *per annum*, subject to a pension of 20s. *per annum* to the bishop of *Winchester ;* 20s. to the archdeacon of *Surrey* for procurations, and 13s. 4d. pension to the Cathedral Church of *Winchester*] devolved on the Crown; and was granted, in 33 *Henry VIII.*, to *William* lord *Howard* of *Effingham* (fourth son of *Thomas* duke of *Norfolk*, and *Margaret* his wife, and the heirs of their bodies, which *Margaret* died seised of it 1581). *Charles* earl of *Nottingham*, their son, inherited it after them, and died 1624. *William*, the son of *Charles*, died in his father's lifetime, A° 1614, leaving an only daughter, *Elizabeth*, who became heir to her grandfather, and with whom this estate went in marriage to *John* earl of *Peterborough*, who died 1642. In 1660, the said *Elizabeth* having surrendered her term, a fresh grant of the premises in fee was made to *John* viscount *Avalon*, her younger son, in trust for *Mary*, daughter of *Henry* earl of *Peterborough*, her eldest; which *Mary* by act of parliament in 1677, was enabled to sell her estates in this county; and under this act it was purchased by sir *John Parsons*, knt., alderman of *London*, who died 25 January, 1716-7. *Humphrey*, son of sir *John*, and alderman of *London*, departing this life 21 March, 1740-1, left (one son, *John*, and) two daughters, his co-heirs ; whereof *Ann* married, in 1745, *John*, after sir *John Hind Cotton*, bart., who, on a partition of the estates, became possessed of this rectory ; which he sold by auction in 1766.

[The parsonage house, and 86 acres of glebe, and the great tythes, were then let at £330 *per annum*. A water-mill, with a dwelling house, at £31 11s. 0d.]

Edward Walter, esq., of *Bury Hill*, in this parish became the purchaser; on whose death, in 1780, it descended, with his other estates in this place, to the lady viscountess *Grimston*, his only daughter and heir; who died in 1786. (Lord *Grimston* is now possessed of it.*) "Manning's Surrey," Vol. I., p. 591. Fifteen possessors in two hundred and sixty-one years.—[E.]

[WARE Priory.

The alien priory of *Ware* in *Hertfordshire*, which was a cell to the abbey of St. *Ebrulf* at *Utica* in *Normandy*, which the convent enjoyed until the 26 *Henry VIII*., when it was surrendered to the king, who granted the site thereof to *Thomas Byrch*, who held it in the time of *Edward VI*. by a yearly rent of 3s. It was afterwards sold to *James Stanley*, citizen and scrivener, from whom it descended to sir *Thomas* his son, and from him to another *Thomas*, of whom it was purchased by . . . *Haydon*; the devisees of whose will alienated it to *Thomas Felton* of *London*, innholder, who sold it to *Robert Hadsley*, of *Much Mundane*, esq., who left it, with a large fortune, to his friend Mr. *Raymond*, who assumed his name, and died 1778, and his widow now possesses it, and has two daughters. "Manning's Surrey," Vol. I., p. 417. Eleven possessors in two hundred and sixty-six years.]—[E.]

[RICHMOND Priory.

" The site of this priory was granted by king *Henry VIII*. in 1540, to *Edward* earl of *Hertford*, brother of his late queen the lady *Jane Seymour* [afterwards duke of *Somerset* 1546]; and, by *Edward VI*. on the duke's attainder in the beginning of 1552, to *Henry Grey*, duke of *Suffolk*, who resided here. But, on 26 Jan., 1556-7, queen *Mary* resumed this grant, and replaced the *Carthusian* monks here; and, by her letters patent dated 14 Nov., 1558 (in consideration of a surrender made by *Maurice*, their new prior, of certain estates in

* This title is now merged in the Earldom of Verulam.

Essex which had been given them the year before by sir *Robert Rochester*), gave them the following manors, etc. Four different possessors in eighteen years.]—[E.]

[SANDON Priory or Hospital.

The manor of Sandon continued to belong to the Crown after the dissolution of the priory until the 1st Edward VI., when it was granted, with other estates, to John Dudley, earl of Warwick, K.G. But it came again into the hands of the king, and Charles I., in 1630, granted it, together with Ember Court in Thames Ditton, to Dudley Carleton, viscount Dorchester, who, dying in 1631, and his only child (a posthumous daughter) surviving but a short time, the estates fell into the possession of his nephew, sir Dudley Carleton, in consequence of the provisions of his will. This gentleman, with his wife Lucy, and his elder brother, sir John Carleton, the heir-at-law to the viscount, conveyed the manor, with its appurtenances, to William and George Gore. Joanna, the widow of John Gore, who held the property through the bequest of her husband, in 1715, sold it to Charles, earl of Halifax. That nobleman died soon afterwards, and was succeeded by his nephew George, 2nd earl of Halifax, who entered into a contract for the sale of Sandon to John Tournay, esq., then a resident at Esher. The latter died before the purchase was completed, but, being anxious to perpetuate his name as the head of a family, he, by will dated 1732, devised his real estates to his collateral relatives, on condition that they should reside in his house at Esher, and that they should christen their respective eldest sons by the names of John Tournay. His relations were five in number, one of whom, however, died childless during the life of the testator, and three died afterwards, leaving no children. This will had no effect as to Sandon, the conveyance not having been completed, but the coheirs of Mr.

x

Tournay were disposed to carry into effect his purpose as to the purchase, and a bill in Chancery having been filed, a decree was pronounced, July the 13th, 1738, by which it was ordered that the estate should be conveyed to trustees for the benefit of the coheirs. It appeared that a title could not be made without an act of parliament, which accordingly passed, for vesting this and other estates of the deceased earl of Halifax, in Thomas, earl of Scarborough, George, then earl of Halifax, and others, in trust to sell to pay debts, etc., in pursuance of which this estate, August the 15th, 1740, was conveyed to Marsh Dickenson, an attorney in London, and Henry Laremore, in trust for the coheirs of John Tournay; and a partition of the property being made, the manor fell to the share of Nathaniel Bateman, and the old buildings and Sandon chapel to Mrs. Catherine Jenkin. In April, 1741, the manor of Sandon was purchased by the right hon. Arthur Onslow, speaker of the House of Commons, who was then resident of Ember Court, in Thames Ditton. He died in 1768, and in 1780 George, then lord Onslow, and Cranley, his son and heir, sold it to sir John Frederick, bart., of Burwood park, to whose second son and successor, the present sir Richard Frederick, bart., it afterwards devolved, on the decease of his elder brother.—" Brayley's Surrey." Vol. II., p. 432. Nineteen possessors in two hundred and sixty-four years.]—[E.]

[Shene Priory (Carthusian).

Who was the first grantee after the dissolution we cannot ascertain, but in the year 1572 the site of the priory appears to have been in the possession of *Percival Gunston*, gent. Queen *Elizabeth*, by letters patent of June 23, 1584, granted it, for life, to sir *Thomas Gorges* and his wife *Helen*, relict of *William Par*, marquis of *Northampton*. Sir *Thomas* died Mar. 30, 1610, the lady *Helen* in April, 1635. About three years after, viz., 2 May, 1638, king

Charles I. granted it, on the same tenure, to *James,* duke of *Lenox,* who died 30 Mar., 1655. But in the meantime, *viz.,* in 1650, it was sold as crownland, being valued at £92 *per annum,* and purchased by *Alexander Easton,* on which occasion a survey was taken by order of parliament, in which the buildings, according to the state of them at that time, are minutely described. The priory church is mentioned as standing, though very ruinous; the prior's lodgings, of brickwork; the refectory, a stone building; the lady St. *John's* lodgings; the hermitage, or anchorite's cell; and the gallery.

On 8 Aug., 1660, king *Charles II.* granted a lease of the priory, or some part of the site of it, for *sixty* years, to *Philip,* viscount *Lisle,* son of *Robert* [*Sidney*], earl of *Leicester,* who, in 1661, assigned it to *John,* lord *Bellasyse,* to whom, on his surrender of it to the crown in 1662, a new grant was made for sixty years more. In 1675 a lease of the priory was granted to *Robert Raworth* and *Martin Folkes,* in trust for *Henry Brouncker* (afterwards viscount *Brouncker*) and sir *William Temple.* But sir *William* had occupied those premises, or some other in *Shene,* before he obtained this lease, as appears by his letters. He quitted public business in 1680, but continued at Shene till 1685, when he gave it up to his son, and, in 1686, retired to an estate he had purchased at *Moor Park,* near *Fernham* in this county, where, a small interval excepted, in which he retired to his son at *Shene* during the commotions in 1688, he resided till his death in the latter end of January, 1698-9.

An ancient gateway, the last remains of the priory, was taken down about the year 1769, at which time, also, the little that remained of the hamlet of *West Shene* was annihilated, and the ground disposed of in the manner already mentioned.—" Manning's Surrey," Vol. I., pp. 421, 422. Thirteen possessors in two hundred and twenty-five years.]—[E.]

[BISHAM Abbey.

The manor of Great Bookham was one of the estates belonging to the abbey of Chertsey which Henry the Eighth settled on the abbey of Bisham after he had refounded it in 1538. But that foundation being also suppressed, the manor again reverted to the Crown, and in 1551 this, with other manorial estates, was granted to lord William Howard, baron of Effingham. He died seised of this manor in 1572, having settled it on his third son, Edward, with remainder to his second son, sir William Howard, knt., who, on the death of his brother without issue, became possessed of it, and from him it descended to his great-grandson, Francis, who succeeded to the title of baron Howard of Effingham on failure of the issue of the eldest son of Charles, earl of Nottingham and baron of Effingham, the former title becoming extinct. Francis lord Effingham, was governor of Virginia in the reign of Charles the Second. Francis, his third son, who at length succeeded to the title and family estates, was created earl of Effingham by George the Second. He died in 1743, and his son and successor, Thomas, who was deputy earl-marshal and secretary of state, died November 19th, 1763. He left two sons, the elder of whom, Thomas, inherited his honours and estates, and was appointed governor of Jamaica. On his death without issue in 1791 he was succeeded by his brother Richard, who in 1801 sold the estate of Great Bookham to James Lawrell, esq. In 1809 his property came into the possession of Louis Bazalgette, esq., and was purchased of his executors in 1833 by David Barclay, esq., the present owner.—" Brayley's Surrey," Vol. IV., p. 469. Fifteen possessors in two hundred and ninety-five years.]—[E.]

[LINGFIELD Collegiate Church.

Thomas Cawarden, gentleman of the privy-chamber to the king, obtained a grant of the collegiate church of Lingfield, with the estate belonging to it, in May, 1544, which he resigned in 1547 for the purpose of having it renewed with additions, and in the reign of Edward the Sixth the grant was confirmed by act of parliament. He was the first "Master of the Revels at Court," to which office he was appointed in 1546. Wm. Cawarden, nephew and heir of sir Thomas, in 1560 had a license to alienate the manor of Lingfield, with other estates, to William lord Howard of Effingham. This property descended to Francis, the 7th baron of Effingham, who settled it on his 2nd wife, Anne Bristow, and she, having survived his lordship, devised these estates by will, in 1774, to trustees for sale. In 1776 Dr. Frank Nicholls became the purchaser of the manor or college of Lingfield, the manor of Billeshurst, the rectory, the patronage of the vicarage, all tithes, etc. He died in 1778, and his son and heir, John Nicholls, esq., after having disposed of part of the tithes, sold the remainder of the rectory, the farms and lands, and the manor of Billeshurst, to the trustees of Robert Ladbroke, esq., in 1803.— "Brayley's Surrey," IV., 164, and "Debrett's Peerage." Fourteen possessors in two hundred and fifty-six years.]—[E.]

[HYDE Abbey.

The manor of *Felcourt* anciently belonged to the abbey of Hyde. After the suppression of the convent it was granted by Henry the Eighth to sir John Gresham, one of whose descendants, in 1589, sold it to John Valentyne. In the seventeenth century it was held by the family of Turner till 1684, when part of the estate was purchased by Anthony Farindon, whose grandson sold Felcourt to Mr. John Field in 1787. Mr. William Tooke, of Gray's Inn, bought it in 1802, and afterwards sold it to Francis Lawrence Dillon, esq., who resided there in 1808. By that gentleman it was sold to sir Thomas Turton, bart., who died in April, 1844, and was succeeded by his only son, sir Thomas

Edward Michell Turton, the present baronet and owner of the estate.—Brayley, IV., 157. Here we have no means of reckoning the exact number of possessors, but it is evident that the property passed into eight different families during the time named, and did not stay in any.]—[E.]

Hence we proceed to Gloucestershire; deriving our materials from Atkyns's and Rudder's Histories.

I. In GLOUCESTER the Benedictine monastery of S. Peter (value £1,946, equalling, perhaps, all things considered, £150,000 of the present currency, and one of the wealthiest in England), and the Augustinian Priory of S. Oswald (£90) were suppressed, as well as other less important foundations; and thirteen other parcels of Abbey lands came into lay hands. Remembering this fearful sacrilege, it is somewhat remarkable, one hundred and sixty years later, to read the following account:—"The city hath no nobleman; no knights; of esquires, so to be entitled, not four: of gentlemen, of any proportionable living, not six: free-holders, not fifty."—[*Atkyns*, p. 64.]

II. IRON ACTON. The Pointzes, a very ancient county family, were settled in this place. In the fifteenth generation, sir Nicholas Pointz acquired (1542) certain tenements belonging to the Abbey of Kingswood, and lying in this parish; and the family of Pointz became extinct in the nineteenth generation.

III. AVENING, which belonged to Sion House, was granted in 1542 to Andrews lord Windsor. He died next year; and the family became extinct a century after they had meddled with Church property, namely, in 1642.

IV. BARNSLEY. Lands here, belonging to Lanthony Priory, were granted, in 1539, to William earl of Southampton. The family became extinct in 1543.

V. The history of the BERKELEYS is highly instructive. No family, except the royal family, founded so many abbeys. Among other things, we are indebted to it for the lands which support the bishopric of Bristol. Its power and influence, up to the reformation, for seventeen generations, is well known. Henry lord Berkeley, in the eighteenth, acquired Church property. What followed ? " Maurice, this lord's uncle, bore a hate to his sister-in-law, the dowager, and came . . . with design to burn down the house; but it happened that there was a party of deer stealers in the park at the same time; these frighted one another, and so the mischief was prevented." Again, this same Henry " was much embroiled in lawsuits," and many of his title-deeds were stolen by the earl of Leicester. His son Thomas died before him. The eldest son of George lord Berkeley was drowned in his passage to France, 1641. The unhappy results of the disputed marriage of the fifth earl, and the decision of the House of Lords against the claims of his eldest son are well known. Atkyns says, " This family had the presentation of above twenty abbeys and priories . . . and in all those places were daily prayers said for the family ; all which privileges were lost by the dissolution of abbeys."

VI. CHARLETON ABBOTS. The tithes, which belonged to Winchcombe Abbey, as well as those of COW-HONEYBORNE, were granted to sir Thomas Seymour 1547 ; he was attainted 1549.

VII. CIRENCESTER. The monastery of Black Canons of S. Augustine, founded by king Henry I. in 1117, in honour of SS. Mary and James, was valued at the dissolution, at £1,051. Most of the lands in the parish belonged to the monastery. The first outbreak in the great rebellion took place at Cirencester. Lord Chandos, in 1641, executing the commission of array, was surrounded by a mob, and compelled to sign a promise that he would never be engaged in that office again. He fortunately escaped ; but the rabble cut his carriage to pieces in revenge. Cirencester was taken and retaken many

times, and garrisoned both for the king and the
rebels.   The first blood was here shed in the revolution of 1688.   Lord Lovelace was seized, and
several gentlemen slain on both sides.

VIII. Deerhurst. A small priory, founded in
715, by Dodo, one of the founders of Tewkesbury.
S. Alphege was a monk here; and S. Edward the
Confessor enlarged the foundation.   Afterwards the
lands were divided between Tewkesbury and Fotheringhay College.   These lands afterwards belonged
to the earl of Coventry, lord Deerhurst; the family
became extinct in the male line in 1719.   Of this
family was sir John Coventry, whose mutilation
gave rise to the *Coventry Act*.

IX. Driffield, which belonged to Cirencester,
was granted in 1546 to sir Humphrey Brown, who
died in 1562 without heirs-male.

X. Dumbleton.   The manor belonged to the
Abbey of Abingdon.   It was granted, in 1543, to
Thomas lord Audley and sir Thomas Pope.   Lord
Audley died 1544, and his title became extinct in
him.   The wretched history of the Popes will be
more fully told in writing of S. Albans; they having
a grant of much of that property.

XI. Farmington.   The manor belonged to S.
Peter of Gloucester.   It was granted, 1541, to
Michael Ashfield; he died the same year; it afterwards belonged to sir Henry Jones, who was slain
in Flanders, leaving no heirs-male.

XII. Oxley.   A manor belonging to Tewkesbury.
Granted, in 1552, to lord Clinton.   The family is
extinct in the male line.

XIII. Frocester, which belonged to S. Peter,
Gloucester.   Granted, 1552, to that duke of Somerset who was beheaded for high treason.   It afterwards came to sir William Doddington, who died
without heirs-male; then to lord Brooke, who was
murdered by his servant; afterwards to a second
lord Brooke, the church spoiler, who was almost
supernaturally slain before Lichfield cathedral.

XIV. The Rectory of FROCESTER was granted to Giles Huntley. Sir George Huntley "came by a violent death in the park."

XV. FARMCOT. Certain lands here, belonging to Hales Abbey, were granted to the marquis of North-ampton in 1547. He was attainted 1553 ; and the family became extinct in 1571.

XVI. MINCHIN HAMPTON. It was given to the Abbey of Worcester 1061. Roger de Ivory, who came with the Conqueror, obtained a grant of it for himself. He afterwards offended King William, and had to fly for his life. His lands were seized, and given first to the nuns of Caen; on the suppression of alien monasteries, they were transferred to Sion House. At the dissolution, they were granted to that Andrews lord Windsor, of whom see (III.).

XVII. HARTPURY. The manor was given to the *nunnery* of Gloucester, about 760, before the house was made a Benedictine Monastery. Having been dedicated to GOD's service nearly 800 years, it was granted to the Comptons, a then powerful county family, now extinct.

XVIII. HAWLING belonged to Winchelcombe Abbey. It was granted, 1536, to Mr. Harwood, who died without heirs-male, 1546.

XIX. HALES. A Cistercian house, valued at £357. It was granted, at the dissolution, to sir Thomas Seymour; see (VI.) ; and afterwards came to the marquis of Northampton; see (XV.).

XX. KINGSWOOD. A Cistercian house, founded by the Berkeleys, 1139. It was valued at £254. There is an old Somersetshire rhyme :—

" Portman and Horner, Windham and Thynne,
When the Abbat went out, they came in."

Kingswood fell to the Thynnes. There was a failure of heirs-male twice ; and of this family was Thomas Thynne, esq., barbarously murdered in his carriage, whose monument is to be seen in the south choir aisle of Westminster Abbey. See also the next chapter.

XXI. LANTHONY. A house of Black Canons, valued at £748. Lanthony the first was founded in Wales in 1108; Lanthony the second near Gloucester, as a cell to the first, 1136, and made the principal house 1483. This was the first Abbey surrendered in Gloucestershire. The noble tombs of the great family of Bohun, earls of Hereford and lords of Brecknock, are now heaps of rubbish in the open air, says Atkyns. Among others were those of Margery de Bohun; Humphrey de Bohun and Eleanor his wife; Henry the Good, earl of Hereford, Maud his wife, and Alice their daughter; Humphrey, the fifth earl of Hereford, and Maud his wife. It was granted to sir Arthur Porter, whose son died without heirs-male; then it passed to the Scudamores, who lived in the Prior's house; the family is now extinct.

XXII. LONG MARSTON belonged to Winchcombe. It was granted in 1566, to Robert earl of Leicester; his miserable end is well known.

XXIII. NEWNHAM, which belonged to Flaxley. Granted, 1555, to Henry lord Stafford. 2. Edward lord Stafford. 3. (1605) Edward lord Stafford, whose son died before him. 4. Henry his son, who died unmarried, 1637. Then, 5. to sir William Howard lord Stafford, in old age beheaded on a false accusation, 1678.

XXIV. SNOWSHILL, belonging to Winchcombe Abbey. Granted by Edward VI. to the earl of Warwick; the family became extinct 1589.

XXV. TEWKESBURY. A large Benedictine house, mitred and valued at £1,595. It was the last surrendered in Gloucestershire. It had the patronage of twenty-one rectories and twenty-seven vicarages; the vestments, which were sold, brought £194; the plate weighed 1,431 ounces, the lead 180 fodder; the bells 14,600lbs. And all this besides jewels. It fell to the lot of sir Thomas Seymour; see (VI.) and (XIX.).

XXVI. WINCHELCOMBE. A mitred Benedictine

house, value £759. It was founded by Offa, 787;
and much enlarged by king Kenulph, of blessed
memory, 798. It was granted to sir Thomas Seymour, see (XXVI.); and the marquis of Northampton, see (XV.).

— —

NEWSTEAD Abbey. It is the more important to
dwell on the history of this house, because Tanner
brings it forward as one of his proofs that no special
curse attaches itself to Sacrilege. We will, as nearly
as we can, avail ourselves of Moore's words, in his
"Life of Lord Byron."

Sir (John?) Byron, made a knight of the Bath by
king James I., was deeply involved in debt. His
son, the first lord Byron, died without issue. The
second and third barons left each only one surviving
son. The fourth baron was thrice married. By his
first wife he had no issue; by his second three sons
and one daughter, who all died unmarried; by his
third, among other children, Admiral Byron, whose
wreck off the coast of Chili, and five years' hardships,
attracted public attention. " Not long after," says
Moore, " a less innocent sort of notoriety attached
itself to two other members of the family; one the
grand uncle of the poet, and the other his father.
The former, in the year 1765, stood his trial before
the House of Peers for killing in a duel, or rather
scuffle, his relation and neighbour, Mr. Chaworth;
and the latter having carried off to the Continent
the wife of lord Caermarthen, on the noble marquis
obtaining a divorce from the lady, married her."
This lady " having died in 1784, he, in the following
year, married Miss Catherine Gordon. It was known
to be solely with a view of relieving himself from his
debts, that Mr. Byron paid his addresses to her. The
creditors lost no time in pressing their demands;
and not only was the whole of her ready money,
Bank shares, fisheries, etc., sacrificed to satisfy them,
but a large sum raised by mortgage on the estate for

the same purpose." "I have been thinking," says
lord Byron himself, "of an odd circumstance. My
daughter (1), my wife (2), my half sister (3), my
mother (4), my sister's mother (5), my natural
daughter (6), and myself (7), are, or were, all *only*
children. My sister's mother had only my half
sister by that second marriage (herself, too, an only
child), and my father had me, an only child, by his
second marriage with my mother, an only child too.
Such a complication of only children, all tending to
one family, is singular enough, AND LOOKS LIKE
FATALITY ALMOST." We need not remind the reader
of the separation of Mr. and Mrs. Byron, and of lord
and lady Byron ; nor of the miserable tenor of the
poet's after-life. Newstead no longer belongs to the
Byrons; the present baron has six surviving children,
of whom three are married, whereas colonel Wildman, the present possessor of Newstead, is without
heirs-male.

COLCHESTER S. JOHN'S. Granted to sir Thomas
Darcy. It passed to Thomas Dudley, earl of
Warwick, who gave it, in payment of a debt, to F.
Gibson, and afterwards forced him to sell it to John
Lucas. It stayed in the family of the Lucases till
sir Charles Lucas, who was murdered by order of
lord Fairfax, in Colchester castle-yard. It then
came to one Walkeden, an exile with king James
II. ; then to —— Bartlett ; then to Currie, a
scrivener; next to Styles, a woollen-draper; then
to R. Simmons, deputy cashier of the South Sea
Company, and seized for the debts of that body;
next to the Rev. E. Arrowsmith, who dying, it
appears, without heirs-male, left it to his daughter,
Mrs. Robarts.

ABBOTSFORD, Dorset, belonging to Milton, was in
the Strangways. The house was, during the civil
wars, blown up with great loss of life.—*Hutchins'
Dorsetshire.*

MINSTER IN SHEPPEY.   Granted to,   1.[1] Sir
William Cheney;   2. Henry Cheney, lord Cheney
of Tuddington (family extinct 1587) ; sold to,   3.
Sir T. Hoby, died 1596.   4. Sir E. Hoby; sold,
about 1614, to,   5. Gabriel Livesey, died 1618.   6.
Sir Michael Livesey ; sold, in 1623, to,   7. Sir John
Hayward, died without issue, in 1636, and left the
estate to charitable purposes.   Seven owners, and
four families, in ninety-six years.

FAVERSHAM.   Granted to,   1. John Wheler, who,
in 1540, sold it to,   2. Sir T. Cheney, who, in
1545, sold it to,   3. Thomas Arderne, gentleman,
murdered by connivance of his wife, Feb. 17, 1550.
4. Margaret Arderne, married Thomas Bradburne,
who soon died.   Passed in 1576 to,   5. Nicholas
Bradburne, who, in 1581, sold it to,   6. Thomas
Straynsham and others.   7. George Straynsham;
died without male heirs.   8. — Appleford.   9. —
Appleford.   10. E. Appleford, sold it to,   11. Sir
G. Sondes, created earl of Feversham ; died without
male heirs.   12. Catherine, his daughter, married
Lewis earl of Rockingham.   13. Lewis earl of
Rockingham ;   his grandson died without issue
1746.   14. Thomas marquis of Rockingham, his
brother ; died without issue ; family extinct 1782.[2]
15. Hon. Lewis Monson (Watson), created, 1760,
lord Sondes.

In two hundred and twenty years fifteen possessors, nine families.

LEEDS, Kent.   Granted to,   1. Sir Anthony St.
Leger, died 1559.   2. Sir Warham St. Leger ; sold
in 1572, to,   3. Robert Hampden, etc., who sold it
to,   4. — Norden, who sold it to,   5. F. Cole-
pepper, who resold it to,   6. — Norden, who sold
it to,   7. William Covert.   8. William Covert :—
sold in 1609 to,   9. Sir William Meredith.   10.
William Meredith.   11. Sir R. Meredith.   12. Sir
W. Meredith, died without heirs-male.   13. Sir R.
Meredith, his brother, died without heirs-male.   14.

---

[1] HASTED'S Kent, II. 648.   [2] HASTED, II. 705.

Sir Roger Meredith, his brother, died without issue :
family extinct. 15. Susannah Meredith, by a flaw
in her uncle's will, enabled to leave it to, 16. William Hooper, who possessed it ten months; then
died, and left it, 1758, to, 17. William Jumper.
18. John Calcraft, died 1772. 19. John Calcraft.[3]

In two hundred and thirty years nineteen possessors, nine families.

AYLESFORD Priory, Kent. This was the earliest
Carmelite house in England, and the place where
the first European Chapter was held, in 1245.

Granted to,

1. Sir Thomas Wyatt, who died the year fol-
lowing. 2. Sir Thomas Wyatt, beheaded 1553.
Reverted to the crown. Granted to, 3. John
Sedley, died without issue. 4. Sir W. Sedley, his
brother. 5. Sir H. Sedley, died without issue. 6.
Sir W. Sedley, his brother, died without issue.
[N.B. Sir Charles Sedley, his brother, the notorious
debauchee, died without issue-male, and family became extinct.] 7. Sir Peter Ricaut. 8. — Ricaut,
who sold it, in 1657, to, 9. Caleb Banks. 10.
John Banks; his two sons died before him. 11.
Heneage Finch, created earl of Aylesford, 1695;
whose descendants possess the estate.

One hundred and fifty years, twelve possessors,
five families.

KIRKBY[4] BELER, Rutland.
Granted, 1555, to,
1. John lord Grey. Passed, in 1575, to, 2.
Brian Cave. 3. Ralph Browne; sold to, 4. Thomas Markham, who died without heirs-male. 5.
Elizabeth, his daughter, married E. Sheldon, who
sold it to, 6. Erasmus de la Fountaine. His house,
built on the site of the priory, burnt, Feb. 25, 1645.
7. John de la Fountaine, married twice, left no
child. 8. Anne Meres. 9. John Meres, died without
children, 10. Elizabeth Peltus, his sister. 11.

[3] HASTED, II. 479.   [4] BLORE'S Rutland, s. n.

Thomas Hayley, her nephew. 12. — Sanderson. 13. — Sanderson. 14. Rev. W. Sanderson; exchanged it to,   15. S. C. Bedley, died without children. 16. Sedley Burdett, his nephew, drowned (as afterwards).

Two hundred and thirty-eight years, sixteen possessors, twelve families.

———

NEW SHOREHAM, SUSSEX. John Butler, aged ninety-one, now [January, 1846] living in this parish, says that his father and master always told him, that the stones, which form the front-wall of the vicarage, were brought from Aldrington church by a captain Arthur, who built the house. (S. Mary, Aldrington, is a ruin near the Portslade station of the Shoreham railway; the rectory is worth £294 a year). Whilst captain Arthur was living there, a poor man begging asked an alms, and was refused by the wife of captain Arthur, then with child. On this the beggar repeated the imprecatory verses of the cixth Psalm, and departed. The children of these parents died in the workhouse, though there had been a good property in the family. The house, with the adjoining, is built on the supposed cemetery of the Abbey. It has the reputation of being haunted; and those who inhabit it are said never to prosper. Many of the townspeople say, that they would on no account possess it. And all this is commonly known and reported in the town.

Here was a priory of Carmelite Friars, founded by sir John Mowbray. Since the dissolution, Shoreham has lost a great part of its trade, on account of the deterioration of its harbour, from the river Adur having altered its course.

In the north transept of this church the election of borough members used sacrilegiously to be held. The borough, for its notorious corruption, was forced to extend its franchise to the whole Rape of Bramber.

The following fragments from sir HENRY SPEL-
MAN's *History of Sacrilege*, may appropriately be
placed here :—

"Lodwick Grevil,* owner of MICKLETON, a
manor belonging to Eynsham Abbey, in Oxford-
shire, had two sons, whereof Edward, the younger,
shooting a piece, by chance slew his elder brother,
and thereby succeeded in the inheritance. Lodwick
himself in the —— year of Elizabeth, standing
mute upon his arraignment, for poisoning of ——,
whose will he had counterfeited, was pressed to
death. Edward, afterwards knighted, mortgaged
the Abbey to —— Fisher, a skinner of London, for
a small sum, and growing farther in with him by
borrowing, and use upon use, it came at length by
forfeiture and entanglement, to be Fisher's absolutely; and sir Edward Grevil having wasted his
whole patrimony, and sold some part thereof in
Warwickshire to the lord treasurer Cranfield, became
bailiff to the lord treasurer of the same land. Old
Fisher put over the Abbey to his son sir Edward
Fisher, who with extreme suits, bribery, etc., so
consumed his estate, that he was judged to be
eleven thousand or twelve thousand pounds in debt,
and driven to sell his great lease of Wormgay,
Blackborough, and Grandcourts in Norfolk, and
yet liveth in fear of bailiffs, etc.   12th of October,
1644. *Ex relat. Johan. Wrenham, partim Rob. Mor-
dant. Mil.*

" Sir Edward Grevil had a son, that breaking his
leg over a style, dyed; his daughters are one
married to sir Arthur Ingram, to whom he sold the
reversion of his chief seat Milcote, etc., and hath a
hundred pound per annum during his life, and the
house."

———

" An esquire in the county of Derby, by name
Mr. G. Thacker, who had the tithes of three villages,

* This passage, in the original edition, makes its appearance
without sense or connection after the account of Sherborne Abbey.

Repton, Ingleby, and Foremark, the two former whereof are very large, and in the first whereof his dwelling-house stands upon the ruins of the dissolved Abbey (Repton Abbey), allows to the minister about some twelve pounds per annum for his pains with, and care over, so large a congregation as Repton itself affords, the two villages having chapels of ease. The annual salary was no greater twelve years since; but whether it hath since augmented, I know not.* This gentleman hath not at any time either by any very great housekeeping, or by any other payments extraordinary, either in behalf of himself, or his predecessors, or successors, had any apparent cause of decay in his estate, which make his neighbours to wonder how or whence it comes to pass that at this time he is brought so low.

"In the county aforesaid is a village called Church-Gresly, where once was a religious house. To this parish church belong three more large villages, viz., Castle-Gresly, Linton, and Swadling-Coat, and some other Lordships. The tithes to all these are impropriate. The minister who serves ·Gresly church, whither all the rest (having no chapels) weekly repair, used to have for his stipend eight pounds per annum, and I doubt it is but little increased.† The tithes were challenged by two impropriators, one Mr. Ketling, and the other Mr. Wilmore. I am not for the present sure whether the tithes of the whole parish were challenged by either, but of a great part I am certain. Perhaps there might be a third impropriator that peaceably enjoyed some part of these tenths. I can soon learn. These two antagonists had had many bickerings, and quarrels, and frays at several harvests in taking of tithes, which was sometimes done *vi et armis*. About some fourteen years since, Mr. Ketling encouraged his servants to fight stiffly for the tithes. Mr. Wilmore the old man, and his

[* It is now £123, with a house.—Edd.]
[† It is now £108.—Edd.]

Y

eldest son Mr. John Wilmore, both gentlemen, did so likewise, and somewhat more. For they promised their servants if any blood was shed, or lost in the fray, to bear them out in it. The next day they fell to it in Swadling-Coat Field, and one of Mr. Ketling's men, by name Stopford, was slain. Upon this both Mr. Wilmore and his son were committed to Derby gaol, and at the assizes (though they expected freedom, and thereupon sent to their wives a little before to make provision), were both executed. The same year (1619) the fore-mentioned Mr. Thacker was sheriff of Derbyshire."*

Fuller relates in his Church History (book vi. p. 358), on the authority of " that skilful antiquary and my respected kinsman Samuel Roper, of Lincoln's Inn," how one Thacker, " being possessed of Repingdon Abbey, in Derbyshire, alarmed with the news that Queen Mary had set up these Abbeys again (and fearing how large a reach such a precedent might have), upon a Sunday (belike, the better day the better deed), called together the carpenters and masons of that county, and plucked down in one day (Church work is a cripple in going up, but rides post' in coming down), a most beautiful church belonging thereunto, adding, he would destroy the nest for fear the birds should build therein again."

We have just noticed Mr. Godfrey Thacker of Repingdon. Gilbert Thacker, the last male of this family, died in 1712, leaving an only daughter, Mrs. Elizabeth Thacker, who died in 1728, and who bequeathed the Priory estate to sir Robert Burdett, bart., grandfather of sir Francis Burdett, bart., the late proprietor.

* The above fragment is preserved by Hearne in the sixth volume of his edition of Leland's Itinerary, p. xv. He calls it a " fragment of sir HENRY SPELMAN's *History and Fate of Sacrilege*, communicated to me by my reverend and learned friend, Mr. Francis Giffard, formerly vicar of Patshull, in Staffordshire, and afterwards rector of Rushall, in Wilts."

BROUGHTON, Leicestershire, belonging to the Premonstratensian Abbey of Croxton.
Granted 1593, to,
1. Sir A. Noel, died 1607. 2. Sir E. Noel, who sold it about 1612, to, 3. George Villiers, duke of Buckingham, assassinated 1628. 4. George, duke of Buckingham (family extinct), who sold it, 1670, to, 5. Christopher, duke of Albemarle (family extinct), who sold it, 1687, to, 6. The infamous lord Jefferies, who died a prisoner in the Tower. 7. Sir C. Duncombe. 8. Lord Feversham, his nephew; thrice married; died childless, 1763.

One hundred and seventy years; eight possessors; six families.

POWDERHAM, Devonshire. The history of this place is a specimen of the fate of those families who did retain possession of Church property. The motto of the Courtenays was, UBI LAPSUS ? QUID FECI ?
1. Sir William Courtenay, "the Great," succeeded to the family estates in 1512. 2. Sir William Courtenay, the grantee of church lands in and about Powderham, had a son, George, who died before his father. His son, 3. William Courtenay, succeeded, and was slain at S. Quentin, 1557. His son, 4. William Courtenay, not only spent his great estate in Ireland, but impaired that of his ancestors. His son, 5. Francis Courtenay, was blind some time before his death. His son, 6. William Courtenay, when a middle-aged man, was struck with paralysis, and lingered in a miserable condition many years. Of his sons, William died young; Francis Edward was drowned in the Thames; and several died unbaptized. William Courtenay was succeeded by, 7. Richard Courtenay, a younger son; he, with one of his sons, was drowned in their passage to Leghorn; another son, William, drowned in the Piava. 8. Francis Courtenay. 9. William Courtenay. 10. William, died ten days after being created viscount

Courtenay (May 16, 1762). A brother of his was drowned at Torquay. 11. William viscount Courtenay had thirteen daughters, one of whom was burnt to death, March 5, 1781 ; and one son. 12. William, third viscount, who claimed and was allowed the earldom of Devon. He died unmarried, 1835 ; and the earldom devolved on, 13. William, present earl.

———

LYOMINSTER, Sussex.
Granted to,
1. Henry earl of Arundel, who sold it, 1579, to, 2. R. Knight. In that family it continued one hundred years ; then sir R. Knight, dying childless, left it to, 1. R. Martin, who took the surname of Knight. Dying without children, it passed to his brother, 2. Christopher Martin, who took the surname of Knight. His daughter, 3. — Knight, twice married, and both husbands took the surname of Knight, but she died childless ; and it passed to, 4. B. May, who took the surname of Knight. 5. T. Knight, his son died childless, 1794. 6. E. Austen, who took the surname of Knight; and from whom it passed to the Gobeys.
Note the perseverance with which it was endeavoured to keep the lands in the same name, and the way in which those efforts were baffled.

———

S. EDMUND'S BURY, Suffolk.
Granted, February 14, 1560, to,
1. John Eyre; sold, March 1, 1560, to, 2. Thomas Badby; in 1581, to, 3. — Blagge; in 1592, to, 4. Sir R. Jermyn; in 1594, to, 5. Edward Cope; left, in (?), to, 6. Erasmus Cope; sold, in 1621, to, 7. Lord Spencer and others ; in 1625, to, 8. Sir G. Hastings; in 1626, to, 9. Dorothy Perkins, afterwards married to — Tyrrell; in 1664, to, 10. Roger Barnes; in 1672, to, 11. John Halls; in 1780, to, 12. Major Park. In two

hundred and forty-four years, twelve families, the estate never descending from father to son. Sold in ——, to, 13. Sir Jermyn Davers; left to, 14. S. R. Davers; to, 15. Lady Davers; in 1804, to, 16. Sir C. Davers, in whom, in 1806, the title became extinct.

CRESSING, Essex. A Preceptory, first of Templars, then of Hospitallers.
1. Sir John Smyth bought it of Henry VIII. Of his sons, Edward, John, William, and another Edward, died without male heirs. 2. Thomas Smyth, who left it to his son, 3. Clement Smyth, who died without issue, and it passed to, 4. Henry Smyth, his brother, who died without surviving issue, and it passed to his brother, 5. William Smyth, who died without issue, and it passed to, 6. Sir Thomas Smyth his brother. From thence, through the Audleys and Tukes, to sir Thomas Davies; whose eldest son shot himself in the Priory, and the estate was in consequence sold by the family. It passed to the Olmiuses; the family, raised to the Barony of Waltham, became extinct in 1787.

S. BREOCK, Cornwall. " In this parish are the united manors of Sele and Trevore, which belonged to the Prior of Bodmin. Within the short space of sixty-two years it underwent sixteen transfers; which is a greater number than can be instanced in any other property in Cornwall, except Fentongollan, in the parish of S. Michael, Penkivel," also church property. " Adverting to these numerous and rapid revolutions, Hals proposes it as a query, whether the king and parliament did not fall under the denunciation of the original curse, by which the whole was guarded, when by Henry VIII. all religions houses were dissolved, and their wealth was turned into another channel; and whether the various possessors of this manor did not feel the effects of this curse. 'It hath been very restless and uneasy,' he adds, 'in their hands, ever since it was diverted from the end and use to which it was originally given as aforesaid.'"—*Hitchins's Cornwall,* ii. 118.

This passage was omitted in the improved edition of Hals and Tonkin.

S. Columb Major. In the College of Austin Canons, in July 1701, a poor youth was burnt to death under circumstances so horrid, that we forbear to repeat them.—*Hitchins* ii. 165.

Wanstead belonged first to the Abbey of Westminster, then to the bishops of London, who underlet it to various tenants. Before the dissolution, it was for many years in the possession (under the bishops of London) of the families of Hoding and Huntercombe. At the dissolution it was held by sir John Heron. Giles, his son, for refusing the oath of supremacy, was dispossessed. Edward VI. granted the manor to Richard lord Rich; his son Robert alienated it to the 'great' earl of Leicester; his widow married sir Christopher Blount, and took Wanstead with her to him; sir C. Blount alienated it to sir G. Carew in 1589. It then passed to sir Charles Blount lord Mountjoy, who was created earl of Devonshire, and died in 1606 without legitimate issue. He had five natural children by lady Rich during her husband's life, and married her. Wanstead then came to the crown. King James I. gave it to sir Henry Mildmay; he married Ann daughter of sir William Holyday, and settled this estate on her, worth then £1,000 per annum. He was one of the Martyr's Judges, and therefore the estate was confiscated to the crown. Charles II. gave it to his brother, James duke of York, who sold it to sir Robert Brooks; but he, being involved in his affairs, fled to France and died there. Of his heirs it was purchased by sir Josiah Child, a merchant. He was married three times, and had several children; some of his daughters married noblemen.

Two sons by his first wife died in infancy. His son Josiah, by the second wife, was knighted by king William III. and died childless; and was succeeded by his brother Richard, who married Dorothy daughter of John Thynne, and grand-daughter of Francis Tylney, esqs., and had three sons. He was made baron of Newton and viscount Castlemaine; his heirs took the name of Tylney: he was succeeded by his second son, earl of Tylney; he died childless. Wanstead then came to his nephew sir James Tylney Long, who was succeeded by his only son James. The last of the family in lineal descent was Miss Tylney Long, whose sad history is well known. She married Mr. Wellesley Pole, now earl of Mornington, and had two children, the elder of whom inherits the estate. Wanstead House,—the glory of Epping Forest, and the abode of Louis XVIII. during a part of his exile from France,—is no more; it is levelled to the ground.—See *Morant's and Wright's Essex.*

WHALLEY. This was granted to the Asshetons. Sir Ralph Assheton, in 1660, pulled down part of the church and steeple. He died without issue, and was succeeded by a brother, who died without issue; and he by a second brother, who also died without issue. Hence the estate came to his sister's son, who left daughters only, and the family became extinct.—*Baines's Lancashire,* iii. 189.

CLERKENWELL. Granted to sir Thomas Chaloner. His son, sir Thomas, seems to have thought lightly of the matter; for he caused these lines to be inscribed in front of the nunnery, which he occupied as his house :—

Cæsta fides superest, velatæ tecta sorores
　Ista relegatæ deseruere licet:
Nam venerandus Hymen hic vota jugalia servat,
　Vestalemque focum mente fovere studet.

He had four sons : sir William, who died without issue, when the baronetcy became extinct; Edward, in holy orders,‘who died of the plague; Thomas, who was one of the regicides, and exempted in the act of oblivion, shortly after which he died; and James, who was also concerned in the great rebellion, and is said to have poisoned himself.

HURLEY, Berks. From the Howards this estate passed to the Kempenfelts. Admiral Kempenfelt's melancholy death, in the Royal George, is well known.

MONK BRETTON, Yorkshire, granted to William Blitheman. His relative, Jasper Blitheman, sold it to George earl of Shrewsbury, whose four sons died without heirs-male. The estate came to Mary, daughter of Henry Talbot, the fourth son, who married twice, but had no children.—*Burton's Monasticon*, 99.

PENMON, Anglesea. “Nothing whatever is known in the parish relative to John Moore, to whom the Priory was granted, neither are there any of his descendants in it. Penmon and Llanvaes afterwards became the property of a family of the name of White, now extinct, and were purchased by the late lord Bulkeley, whose line is also extinct.”— *Information received from Penmon.*

AUDLEY END, Essex. The miserable termination of lord Audley's own family we shall notice in Table III. The descendants of his brother, to whom he left very considerable property, were seated at Bere Church, in Essex, where the family became extinct by the death of Thomas Audley, who died in very reduced circumstances. The first lord Howard of Walden, created earl of Suffolk, was most un-

THE HISTORY AND FATE OF SACRILEGE.

fortunate in his wife and two of his children. His widow was compelled to abscond for fear of arrest. The estate has been subsequently expensively litigated.—*Lord Braybrooke's Hist. of Audley End,* pp. 23, 39.

HOLCOMBE-BARTON Chapel, Devonshire, was pulled down, and an upping-stock built with its materials; but the tradition of the country people is, that it would never stand.

LEOMINSTER. Granted, 1620, to the duke of Buckingham, assassinated 1628; king Charles was at Southwick *Priory* when he heard the news. His son, a minor, succeeded in 1662; great part was sold for debt in 1675. Major Wildman, the notorious hypocrite, purchased the estate; in 1680 he was obliged to fly the country. In 1693 lord Coningsby had it; he left two daughters. The first died without issue, the second had only two daughters.— *Price's Leominster.*

CHELLISCOMBE, Devonshire. " In 1554, in the north part of the village was a chapel entire, dedicated to S. Mary. The walls and roof are still whole, and served, some years since, for a dwelling-house, but are now in ruins. Superstitious fear prevents any from living in it. I could not prevail upon any husbandman living in the village, by entreaties or offers of money, to sleep in it one night." —*Dunsford's Tiverton.*

KENILWORTH. " The site of the Monastery, which had been given by king Henry VIII. to sir Andrew Flamok, a courtier of those days, descended to sir William Flamok, his son and heir, who died seised thereof, July 11, 2 Eliz., leaving Katherine his daughter and heir, about three years old, afterwards married to John Colburn, of Morton-Morrell, in this county, esquire. Which John, having bought certain horses, stolen out of the earl's stables here at Kenilworth Castle, as was pretended, was so terrified by Leicester, that he quitted to him all his right therein upon easy terms, as I have heard."—*Dugdale's Warwickshire*, 159.

WARWICK. "The next most memorable thing relating to this place, is that purchase by the City, made in 34 Hen. VIII. from the crown, of much Monastery land lying in and near thereto, . . . for the sum of £1,378 10s."—*Dugdale*, p. 95. "To so low an ebb did their trading soon after grow . . . that many thousands of the inhabitants, to seek better livelihoods, were constrained to forsake the City; insomuch as in 3 Edward VI., there were not at that time above 3,000 inhabitants, whereas, within memory, there had been 15,000."—*Ibid.*, p. 96.

CROSSED FRIARS, Aldgate. "The Friars' house was made a glass-house; . . . which house, in the year 1575, on the 4th of September, burst out into a terrible fire; . . . the same house, . . . having within it about 40,000 billets of wood, was also consumed *to the stone walls*, which, nevertheless, greatly hindered the fire from spreading any farther."—*Stow's Survey*, p. 291.

CERNE. The old "abbey house" and farms were inhabited and used, but burnt down some fifty years ago.—*Hutchins' Dorset*.

SHELFORD. "After the Priory of Shelford had Saxendale, the provision for the cure was little; and since that Priory came to the family of Stanhope, with which it yet (1677—that branch of the family is now extinct) continueth, they had . . . to swear it was but a chapel of ease, and that Saxendale was ever parish to Shelford; and so, to save a small allowance, they pulled down the church, and some of the *few inhabitants now left* have taken up stone coffins, and do still use them as troughs for their swine."—*Thoroton's Notts*, p. 146. " The house [of these same Stanhopes] was a garrison for the king, and commanded by colonel Philip Stanhope ; which, being taken by storm, he and many of his soldiers were therein slain, and the house afterwards burned. Ferdinando Stanhope, his brother, was slain at Bridgnorth, while doing a charitable action, by a parliament soldier."—*Ibid.* 148.

ALCESTER. Fulke Grevil " much enlarged his manor-house at Beauchamp's Court, taking stone and timber from the then newly-dissolved Priory of Alcester."—*Dugdale's Warwickshire*, p. 570.

His grandson, lord Brooke, the poet, " delaying to reward one Hayward, an ancient servant that had spent the most of his time in attendance upon him, being expostulated with for so doing, received a mortal stab in the back by the same man, then private with him, at his chamber at Brook House, London, Sept. 30, 1628 ; who, to consummate the tragedy, went into another room, locked the door, and pierced his own bowels with the sword."—*Ibid.* p. 572. This lord Brooke had himself procured a grant from king James I., of Knoll, part of the possessions of Westminster Abbey.—*Ibid.* p. 702. Of this family was the celebrated lord Brooke, of whom we have spoken already.

STRETTON BASKERVILLE, Warwickshire. " H. Smyth, 9 Henry VII., inclosed 540 acres of land more, whereby twelve messuages and four cottages fell to ruin, and eighty persons there inhabiting were constrained to depart thence, and to live miserably. By means whereof the church grew to such ruin, that it was of no other use than for the shelter of cattle; being, with the churchyard, wretchedly profaned, to the evil example of others, as are the words of the Inquisition."—*Dugdale*, 34.

We abridge the sad history of this family from the same work (p. 37) :—

" This sir Walter being grown an aged man at the death of his first wife, considering of a marriage for Richard his heir, made known his mind to Mr. T. Cherwin of Ingestre in Staffordshire, in behalf of Dorothy, one of his daughters. But no sooner had the old knight seen the young lady, than he became a suitor for himself, whereupon the marriage ensued accordingly, but with what a tragic issue will be seen. For it was not long ere she gave entertainment to one Mr. W. Robinson, son to George Robinson, a rich mercer of London; and grew so impatient at all impediments which might hinder her full enjoyment of him, that she rested not till she had contrived a way to be rid of her husband. For which purpose, corrupting her waiting gentlewoman and a groom of the stable, she resolved, by their help and the assistance of Robinson, to strangle him in his bed, appointing the time and manner how it should be effected. And though Robinson failed in coming on the designed night, she no whit staggered in her resolutions; for watching her husband till he was fallen asleep, she then let in those assassins; and casting a long towel about his neck, caused the groom to hinder him from struggling, whilst herself and the maid straining the towel, stopt his breath. It seems the old man little thought his wife had acted therein ; for when they first cast the towel about his neck, he cried out, ' Help, Doll, help!' But having thus dispatched the work, to palliate the business, she made an outcry in the house, wringing her hands, pulling her hair, and weeping extremely, which subtle and feigned signs of sorrow prevented all suspicion of his violent death ; and, not long after, went to London, setting so high a value upon her beauty, that Robinson, her former darling, became neglected. But within two years following, it so happened that this woeful deed was brought to light by the groom; who being entertained with Mr. R. Smyth, son to the murdered knight, and attending him to Coventry with divers other servants, became so sensible of his villainy that he took his master aside, and upon his knees besought forgiveness from him for acting in the murder of his father, declaring all the circumstances thereof. Whereupon Mr. Smyth gave him good words, but wished some others, whom he trusted, to have an eye to him, that he might not escape when he had slept and better considered what might be the issue thereof. Notwithstanding which direction he fled away with his master's best horse, and hasting presently into Wales, attempted to go beyond sea; but being hindered by contrary winds, after three essays to launch out, was pursued by Mr. Smyth, that he was found out and brought prisoner to Warwick, as was also the lady and her gentlewoman, all of them denying the fact: and the groom most impudently charging Mr Smyth with endeavour of corrupting him to accuse the lady, his mother-in-law, falsely, to the end he might get her jointure. But upon his arraignment, so smitten was he with apprehension of the guilt that he publicly acknowledged it, and stoutly justified what he had so said to be true to the face of the lady and her maid, who at first, with much seeming confidence, pleaded their innocence; till, at length, seeing the circumstances thus discovered, they both confessed the fact. For which the lady was burnt at a stake near the hermitage on Wolsey-heath, where the country people, to this day, show the place; and the groom, with the maid, suffered death at Warwick. This was about the third year of queen Mary's reign, it being May 15, 1·Mariæ, that sir Walter's murder happened.

" To whom succeeded Richard, his son and heir,

who was strangely juggled out of a fair inheritance. For he, having but one only daughter, Margaret, by his first wife, and doubting of issue-male, treated with sir J. Littleton, of Frankley in Worcestershire, for a marriage betwixt his said daughter and William Littleton, third son to sir John. In consideration whereof, he agreed to settle all his lands, in remainder, after his own decease without other issue, upon the said William and Margaret, and the heirs of their bodies lawfully begotten; but, failing such issue, to return to his own right heirs: and having writings drawn accordingly, trusted to the said sir J. Littleton to get them engrossed. The day being appointed for sealing, Mr. Smyth came over to Frankley, where he found some of sir John's friends to bear him company, in whose presence the writings were brought forth and begun to be read; but before they came to the uses, stept in sir J. Littleton's keeper, and told them that there were a brace of bucks at lair in the park, but if they made not haste, those market people which passed through the park would undoubtedly rouse them. Whereupon sir J. Littleton earnestly moved Mr. Smyth to seal the writings without further reading, protesting that they were according to the draughts he had seen, and without any alteration. Which bold asseverations caused him forthwith to seal them, and to go into the park.

"Hereupon the two children (for they were not above nine years old apiece) were married together, and lived in the house with sir John. But so it happened that about six years after the young man died by a fall from a horse; insomuch as Mr. Smyth, considering that his daughter had no issue, resolved to take her away, and signified as much to sir John; who, designing to marry her again to George, his second son, refused to deliver her, till which time Mr. Smyth never suspected anything in the deed formerly sealed; but then it appeared, that for want of issue by William and Margaret, the lands were to

devolve to the right heirs of the said William, which
was Gilbert Littleton, his eldest brother, contrary to
the plain agreement at first made.   To make short,
therefore, William, the youngest son, married her ;
George, the second, enjoyed her; and Gilbert, the
eldest, had the estate, as heir to his brother.   Which,
descending to John, his son, was kept from Mr.
Smyth the true heir, with whom he had great suits
at law; and, at length, by his attainder for adhering
to Robert earl of Essex, in 42 Elizabeth, came to the
Crown; for he was drawn into that treason as being
a man much respected for his wit and valour by those
conspirators, and died in prison.

" And as none of the line of Gilbert Littletor
doth enjoy a foot of the lands, so it is no less observable that the son and heir of George by the same
Margaret, Stephen Littleton of Holbeach in Worcestershire, was attended with a very hard fate,
being one of the gunpowder conspirators, for which
he lost his life and estate."

BISHOP'S ITCHINGTON.   "Thomas Fisher, secretary
to the duke of Somerset, being as greedy of Church-
lands as other courtiers in those days were, swallowed
divers large morsels, of which this was one ; and,
indeed, so fair a bit, as that he was loath that any
should share with him therein; and, therefore,
making an absolute depopulation of that part called
Nether Itchington, where the church stood, (which
he also pulled down for the building of a large
Manor-house in its room), to perpetuate his memory
turned the name of it from *Bishop's* Itchington to
Fisher's Itchington. . . .   But how such sacrilegions acquisitions do thrive, though fenced about
with all worldly security imaginable, we have mani-
fold examples, whereof this is one, and not the least
observable; for after the death of the said Thomas,
which happened in 20 Eliz., Edward, his son and heir,
making a shift to consume all those great possessions
which his father left him, excepting only this lordship, and dying in prison, left it to John his son and

heir, who by his deed, bearing date 8th Jac. [I.], sold it," etc. Dugdale then traces its descent, and adds, " So that the third generation never enjoyed it since it was thus aliened from the Bishoprick."— p. 283.

———

CAVERSFIELD (belonging to Burcester Abbey), Bucks.
Granted, 154–, to,
1. John Langstone; he died without issue, 1553. 2. Thomas Moyle, his brother-in-law. 3. In 1558, Joan Langstone, who conveyed it to, 4. Robert Hitchcock, whose claim was disputed by the Moyles. 5. — Bedell. 6. Moyle. 7. Thomas Moyle, died 1649, it seems, without issue. 8. James Davenport; sold it, 1653, to, 9. Maximilian Bard. 10. Nathaniel Bard, his son. 11. Thomas Bard. 12. William Vaux, who held it in 1735.
In one hundred and ninety years twelve possessors, seven families.—*Willis's Buckingham*, p. 166.

———

CANWELL, Staffordshire. " It was purchased by John Vescy, alias Harman, bishop of Exeter. John Harman, son of the bishop's brother, was found his heir, who, it should seem, enjoyed it to 6 Eliz., and left it to Sibil, his daughter and heir, being an infant of six years of age. In this last age sir John Pershall bought it, and gave it to sir William Pershall, his youngest son, who, not long after, sold it to sir Fr. Lawley, after he had filled it with incumbrances ; and likewise sold all the rest of his estates, and became as bad as a beggar, if not worse."— *Erdeswicke; quoted in Shaw's History of Staffordshire.*

———

SYON HOUSE. This, with the exception of Shaftesbury, was the most influential nunnery in England. The site was, on the dissolution, kept in the king's hands ; and Catherine Howard was confined here for nearly three months, leaving this prison for the scaffold. Henry's body lay here in state; and here it was that Father Peto's prophecy was fulfilled, by the dogs licking his blood. Edward VI. granted the place to the duke of Somerset, who perished on the scaffold;—then it reverted to the Crown. Next it came to John Dudley, duke of Northumberland—and here it was that lady Jane Grey was persuaded to accept the crown. In 1557, the nuns having all this time lived together in community, they were recalled and put in possession of the house, and sir Francis Englefield rebuilt two sides of the Monastery. On the re-dissolution by queen Elizabeth it came again to the Crown, and was, by James I., granted to Henry Percy, earl of Northumberland—"one of the most unfortunate," says Aungier, "of his race. On a groundless suspicion of having been concerned in the Gunpowder Plot he was stripped of all his offices, adjudged to pay a fine of £30,000, and sentenced to imprisonment in the Tower for life." In 1613 he offered Syon House in lieu of the fine, but it was not accepted. In 1619, after fifteen years' imprisonment, he was set at liberty, on paying £11,000. In the time of his son it was used as a prison for the children of king Charles; and his grandson, Josceline, eleventh earl, died without issue-male. Lady Elizabeth Percy was heiress of this, and of five others of the oldest baronies in England; and before she was sixteen she had been thrice a wife and twice a widow. She was married, at the age of thirteen, to Henry Cavendish, earl of Ogle, only son and heir of the Newcastle family; he died a few months afterwards. Thomas Thynne, of Longleat, esq., and count Köningsmark, were rivals for her hand. She was married to the former; but before the marriage could be consummated he was assassinated by three ruffians hired by Köningsmark. She was married three months afterwards to Charles "the Proud" duke of Somerset. The character of this man is

well known. The roads used to be cleared when he
rode out; he made his daughters stand while he
slept in the afternoon; and left one of them
£20,000 less than the other for sitting down
at that time when tired. He had many children,
but one son only survived him. In this son the
male line failed again, sir Hugh Smithson succeeding.

While the lay possessors of Syon, notwithstanding
their riches and honours, were thus made like a
wheel, and as stubble before the wind, the poor nuns
were pilgrims indeed, but still remained a community. They first went to Dermond in Flanders, then
to Zurich-zee in Zealand, then to Mishagan, then to
Antwerp, and then to Mechlin. In great danger
when that city was taken by the Prince of Orange,
they nevertheless escaped; going first to Antwerp,
then to Rouen, and, last of all, to Lisbon. Here, in
process of time, they were enabled to build a Syon
House of their own; here, though their house was
burnt down in 1651, and overthrown by the earthquake in 1755, they still remained; and here, though
their house was for a while taken possession of by
the Peninsular army, and a part of the sisterhood
sought refuge in England, where they continued,
they still prosper; and Syon House at Lisbon was
untouched in the dissolution of the religious houses
of Portugal. They keep the original keys of the
house in token of their continued right to the
property.

[S. Mary's Priory, Bishopsgate (Manor of Ditton).
14th June, Edward VI., 1553, then king, granted
the manor of Ditton, *alias* Long Ditton, late belonging to the Priory of "the Blessed Mary without
Bishopsgate," and all lands, etc. (and other estates
in Northamptonshire), to (1) David Vincent, esq.
In 1542, Henry VIII., Anno. 33., he had a grant
with Robert Bocher, gent., of the site of the Grey

Friars in Grantham and the Black Friars in Stamford, and had a legacy of a hundred pounds in the king's will, to which he was one of the witnesses. He married, first, Elizabeth, daughter of — Spencer, of . . . *com.* Northampton; second, Jane, daughter of William Roffey, esq., . . . *com.* Worcester. He died 22nd August, 1565. (2) Thomas, his son and heir, by deed dated April 1, 9 Elizabeth, 1567, conveyed this manor and advowson to (3) George Evelyn, esq., who died May 29th (1 James), 1603, leaving a son and heir (4), Thomas, aged 50. He had fifteen children by his first wife and two by his last. His great-grandson (7) Edward, who possessed this estate, was created a baronet Feb. 17th, 1682-3. Thomas (8), the eldest son, who remained here when his father removed to Godstone, died 24th October, 1617, leaving a son (9) and heir of the same name, who was a knight, and died October 4th, 1659. His son and heir was sir Edward Evelyn (10). His heir, George, died without issue 13th September, 1685, in his father's life-time. Sir Edward died 1692, leaving a grandson (11), Edward Hill, and two daughters, Mary and Penelope, his co-heirs at law. This manor passed by settlement to (12) sir Joseph Alston, the husband of Penelope. There were three sons of this marriage, of whom (13) Joseph, the eldest, succeeded his father in titles and estate. He died without issue, and (14) Evelyn Alston, his next brother, became his heir. He, previous to 1721, sold the manor to sir Peter King (15), afterwards lord high chancellor, and created lord King, died 1734, leaving four sons, John (16), Peter (17), William (18), and Thomas (19), all of whom took the title and estate in succession, the youngest only leaving issue. He died 1779, succeeded by Peter, lord King (20), and owner of this manor 1810, succeeded, 1833, by (21) William, now earl of Lovelace.]—"Manning's Surrey," and "Debrett's Peerage." Twenty-one possessors in two hundred and eighty years.—[E.]

APPULDURCOMBE. An alien Priory in the Isle of Wight, and suppressed in the time of Edward III. It came into the hands of Richard Worsley, who was one of the commissioners, under Edward VI., for the sale of Church plate. Two of his sons were blown up with gunpowder at Appuldurcombe Sept. 6, 1557.—*Hist. Isle of Wight*, p. 189, and *Burke's Extinct Baronetage*, p. 581.

ASHEY, Isle of Wight, a cell to Whorley in Hants. Granted to Giles Worsley. His son died a minor shortly after his father. The half-brother and the heir-at-law were involved in a lawsuit, and so the property passed from the family.

MILTON ABBAS, Dorsetshire. It is traditionally reported that at the time of the removal of the ancient parish church, as they were levelling a portion of the churchyard, the then earl of Dorchester came to the men, and kicking a skull, and using blasphemous language, ordered them to move " the *lousy* skull ; " and was soon after and to the day of his death afflicted with the *morbus pedicularis*.

CARDIGAN Priory belonged, in 1666, to James Phillips, one that had the fortune to be in with all times, and thrived by none. He married thrice, and left one daughter only.—*Cambrian Register*, 1795. (167.)'

Instances of the misery which has attached itself to the possessors of this house, are to be found in its sale for debt by Thomas Pryse in 1744; and in the destruction of the magnificent Hafod Library, the property of Thomas Johnes, the possessor of Cardigan.

ROCK-LANE Chapel, Exeter, " was pulled down by a person who built several tenements with the materials ; but no inhabitant of these houses hath prospered either in body or purse."—*Polwhele's Devon*, p. 21.

COPLESTONE Chapel " was a large building, pulled down by sir John Coplestone, and the materials sold to a blacksmith and others."—*Ibid.* p. 36. " This manor of Coplestone is now divided into several little farms; and scarcely are there any remains at present of a mansion-house, heretofore so noted for one of the first in the country."—*Ibid.* p. 35.

" The heir-male of this stock was a hopeful young gentleman who, lately dying issueless, has left his lands unto his two sisters, married into the families of Bampfylde and Elford."—*Ibid.* From the former stock came colonel Hugh Bampfylde, who riding swiftly down hill, his horse tripped and threw him with such violence that he fractured his skull. Before which fatal end, says Prince, there were observed some unusual foreboding circumstances.— *Ibid.* p. 125. His son, sir Coplestone, making a visit to his son's relict, said, as soon as he entered the house, that he should never more go thence alive—which accordingly happened.—*Ibid.*

FERRYTON Bridge. There was a chapel here, profaned by a blacksmith. Not long since his son, a very promising young man, fell down dead in S. Mary Ottery churchyard ; and a greater number of people have been drowned at that water than at any other place in Devon.—*Polwhele's Devon*, p. 276.

UPHAM. A land belonging to Glastonbury, granted to the Drakes. Sir B. Drake, for giving the celebrated Francis Drake a box on the ear within the precincts of the court, was disgraced. Sir John Drake rebuilt his house, ruined in the civil wars: " But he lived," says Polwhele, " but a short time to enjoy that pleasant place,"—and the family became extinct in 1736.

LUPPIT. Also Abbey-lands ; they were in the Carews. Sir G. Carew, the grantee, sunk in harbour at Portsmouth in his ship the Mary Rose, in 1546, and left no issue.

BURWELL, Cambridgeshire, held of Ramsey, and alienated at the dissolution.   Here, Sept. 8, 1727, seventy-eight persons were burnt to death in a barn.

BURTON LAZARS, Notts.   The mansion-house erected on the abbey-lands was blown down 1703.

ABBOTSFORD.   Belonged to the Abbey of Melrose.   It is a deeply affecting thing to observe how after he had purchased this property, sir Walter Scott's affairs never prospered : the end is known to all.   And with this knowledge, it is painful to read his light allusions to the appropriation of a Cross, as "a nice little piece of sacrilege from Melrose."

DUNFERMLINE.   A Benedictine Abbey in Fife. The commendator at the Reformation was secretary Pitcairn, who was also archdeacon of S. Andrews. He joined the reformers, and secured his temporalities.   For the part he took in the "Raid of Ruthven," he was denounced rebel, and banished the country.   The next who obtained the revenues of Dunfermline was Patrick master of Gray, the twelfth of a family succession.   He was banished in 1587 ; his son Andrew was also banished, and left no surviving male issue.   George, the sixth earl of Huntly, was the next who got the Abbey; his son was executed at Edinburgh, and *his* son killed at the battle of Alford in 1645, leaving no family. Alexander Seton, lord Fyvie, president of the Court of Session (a younger son of the fifth lord Seton), was created earl of Dunfermline by James VI. in 1605.   He only got part of the temporalities; but he was commendator besides of the rich Abbey of Pluscardine, in Morayshire.   He was married three times, and had only one son, whose grand-nephew and heir was forfeited, and died childless.   The other individual who shared the temporalities of

Dunfermline, was no less a personage than the queen of James VI., who received them as part of her marriage settlement ; though not without several complaints from pensioners, who alleged that they were thus robbed of their incomes. The fate of the queen's son, Charles I. (who by the way was born in the Abbey), and her daughter Elizabeth (the only two who survived out of seven children), and of her grandson James and posterity, need not be told.

BALMERINO. A Cistercian Abbey in Fife. John Hay, master of Requests to queen Mary, obtained from her this Abbey in 1565. We have not been able to trace his history, but we presume the Abbey passed to the crown under the "Annexation Act" of 1587; for in 1603 it was given to sir James Elphinston, who was created lord Balmerino. He died soon after of a broken heart. His descendant Arthur was executed in 1746, in whom the line became extinct. The Balmerino family were also in possession of Restalrig near Edinburgh, which had belonged to a religious establishment founded by James III., for a dean and eight prebendaries.

PITTENWEEM. An Augustinian Priory in Fife. The lord James Stewart was commendator of this Priory at the Reformation, whose conduct and fate we have seen. Before his death he gave it to sir James Balfour, governor of Edinburgh castle (one of the murderers of Darnley), as the price of receiving over that fortress from him. Another of the conditions was, that sir James's son, Michael (afterwards lord Burleigh), should enjoy, for himself and his heirs, a pension out of the priory-lands of S. Andrews. Sir James was forfeited in 1579, and lord Burleigh left only one daughter, as we have already seen under the head of Cupar. Next we find this Abbey ratified to captain William Stewart in 1592. Frederick Stewart, his son, was created lord Pittenweem in 1609; but dying without issue, the title and family became extinct.

LINDORES. A Tyronensian Abbey in Fife. The last Roman Catholic abbat was the celebrated John Lesley, afterwards bishop of Ross. It is probable that, owing to his fidelity to queen Mary, James VI. permitted him to retain his Abbey, or a portion of its rents, till 1592; as in that year it was bestowed on sir Patrick Lesley, second son of the earl of Rothes, who was made lord Lindores. Balfour, in his " Annals," August 12, 1640, says of this lord :— "On Sunday, about three o'clock in the afternoon, died Patrick lord Lindores. He was never married, but he had sixty-seven base children, sons and daughters." His brother James succeeded him, whose grandson, David, died childless.

INCHCOLM. An Augustinian Priory on the Forth. In 1581 the grant of this priory is ratified to Henry Stewart, son of sir James Stewart of Doune. In 1611 James VI. created him lord St. Colme. He had only one son, who entered the service of Gustavus Adolphus, and died without children.

CULROSS. A Cistercian Abbey on the Forth. Alexander Colville was commendator in 1584. His son John succeeded; who, having no family, resigned in favour of his nephew sir James Colville, who was made lord Colville in 1609. His grandson James, second lord Colville, died issueless in 1640.

CUPAR. A Cistercian Abbey in Angus. The last Roman Catholic abbat was Donald Campbell, a younger son of the earl of Argyll. He joined the reformers, kept his abbey, and died (unmarried, we believe) in 1562.[1] One Leonard Leslie succeeded,

[1] There is a tradition in the neighbourhood of Cupar-Angus to this day, that this Donald Campbell, in the true spirit of clanship, invited a number of his relations from Argyllshire to come and settle on his monastic lands, which he let out to them on easy terms. Thus the vicinity of Cupar was soon peopled with Campbells; and yet there is not a single proprietor of that name now to be found near it!

nd was forfeited. Next we find that sir Thomas Lyon of Auldbar, second son of the seventh lord Glammis, got "the patronage, advowson, and donation of the parish kirk of Nether-Airley, parsonage and vicarage thereof," which had belonged to this Abbey. This sir Thomas had also some monks' portions from the Abbey lands at Arbroath. He had only one son, who married a daughter of Gladstones, archbishop of S. Andrews, and died without issue. In 1569, sir Michael Balfour, afterwards lord Burleigh (the ninth of a lineal descent) obtained the lands of Cupar. He left only a daughter, through whom the title was allowed to be continued till it expired. In 1607, James VI. made lord Elphinstone (second son of lord Balmerino) lord Cupar, with the temporalities of the Abbey. He married twice, but died in 1669 without issue. The property was then granted to his nephew John, lord Balmerino, of whose family see below.

ARBROATH. A Tyronensian Abbey in Angus. Lord John Hamilton, second son of the duke of Chatelherault, got this Abbey at the Reformation. In 1579 he was forfeited and banished. William Erskine, one of the Mar family, next obtained the Abbey, who was forfeited for his concern in the "Raid of Ruthven" in 1584. The first duke of Lennox succeeded, concerning whose family see under the head of "Priory of S. Andrews." In 1606, the above lord John Hamilton was restored, and his son created marquis of Hamilton and lord Arbroath. His son, the first duke of Hamilton, was executed in London in 1649, leaving no surviving son. The earl of Dysart next obtained the property, who sold it, together with the patronage of thirty-four churches, to Mr. Maule, of Panmure. This earl left no male issue. Mr. Maule took part in the rebellion of 1715, and was forfeited. His son William bought back the property, but died unmarried in 1782, leaving it to a nephew who is still alive.

Scone. An Augustinian Abbey near Perth. Provost James Halyburton, of Dundee, a friend of John Knox, had a pension out of this Abbey, as a reward for his reforming zeal; but we have not been able to trace his progeny, if he had any. In 1581, James VI. made the first earl of Gowrie (the fifteenth of a family descent) commendator of Scone, who was attainted and executed in 1584. His eldest son James died without issue; and the latter's brother John, third earl of Gowrie, who succeeded to Scone, was killed in the Gowrie conspiracy; on which occasion the whole family was banished, their posterity denounced and disinherited for ever, and the name of Ruthven declared to be abolished in Scotland. Next, sir David Murray obtained the lands of Scone and Elcho (a nunnery), together with " ten chalders of victual " annually from the Priory of S. Andrews; with a substitution, failing himself and heirs, of different branches of his family and their heirs. This sir David died without issue. Sir Mungo Murray, a younger son of the earl of Tullibardine, succeeded, and died without issue. James Murray, second earl of Annandale, succeeded, and died in 1658, without issue; thus terminating a line of eighteen descents. The title and lands then went to William Murray of Letterbannathy, who is the ancestor of the present proprietor.

Lands of the Knights Templar of S. John of Jerusalem. Sir James Sandilands, then Preceptor of that order in Scotland, and the ninth of a family descent, joined the Reformation, obtained the estates, married, and was created lord Torphichen. Leaving no issue, the title and property devolved on his grand-nephew, James Sandilands of Calper.

Elcho. A Cistercian Nunnery in Strathearn. Lord Scone, as we have seen, got the lands of this religious house in 1605, and died issueless. In 1628, sir John Wemyss was made lord Wemyss of Elcho. His only son, David, was married three times, but left no surviving male issue.

INCHAFFERY. An Augustinian Abbey in Strathearn. The commendator at the Reformation was Gordon, bishop of Galloway, who, like most other prelates of the period, changed with the times, and dropt his episcopacy in order to keep his church preferment. He died in 1579, leaving three sons, none of whom had any male issue. We next find Alexander Ruthven commendator, who was killed in the conspiracy of Gowrie in 1600. James VI. then made James Drummond, second son of lord Drummond, commendator, with the title of baron Maderty, afterwards viscount Strathallan. The direct line failed in his grandson, who died issueless, in 1711. The property then passed to the sixth earl of Kinnoul, whose grandson Thomas, the eighth earl, died without children, in 1765.

———

SWEETHEART, Galloway, a Cistercian Abbey. Sir Robert Spottiswood (son of the archbishop) got it from Charles I. He was executed by the Covenanters, in 1646. One of his sons was also executed by them.

S. GILES, Edinburgh. John Knox, the sacrilegious Reformer, was twice married. By his first wife he had two sons, matriculated at S. John's College, Cambridge, eight days after their father's death in 1572. "It appears," says M'Crie, Knox's biographer, "that both of them died without issue, and the family became extinct in the male line." For, by his second wife, John Knox had no male issue. Knox himself is buried in the highway, and the very spot is unknown. His remains were interred in the churchyard of S. Giles, Edinburgh, which soon after was converted into, and still remains, a paved street.

HOLYROOD-HOUSE. An Augustinian Abbey in

Edinburgh. Lord Robert Stewart, natural son of James V., was abbat at the Reformation. He joined the Reformers, married, and retained his temporalities. He exchanged his Abbey with Bothwell, bishop of Orkney (also a love-lucre reformer), for the latter's diocesan lands and revenues; and was created earl of Orkney in 1581. His eldest son, Patrick, was forfeited, and executed at Edinburgh in 1614, leaving no issue. John Bothwell, a son of the bishop's, was made lord Holyrood-house in 1581. In 1587 the property was annexed to the crown, under the Annexation Act. In 1606, James VI. restored the title and lands to John Bothwell of Alhammer, another son of the bishop's, whose line also soon became extinct.

KELSO. A Tyronensian Abbey in Teviotdale. On the death, in 1558, of the eldest natural son of James V., who was abbat of this Monastery, the queen-regent bestowed its temporalities, with those of Melrose, on her brother, the cardinal of Guise; but it is doubtful if he ever drew any of them. Queen Mary gave these two abbacies to her husband, the earl of Bothwell. He was outlawed, forfeited, and died childless in 1577, thus ending a line of ten successions. In 1587, we find sir John (afterwards lord) Maitland of Thirlstane, commendator, the thirteenth of a lineal descent. He was succeeded by his son John, father of the well-known duke of Lauderdale, who left no male issue. Meanwhile the Kelso property had passed to the Crown in 1592, which, in 1607, erected it into a temporal lordship in favour of lord Roxburgh, the eleventh of a lineal succession. The same nobleman shared largely in the spoils of Holyrood-honse. His only surviving son, Harry, left four daughters, but no son.

HADDINGTON. A Cistercian Nunnery in that town. Sir W. Maitland of Lethington, the thir-

teenth of a family succession, had some of the lands
belonging to this house, but which were subsequently
taken from him on a charge of treason; after which
he was attainted, and ended his days by poison in
1573. He married twice, but had only one son, who
died childless.   James VI. next gave the lands to
sir John Ramsay in 1606, and created him viscount
Haddington. He married twice, but left no surviving children, in consequence of which the family
became extinct.   In 1621 the Nunnery lands were
bestowed on John, the second lord Thirlstane, whose
male line ended with his son, as mentioned above.

MELROSE.   A Cistercian Abbey in Teviotdale.
Queen Mary gave the revenues to her husband
Bothwell, whose fate has been mentioned.   Sir W.
Maitland of Lethington next came in for a considerable share of them, whose destiny we have noticed.
In 1592, Archibald, grandson of the sixth earl of
Morton, got six monks' annual portions from the
same source; but we have learnt nothing farther
concerning this pensioner. In 1609 sir John Ramsay
was made lord Melrose cum Haddington, whose end
we have seen.   Finally, sir Thomas Hamilton, who
had other monastic lands, was created lord Melrose
in 1619.   His eldest son, Thomas, was blown up by
gunpowder in 1640, along with a brother who was
beside him; and the only son of this Thomas died
issueless.

COLDSTREAM.   A Cistercian Nunnery on the
Tweed.   In 1621 this was erected into a temporal
barony in favour of sir John Hamilton, third son of
the above sir Thomas, earl of Melrose. He had only
one son, who died without issue.

JEDBURGH.   An Augustinian Abbey in Teviotdale.
One Andrew, commendator of this Abbey in 1593,
complains that, owing to the number of pensions
and monks' portions that had been granted to

private persons, he had little or nothing left to himself. This Andrew had also the Priory of Restennot; but who he was, and what became of him, we have not learnt. In 1606 Jedburgh and Coldingham were erected into a temporal lordship in favour of Alexander, first earl of Home, who was the fifteenth of his line. He had also some of the Abbey-lands of Kelso and Lesmahago. His only son, James, was twice married but had no issue. James VI. next made sir Andrew Ker of Fernihurst, lord Jedburgh, in 1622, who was the twelfth of a lineal family descent. He died without surviving issue. His brother James succeeded, whose son, the third lord, left no issue. The title and lands then passed to W. Ker of Ancrum, who was assassinated.

DRYBURGH and CAMBUSKENNETH. The first a Præmonstratensian abbey on the Tweed, the second an Augustinian Abbey on the Forth. John, the sixth earl of Mar, was the first lay commendator of these two Abbeys, after the Reformation. He became regent of Scotland, and died in 1572, "not without suspicion of poison." David Erskine was then made commendator of Dryburgh, and Adam Erskine, his cousin, commendator of Cambuskenneth. They were both forfeited and banished in 1572, for their concern in the "Raid of Ruthven." The Abbeys were then annexed to the Crown; but the greater part of both was, in 1606, erected into the temporal lordship of Cardross, in favour of the son of the seventh earl of Mar. The proprietorship of these lands has undergone various changes, but part of them still belong to the earl of Buchan, who is the descendant of the above lord Cardross.

COLDINGHAM. A Benedictine Abbey in Berwickshire. Lord John Stewart, natural son of James V.,

was prior of this Abbey at the Reformation.[1] Like
his brothers he changed with the times, kept his
temporalities, and married. His eldest son, Francis,
was created earl of Bothwell, but was outlawed and
forfeited. The Abbey was next granted to John,
one of the Maitlands of Lethington, who were all
forfeited in 1571. In 1581, Alexander, son of Alexander Home of Manderstone, was made commendator, under several protests from persons who had
previous claims upon the revenues. Why the Abbey
should have passed from the family we are not
aware ; but in 1592 it was annexed to the Crown
with a few exceptions. In 1606 it was given, along
with Jedburgh, to earl Home ; the fate of whose
family we have seen under the head of that Abbey.
In 1621, John Stewart, son of the forfeited earl of
Bothwell above mentioned, obtained Coldingham ;
but the family declined, and soon became extinct.

NEWBOTTLE. A Cistercian Abbey in Midlothian.
Mark Ker, son of sir Andrew Ker of Cessford, was
abbat at the Reformation. He joined the Reformers,
was made perpetual commendator, married, and had
a son Mark, who was created lord Newbottle and
earl of Lothian. His eldest son, Robert, died in
1624, leaving only two daughters.

ELBOTTLE. A Cistercian Nunnery on the Forth.
Charles I. gave this to sir James Maxwell, and
created him earl of Dirleton and lord Elbottle in
1646. He left only two daughters, and thus the
title and family became extinct.

CHURCH LANDS OF ABERNETHY. These were given
to David, the ninth earl of Crawford, in 1584. He
had only one son, who died in 1621, without issue.

[1] James V. drew the revenues of S. Andrew's Holyrood-house,
Kelso, and Coldingham, during the minority of his four natural
sons. He left no surviving male issue. His only daughter
Mary, and her son James VI., were still more contaminated by
sacrilege by giving away so many Church-lands to lay persons.
The final fate of the family is well known.

PRIORY OF S. ANDREWS.   An Augustinian Monastery in Fife.   The lord James Stewart, natural son
of James V., was the last prior.   He changed with
the times, and applied a large portion of the revenues
of S. Andrews and Pittenweem to his own use.   He
was shot at Linlithgow in 1571, leaving no male
issue; but his earldom of Moray was allowed to go
to one of his daughters, who married a Stewart.
The next commendator of the Priory was Robert
Stewart, brother of the earl of Lennox, who died
in 1586, without children.   Next to him was his
nephew Ludovick, second duke of Lennox, who was
married three times, but had no issue.   The property then passed to his brother Esme, third duke
of Lennox, whose grandson and heir died unmarried
in 1660.   The Priory was finally annexed to the
archbishopric of S. Andrews, and thus shared the
same fate with the other Scottish sees, which we
shall have to notice afterwards.

PORTMOAK.   An Augustinian Priory on Lochleven.
John Wynram, the Reformer, was made commendator.   In his old age, having no family, though
married, he made it over to S. Leonard's College,
S. Andrews, on the condition of drawing the income
during his life.

DEIR, in Kirshan, an Abbey of the Cluniac monks
(see Keith's Catalogue of the Scots Bishops, p. 422).
King James VI. first gave this abbey to Robert
Keith, son of William earl Marischall, and created
him lord Altrie.   Leaving only a daughter, the king
transferred the abbey to George earl Marischall,
whose wife had the dream here annexed:— . . .
" This was a fearfull presaige of the fattall punishment which did hing over the head of that noble
family, fortold by a terrible vission to his grandmother, efter the sacraleidgious annexing of the
abace of Deir to the house of Marshell; which I think

not unworthie the remembrance, were it bot to adwyce other noblemen therby to bewar of meddling with the rent of the Church ; for in the first foundation thereof they were given out with a curse pronounced in ther charactor, or evident of the first erectione, in those terms : ' *Cursed be those that taketh this away from the holy use whereunto it is now dedicat ;*' and I wish from my heart that this curse follow not this ancient and noble familie, who hath, to their praise and never dieing honour, conteinued ther greatness, maintained ther honor, and both piously and constantly hes followed forth the way of virtue, from that time that the valoure, worth, and happy fortune of ther first predecessores planted them ; and ever since the currage of his heart, strenth of his arme, and love of his contrey, made him happily to resist the cruell Danes in that famous field of Barry, wher he gained to his nation a nottable victorie, to his contrey a following peace, and to his posteritie both riches and dignitie by that noble and high preferment to be marishell of the whole kingdom.

"George, earle Marishell, a learned, wyse, and upright good man, got the abacie of Dier in recompence from James the Sixt, for the honorable chairge he did bear in that ambassage he had into Denmerk, and the wyse and worthie accompt he gave of it at his returne, by the conclusion of that matche whereof the royal stock of Brittanes monarchie is descended.

"This earle George his first wife, dochter to the lord Home, and grandmother to this present earle, being a woman both of a high spirit, and of a tender conscience, forbids her husband to leave such a consuming moth in his house, as was the sacraledgeous medling with the abisie of Deir ; but fourtein scoir chalderes of meill and beir was a sore tentatione, and he could not weel indure the randering back of such a morsell. Vpon his absolut refusall of her demand, she had this vission the night following.

"In her sleepe she saw a great number of religious men in ther habit com forth of that abbey to the strong Craige of Dunnothure, which is the principall residence of that familie. She saw them also sett themselves round about the rock to gett it down and demolishe it, having no instruments nor toilles wherewith to perform this work, but only penknyves, wherewith they follishly (as seemed to her) begane to pyk at the craige. She smyled to sie them intende so fruitless ane interpryse, and went to call her husband to scuffe and geyre them out of it. When she had fund him and brought him to sie these sillie religious monckes at ther foolish work, behold, the whole Craige, with all his stronge and stately buildings, was by ther penknyves undermynded, and fallen in the sea, so as ther remained nothing but the wrack of the riche furnitore and stufe flotting on the waves of a rageing and tempestous sea.

"Some of the wyser sort, divining upon this vission, attribute to the penknyves the lenth of tym befor this should com to pass, and it hath bein observed by sundrie that the earles of that house befor wer the richest in the kingdom, having treasure and store besyde them, but ever since the addition of this so great a revenue, theye have lessed the stock by heavie burdenes of debt and ingagement."

Extracted from "A Short Abridgment of Britane's Distemper, from the year of God M.DC.XXXIX. to M.DC.XLIX., by Patrick Gordon of Ruthven," pp. 112, 113, 114. Ed. Spalding Club.

N.B. The author died previous to the restoration, and consequently long before the downfall of the noble family of Marischal, in 1715.

S. Alban's* and its Manors. Sir Thomas Pope (founder of Trinity College, Oxford), was one of the

* For these particulars we are indebted to a very interesting article in the *Christian Remembrancer* of August 2, 1843, on S. Alban's Abbey.

commissioners for the surrender of the Premier Abbey:—he obtained for himself Tittenhanger, the abbat's country house.

Sir Thomas was thrice married, and left only one daughter, Alice, who died very young. His third wife was Elizabeth, daughter of Walter Blount. Thomas Blount, the heir of her brother William, inherited Tittenhanger from his uncle sir Thomas Pope, and called himself Pope-Blount. Of this family sir Henry Blount was a sceptic, and pulled down the house. His son, Charles Blount, "inherited his father's philosophy," and was the notorious infidel author of the "Anima Mundi," and "Oracles of Reason." After his wife's death, this wretched man shot himself, because he could not form an incestuous marriage with his wife's sister, which account Warton (in his life of sir T. Pope) says, that he received from "the late sir H. Pope-Blount, the last of the family." But to pursue the subject; and we have been at some little pains to trace the descent of other church-lands in this immediate neighbourhood.

The site and buildings of Sopwell Nunnery, founded by Robert de Gorham, the sixteenth abbat, were granted by Henry VIII. to a sir Richard Lee, as well as the monastic buildings of S. Alban's Abbey and the parish church of S. Andrew, all of which he pulled down: according to Newcome, he was indebted for this wicked grant to the charms of his wife, one Margaret Greenfield, "who was in no small favour with the king:" he died without male issue, and his lands passed into the Sadleir family. At the time of the restoration, the male line of the Sadleirs became extinct, and the property passed to the Saunders' family; the male line of which being extinct, it was sold to the Grimston family, the present possessors.

Again; the hospital of S. Mary de Prè, near S. Alban's, was suppressed by Wolsey, who afterwards obtained a grant of these lands for his own use; his fate is sufficiently notorious; after his attainder, it was forfeited to the crown, and granted to Ralph Rowlat, esq., on the failure of whose male line, it was purchased from a female descendant, by sir Harbottle Grimston, the ancestor of the earl of Verulam, the present possessor.

Again ; Gorhambury, the seat of the earl of Verulam, was originally part of the abbey-lands, and granted by abbat Robert de Gorham to a relation of the same name, who erected a mansion on it, hence called Gorhambury : it was reannexed to the abbey by abbat De la Mare, and at the dissolution, was granted to the above Ralph Rowlat, esq. ; on the failure of his heirs male, his daughter conveyed it to —. Maynard ; he sold it to lord chancellor Bacon, who died without issue, and, as is well known, the title and family of the Bacons became extinct.   Sir Thomas Meautys, lord Bacon's private secretary, inherited Gorhambury as cousin and next heir ; he died heirless, leaving an only daughter, who died unmarried ; sir Thomas's elder brother succeeded him, who (or his representative) sold the estates to sir Harbottle Grimston above-mentioned.

Again, the manor of Childwick, formerly belonging to the abbey, was held by Thomas Rowse in 1561.   He died leaving one son, who died without issue.

Again, the manor of Newlend Squillers, formerly belonging to the abbey, was granted to sir Richard Lee above-named : on the extinction of his race it was conveyed to Richard Grace, who died without male issue.

Again, the manor of Aldenham belonged either to this abbey or to S. Peter's, Westminster ; at the dissolution it was granted to Ralph Stepneth and his heirs for ever, but he died without male issue ; from his collateral heirs it passed into the Cary family, the last of whom, the celebrated Lucius lord Falkland, was killed in a particularly strange and awful manner at the battle of Newbury : it then passed into the Harby family, the male line of which became extinct in 1674 : and from them to the Holles family, the direct line of which became extinct in 1711, by the death of the duke of Newcastle, who left an only daughter who carried the property into the Pelham family.

We have only selected the first seven estates, formerly belonging to the Church, from a common county history, and here we find the families of Pope, Blount, Lee, Sadleir, Saunders, Wolsey, Rowlat, Bacon, Meautys, Rowse, Grace, Stepneth, Cary, Harby, Holles, invariably failing in the male line; fifteen families in succession possessed these abbey-lands, and every one of them is extinct.

NETLEY Abbey, three miles from Southampton. " The destruction of the Abbey Church or Chapel," according to Browne Willis, " commenced about the period when it was inhabited by the marquis of Huntingdon, who converted the nave, or west-end, into a kitchen and offices. Sir Bartlet Lucy," as appears from this writer (but others say the marquis of Huntingdon), " sold the materials of the whole fabric to Mr. Walter Taylor, a builder, of Southampton, soon after the beginning of the last century, for the purpose of removing them to erect a townhouse at Newport, and dwelling-houses at other places. An accident which befel Mr. Taylor, in consequence of this purchase, and which afterwards led to his death, has been regarded by the vulgar as a judgment inflicted by Heaven, for this presumed guilt, in undertaking to destroy a sacred edifice; but more enlightened understandings can only regard it as the effect of a fortuitous combination of circumstances in perfect accordance with the established laws of nature." The original narrative of this event, as given by Browne Willis, is in several particulars erroneous, as appears from an inquiry made of Mr. Taylor's family; and the substance of

which is as follows :—" After Mr. Taylor had made
his contract, some of his friends observed in conver-
sation, that they would never be concerned in the
demolition of holy and consecrated places ; these
words impressed his memory so strongly that he
dreamed, that, in taking down the Abbey, the key-
stone of the arch of the east window fell from its
place and killed him.   This dream he related to Mr.
Watts (father of Dr. Isaac Watts), who advised him
not to have any personal concern in pulling down
the building; yet this advice being insufficient to
deter him from assisting in the work, the creations
of sleep were unhappily realized ; for in endeavouring to remove some boards from the east window to
admit air to the workmen, a stone fell and fractured
his skull.   The fracture was not thought mortal ;
but in the operation of extracting a splinter, the
surgeon's instrument entered the brain and caused
immediate death.   Whether this accident caused
a direct stop to be put to the demolition of the
Abbey is uncertain, but the superstitious gloom
which it generated has evidently tended to preserve
the ruins in more modern times."—*Partington's
British Cyclopædia, Geography*, vol. iii., under the
head " Netley Abbey."

———

" The nunnery of EASEBOURN or ESSEBURN, was
founded about the reign of Henry III., by John
Bohun, baron Midhurst, for a prioress and five nuns
of the Benedictine order.   Their revenues were small,
and there is a singular variation in the amounts
stated—by Dugdale, £29 16s. 7d. ; by Speed,
£47 13s. 9d.   These possessions, with the site,
were granted by Henry VIII. A.D. 1537, to William,
earl of Southampton, including the demesnes of
the priory, the manor of Worthing in Broadwater,
the rectory of Compton, with the chapels of Midhurst, Fernhurst, and Lodsworth.   The nunnery
house and remains are still extensive, situated

on the N.E. side of Cowdray Park. It retains the dormitory and cells, with the refectory, the windows of all which were uniformly pointed, but which are now walled up; which alteration took place when sir David Owen converted the whole into a dwelling house. Queen Elizabeth was entertained here during her visit at Cowdray. The refectory is now used as a barn; the cloister which connected the house with the south aisle of the parish church (which was the nuns' chapel) no longer remains; and the aisle afterwards used for sepulture is ruinous and roofless. The nuns had their own chaplain and heard mass through internal windows or grates, the neglect of repairing which was exhibited among other complaints at an episcopal visitation. (Bp. Story, 1478.) No documents furnish a list of the prioresses in succession,—the following names only have occurred:—In 1472, Agnes Tawke; in 1521, Joan Sackfylde; in 1534, Elizabeth Sackville; and 1535, Margaret Sackville, who was then prioress, and resigned the convent into the hands of the king's visitors."

The above is *verbatim* from Dallaway; what follows is gathered from his Genealogy of the Montague Family.

Sir Willian Fitz William, who was created earl of Southampton, by Henry VIII., A.D. 1537, and to whom the same king gave the nunnery of Easebourne, died *sine prole*, A.D. 1542. At his death the estate went to the Montague family, the earl's father having married Lucy, fourth daughter and coheiress of John Nevil, marquis of Montague. This lady appears to have married secondly sir Anthony Brown, knt., by whom she had Anthony, who became the heir of the earl of Southampton, A.D. 1542. He was knighted for his eminent services in winning Morlaix, in Brittany. Sir Anthony died A.D. 1548, and was succeeded by his eldest son, Anthony, who, on the first of May, was advanced to the dignity of baron and viscount Monta-

gue. His only son and heir dying in his lifetime,
he was succeeded by his grandson, who had one son,
Francis, who became his heir, and six daughters.
Francis had Anthony, the first-born, who died in
his father's lifetime unmarried; Francis, Henry, and
Elizabeth.

Francis, the eldest *surviving* son, succeeded to the
title and estates A.D. 1682, and died *sine prole*, A.D.
1708.

Henry, his brother, became heir. He had six
daughters and one son, Anthony, who succeeded
him A.D. 1717.

Anthony had two sons, the eldest of whom died
at Rouen, aged one year; the second, Anthony,
became his heir in 1767.

Anthony died in 1787, and was succeeded by his
son,

George Samuel, born 1769; he enjoyed the title
but six years, being drowned at the age of twenty-
four, in an unfortunate attempt to descend the falls
of Schaffhausen, in October, 1793, accompanied by
Mr. Sedley Burdett, who shared the same fate.*
The previous month, September 24th, 1793, his
splendid residence at Cowdray, founded by the earl
of Southampton,—in which, A.D. 1591, Queen Elizabeth had been entertained,—with its noble hall and
chapel, was totally destroyed by fire, and remains a
ruin to this day. Lord Montague lost his life
before the news of this calamity could reach him,
and his estates passed by will to Elizabeth Mary,
his only sister and heiress, wife of W. S. Poyntz,
esq. The title passed to another branch of the
family, and very soon became extinct.

Since Dallaway's history was published, the following events have occurred to the holders of this
property.

Mr. Poyntz, by Elizabeth Mary, sister and heir of
viscount Montague, had two sons, twins, and three
daughters. These ladies are now living; the two

* See more on this attempt in Appendix II.

sons came to an untimely end, being upset in a boat with their father off the coast of Bognor. Mr. Poyntz was hardly saved—his sons both perished; and consequently on his death, two or three years since, his daughters succeeded to the estate, which they sold to its present possessor, the earl of Egmont, who is *sine prole*.

WEST DEAN Priory, Sussex. Sir — Peachy, citizen of London, purchased the estates of this priory and its site, formerly called Canon Park, and by act of parliament had it enfranchised from the claims of the Dean and Chapter of Chichester. In 1794, the then baronet was created baron Selsey. The family in the male line became extinct in 1839; on which the estates devolved on the honourable Mrs. V. Harcourt, who has no issue. The property is entailed on the marquis of Clanricarde, whose interest in it is already disposed of.

BATTLE Abbey, Sussex. This place came into the possession of the Websters in the last century. Sir Thomas Webster, first baronet, had issue sir Whistler, second baronet, who was married, but died childless, and was succeeded by his brother, sir Godfrey, who had one son, sir Godfrey. He married Elizabeth Vassal; the marriage was dissolved by act of parliament,—he committed suicide, June 3, 1800, and the lady married lord Holland.

BOXGROVE Priory, Sussex. It is in the duke of Richmond. Charles, fourth duke, had issue, besides other children, lord Henry Lennox, who was drowned in Port Mahon. His grace died in Canada, from the bite of a mad fox. The present duke, besides other children, had issue lord William Lennox, supposed to be lost in the President steamship.

The impropriation of SALEHURST, Sussex, which belonged to the abbey of Robertsbridge, was in the Peckhams.

William Peckham died April 5, 1679. From him the property descended to William Peckham, who

died January 24, 1765. He had five sons and
two daughters, who all died single, except the
younger daughter, married to John Micklethwait,
esq. From William Peckham, the tithes passed to
his son George Peckham. He died May 28, 1788,
and was succeeded by John Micklethwait, son to
the before-named John. He, dying without issue,
devised these, with other estates, to his nephew, the
present sir S. B. Peckham-Micklethwait, married in
1809, but without issue. Under the will of his
uncle, the estates will pass to the rev. J. N. Micklethwait, a bachelor. It appears that from 1679 to
1845, the estates have only twice passed in the direct
line of descent. The abbey-lands of Robertsbridge
were, as is well known, sold to pay the debts of the
late sir Godfrey Vassal-Webster, father of the present
baronet.

The family of EGREMONT, lately extinct, is a strange
instance of the curse of Church property. The last
earl but one possessed vast estates in England and
Ireland; but he left all that he could among three
illegitimate sons, and several daughters. The last
earl was, comparatively, heir to but little.

Lands of CHERTSEY Abbey. Of the abbey-site we
have already spoken. The hundred of Chertsey is
still called in all legal documents " Godsley," that
is to say, GOD'S Ley or Land, from the fact that
almost the entire land contained in it was Church
property, and appertained to the abbey. The estates
which seem chiefly to possess it at the present time
are those of Botleys, Ottershaw, S. Ann's Hill,
Simplemarsh, and Thorpe Manor.

Botleys. This manor was purchased by the crown
in 1541, of sir Robert Cholmeley, and conferred with
a portion of the abbey-lands, upon George Salter
and John Williams, by James I., May 22, 1610. In
August, the same year, the estate was conveyed to
William Garwaie and his heirs. This family becoming extinct, it was bought by Mr. Samuel Hall,

whose widow sold it (on the death of her only son) to Joseph Mawbey, esq., who was created baronet in 1765. In 1761, died his first-born daughter, Elizabeth, aged twelve days. In 1766, died his second son, Onslow, aged six months. In 1770, died his last-born son, Pratt, aged eight years. In 1775, died his daughter, Sophia, aged four years. In 1785, died his daughter, Emma, aged ten years. In 1790, died Dame Elizabeth Mawbey, wife of sir Joseph. In 1798, died sir Joseph, leaving issue Joseph, who succeeded him in his estate; Emily, who died in 1819, aged twenty-nine, unmarried; Catharine, who died without issue; and Mary, who died 1800. Sir Joseph II. left one daughter, who is married to J. Brisco, esq., without hope of heirs. The present possessor is — Gosling, esq.

Ottershaw. The first mention of this estate after the dissolution is in 1540, at the death of John Bannister, esq., leaving one daughter, who married Owen Bray, esq., of Chobham, and died without heirs-male. It now fell into the hands of a yeoman, named Roake, whose son married Margaret Porter, of Woking, in 1684, and died in 1722, without issue. He was succeeded by his brother, who sold it the same year to Law Porter, esq. This gentleman parted with it to Thomas Woodford, of Threadneedle Street, who in 1758 bequeathed it to his son the rev. W. Woodford. In April, 1761, he sold it to Thomas Sewell, esq., who married, 1. Catharine Heath, by whom he had several children; 2. in 1773, Mary Elizabeth Sibthorpe, by whom he had one child, who died in infancy. He died 1784, leaving a son, who married the daughter of the earl of Louth, whom he divorced in 1779, before his father's death. He having no children, the estate was sold in 1795, to Edmund Boehm, esq., who was ruined by smuggling 1817. It then fell to Mr. James Bine, afterwards to (sir—and) lady Wood, whose son losing his fortune, sold it to — Crawshaw, esq., the present possessor.

S. Ann's Hill.—This estate was in possession of
the crown until 1728, when it belonged successively
to Catharine Barton, John Barton, and Mary Trevor,
spinster, whose family afterwards surrendered it to
lord Charles Spencer, from whom, in 1778, it fell
to the duke of Marlborough, who sold it to Mrs.
Armistead, afterwards wife and widow of Mr. Fox.
Lord Holland is the present possessor.

Simplemarsh. In 1614, this estate was granted
by the crown to Francis Morris and Francis Philips,
who sold it to Richard Tylney, esq., in 1616. It
afterwards came to John Tylney, viscount Castle-
main, who sold it to Aaron Franks, 1737. In 1807,
it was again sold by his descendants to Mr. Pem-
oroke, attorney. In 1810, it was bought by George
Holme Sumner, esq., whose son possesses it at the
present time.

Thorpe Manor. At the dissolution, the abbey-
lands in the parish of Thorpe remained in the possession of the Crown until 1590, when they were granted
by Elizabeth to her Latin secretary, sir John Woolley.
His only son, sir Francis Woolley, succeeded him,
and died at the age of twenty-eight without issue.
He bequeathed the estate to his cousin, William
Minterne, who also died without heirs-male, and the
estate by the marriage of his daughter Elizabeth
passed to sir Francis Leigh, bart. It then by default
of heirs-male fell to Mary and Ann Leigh, who
married respectively into the families of Spencer
and Bennett, in 1731 and 1737. Upon a consequent
division of the estates, the manor, rectory, and abbey-
lands, came into the hands of the Bennett family,
with whom they still remain, the present heir being
grandson of the original possessor of that name.

NEWARK Priory. The temporalities of this foundation seem to have been the manors of Hertmere
(Godalming), Puttenham, and Send; besides divers
other small farms, still in possession of the crown.

Manor of Hertmere. In the reign of Henry III.
Thomas de Hertmere conferred this estate upon the

prior and convent of Newark. In the year 1540, Henry VIII. resolved to obtain for himself the manor of Stanwell, in Middlesex, the property of lord Windsor, whose ancestors had occupied it since the Norman conquest. He, therefore, signified to the baron that he must surrender his estate, and offered him in exchange the manor of Hertmere, late in the possession of Newark. Lord Windsor, sorely against his will, was compelled to obey, and in the year 1549 his family was totally extinct. Eustace More was the next possessor, who, in 1556, died without issue ; and left the manor to his nephew, Edward More, whose family shortly becoming extinct, it again reverted to the Crown. It was next divided between a distant relation of the last family and one Anthony Gooch, esq., who died without heirs. The estate was then united under sir Edward More, whose only child died in infancy. It was afterwards sold to — Bennet, esq., and in default of heirs-male it passed to the earls of Salisbury, one of whom sold it to John Richardson, whose son occupied it in 1811.

Manor of Send. (See p. 181.)

Manor of Puttenham. Henry VIII. granted this part of Newark priory to Edward Elrington and Humphrey Metcalf, but nothing more appears to be known of it till 1627, when it belonged to William Minterne. In 1636 it was possessed by the Leighs, and passed quickly through the hands of six generations, when the family becoming involved, it was mortgaged to John Kenrick, esq., who retained it until the only child of the last Leigh, a daughter (who married J. Jones, esq.), became re-possessed of it. Her husband sold it to James Oglethorpe, esq., in 1744, who, in 1761, parted with it to Thomas Parker. In 1775, the whole was sold by auction, and the property became separated. The manor-house was bought by Admiral Cornish, who died without heirs. Richard Sumner is the present owner.

POSSESSIONS OF THE ABBEY OF WESTMINSTER, in
Surrey. *Manor of Claygate*, Thames Ditton. In
the reign of Edward the Confessor, this estate was
granted to the abbey of Westminster, but by whom
is not known. At the dissolution, it was granted
to sir Thomas Heneage, but shortly after reverted
to the Crown. Edward VI. gave it to John Child,
esq., who soon sold it to David Vincent, esq. He
died in 1565, leaving it to his son, who died childless. The lands then fell to his sister, married to
George Evelyn. Their grandson leaving no heirs-
male, the manor was divided between his two
daughters, who married respectively sir Joseph
Alston and sir Stephen Glyn. They both appear
to have died childless. The whole was shortly
purchased by lord chancellor King. He left five
sons, who at his death, in 1734, possessed it one
after another, and left no heirs except the youngest,
who died in 1779, leaving an only child, whose son
inherits the estate.

Manor of Pirford. By the surrender of the
abbey of Westminster, 1539, this manor became
vested in the Crown; and by letters patent was, in
1558, granted to the monastery of Shene, refounded
at this time. This being also dissolved in less than
a year, it reverted to the Crown. Queen Elizabeth
granted it to Edward, earl of Lincoln, but in less
than six years after his death (which happened in
1584) we find it in possession of John Woolley, esq.
He married Elizabeth, daughter of sir William More,
of Losely, by whom he had one son Francis. He
was knighted in 1592, and died in 1595. He left
only one legitimate child, Francis, who succeeded to
the abbey-lands, the greatest part of his remaining
property falling to a natural daughter. This son
died without issue at the age of twenty-seven, 1610.
The manor then fell to sir Arthur Mainwaring, a
distant relation, who, in 1635, sold it to Robert
Parkhurst, citizen of London. This gentleman died

in 1636, his son in 1651, his grandson in 1674, whose children being in want of money, sold it to Denzil Onslow, esq. Thomas Onslow his son succeeded him in 1717, and was twice married, but had issue by neither wife. He dying in 1721, the manor of Pirford was occupied by his second wife till her death in 1729, when it passed to another branch of the family, which becoming extinct with the next heir, it descended to the earls of Onslow, the third earl being the present possessor.

BINDON, Benedictine House, Dorsetshire.
Granted to,
1. Thomas lord Poynings, married, but died without issue; in 1546, to, 2. Thomas, afterwards lord Howard of Bindon; in 1582, to, 3. Henry his son, died without male issue; in 1590, to, 4. Thomas his brother, died without issue; in 1619, to, 5. Thomas earl of Suffolk; in 1626, to, 6. Theophilus his son; in 1640, to, 7. James his son, died without male issue; in 1641, sold to, 8. W. Humphrey Weld; 9. *sequestered;* in 1685, sold to, 10. William Weld, nephew of Humphrey; in 1698, to, 11. His son Humphrey; in 1722, to, 12. His son Edward; in 1761, to, 13. His son Edward.
SHAPWICK, Carthusian House, Dorsetshire.
Granted, in 1545, to,
George Rolle; in 1546, to, 2. Robert Ryves; to, 3. John Ryves; to, 4. George Ryves; to, 5. Thomas Shovel; to, 6. George Turberville; to, 7. J. Gundry; to, 8. William More; to, 9. John Harding; to, 10. William Fry; to, 11. Henry Banks. In two hundred and twelve years, only twice descended from father to son.
DORCHESTER, Franciscan Friary.
Granted, 1544, to,
1. Sir Edward Packham; to, 2. Wriothesley earl

of Southampton; to, 3. John Strangeman; to, 4. John his son; to, 5. — Harben; circ. 1610, to, 6. Robert Samways; 1621, to, 7. His grandson Bernard Samways, died without male issue; 1645, to, 8. Sir Francis Ashley, died without male issue; to, 9. Denzil lord Holles, who by three marriages had only one son that survived him, and in whose grandson the family became extinct; to, 10. John earl of Clare, died without issue; to, 11. Thomas duke of Newcastle; to, 12. John Browne.

In about two hundred and twenty years it descended once only from father to son.

CERNE ABBAS, Benedictine Monastery, Dorsetshire.

In 1539, to, 1. Philip Vanwelder; 1564, to, 2. John Fowler; 1574, to, 3. John Dudley, &c.; 1574, to, 4. Edmund Downing, &c.; 1612, to, 5. Henry prince of Wales, died young; 1618, to, 6. Sir Francis Bacon; 1618, to, 7. Charles prince of Wales; 1628, to, 8. Edward Ditchfield; 1628, to 9. City of London; ——, to, 10. Sir Thomas Freke; 1633, to, 11. His son John Freke, who appears to have died the same year; 1633, to, 12. His son John Freke, died without issue; 1657, to 13. His brother Thomas Freke, died without issue; 1698, to, 14. Thomas Pile, in whose time the abbey-house was burnt down; 1702, to, 15. Thomas Freke; 1714, to, 16. George Pitt of Strathfieldsay; to, 17. His son George Pitt.

In two hundred and twenty years the estate passed only twice—we might almost say only once—from father to son.

——

[FOUNTAINS, a Cistercian Abbey, was granted at the dissolution to sir Richard Gresham. It passed through various families, and was at length purchased by William Aislabie, esquire, of Studley.

(This estate was brought into the Aislabie family by marriage with the daughter and heiress of sir John Mallorie, a distinguished loyalist.)

About 200 yards from the abbey is Fountains Hall, built from a part of its ruins by sir Stephen Proctor, one of the esquires to James I., but is not now occupied as a mansion.—S. R. Clarke, " Yorkshire Gazetteer."]—[E.]

GUISBOROUGH Priory, Yorkshire. The lands were in the family of Chaloner. The late possessor became a banker at York and Leeds, failed, and is now land-steward to earl Fitzwilliam, in county Wicklow, Ireland.

RIEVAULX Abbey. The property of this once noble Cistercian abbey and the adjoining town and castle of Helmsley, will remain a monument of the curse on spoilers so long as Pope's lines exist, beginning —

" In the worst inn's worst room,"——

and ending,

" And Helmsley, noble Buckingham's delight,
Slide to a scrivener or a city knight."

[The facts are stated somewhat indistinctly above. Rievaulx, at the dissolution of the monasteries, was granted to Thomas, earl of Rutland, by Henry VIII.* It cmae into possession of George Villiers, first duke of Buckingham, by his marriage with the heiress of the Rutland family; the trustees of his dissipated son sold it in 1695 to sir Charles Duncombe, the ancestor of its present proprietor (now earl of Feversham).—S. R. Clarke, " Yorkshire Gazetteer."]—[E.]

[TEMPLE NEWSAM (Yorkshire) was a manor of the Knights Templars, having been bestowed upon them by William de Villers about 1180. At the suppres-

* His eldest son Henry succeeded as earl, and had issue Edward, the third earl, who died without male issue, leaving a daughter only.

sion of the Order it was given to the Darcy family, which possessed it until it was forfeited by lord Darcy for the active part which he took in the insurrection called the Pilgrimage of Grace. Henry VIII. conferred it on the earl of Lennox, father of Henry earl of Darnley, husband of Mary queen of Sc)ts. He was born here, and his murder at Kirk-of-Field, near Edinburgh, is well known. The estate reverted again to the crown in the reign of James I., who gave it to his kinsman, Esme Stuart, duke of Richmond. Of him it was purchased by sir Arthur Ingram, the son of a wealthy citizen of London, who was afterwards created lord Irvine. That peerage is extinct, but the manor has passed into the Hertford family. " The embayed and spacious windows and the deep, projecting wings of this mansion give it much the appearance of a college, and the resemblance would have been more complete had not the chapel been converted into a kitchen."—S. R. Clarke, " Yorkshire Gazetteer."]—[E.]

———

ETWALL Manor, Derbyshire : belonged to the priory of Beauval, in Nottinghamshire. The appropriate rectory to Welbeck Abbey, in the same county. It was granted to sir John Port, whose son, sir John, died without heirs-male. His elder daughter brought it to sir Thomas Gerard, whose great-grandson, sir William Gerard, sold it in 1641, to sir Edward Mosley ; the family is extinct. From him it was purchased, 1646, by sir Samuel Sleigh, thrice married, but left only one daughter, who married Rowland Cotton, of Bellaport, in Salop, esq. The manor, etc., are now vested in the trustees of William Cotton, esq., a lunatic.

———

CHICKSANDS Priory, Beds. This priory has brought

great misery on its lay-occupants; but we are not at liberty to enter into the particulars.

CALDER Abbey, Cumberland, granted to Thomas Leigh, LL.D.; in his family it continued till the time of sir Ferdinando Leigh, who sold it to sir R. Fletcher, who gave it in marriage with his daughter Barbara to Mr. John Patrickson, whose son Richard Patrickson sold it to Mr. Tiffin, who gave it to his grandson Joseph Seahouse, whose daughter, married to Captain Irwin, is in possession of the property. Thus it seems to have only twice passed from father to son.

CATESBY Nunnery, Northamptonshire. On the extinction of the family of the Onleys, to which it was originally granted, it came to that of the Parkhursts. Charles Parkhurst, esq., who lived at the beginning of this century, was the last of the name; he had one son, who died an infant; and the property came, by a daughter, into its present possessors, the Baxters. The proprietors of Catesby have, within the last hundred years, been two or three times in the Fleet. Our informant speaks of Catesby as " this unhappy estate." It is remarkable that the adjacent estates, Fawsley and Thuckburgh, were each in the family of its present possessor for several generations previous to the Reformation.

COFTON CHAPEL, near Dawlish, is said to be connected with a strange tale of the fate of sacrilege; but we are not able to relate the full particulars.

GLASTONBURY. " The next building, worth most observation, that is now in being, is the Market-house. It is a neat pile of building, built of late years with some materials the town had from the old abbey. But I was told by a man of credit, living in the neighbourhood of Glastonbury, that the town hath lost, in a great measure, their market since its building, which he imputed to its being built with materials that belonged to the church; and whoever reads sir H. Spelman's History of Sacrilege will not wonder that such a fate should attend it."—*Hearne's* [*Rawlinson's*] *Hist. of Glastonbury*, p. 104.

CHAPTER VIII.

Of Families, wherein Church Property has, or is said to have, continued.

THE younger Tanner says,—" If the abbey-lands did not continue long in some families, they continued a great while in others. Tavistock, Woburn, and Thorney Abbeys were granted to John lord Russell, and are yet the duke of Bedford's. Burton-upon-Trent was granted to sir William Paget, 37 Henry VIII., and is now the estate of the earl of Uxbridge. Thetford and Bungay were granted to the duke of Norfolk; Newstead, in Nottinghamshire, was granted to sir James Byron, and is still lord Byron's; Margan was granted to sir Rice Mansell, and is still lord Mansell's,* etc., etc."— (*Nasmith's Ed. Pref.* p. 25, *Note* 2.)

The case of the Russells we shall notice presently. The Pagets—and it is difficult to believe that Tanner could have been ignorant of it—are not a case in point; the original family are extinct in the male line; and that now assuming the name is properly Bayly. The pedigree is this:—

Sir William Paget, the original grantee, created lord Paget, 1549, was succeeded by his eldest son, who died without children. To him succeeded his brother Thomas, third baron Paget; to him his son, William, fourth baron; to him his son, William, fifth baron. This William had two sons. The elder, William, sixth baron, had one son, Henry, created earl of Uxbridge, 1714. The earl had one son who died before his father; and on his son dying without heirs, the earldom became extinct. But the barony of Paget, being a barony in fee, devolved on the other branch of the family.

For Henry, second son of the fifth baron, settled

---

* This peerage is apparently extinct.

in Ireland, and had issue one son, Thomas, who died without heirs-male; his only daughter, Caroline [or Catherine] married sir Nicholas Bayly, and their son succeeded to the barony of Paget, and was afterwards created earl of Uxbridge.

Thetford was granted to the duke of Norfolk; but is now in lord Petre.

Bungay, when Taylor wrote, was in Wolfran Lewis, esq., and others.

Newstead was a most unhappy example at best; but the abbey belongs now to Colonel Wildman, who has no issue.

The family of the Mansells became extinct in the male line six years after Tanner wrote.

So that of all Tanner's instances, the Russells are the only case that is pertinent at the present time.

We believe that the following list embraces nearly, if not quite, all those families which have held abbey sites in the male line from the Dissolution to the present time. There may be, here and there, a detached abbey manor remaining in the same family; had we, however, discovered any such not heretofore named, they should have been stated here.

Brooke......of Norton, Cheshire.
Cecil ....of Woolstrop (marquis of Exeter).
Croke ......of Stodely, Oxon.
Cotton ......of Combermere, Cheshire (viscount
                        Combermere).
Fortescue...of Cokehill, Worcestershire.
Giffard ......of Brewood, Staffordshire.
Heneage ...of Sixhills, Lincolnshire.
Luttrell ...of Dunster, Somersetshire.
Manners ...of Belvoir, Notts (duke of Rutland).
Nevill ......of Brading, Leicestershire.
Russell ......of Woburn, Beds (duke of Bedford).
Somerset ...of Tinterne, Monmouthshire (duke
                        of Beaufort).
Thynne......of Longleat, Wilts (marquis of Bath).
Wynne ......of Conway, Caernarvonshire (baron
                        Newborough).

Among these families we notice the following :—
CECIL, marquis of Exeter.   The second, seventh,
and ninth earls died without issue-male.

———

COTTON, of Combermere.—Sir George Cotton, first
grantee, had one son, Richard Cotton, esq., who
was succeeded by his eldest son, George Cotton;
and he by his eldest son, Thomas.   This gentleman
had one son, sir Robert Cotton, first baronet, whose
three eldest sons died in their father's lifetime, and
without issue-male; the fourth son, sir Thomas,
succeeded.   He had seven sons, all of whom, except
the youngest, died without issue-male.   Sir Robert,
the eldest, was third baronet: sir Lynch, the
youngest, the fourth; his son, sir Robert, was the
fifth; and his son, sir Stapleton, created first
viscount Combermere.   His lordship has lost his
three eldest sons.

———

Of John Russell, first earl of BEDFORD, it will be
sufficient to refer to Burke's character.   He had
but one son, Francis, second earl, whose eldest son,
Edward, died in his father's lifetime, without children; the second son, John, died also in his father's
lifetime, without heirs-male; the third son, Francis,
was slain the day before his father's death.   Edward,
son of this Francis, succeeded as third earl, but
died childless.   His cousin (Francis, grandson of the
second earl by his fourth son), succeeded as fourth
earl.   He was succeeded by his eldest son, William,
fifth earl and first duke; of his sons, Francis, the
eldest, died young; William was beheaded on a
charge of high treason; John died young; Edward
and Robert died without children; George left one
son, who died without children.   Wriothesley, son
of the beheaded lord Russell, succeeded as second
duke.   Of the second duke's sons, William died
young; Wriothesley succeeded as third duke, but
died without children; John succeeded as fourth

duke ;—he had but one son, Francis, who was killed by a fall from his horse ; and was succeeded by his grandson, Francis, fifth duke, who died without issue. His brother, John, succeeded as sixth duke ; who was succeeded by his eldest son, Francis, present duke ; and he has one son, the present marquis of Tavistock. We add the following to this account.

" Sir Francis Russell, third son of the second earl of Bedford, was slain the day before his father's death. This youth and his elder brother, Edward, lord Russell, are (in the Woburn Gallery) represented in small full lengths in two paintings, and so alike as scarcely to be distinguished ; both dressed in white close jackets, and black and gold cloaks, and black bonnets. The date by lord Edward is October 22, 1573. He is represented grasping in one hand some snakes, with this motto, ' Fides homini serpentibus fraus ; ' and in the background he is placed standing in a labyrinth, and above is inscribed, ' Fata viam invenient.' This young nobleman also died before his father. His brother Francis has his accompaniments not less singular : a lady, seemingly in distress, is represented sitting in the background surrounded with snakes, a dragon, crocodile, and cock. At a distance the sea, with a ship under full sail. The story is not well known, but it certainly alludes to some family transaction similar to that in Otway's Orphan, and gave rise to it. He by the attendants was perhaps the Polydore of the history. Edward seems by his motto, ' Fides homini serpentibus fraus,' to have been Castalio, conscious of his own integrity, and indignant at the perfidy of his brother. The ship alludes to the desertion of the lady. If it conveyed sir Francis to Scotland, it was to his punishment, for he fell there July 27th, 1585, in a border fray."—*Pennant's Journey from Chester to London,* p. 369.

On which family we remark : (1.) In ten generaᴜns, the eldest son has succeeded his father thrice only. (2.) There have been four violent deaths (not in the field of battle), namely, William lord Russell, beheaded 1683; the marquis of Tavistock, killed 1767; lord William Russell, murdered 1840; lord Henry Russell, killed on ship-board by a block falling on his head, 1842. (3.) That the tenuity of the line, by which succession has been maintained, is, considering the number of births iu the family, very singular.—See also note at the end of Appendix A.

THYNNE, of Longleat. Longleat, the family seat, was a priory of Black Canons.

Thomas Thynne, created, 1628, baron Thynne, and viscount Weymouth, had one son, Henry, who died in his father's lifetime, without heirs-male. On which the title passed to Thomas, only son of Thomas, only son of Henry, the viscount's brother, according to the limitation of the patent. He had two heirs. The younger was created lord Carteret: he died without issue; and was succeeded by his nephew, who died without issue; and was succeeded by his brother the present baron, who, marrying a daughter of Thomas Master, esq., of Cirencester Abbey, has no issue; and in him the title will expire. The eldest son was created marquis of Bath; and was succeeded by Thomas, second marquis. His eldest son, Thomas viscount Weymouth, died without heirs; his third son, lord John Thynne, has lost his three eldest sons; his second son, the third marquis, succeeded, but dying in the prime of life, left his eldest son, a minor, his successor,—the present marquis. Of this family was Thomas Thynne, esq., murdered in his carriage (see p. 217).

WYNNE, of Conway and Bardsey. This family is descended from the third son of the original grantee. Sir Thomas, first baronet, had one son, sir John,

second baronet.   He was succeeded by sir Thomas,
first baron Newborough, who had three sons; John,
who died in his father's lifetime, without issue;
Thomas John, second baron, who died without
issue; and the third and present baron, who has
one son.

We do not say that these are all the parties who
have held an abbey site in an uninterrupted male
line from the time of Henry VIII. to the present
day.   We cannot discover more ;—we shall be glad
to be informed of any that we have omitted.   But
it is surely a remarkable, and almost supernatural
fact, that fourteen such owners only can be discovered out of six hundred and thirty grantees.
Allowing that we have reckoned only half—an impossible supposition)—then the crime of sacrilege
has been punished on six hundred families out of
six hundred and thirty.

CHAPTER IX.

Of Sacrileges committed under Queen Elizabeth, and in the Great Rebellion, and till the present time.

WE will now leave the sacrilege connected with, or springing from, the Dissolution of the Abbeys—and will proceed, very briefly, to notice a few particulars respecting that committed by Queen Elizabeth, and that of the Great Rebellion.

Queen Elizabeth's sacrilege consisted in forced exchanges of bishops' lands, and by keeping sees vacant, that the revenues might fall to the crown. From the former species of tyranny Ely perhaps chiefly suffered ; from the latter, Oxford. Oxford, of the first sixty-two years subsequent to its erection into a bishopric, was vacant forty-two. The persons who appear to have profited most largely from these acts of sacrilege were s.r Christopher Hatton, the earl of Essex, and the earl of Leicester.

Sir Christopher Hatton, who robbed Ely, after having long enjoyed the especial favour of Elizabeth, died of a broken heart, or rather of fear, on her re-demanding a sum of money which she had lent him, and which he was unable to pay. Leaving no children, he adopted sir William Newport as his heir, who also died childless. Then the estates passed to Christopher Hatton, a godson of the first; —his family was ennobled by Charles I., but became extinct in 1762.

The earl of Leicester ran a course of wickedness almost unparalleled ; extortions, treacheries, intrigues, adulteries, assassinations, rendered it infamous. His first wife he caused to be murdered;

his second he poisoned; the third he seduced, and, having poisoned her husband, married her. He died either of a broken heart, or as some say from poison, administered by his wife and her paramour.

The miserable end of the earl of Essex is too well known to be repeated.

———

" As for sir Henry Seimour . . . he was afterwards enducted in the manours of Marvell and Twyford, in the county of Southampton, dismembered in those broken times from the See of Winchester. To each of these belonged a park . . . the first being also honoured with a goodly mansion-house, belonging anciently to those bishops, and little inferior to the best of the wealthy bishopricks. There goes a story that the priest officiating at the altar in the church of Owslebury, of which parish Marvell was a part, after the Mass had been abolished by the king's authority, was violently dragged thence by this sir Henry, beaten and most reproachfully handled by him, his servants universally refusing to serve him, as the instruments of his rage and fury; and that the poor priest having after an opportunity to get into the church, did openly curse the said sir Henry and his posterity, with bell, book, and candle, according to the use observed in the Church of Rome. Which whether it were so or not, or that the main foundation of this estate being laid on sacrilege, could promise no long blessing to it, certain it is that his posterity are brought beneath the degree of poverty. For having three nephews [grandsons] by sir John Seimour his only son; that is to say, Edward, the eldest, Henry and Thomas, younger sons, besides several daughters, there remains not to any of them one foot of land, or so much as a penny of money to supply their necessities, but what they have from the munificence of the marquis of Hertford, or the charity of other well-disposed people, which have affection or relation to them."—*Heylyn's History of the Reformation*, pp. 4, 5.

———

Sir Horatio Palavicini was descended from a famous Genoese family. He left Genoa, the place of his birth, and went to the Low Countries, and thence to England. Queen Mary employed him to collect the papal taxes; when she died he had a very large sum of money, collected for this purpose, in his hands; this he most wickedly appropriated, having previously abjured the Roman faith. His riches were immense; the fate of this kingdom is said to have hung upon him. He lent money to Queen Elizabeth, for which he exacted an enormous interest. He lived at Babraham, in Cambridgeshire. He married twice, and by his first wife had one son, Edward, who to please his stepmother, his father's second wife, was declared illegitimate and disinherited. Henry, his eldest son by his second wife, died without issue, having been married nine years. His brother, sir Toby Palavicini, inherited the estates, and also the impropriation of Westacre Abbey; he also purchased part of Great and Little Shelford, and built a house there, which, as soon as built, he sold to John Gill, of Gillingham, esq.; and he quickly squandered the rest of his property with as great indifference as his father had procured it by rapacity and sacrilege; he was obliged to sell part of his estate in 1624, to pay his debts; he soon after parted with the impropriation of Westacre to alderman Bushan, and then estate went after estate, until there was no more to dispose of; and then, being still in debt, he was committed to the Fleet Prison; it is not known if he ever regained his liberty. He had three sons and one daughter, all of whom died without issue, and all, with the exception of the eldest, very young. Sir Horatio had also a daughter, Baptina, who married Henry, eldest son of sir Oliver Cromwell, uncle of the usurper, and had issue only one daughter, who died when two years old. Thus we see that in the second generation the name of the sacrilegious sir Horatio Palavicini, once so famous in England, was clean put out. The family of Palavicini, which rose so rapidly by fraud and sacrilege, is now unknown in England. The seats of Babraham and Shelford were destroyed, and no traces of them now remain. There is still a mansion at Babraham, but not that of the Palavicinis. Westacre, and Cranbrook, and Ilford, are gone too. All the vast personality was dissipated before the estates.—See *Noble's History of the Cromwells*, vol. ii., p. 180.

———

Let us next consider the fate of the Scottish bishoprics, and of those who plundered them. At the Reformation, as a general rule, the papal incumbent, whether he joined the reformers or not, was allowed to retain two-thirds of his benefice during his life, the other third being divided between the royal household and the protestant ministers. After the restoration of episcopacy, the bishoprics were rightly appropriated; though from various causes, shorn considerably of their former wealth. But to make up for this, in some measure, the smaller ones were augmented from time to time, previous to the Revolution, by grants of some of the monasteries which had been either annexed to the crown, or purchased by it from those to whom they had been given. These monasteries were, S. Andrew's, Tungland, Whitehorn, Dundrennan, Monymusk, Crossraguel, Forne, and perhaps a few more.

Archbishopric of S. ANDREWS. After the death of the Roman Catholic archbishop (Hamilton), the regicide James, fourth earl of Morton, obtained the temporalities of the see. He suffered a violent death, and left no legitimate male issue; thus terminating a family line of ten successions. Next to him succeeded Ludovick, second duke of Lennox, who held the temporalities till 1606, when on the

restoration of episcopacy, he gave up the archbishopric, and received in exchange the priory of S.
Andrews, which was nearly of equal value. He was
married three times, but had no children. During
the rebellion, the temporalities of the see were bestowed on the university of the city, and at the
revolution they were annexed to the Crown.

Archbishopric of GLASGOW. The above-mentioned duke of Lennox obtained a temporary grant
of this see also, whose childless fate we have seen.
After some years it was restored, though much
dilapidated, to the Roman Catholic archbishop,
James Beaton, then in Paris, who kept it till his
death in 1603. It then passed to the Church.
During the rebellion it was given to the university
of Glasgow, and finally fell to the Crown at the
revolution.

CAITHNESS, MORAY, ROSS, DUNKELD, and DUN-
BLANE. It is not easy to trace the property of
these sees separately, from the Reformation downwards, when not possessed by the Church. Caithness was held at the Reformation by Robert Stewart,
brother of the earl of Lennox. He joined the
Knoxian reformers, kept his revenues, married a
daughter of the earl of Athol, and died issueless in
1586. The episcopal lands of Moray were given to
sir Alexander Lindsay, third son of the eighth earl
of Crawford, who was created lord Spynie by James
VI. He was killed in 1606 ; and though the lands
were restored to the Church, his grandson died without issue in 1670. A brother succeeded, who also
died without issue, and thus the line became extinct.
During the rebellion, the temporalities of the five
foregoing sees were granted to the fourteenth earl of
Crawford, as the reward of his treason against his
king. His eldest son, the fifteenth earl, joined the
Prince of Orange at the revolution, and endeavoured
to recover these bishoprics for himself, in which he
did not succeed; but he got some other lands in
their stead which had belonged to the Church. His

grandson died issueless in 1746, and thereby closed a very long line of ancestors.

BRECHIN, ARGYLL, and the ISLES. The earl of Argyll obtained these three sees as his share of Church plunder, at the reformation, drawing their revenues through the medium of tulchan or titular bishops. He was twice married, yet had no off-spring. At the rebellion the then marquis of Argyll got the bishoprics of Argyll and the Isles, as a reward for the part he took with the Covenanters, Both he and his son were executed for high treason. The latter's grandson had five daughters, but no son. The bishoprics are now of course with the Crown.

GALLOWAY. Alexander Gordon was bishop at the reformation. He changed with the times, and renounced his episcopacy, in order to secure his Church preferment. He died in 1579, leaving three sons, none of whom had any issue.

ORKNEY. Adam Bothwell was bishop at the reformation. He followed the example of his brother reformers, and then exchanged his diocesan lands and revenues with lord Robert Stewart, for the latter's abbey of Holyrood-house. Bothwell's line became extinct in two generations, and Patrick, eldest son of lord Robert, who had been made earl of Orkney, was forfeited and executed at Edinburgh in 1614, leaving no issue.

In descending to the Great Rebellion, we have not thought it necessary to accumulate, from every possible quarter, the largest number of facts that we could collect, because they convey a less practical lesson at the present time, inasmuch as the Church was, for the most part, replaced in the enjoyment of her own at the Restoration.

But we desire to call especial attention to the writings, as taken in comparison with the fate, of Cornelius Burgess. The whole story is so remark-able, that we may be excused for dwelling on it.

Dr. Burgess, a Puritan divine, living in London, sided, as was natural, with the parliament at the commencement of the Great Rebellion. When a voluntary loan was raised, to supply troops for Ireland, he offered £300 ; and paid in £700 more, to be laid out in the purchases of the confiscated property of the insurgents. When the king's standard was set up, and another loan was requested, the same divine again subscribed, though it does not appear to what amount.

In due time, the Commons, finding that the repayment of these loans, and the other charges of the war, was impossible, ordained, by a vote of October 9, 1646, that all cathedral lands should be sold, and the produce vested in such trustees as parliament should appoint, " subject to such trusts as it should declare." £200,000 were to be raised by these means, and vested accordingly. But it would appear that even the boldest rebels had some fears of participating in such sacrilege ; for soon after, persons that had contributed to the voluntary loan, were invited to double their quotas, and to take them out in bishop's lands ; and it was intimated that till *doublers* should be paid, none else need look to be so.

Dr. Burgess, now thoroughly involved in the snare, doubled ; and, in July, 1648, he found himself with a wife and ten children, creditor to the state for about £3,400. " Since that purchase," he says, " it hath pleased the wise GOD to exercise him with many sharp afflictions ; . . . his ministry also hath been of small use."

But still this man would not own GOD's Hand ; and, though growing poorer and poorer, and involved in a lawsuit with the Corporation of Wells, in which diocese his ill-gotten possessions lay, he still asserted that his course was justifiable, and that the sale and purchase of church-lands was not sacrilege. But, in 1659, when symptoms of a change became visible, Dr. Burgess, in common with others, began to tremble for their property; and he published a book entitled "A Case concerning the buying of Bishops' Lands, with the lawfulness thereof, and the difference between the contractors for sale of those lands, and the Corporation of Wells." The book seems to have had a considerable sale; for in the following year we find a *third* edition (we have not seen the second) published under an altered title, and in a much enlarged form. It now bears the name, "No Sacrilege nor Sin to alienate or purchase cathedral-lands, as such; or, a Vindication not only of the late Possessors but of the ancient Nobility and Gentry, yea, of the Crown itself; all deeply wounded by the false charge of Sacrilege against new purchasers."

His definition of Sacrilege is as follows, in the first edition.

"Sacrilege is the robbing of GOD, by alienating, detaining, purloining, or perverting that which is GOD's own by Divine Right, and thereupon due to the ministers of the Gospel; whether the things be set apart by Divine Commandment, or voluntarily given by men, by virtue of some special warrant or direction from GOD." It is evident that nearly the whole question turns on the admissibility or inadmissibility of the last clause. In the third edition, Dr. Burgess, apparently desirous of turning the tables on his opponents, adds—"or by retaining or perverting to man's use what GOD hath ordered to be destroyed, as a service to Himself, denounced not by man, but by GOD himself."

His general arguments are miserably poor; those from Holy Scripture ingenious enough. He argues that, under the old law, the Priests were prohibited from holding land. (Numbers xviii. 20.) That the number of cities appropriated to the Levites was limited, and those cities were not held by Levites alone (Joshua xv. 13; xxi. 10, 11; xiv. 13, 14); that the Levites might sell their lands, nay, that they might redeem their houses at any time, while others must do it within a year (Lev. xxv. 31, 32); and, finally, that Ezekiel's temple, though seemingly opposed to this view, is so thoroughly typical that it cannot be urged as an argument.

It would almost seem as if GOD had taken the controversy out of man's hand. "Dr. Brittain of Deptford," says M. Durel, in a letter to Dr. Basire, bearing date January 9, 1668, "told me he had seen, in the hands of major-general Brown, a letter of Dr. Cornelius Burgess, wherein he acquainted him that he was brought to great poverty, and that he was eaten up with a cancer in his neck and cheek; I desired sir Richard [Brown] to do me the favour to show me Dr. Burgess his letter, which was presently granted me; and there I read these very words to the best of my remembrance, ' I am reduced to want a piece of bread, and am eaten up with a cancer in my neck and cheek, as this bearer, my son, may better inform you.' Yet the man was not so humbled by that heavy and exemplary judgment of GOD, but that he presently added, ' sir, mistake me not; I do not beg; I only acquaint you with my condition, and do you what is fit.' 'Tis known this man had a great yearly income; he was besides a purchaser of a considerable estate of the lord bishop of Bath and Wells' lands, which he enjoyed long enough to reimburse himself and much more than so; and how he could be reduced to that extreme poverty, is not easily to be guessed at. . . . I must not omit that I am told Dr. Burgess died a very penitent man, frequenting with great zeal and devotion the Divine Service of the Church of England till his death, which happened about two years ago." (*Basire's Sacrilege Arraigned.* Ed. 2. London: 1668. Preface, last page but one.)

We will now bring forward some instances of GOD's judgment on sacrilegious offenders, from Walker's *Sufferings of the Clergy.* Sacrilege of person will be chiefly found in these.

William Cottle, one of the perjured witnesses

268   THE HISTORY AND FATE OF SACRILEGE.

against Mr. Bushnell, vicar of Box, Wilts, fell sick
of a burning on his lips, which spread into his
mouth, insomuch that he was forced to cool his
mouth continually with water. After that his
tongue grew black and swelled out of his mouth,
in which condition he continued some days, groan-
ing in such a lamentable manner that he was heard
in the streets, and soon died leaving a wife and
many small children, who were beholden for some
assistance to the parish.—*Walker's Sufferings of the
Clergy.* Part i. p. 191.

The parliamentary agents collected all the growing
rents and arrears of the bishopric of Carlisle for
their own use. The chief of those who were employed at Carlisle was one Barker, who destroyed
the woods, pillaged the castle of Rose (the place of
the bishop's residence), and carried off many of the
stones to build his own house and barns. But, I
observe that by the way in the next generation
Barker's name was clean put out. For he died soon
after the restoration, and his son and posterity,
together with the houses and lands, are in a manner
quite vanished; that is, the latter out of the name,
and the former out of the country.—*Ibid.* Part ii.
p. 9.

Sir Richard Wiseman, who led the mob which
assaulted the house of Dr. Winniffe, bishop of
Lincoln, had his brains beat out with a stone.—*Ibid.*
p. 42.

John West, a very wicked man, a robber, adul-
terer, and murderer, was one of the six commissioners appointed to try Mr. Jeremiah Stephens, a
prebendary of Lincoln [and the intended editor of
the *History of Sacrilege*], carried away his tithes,
etc.; after a course of the most abandoned de-
bauchery, he died under sentence of excommunication in the dungeon of Northampton gaol.—*Ibid.*
p. 45.

One of the chief adversaries of Mr. Robert Joyner,
sub-chanter of Salisbury and vicar of Chew-Magna.

Somerset, was one Peter Lock, a tanner, of which reforming saint there goes this story, That having sold a piece of leather to a cobbler just by, and this cobbler being sick and like to die, out of pure charity to be sure he went to pray by the sick man; and having, out of pretence, made a long prayer, he stole away the poor man's leather from under his bed, and very devoutly retired. Of this fellow, and most of the rest of Mr. Joyner's adversaries, it was afterward observed that the displeasure of Providence was manifested against them by various remarkable judgments, some of them coming to untimely ends, others having monstrous children, others suffering great and judiciary misfortunes in their goods.— *Ibid.* p. 64.

Barrett, the miscreant who murdered Dr. Raleigh, dean of Wells, was a renegade Welshman, and not worth one groat when he came to Wells, but by plundering and such practices he got an estate of about £16 per annum, which is now crumbled into nothing again. The sister of this fellow's wife had her mouth drawn back into her neck in a most frightful and dismal manner, and expired in that posture, crying out on her deathbed that her brother-in-law had made her damn her soul by false swearing, because she had on her oath deposed that Dr. Raleigh struck Barrett first.—*Ibid.* p. 72.

Robert Chestlin, of S. Matthew's, Friday-street, was most shamefully used by the rebels, and brought up before the House of Commons by one Pennington ; but in the midst of his trouble, it pleased GOD to take off the chief promoter of his prosecution.— *Ibid.* p. 166.

Christopher Butson, rector of Chulmleigh, Devon, was much persecuted by the Puritans ; three of his chief enemies died in a most unhappy manner, one by a fall from his horse, another was drowned, and the third expired in a raving and distracted condition.— *Ibid.* p. 192.

One of the two captains who prosecuted Mr.

George Buchanan, vicar of Kirkby Lonsdale, grew very rich, and purchased a field, and built a very large house with the price of iniquity; but before his death he became miserable and poor, and lay some time in prison, where he died, and was daily relieved from the table of one of Mr. Buchanan's sons. A grandson of Mr. B. saw one of the captain's sons begging at Edinburgh, and he asked his charity, which was not denied him.—*Ibid.* p. 211.

Mr. Harrison, rector of S. Clement, Sandwich, was dragged out of his pulpit and much abused, beaten, and threatened to be shot by the rebel soldiers, and was taken to prison. This very Sunday afternoon, by a strange and unaccountable accident, only by Providence, by whatever appeared, the court of guard was blown up by gunpowder, and the man that first laid hands upon him killed dead by taking away his belly at once (his name was Buck), and a great many others of them mortally wounded.—*Ibid.* p. 266.

Dr. Hudson, one of the king's chaplains, and a very active person in the royal service, was murdered thus. He was besieged at Woodcroft-house, at Etton, in Northamptonshire; the house was taken, but he with some of the bravest of his men retired to the battlements; he then surrendered upon promise of quarter; but the rebels having got possession denied quarter, and threw the doctor over the battlements; he caught hold of a spout and there hung; his hand being cut off, he fell into the moat much wounded, and desired to come to land that he might die there. Whereupon one Egborough knocked him on the head with the butt-end of a musket, and one Walker cut out his tongue and carried it for a trophy about the country. His body was denied burial. Yet after the enemy left, he was by some Christians committed to the earth. As for Egborough, he was not long after torn in pieces with his own gun, which burst whilst under his arm. Walker quitted his trade, and became a scorn and a by-word as he passed

through the streets of Stamford, where he lived.—
Ibid. p. 270.

Mr. William Holway, rector of North Cheriton,
Somersetshire, was seized on in time of sermon by
some fellows who threatened to shoot him. He
foretold the death of one of his persecutors, which
fell out accordingly, he being devoured with lice and
worms, as many of the parish testified.—*Ibid.* p.
273.

Mr. Richard Long, vicar of Chewton Mendip, in
Somersetshire, was vilely treated by the rebels, and
died of poison. The four persons chiefly concerned
in his persecution, were Job Emlin, Robert Wilcox,
James Hoskins, and Thomas Philips. The first died
soon after, the second was taken speechless and
never spoke more, the third was distracted in his
head before, and after grew downright mad, and the
last died in a barn. Two others who were going to
London to swear against Mr. Long, died on the road
thither of small-pox.—*Ibid.* p. 298.

The persons who principally plundered Dr. Manby,
of Cottenham, were Wright and Taylor. They grew
rich in those times, but Wright's children and grand-
children became wretched and miserable. Taylor's
wife and daughter came to be relieved by the parish,
and Dr. Manby lived to bury them both after he was
repossessed. Another man, named Nye, also a rebel
and persecutor of the doctor, and who was thrust
into the living, buried his wife and six children who
were born at the parsonage.—*Ibid.* p. 304.

Dr. William Odis, vicar of Adderbury, was betrayed by a neighbour to the rebel soldiers, and shot
in his flight with a pistol. The man who betrayed
him, fell down dead on the very spot where the
doctor was shot.—*Ibid.* p. 323.

Mr. Richard Powell, rector of Spaxton, Somersetshire, was with several other clergy put on board a
ship to be sent to London. Upon Sunday he and
the others were at prayers on the deck, when the
children pelted them with stones, and called them,

"Baal's priests;" one of these children fell down
dead.—*Ibid.* p. 333.

Mr. Rosington, vicar of S. Allen's, Cornwall, was
persecuted and robbed by the sequestrators; his
enemies themselves came to beg their bread at his
door, and were relieved by him.—*Ibid.* p. 340.

Mr. Francis Rowley, rector of Coppenhall, Lancashire, was most shamefully abused by the rebels,
his house being fired over his head, and his cattle
destroyed, and corn burnt, etc. In this villainous
work the chief was one Wettinghall, his next neighbour, who afterwards came to the extremest poverty
and died miserably, being eaten of lice.—*Ibid.* p. 344.

A miserable man, John Blanchard, attempted to
keep Mr. Joseph Shute, rector of Meavy, Devon,
out of his church, and caught hold of his legs as he
attempted to enter the chancel-door. He was immediately smitten with an incurable disease, an ulcer
in his own leg, which brought him to the grave.—
Ibid. p. 355.

One of the chief persecutors of Mr. Tournay,
rector of Wittersham, Kent, declared when he was
sent to prison, that he should not come out again as
long as his eyes were open to see it. This person was
afterwards drowned on the sands, and on that very
day Mr. Tournay was released from prison.—*Ibid.*
p. 379.

Mr. Edward Vaughan, rector of Pisford, was
robbed by the rebels, and particularly by one
Robbins. The stolen goods proved a canker to him,
for his family soon came to utter ruin and beggary.
Ibid. p. 388.

When Mr. Vaughan returned to his living, he
was refused entrance into his house by his clerk,
and was obliged to force a way in. This old clerk
had taken the surplice and put it to the uses of his
own family, as also the bells, etc. But he lived to
be a walking monument of his sacrilege, being forced
to beg his bread, and being eaten up by vermin.—
Ibid. p. 389.

Mr. Cæsar Williamson, rector of Wappingham, Northamptonshire, was ejected, and one Theophilus Hart was thrust in. This Hart was a most profane wretch; when he made a mockery of administering the Communion, the people, by his direction, when giving the cup to each other, said, "Here's to ye, neighbour." He conformed after the restoration, but never read the Common Prayer, a curate whom he kept doing it for him. He was found in the act of adultery with a butcher's wife: the butcher cleft his skull with an axe. Before his death he fell into lawsuits, etc., so that of his temporal estate, to which he had added largely from the church, not one foot was left.—*Ibid.* p. 403.

Mr. John Watson, of Woolpit, Suffolk, was ejected by the earl of Manchester. The three persons of the parish who articled against him remarkably decayed, and came to nothing soon after.—*Ibid.* p. 405.

Mr. Whitly, of Earl Soham, Suffolk, was ejected. The following wonderful account is given, as is supposed, by bishop Hall, concerning one Clark, a schoolmaster, who succeeded him. Some of the parish who had chosen him, being with him late on the Saturday before he was to make his publick appearance, were partakers of his prayers in his chamber; when he prayed GOD that if his calling to that place were not lawful and according to His will, He would show some sign or token upon him; and the same prayer he renewed the Sunday morning in the pulpit before his intended sermon to the congregation; which done, he no sooner read the text but he was stricken dumb, and was not able to speak to the people. When he had endeavoured it in vain about half an hour, he no sooner laid his hand upon the pulpit door to go away, but his voice came again to him, and he then told the people that according to his prayer GOD had showed His token upon him in their sight of His dislike of his calling to that place, professed that he would not meddle with it any more, and willed them to receive again their own minister, etc. Neither would he be entreated to attempt the work again.—*Ibid.* p. 406.

Mr. Wethers, of Wetheringset, Suffolk, was sequestered. Five or six of the more substantial freeholders who were instrumental in his sequestration, came afterwards to nothing.—*Ibid.* p. 406.

William Bartholomew, vicar of Campden, Gloucestershire, was miserably harassed by the rebels. Not one of his persecutors was there but what came to some untimely end, or had some signal misfortune befal them.—*Ibid.* p. 412.

One Greenway, a butcher, during the rebellion, got a considerable estate by plundering, which he wasted as fast as he got it, and his children wanted bread before they died.—*Ibid.* p. 416.

———

If, as Andrew Marvell broadly hints in one of his lampoons, lord Clarendon's house in London was partly built with some stones intended for S. Paul's Cathedral, we have another wonderful instance of the fate of sacrilege. Clarendon himself imputes to the building of his house in London the greater part of the envy and calamity which overwhelmed him ; but in acknowledging his folly, he seems totally unconscious of any sacrilegious taint.—(See *Continuation of the Life of Clarendon,* p. 276. Ed. 1848.)

———

Bishopric of OSNABURG. Ernest-Augustus, created duke of York by his brother, George I., was bishop of Osnaburg, the title being sacrilegiously usurped ; he died unmarried, 1728.

Edward-Augustus, brother to George III., was created duke of York and bishop of Osnaburg in 1760 ; died young and unmarried, 1767.

Frederick, second son of George III., was created

bishop of Osnaburg; but died 1827, though married, without issue. And these three are the only instances of an English Prince having borne this title.

———

By way of conclusion to this chapter, we will remind the reader of bishop Cosin's conduct. " He," says Dugdale, "shortly after his consecration to Durham, taking notice that the greater part of the materials made use of in that building,"—the castle, as erected by sir Arthur Haslerigg, the rebel,— "were what were taken for the purpose from the consecrated chapel, not only refused to make use of it for his habitation, though it was most commodiously contrived, and nobly built, but took it wholly down, and with the stone thereof built another beautiful chapel on the north side of that great court."

CONCLUSION.

WE thus close the additions which we have thought desirable to make to sir Henry Spelman's *History of Sacrilege*. They might have been indefinitely increased; but we were afraid of wearying the patience of the reader, and of swelling the book to an inconvenient size. Enough, we think, has been said to convince those who are capable of conviction; more examples to the same end to them would be useless, and to others superfluous.

We have reserved for the following Appendices a systematized view of the fate of those abbey-sites of which we have been able to learn the history; and we trust that the Tables, which we are about to present, will not be without their use. They, as well as what we have hitherto written, will confirm the words of good king Wihtred in the Council* of Beccancelde. " It is a horrible thing for men to rob the living GOD, and to divide His portion and raiment among themselves."

* LANDON's Manual of Councils, p. 76.

APPENDIX I.

THE MITRED ABBEYS OF ENGLAND.

Fate of the First Possessors of the Sites.

Name.	Grantee.	Fate.
Hyde, Benedictine Abbey, Hants; value £865	Bethell, Richard	Of him we can learn nothing, either from books or from inquiries at Winchester. At all events, his family never took root in the county.
Battle, Benedictine Abbey, Sussex; value £937	Browne, sir Antony	The end of this family is deplorable; George Samuel Montague, last lineal descendant of sir Antony Browne, in the direct line, determined, in company with Sedley Burdett (also the representative of a family involved in Sacrilege), to pass the falls of Schaffhausen. Eluding the vigilance of the magistrates, who placed guards to prevent the attempt, and extricating himself by force from the grasp of a faithful servant, he pushed off in a flat-bottomed boat. The adventurers passed the first fall safely; they went down the second, and were never more heard of. In that same year, Cowdray House, the magnificent mansion of the Montagues—from whom it passed to the Poyntzes—was burnt to the ground.

Croyland, Benedictine Abbey, Lincolnshire; value £1217 ... } Clinton, Edward, lord { Extinct in the direct male line, 1692. Abeyance of barony determined in favour of Hugh Fortescue, esq., 1721; he died without issue, and the barony passed to his sister Margaret, who died unmarried. Among other possessors of the abbey was Adrian Scrope, the regicide, beheaded at the Restoration.

Canterbury, S. Austin; Benedictine Abbey; value £1413... } Cobham, William, lord (1564.) { In Appendix II. we have related at length the miserable fate of his sons, and the extinction of the family in the male line.

Coventry, Cathedral and Benedictine Priory; value £731 ... } Coombes, John . { His co-grantee was Richard Stansfield; of them we can learn nothing.

Ramsey, Benedictine Abbey, Hunts; value £1983.......... } Cromwell, sir Richard { Both lines of Cromwells were deeply involved in Sacrilege; both miserable. Sir Richard Williams, grantee of Ramsey, who assumed his wife's name, she being sister to Thomas Cromwell, must have had estates from the Dissolution producing an annual income of £80,000 or £90,000, present value. And yet his grandson, Robert, father of Oliver Cromwell, was in reduced circumstances.[1]

Colchester, S. John's Benedictine Abbey; value £523 ...... } Darcy, Thomas, lord { Family extinct in the fourth generation.

Waltham, Augustinian Abbey; value £1079 .... } Denny, sir Antony .. { Family extinct in the third generation. Of a collateral branch, we believe, was sir William Denny of Gillingham, bart, who died in great indigence, 1642, and was the last of his family.

Abbey	Grantee	Note
S. Edmund's Bury, Benedictine Abbey; value £2336	Eyer, John	Died childless.
Shrewsbury, Benedictine Abbey; value £615	Forster, Thomas	Of him we can learn nothing; he only held the estate four years. The next grantee was Edward Watson, of Rockingham; family extinct.
Evesham, Benedictine Abbey; value £1268	Hoby, Philip	Died childless. The family of sir Thomas Hoby, his half-brother, whom he made his heir, likewise extinct.
S. Alban's, Benedictine and Premier Abbey; value £2510 ...	Lee, sir Richard	Received as the price or reward of his wife's adultery with the king; died childless.
Tavistock, Benedictine Abbey (but _quære_ if mitred); value £902 .... Thorney, Benedictine Abbey; value £508	Russell, John, lord	Of this family we have treated in Chap. viii.—See note 2.
Selby, Benedictine Abbey; value £819	Sadler, sir Ralph .	Family extinct in the direct line.
Abingdon, Benedictine Abbey; value £2042 .... Cirencester, Augustinian Abbey; value £1051 .... Winchelcombe, Benedictine Abbey; value £759	Seymour, lord, of Sudeley	Beheaded for high treason, 1549.
Glastonbury, Benedictine Abbey; value £3508 .... Reading, Benedictine Abbey; value £2116	Somerset, Edward, duke of	Beheaded for high treason, 1552.

Name.	Grantee.	Fate.
Tewkesbury, Benedictine Abbey; value £1598	Stroude, Thomas	His co-grantees were Walter Erle, and James Paget; but of none of these can we learn anything.
Malmesbury, Benedictine Abbey; value £803	Stump, William	The descendants of this wealthy merchant now exist *as labourers* in or near Malmesbury. (Information received from the place.)
Bardney, Benedictine Abbey; value £482	Tyrwhitt, sir Robert .. .	See under next Appendix.
York, S. Mary, Benedictine Abbey; value £2091 .... (So far only as related to the abbat's palace.)	Wriothesley, Thomas, lord	His son, grandson, and great-grandson, all involved in much political trouble; the grandson actually condemned for high treason, but pardoned. The great-grandson married thrice, but left no surviving male issue; and in him the honour became extinct.
Gloucester, S. Peter's, Benedictine Abbey; value £1946............ Peterborough, Benedictine Abbey; value £1972 .... Westminster Benedictine Abbey; value £3977	..	Sites, and some of the lands granted for cathedral churches.
S. Bene't Hulme, Benedictine Abbey; value £677.	..	Granted to the bishop of Norwich in Exchange for the old estates of the see; the bishop is still titular abbat.

FIRST GRANTEES OF THE SITES OF ABBEYS NOT MITRED : THEIR FATE.

"Such as are of death, to death : and such as are for captivity, to captivity ; and such as are for the sword, to the sword."

Grantee.	Name.	Fate.
Aglionby, Edward	Truro,[1] Black Friars.............	Family extinct.
Andrews, Richard	Blythe, Benedictine Priory, Notts: (half) .... Caermarthen, Austin Canons: (half) Denbigh, White Friars: (half) ... Gloucester, White Friars: (half) Malvern, Little, Benedictine Cell: (half) .... Norwich, White Friars: (half) ... Oxford, Black Friars: (half) ...... —— Grey Friars: (half)............ Sele, Sussex, White Friars: (half) Shrewsbury, Austin Friars: (half) —— Black Friars: (half) ...... —— Grey Friars: (half) Temple Comb, Somersetshire: (half) .... Yarmouth, Black Friars: (half)....	Of this fearful amount of Sacrilege, nothing appears to have remained in the family; and all trace of the family itself, whether from indigence, or extinction, has long been lost.

Name	Grant	Fate
eton, Richard	Whalley, Lancashire : Cistercian Abbey : (half)	Died[2] without children.
her, sir Antony	Swingfield, Kent, Knights of S. John	Slain[3] at S. Quentin, 1557.
ley, lord, of Walden	..at, Benedictine Cell: (half) .... uban sons : Ged Fars ...... S. Ives, Hunts, Benedictine Cell London, Charter House .... —hfirst Gth, Aldgate : —Austin ; ans; (the first church granted to a layman) .... Prittlewell, Essex, Cluniac Priory : (half) .... Tilt y, E. xx Cistercian Abbey... Men, Essex: Benedictine Abbey	Died 1544, and the title became extinct : His only daughter married—1. Lord Henry Dudley, slain at S. Quentin, 1557 :—2. Thomas, duke of Norfolk, died 1572. She died at the age of 23 : and the duke of Norfolk, though the rich in the realm, was little better than a beggar.
dwin, sir John	Aylesbury, Grey Friars	Died without heirs-male.
kwith, Leonard	York, Christ Church, Benedictine Priory .... York, Grey Friars	Had two sons, who both died without heirs, and the family became extinct.[5]
reton, William ..	Lesnes, Kent, Austin Canons	Beheaded[6] for High Treason in the matter of queen Catherine Howard, 1542.

Louther, Henry ...	Nunnery............	...... manor house on a different site, but died in the course of the work.
Candish, John	Epworth, Lincoln, Carthusian Priory....	He turned the Priory "into a goodly place,"[8] but the family in the male line appears to have become very soon extinct.[9]
Carnaby, sir Reginald .	Hexham, Austin Canons, & Hospital	Died without heirs-male.
Carne, Sir Edward	Ewenny, Glamorganshire, Benedictine Priory ....; Newport, Monmouthshire, Black Friars	Family extinct.[10]
Cheke, sir John	London, S. Laurence Poultney, Collegiate Church............; Spalding. Benedictine Abbey ......; Stoke by Clare, Suffolk, Collegiate Church: (half)	Seized in Germany[11] as an heretic during queen Mary's reign: sent prisoner to London: recanted to save his life: forced to surrender these estates to the queen: died of shame and a broken heart, 1556.
Cheney, sir Thomas	Davington, Kent, Benedictine Nunnery ....; Faversham, Benedictine Abbey ...; Minster-in-Sheppey, Benedictine May ....; Patricksbourne, Kent, Austin Nuns	His son sold the chapel[12] of Minster, where his father was buried: family extinct, 1578.

APPENDIX II. CONTINUED.

Grantee.	Name.	Fate.
Clinton, Edward, lord ...	Alvingham, Lincolnshire, Gilbertine Priory	See in Appendix I.[15]
	Barking, Essex, Benedictine Abbey	
	Flitcham, Norfolk, ... in Cell	
	Folkestone, Kent, Benedictine Priory	
	Haverholme, Lincolnshire, Gilbertine Priory	
	Holland Brigge, Lincolnshire, Gilbertine Priory	
	Richmond, Yorkshire, Benedictine Cell	
	Sempringham, Lincolnshire, Gilbertine Priory	
	Swineshead, Lincolnshire, Cistercian ...	
	Stamford, Austin Friars	
	Wormley, Herefordshire, Austin ...	
	...ly, Lincolnshire, Knights of S. John.	
Cobham,[14] George, lord ...	Burnham Norton, Norfolk, White Friars	See the next.
	Cobham College, Secular Priests ...	

Cobham, William, lord (son of the above) ......} Maidstone College, Secular Priests

Of his sons, Maximilian, the eldest, died with ut children; Henry, his on died also without n : the third, was beheaded for participating in "Raleigh's pl" and William was killed in 95. Henry was tried for participating in the ame plot: and, "on his trial, ever was there so poor and abject a spirit."—He died full of , for want of apparel and linen: " h," says Banks,[15] "was a singular judgment, that a man of near £7,000 a year, and a personal estate of £30,000, should die for want.—The lady Cobham, his wife, though ry rh, would not even give him the crumbs from her table."—Sir John Brooke, nearest heir-male, was restored to the le ard dignity of Lord l, by King Charles I., but died without issue, 1651; on which the title ue extinct.

Constable, sir Marmaduke .... {
Drax, Yorkshire, Austin Canons... Nuneaton, Warwickshire, Fontevraud Nuns......

The elder branch, Constable of Flamborough,[16] extinct 1655: the younger extinct 1746.

Cranmer, Thomas, Archbishop of Canterbury... {
Arthington, Yorkshire, Benedictine Nuns ...... Kirkstall, Yorkshire, Cistercian Abbey ...... Malling, Kent, Benedictine Nuns

Burnt alive, 1555.

Cromwell, alias Williams, sir Richard	Hinchinbrooke, Hu ts,n Benedic-tine Nunnery.................. Huntingdon, ▪in Canons ...... London, S. Helen, Benedictine Nunnery.................. Neath, Glamorganshire, Cistercian Abbey .... S. Neots, Hunts, Benedictine Priory.................. Sawtry, Hunts, Cistercian Abbey	See note on Appendix I.
Dacre, William, lord[17] ...	Lanercost, Cumberland, Austin Canons	His son Thomas died[18] shortly aft rehirm : and his son, ..g, was killed by the fall of a wooden horse on ..h he was used to ..p. On this the bar ny ..e extinct. But Leonard, ..le to George, claiming to ..d as ..ir in tail ..e, and being refused, joined Northumber-land's rebellion, and with his two brothers was attainted for high treason. The family became extinct in the ..t generation.
Dudley, John, lord	Dudley, Cluniac Cell, Staffordshire Wymondham Hospital, Norfolk...	"This John L rde Dudley,[20] being a ..n of weak understanding, so ..spd ..elf to the snares of usurers, that John .. ..y, then ..t ..le, afterwards duke of Northumberland, thirsting after Dudley Castle, the chief seat of their family, ..le ..se money-merchants his means to work him out of it: which by some ....

la Warr, Thomas, rd	Wherwell, Hants, Benedictine Nunnery......	among them, was commonly called the lord *Quondam*." / Died childless.
ereux, Richard	Pembroke, Benedictine Cell	Died in his father's lifetime; his grandson, the unfortunate earl of Essex, beheaded for high treason. Property now in trustees, for payment of owner's debts.[19]
bar, George, earl of	Holystone, Northumberland, Benedictine ... the My, 1605	Died without heirs-male, 1611.
ex, Thomas Cromwell, earl of	Mr, Benedictine Abbey ...... uhd, Leicestershire, Austin ... aths .... Lewes, Wc Priory ...... Mon My, Wc Cell ... Michelham, Sussex, Au tin Canons ... S. O yth, Essex, Austin Canons ... Yarmouth, Grey Friars......	Cromwell's wretched end is known to all. Beheaded, 1541.
re, William, lord .. .	Jarrow, Benedictine Cell, Durham	His eldest son[21] slain in his life time. William, foh ban, lnd issue:—Ralph, who died in his father's fene: William, fifth baron, William, sixth, was slain at Marston Moor, having had a son, who was slain in his lifetime: George, wth, died unmarried: Ralph, eighth, died lHis, 1698: and in him the title b came extinct.

Grantee.	Name.	Fate.
Fulmerstone, sir Richard	Thetford, Sons of the Holy Sepulchre .... Thetford, Benedictine Nuns.......... Austin Friars .... Black Friars .... Weybridge, Norfolk, Black Canons	Died without heirs-male.
Gale, George	Wilberfoss, Yorkshire, Benedictine Nunnery	Family appears to be extinct,²² or reduced to indigence.
Goodere, Francis	Polesworth, Benedictine Nunnery, Warwickshire	Sir John Dineley died²³ had an only son, who died before his father unmarried. "Sir John having for a series of years lied on bad terms with his younger brother Samuel, threatened to disinherit him. This circumstance so alarmed captain Goodere that he formed the horrid purpose of murdering his brother. A friend at Bristol invited them both to dinner in the hope of reconciling them, and they had parted in the evening in seeming amity. Captain Goodere had, however, watched his opportunity. Several of his crew, placed in the street near College Green, seized sir John as he passed, and under pretence that he was disordered in his mind, hurried him by violence to the ship, where he was strangled by two sailors, captain Goodere himself standing sentinel at the door while the

		crime was commi[tted] ... ir[?] Samuel Goodere was hung for this murder April 15, 1741; sir Edward Dinely Goodere, his son, died a lunatic; and sir John Dinely, who succeeded his brother, dying unmarried, the title became extinct.
...imstone, Edward	Chiltern Langley, Black Friars ... (the largest friary in England)	Extinct in male line, 1700.[24] (The present Grimstone family are properly Luckyns.)
...ll, Richard	Hartley Wintney, Hants, Cistercian Nunnery.................	Family either extinct, or reduced to indigence; nothing known of them.
...pton, Ralph	Witham, Somersetshire, Charterhouse	Family extinct in the male line, 1652, by the death of lord Hopton in exile.
...timer, John, lord	Nun Monketon, Yorkshire, Benedictine Nunnery	Extinct in the male line, 1580.[25]
...antel, Walter	(Second grantee of) Monks' Horton, Kent, Cluniac Cell..............	Beheaded for participation in Wyatt's rebellion 1553.[26]
...eautis, Peter	Stratford Langthorne, Cistercian Abbey	Family in the male line xtinct, or in the deepest indigence. "The abbey-lands are so often ¶den ¶¶ed by sale, that it is ¶¶le to trace their ¶¶ possessors." (Information received at the ¶¶¶e. The only memorial of ¶¶tis himself, at Stratford, is, that a wall near the abbey-site g es by the ¶¶e of 'Meautis's-wall.)

Founder.	Name.	Fate.
Mildmay, Thomas	Pentney, Norfolk, Austin Canons; Shouldham, Norfolk, Gilbertine Priory	Family extinct in its two male lines, Mildmay, of Moulsham, Warwickshire, and Mildmay, lord Fitz-Walter.[27]
Montjoy, Charles, lord ...	Kirkby-Beler, Austin Canons, Rutland ....; Spectesbury, late Alien Priory, Dorsetshire ....; Yevely, Preceptory, Derbyshire ...	Died three years ...... His grandson, William, dying without ...e issue, was suc-eeded by ; ...d, his brother, ...ed earl of Devonshire. He had been ...ngaged to Penelope, sister to the earl of E ...x; she was marri..d to Robert lord Rich, but having had ...al chil-dren by the earl of , ... was divorced by her husband, and ... the earl, ...d offi-ciating. This great ...al shortened the ...el's days; he ...d the marriage little ...e than three months. "He left ...this life," says the con-temporary ...n, "soon and early for his year, ...but late enough for ...lf; and happy had he been, if he had g...ne two or three year s ...se, before the world were weary of ...m, or that he had left that ...al him."[28]
Moore, John	Penmon, Anglesea, Benedictine Priory	Family, it appears, is extinct.
Mordaunt, Edward	Stanesgate, Essex, Cluniac Priory	Family supposed to be extinct. Not mentioned in parish register, which begins 1662.

Nedeham, James .	Wymondley Parva, Herts; .... Austin Canons	Family extinct.[29]
Norfolk, Thomas, duke of	Bungay, Suffolk, Benedictine Nunnery...... Butley, Suffolk, Austin Canons;...... Castle Acre, Norfolk, Cluniac Priory...... Cokesford, Norfolk, Austin Cns Deping, Lincolnsh: Benedictine Cell Felixstowe, Suffolk, Benedictine Cell...... Hitcham, Norfolk, Cluniac Cell ... Newenham, Devon, Cistercian Abbey...... Norwich, S. Catherine, Benedictine Cell...... Snape, Suffolk, Benedictine Priory Thetford, Norfolk, Cluniac Priory ———, ———, College ...... Wangford, Suffolk, Cluniac Cell...	He had two sons: 1. Henry, earl of Surrey, beheaded for high treason, [Ma]y 20, 46, and Henry the Eighth's last ꝟn. Of the earl of Surrey's ꝟn, the eldest, Th duke of Norfolk, was ꝟed for high treason, 1572; the youngest, Henry, earl of Nort ꝟn, di de unmarried, and is reported to have be ꝟ the most contemptible and d ꝟicable of ꝟd." 2. ꝟs, viscount ꝟn, whose family became extinct in the next generation.
Northampton, William, marquis of	Edith Ws̄n, Rutland (once an Adn Priory, then belonging to the Chartreuse at Coventry) ... Halsted, E ꝟp College ... . S. Mary du Pré, Leicestershire, s̄tin ꝟns ...... Pipewell, Northampt ꝟse, Cistercian Aꝟey	Died without legitimate issue, and the title became extinct. His children by his first wife were bastardized; and by his two others, he had none.[30]

Grantee.	Name.	Fate.
Northumberland, John, duke of	Balsall, Warwickshire, Preceptory Brinkeburne, Northumberland, Austin Canons .... Calke, Derbyshire, Austin Cell ... Nost, Northu...d, Benedictine Cell ...., Grey Friars .... Hyrst, Lincolnshire, Austin Canons Kilburne, ..., Benedictine Nunnery .... Lambley, Northumberland, Benedictine Nunnery .... Melsa, Yorkshire, Cistercian Abbey Newcastle-on-Tyne, Austin Friars Penkridge, Staffordshire, College Stratfor ..., College .... Snaith, Yorkshire, Benedictine Cell Tynemouth, Northumberland, Benedictine Cell ...., Black Friars ...., White Friars ...., B... ... Abbey .... Wolverhampton, College	Beheaded for high treason, 1553. He left several sons, all unhappy. Henry died at the siege of Boulogne; John, by courtesy earl of Warwick, died in his father's lifetime, with no issue; ..., afterwards restored in blood and earl of ... r W...k, thrice ..., but died without issue; G..., ... with his father; Robert, afterwards earl of Leicester, whose crimes and misfortunes are well known; ... Henry, who was slain at S. Quentin; and ..., who died a child.[31]

Palmer, sir Thomas	Snelleshall, Buckinghamshire, Benedictine Priory ...... South Malling, Sussex, College ... Wigmore, Herefordshire, Austin Canons	Attainted and beheaded.
Palmer, sir Henry .. .	Wingham, Kent, College......	Slain at the siege of Guisnes,[32] aged seventy.
Page, sir Richard	Thoby, Essex, Austin Canons...... Flamstead, Hertfordshire, Benedictine Nuns	Died without heirs-male.
Paston, Thomas	Binham, Norfolk, Benedictine Cell Sudbury, Suffolk, College	Family extinct.[33]
Ratcliffe, sir Humphrey	Elstow, Bedfordshire, Benedictine Nunnery......	Family extinct, 1641.[34]
Ramsden, William	Blyth, Nottinghamshire, Benedictine Priory : (half) ...... Northampton, Black Friars... ...... , White Friars ...... Oxford, S. Mary, College (half) ... R ch, Yorkshre, Cistercian Abb ye (half)	Family either extinct or reduced to extreme i digence.
Rowlet, Ralph	S. Mary du Prè, Hertfordshire, Benedictine Nunnery	His son and heir sir Ralph, dying without heir male, the family became extinct.[35]

Grantee.	Name.	Fate.
Sandys, William, lord, of the Vine..............	Mottisfont, Austin Canons, Hants, by exchange	This William was first lord Sandys. William, fourth lord Sandys, died without issue-male, and was [?] by his [?], and Henry Sandys, mortally wounded in the fight at Bram-ber. His son, W... [?], died without issue, and was succeeded by his brother Henry, who died without issue; and he by his brother William, who, dying without issue, the family became extinct in the male line.[36]
Sharington, sir William	Avebury, { originally Alien Priories, afterwards granted to Fotheringay } Notts / Charlton, / Lacock, Austin Nuns	Family extinct. The family of the Talbots, to whom Lacock next passed, also extinct; the present possessor, though bearing the same name, being of a different family; his father gained it by act of parliament. (Information received from the place.)[?]
Seymour, lord, of Sude-ley	Bardsey, Caernarvonshire, Abbey / Coggeshall, Essex, Cistercian Abbey.............. / Edindon, Wilts, Bonhommes ...... / Hales, [?], Cistercian Abbey,................ / South Baddesley, Hants, Precep-tory................	Beheaded for [?] treason, 1549.
	Amesbury, Wilts, Benedictine Nunnery.................... / Eston, Wilts, Trinitarian Friars......	

Founder	Houses	Notes
Southampton, Wriothes-ley, earl of	Beaulieu, Hants, Cistercian Abbey; ..., Bucks, Cistercian Abbey; Tichfield, Hants, Præmonstra... nAbbey; Winchester, S. Elizabeth's College	The earl died 1550. His son, Henry, second earl, was in trouble about Mary, ... of S... ...so... Henry, third ..., ...ed for high treason in the insurrection of the earl of Essex, though pardoned. Thomas, ... "of a nature much in lin de to melancholy," married thrice, but left no surviving ...le. Whereupon the title became extinct.[38]
Shelton, sir John	Carow, Norfolk, Benedictine Nunnery..................	Family either extinct or reduced to extreme indigence.
Southampton, William, earl of	Shaftesbury, Benedictine Nunnery	Died without legitimate issue, 1543.[37]

Grantee.	Name.	Fate.
Stanhope, sir Michael ...	Athelington, Dorsetshire, Hospital (half)............ Beverley College (so far as respects the prebendal houses, half)..... Shelford, Notts, August inn Priory........................... York (S. William's College), half	Beheaded, 1552.[39]
	Barling, Præmonstratensian Abbey, Lincolnshire .... Boston, Black Friars............. Bullington, Gilbertine Priory...... Burcester, Austin Canons, Oxon... Burwell, late Alien Priory, Lincolnshire........................ Ellesham, Austin Canons, Lincolnshire .... Erdbury, Austin Canons, Warwickshire .... Eye, Benedictine Priory, Suffolk Greenfield, Cistercian Nunnery, Lincolnshire .... Goring, Austin Nuns, Oxon ...... Kirksted, Cistercian Abbey, Lincolnshire........................	This despoiler of *thirty* ~~dies~~ was married four times. By his first wife he had no children. By his second, a daughter, ~~My~~, married to lord ~~Me~~, by whom she had three sons, of whom two died without issue; the third left issue only a daughter, and in him the title ~~the~~ extinct. By his third wife, the duke had issue one son, created earl of Lincoln, who died at an early age; and two daughters.

folk, Charles, duke of

Leystone, Præmonstratensian Abbey, Suffolk ....
Lincoln, Gilbertine Priory ....
Louth Park, Cistercian Abbey ...
Malteby, Preceptory, Lincolnshire
Markeby, Austin Canons, Lincoln.
Maxstoke, Austin Canons, Warwickshire ....
Monks Kirby, late Alien Priory, Warwickshire ....
Newhouse, Præmonstratensian Abbey ....
Oldbury, Benedictine Nuns, Warwickshire ....
Revesby, Cistercian Abbey, Lincolnshire ....
Skirbecke, Hospital, Lincolnshire
Stonely, Cistercian Abbey, Warwickshire ....
Ribstone, Preceptory, Yorkshire...
Tattershall, College, Lincolnshire
Stamford, Grey Friars...........
Temple Bruerne, Preceptory, Lincoln ....
Trentham, Austin Canons, Oxon
Vaudey, Cistercian Abbey, Lincoln......................
Wellesford, late Alien Priory......

Frances married Henry, duke of Suffolk, who was beheaded, 1554; and by him she had, 1. Lady Jane Grey, beheaded; 2. Lady Catherine Grey, married Henry, lord Herbert, who divorced her; and then Edward, earl of Hertford, beheaded; and 3. Lady Mary Grey, married to Martin Keys, and died without issue. After the execution of her husband, Frances Brandon married Adrian Stokes; and appears by him to have had no issue. The duke's third daughter, Eleanor, married Henry, earl of Cumberland, and by him had two sons, Henry and Charles, who both died young; and Margaret, married to Henry, earl of Derby. By his fourth wife the duke had two sons, who both, in turn, succeeded; and died of the sweating-sickness in one day, July 14, 5 Ed. VI. A more remarkable instance could scarcely be found wherein, in the next generation, a man's name has been clean put out.

Grantee.	Name.	Fate.
Suffolk, Henry, duke of	Breadsale, Austin Friars, Derbyshire .... Holiwell, Benedictine Nunnery, London .... Oxford, Austin Friars	Beheaded for high treason, bringing ruin on his whole family, as related in the preceding.
Surrey, Henry, earl of ...	Rushworth College, Norfolk ...... Wymondham, Benedictine Abbey	Henry VIII.'s last victim : beheaded, 1546.
Sussex, Robert, earl of ...	Attleborough Colleg , Norfolk ... Dunmow, Austin Canons, Essex... Clyve, Cistercian Abbey, Somersetshire .... Pountney College, London (in part)	He died the year following the grant of Attleborough : see next.
Sussex, Thomas, earl of, grandson of the last	Clyve (regranted)	Died without surviving male heirs : family extinct, 1641, a century after meddling with church property.
		The barony of Talbot, being a barony in fee, passed, at the death of Gilbert, seventh earl of Shrewsbury, without heirs-male, with Alethea, his daughter, into the Howard family. The title was continued in the Talbots. Edward,

Talbot, William, lord ... } Pontefract, Cluniac Priory, York-shire ...... eighth earl, died wi[th]out heirs-male. and was succeeded by his kinsman George, nin[t]h earl, who, dying without heirs-male in 163[.], was [succ]e[ed]ed by his nephew John, tenth ear[l]. He was [succe]ed by his eldest son, [the] duke of Buckingham, March 16, 1667: and it is s[ai]d that hi's own wife [and] as the duke's page. He was succeeded by his son Charles, twelfth earl, created marquis of Alton and duke of Shr[ews]bury: on his death without male-issue, in 1717, th[o]se titles became extinct: but the earldom devolved on his grace's cousin, Gilbert, of right, thirteenth earl: but he being a Roman Catholic Priest, could never use it. He was succeeded by his nephew, George, fourteenth earl: who died without issue, and was [succeeded] by his nephew, Charles, fifteenth earl, who died without issue, and was [succee]ded by his nephew, John, present and sixteenth earl. His lordship has no male-heir:—and the heir presumptive to the earldom is his nephew. Thus, since 1616 the title has only [bee]n [d]escended from father to son.

Tregonwell, sir John ... { Milton Abbas, Benedictine Monas-te[r]y .... } The branch of the family which possessed the Abbey, extinct.

Grantee.	Name.	Fate.
Tyrwhitt, sir Robert ...	Cameringham, late Alien Priory, Lincolnshire .... Irford, Præmonstratensian Nunnery. Stanfield, Benedictine Nunnery...	Family extinct. They built a noble inn & one on the site of the Priory, which fell into great decay, during the time the estate was held by Frances, sister and heiress to the last male descendant, sir John de la Fountaine Tyrwhitt. After his death, the greater part was taken down.
Westmoreland, Ralph, earl of	Keldon, Cistercian Nuns, Yorkshire Rosedale Nuns	His grandson, Charles, joined in the great rebellion of 13 Elizabeth. He saved his life by flight, and retired into the Netherlands, where "he lived meanly and miserably to a great age." His terminated, in disgrace, the barony of Neville of Raby, and the earldom of Westmoreland.
Williams, Roger	Usk, Benedictine Nunnery, Monmouthshire...............	Family extinct. (Information received from Usk.)
Windsor, Andrews, lord	Ankerwyke, Benedictine Nunnery, Bucks .... Bordesley,[40] Cistercian Abbey, Worcestershire .... Minchinhampton, late Alien Priory Gloucestershire............... Pleyden, Hospital, Sussex	Family extinct in the direct male line, 1642.

(¹) The family of the Cromwells, alias Williams, came originally from Wales, and dated back their genealogy as far back as 1066. Sir Richard Williams, alias Cromwell, was first nephew to Thomas Cromwell, earl of Essex. Sir Richard was one of the visitors of Religious houses, and had the nunnery of Hinchinbrooke, in Huntingdonshire, granted him, and also the abbey of Grey Friars in Yarmouth, Norfolk, but more especially Ramsey Abbey, Hunts, was given to him for the sum of £4,963 4s. 2d. He was great-grandfather of the usurper Oliver. He had two sons, Henry and Francis ; sir Henry was grandfather of the usurper : he was knighted by queen Elizabeth : he died in 1604. He was twice married : by his first wife he had many children, none by the second. His children were sir Oliver : Robert, father of the usurper ; Henry, who married twice and had three sons and two daughters, viz.—1st, Richard, who had two children, one of whom, a daughter (the son died in infancy), married her second cousin Henry, grandson and representative of sir Oliver above-mentioned, and in which Henry the elder branch became extinct. 2nd, Henry who died before his father. 3rd, Another son who died before his father ; and two daughters, Elizabeth and Anna. The 4th son of sir Henry was Richard, who died childless ; the 5th was Philip, who had eight children, but who amongst them all (one was hung for murder) had only four heirs ; the 6th was Ralph, who died an infant ; 7th, Joan, who married sir Francis Barrington, whose family in the male line in the Isle of Wight is now extinct. 8th, Elizabeth, married to W. Hampton. 9th, Frances, wife of Richard Keston. 10th, Mary, married to sir W. Dunel. 11th, Dorothy, married to sir Thomas Fleming. Sir Oliver, the eldest son of sir Henry and uncle to the usurper, had many children ; some died childless ; the families of others are gone to decay, so much so, that at the end of the last century, some of the descendants in the female line received parish relief. Henry Williams, alias Cromwell, his eldest son, had several children, both sons and daughters, of whom only three, viz., one son and two daughters, survived him. Henry his son, who married his second cousin, Anna, died suddenly and childless, Aug. 3, 1673, and in him the elder branch was extinct, and Ramsey Abbey passed to his sisters, who disposed of it to colonel Titus, who left it to his daughters, of whom one bequeathed it to her servants, John Smith and Catharine Gofford ; Coulson Fellowes bought it of them, and his son at the end of the last century had it.

" The family of Cromwell, the most opulent in Huntingdonshire," says Noble, the biographer of the Cromwells, " after a gradual decline totally expired, and their great riches fell into various hands : Ramsey, the richest, into those of the celebrated colonel Titus, by purchase : what this monastery was may be guessed by the value of such appendages as were held by the Cromwells, which would now let for perhaps upwards of £80,000 per annum ; but the estates had been so lessened that this Mr. Cromwell alias Williams had only £2,000 per annum, and that probably much encumbered.

(²) The daughters of the house of Russell seem to have brought the usual fate of abbey-lands into the families into which they married. We will trace them out.

1. Anne, daughter of the second earl, married Henry Somerset, first marquis of Worcester—her descendant is the present duke of Beaufort.
2. Anne, eldest daughter of William baron Russell of Thorn-haugh, married Ambrose Dudley, earl of Warwick ;—title extinct.
3. Elizabeth, second daughter of the same, married William Bourchier, earl of Bath ;—title extinct.
4. Margaret, third daughter of the same, married George Clifford, earl of Cumberland ;—title extinct.
5. Catherine, eldest daughter of Francis, fourth earl, married Robert lord Brooke, who died childless.
6. Anne, second daughter of the same, married George Digby, earl of Bristol ;—title extinct.
7. Margaret, third daughter of the same, married,
   (1) James Hay, earl of Carlisle ;—title extinct.
   (2) Edward Montagu, earl of Manchester ; and by him had no children.
   (3) Robert Rich, earl of Warwick ;—title extinct.
8. Diana, fourth daughter of the same, married Francis Newport, earl of Bradford ;—title extinct.
9. Rachael, eldest daughter of the beheaded lord William, married William, second duke of Devonshire—her descendant is the present duke.
10. Catherine, second daughter of the same, married John, second duke of Rutland—her descendant is the present duke.
11. Diana, fourth daughter of the same, married,
    (1) Sir Greville Verney ;—(? if childless).
    (2) William, lord Allington ;—title extinct.
12. Margaret, sixth daughter of the same, married Edward Russell, earl of Orford ;—title extinct in him.
13. Rachael, eldest daughter of Wriothesley, second duke, married,
    (1) Scroop, first duke of Bridgewater ;—title extinct.
    (2) Sir Richard Lyttleton, who died childless.
14. Elizabeth, second daughter of the same, married William, third earl of Essex ;—the present earl is her descendant.

Thus, in the two first centuries after the ennoblement of the House of Russell, we find that its daughters intermarried into eighteen families; but only in four cases have they descendants now existing on the male line. To pursue the inquiry below that period would prove nothing, the times being manifestly too near to our own. The only remaining marriages took place in 1762, 1816, 1829, 1832, 1842.

NOTES TO APPENDIX II.

(¹) Hitchin's Cornwall.
(²) See Whitaker's History of Whalley.
(³) Hasted's Kent, iii. 330.   (⁴) Braybrooke's Audley End.
(⁵) Burke's Extinct Baronetage, 51. (⁶) Hasted's Kent, i. 201.
(⁷) Leland, Itinerary, i. 136.   (⁸) Leland, Itinerary, i. 39.
(⁹) Information received from the parish of Epworth.
(¹⁰) Burke's Commonalty, iv. 482.
(¹¹) Chalmers' Biographical Dictionary, v. 5.
(¹²) Hasted's Kent, ii. 648.
(¹³) Banks' Baronia Anglica, ii. 101, 2.
(¹⁴) Tanner, by mistake, makes *William* lord Cobham first. grantee of Burnham, Norton.   (¹⁵) Banks' Bar. Ang. ii. 108, 9.
(¹⁶) Burke's Extinct Baronetage, pp. 124, 5, 6.
(¹⁷) Tanner makes *Thomas* lord Dacre first grantee. If so, he was hung, in pretence for the murder of a park-keeper of sir Nicholas Pelham : in reality for his great possessions ; Æt. 24.
(¹⁸) Banks' Baronia Anglica, ii. 139.—See Jefferson's Cumberland, i. 60.   (¹⁹) Information received from Pembroke.
(²⁰) Shaw's Staffordshire, 2 Part, i. 143.
(²¹) Banks, iii. 285, 6.
(²²) Information received from the place.
(²³) Burke's Extinct Baronetage, 221.
(²⁴) Comp. Dugdale's Monasticon, vi. 1486, with Burke's Extinct Baronetage, 289.
(²⁵) Banks, ii. 227.   (²⁶) Hasted's Kent.
(²⁷) Burke's Extinct Baronetage, 356.
(²⁸) Banks, iii. 539.   (²⁹) Clutterbuck's Herts. ii. 551.
(³⁰) Banks, iii. 595, 6.   (³¹) Banks, iii. 572.
(³²) Hasted's Kent, iii. 700.
(³³) Burke's Extinct Baronetage, 402.   (³⁴) Banks, iii. 696.
(³⁵) Clutterbuck's Herts. i. 14.   (³⁶) Banks, ii. 457, 8.
(³⁷) But quære whether Tanner is not mistaken in giving Shaftesbury to *William*, earl of Southampton. If right in the person, he is wrong in the date, 1 Edward VI., for this earl had then been dead some years, and Thomas Wriothesley had been created earl of Southampton by patent, three days before the coronation of Edward VI.
(³⁸) Banks, iii. 671.
(³⁹) See Debrett's Peerage, under " Chesterfield."
(⁴⁰) By compulsory exchange for his own seat, Stanwell, **which** his ancestors had held from the conquest.—Banks, ii. 610.

APPENDIX III.

MITRED ABBEYS AND PRIORIES IN IRELAND.

Fate of the First Possessors.

(From *Archdall's Monasticon*).

[It has been thought right to add these, though the want· of Irish County Histories renders it impossible to trace the fate of the greater number of their possessors.]

1. Mellifont . . . . . The Abbey turned into a dwelling-house; which, holding for the king, was besieged by the rebels in 1641. It surrendered on promise of quarter: but many of its defenders were murdered* in cold blood.

2. Baltinglass . . . . Granted to Baron Fitz Eustace, Viscount Baltinglass, in 1541: family extinct in 1583.

3. Jeripoint . . . . . Granted to James, Earl of Ormond: elder branch of family, after suffering great hardships, extinct by the death in exile of the twelfth earl, 1746.

4. Tracton. . . . . . Of its earlier possessors we find nothing: the title, Baron Tracton of Tracton, granted in 1781, is now extinct.

5. Rathtoo. . . . . . Abbey-house seized, and burnt by the rebels, 1600.

6. Louth, S. Mary . Granted to Plunket, Lord Louth: title forfeited 1641.

7. Dublin, S. Mary . James, earl of Desmond, was the grantee. His son, Gerald, earl of Desmond, fifteenth in succession of a family dating its honours from 1329, engaged in the rebellion of 1582. Reduced to extremities, he lived like a wild

* Cox's History of Ireland, ii. 92.

beast, continually hunted by his enemies in Harlow Wood: and once he and his countess only escaped by standing up to their chins in water. In 1583, he was surprised at night:—" One Kilby struck the old man with his sword, and nearly cut off his arm: whereupon the old man cried out, that he was earl of Desmond. And Kilby would have spared him: but finding that he bled so fast that he could not live, he immediately cut off the earl's head, which was sent afterwards to England, and placed on a pole in London."*

8. Dublin, S. Thomas
9. Douske.
10. Bective.
11. Trim, S. Peter's.
12. Caral.

We cannot learn the grantees.

13. Dumbrody, granted to Osborne Itchingham,
14. Monasternenagh, ,, S. H. Wallop,
15. Wothney, ,, Sir E. Walsh,
16. Athassell, ,, James White,
17· Killagh, ,, Thomas Clinton.
Of whom we can learn nothing.
18. Kells, ,, James, earl of Ormond. (See iii.3.)
19. Down.† ,, Lord Baltimore. Family extinct, 1731.
:20· Tintern, Wexford ,, Antony Colcleugh: and the property, when Archdall wrote, (1786,) was in his descendant Vesey Colcleugh. But the last possessor of that name died two or three years ago: and on his widow's death, it must go to another family, as we learn by information received from the place.
:21· Monaster, Evan ,, George, lord Audley: family exists, but the property is not in it.

Hence it appears, that of the possessors of the eleven

* Cox's History of Ireland, ii. 369. (But the book is so badly paged in that part, as to make the numbers nearly useless.)
† But query whether this be the Mitred Abbey.

Mitred Abbeys, of which we have any data, not one family remains in possession of the estate:—one exists. in the direct, and one in the younger line.

[Also the following were suppressed by Henry VIII. and granted as stated: about forty of the lesser ones in. 1528, and the remainder in 1536 and following years.

COUNTY OF ANTRIM.

22. Carrickfergus, a Franciscan Abbey, granted to . . . . Marquis of Donegal..
23. Massareene, a Franciscan Abbey and Estate, granted to. . .   ,,   ,,
24. Ballycastle, Abbey and Estate, to. . . . . Earl of Antrim.
25. Bonamargy, Abbey and Estate, to. . . . . ,,
26. Glenarm, Franciscan Abbey and Estate, to . . . . . ,,

COUNTY TYRONE.

27. Dungannon, Franciscan Friary and Estate, to . . . . . Marquis of Donegal..

COUNTY CAVAN.

28. Ballylinch, Hospital and Estate, to. . . . . Earl of Drogheda.
29. Dromlonman, Hospital and Estate, to . . . . . . ,,
30. Mounterconagh, Hospital and Estate, to . . . . ,,

COUNTY KILDARE.

31. Kilrush, Augustine Abbey and Estate, to . . . . Earl of Ormond.

COUNTY CLARE.

32. Clare, Augustine Abbey and Estate, to . . . . Earl of Thomond.
33. Inchycronane, Monastery and Island of, to . . . . . . ,,
34. Inisnegenagh, Priory and Island of, to . . . . . . ,,

COUNTY CORK.

35. Castle Lyons, Dominican Monastery and Estate, to . . . Earl of Cork.

County Down.

36. Gray, Abbey and Estate, to . Earl of Kildare.
37. Iniscourcey, Abbey and Estate,
to . . . . „
38. Saul, Abbey and Estate, to. . „
39. Downpatrick, two Priories, a
Friary, and a Hospital, to. . „
40. Dundrum, a Castle of the
Templars, to . . . . . . „

County Galway.

41. Gormoghan, Abbey and Estate,
to . . . . Earl of Clanricarde.
42. Aughrim, Augustine Priory and
Estate, to . . . . „
43. Clonthuskert, Monastery of
Canons and Estate, to . . . „
44. Ernan Dune, Nunnery and
Estate, to . . . . „
45. Kilmacduagh, Abbey and
Estate, to . . . . „
46. Loughrergh, Carmelite Friary
and Estate, to. . . . . . „
47. Millick, Franciscan Friary and
Estate, to . . . . „
48. Rosserelly, Franciscan Monastery and Estate, to . . . . „
49. Tuam, Priory of S. John with
Estate, to . . . . „

County Meath.

50. Lough Shillesni, Nunnery and
Estate at, near Cavan, to . . Earl of Kildare.

County Roscommon.

51. Killaraght, Nunnery at, to . . Earl of Clanricarde.

County Kilkenny.

52. Callan, Augustine Friary and
Estate, to . . . . Earl of Ormond.
53. Jerpoint, Cistercian Abbey and
Estate, to . . . . „
54. Inisbirge, Augustine Priory
and Estate, to . . . . . „

Queen's County.

55. Leix, Abbey and Estate, to . . ⚬

COUNTY SLIGO.

56. Clonmel, Franciscan Friary and
    Estate, to . . . .   Earl of Ormond.
57. Holy Cross, Cistercian Monas-
    tery and Estate, to . . . .   „
58. Kilcolly, Cistercian Abbey and
    Estate, to . . . .   „
59. Thurles, Carmelite Monastery
    and Estate, to . . . . .   „

COUNTY WATERFORD.

60. Carrickfergus,   Franciscan
    Friary and Estate, to . . .   „

COUNTY WEXFORD.

61. Kilclogan,   Commandery   and
    Estate, to . . . .   „   „
62. Magere Nuidhere, Monastery
    of S. Saviour and Estate, to .   „   „]

[E.]

APPENDIX IV.

The following may be taken as a fair specimen of the
Curses pronounced on the violators of the privileges and
property of Monastic Institutions. There does not appear
to have been one universal form; the tenor of the imprecation varied according to the will of the Founder. Those
which we give are selected at random, one from Martene,
the other from Horstius' Edition of S. Bernard.

*Tenor Maledictionis ferendæ in pervasores, latrones et præ-
dones rerum Fontanellæ*

Auctoritate Omnipotentis DEI et B. Petri Apostolorum
principis, cui à DOMINO DEO collocata est potestas ligandi
atque solvendi super terram, fiat manifesta vindicta de
malefactoribus, latronibus et prædonibus possessionum et
rerum juriumque et libertatum Monasterii Sancti Wandregisilii de Fontanellâ totiusque congregationis ipsius
Monasterii, nisi de malignitate suâ resipiscant cum effectu.
Si autem prædicti malefactores hoc in quo ipsi commiserint
emendari voluerint, veniat super illos benedictio Omnipotentis DEI et retributio bonorum operum. Si verò in
suâ malignitate corda eorum indurata fuerint, et pos-
sessiones cæteraque reddere noluerint, seu ad statum
debitum redire non promiserint et emendare pœnitentialiter, malitiosè distulerint, veniant super illos omnes
maledictiones quibus Omnipotens DEUS maledixit qui
dixerunt DOMINO DEO, Recede à nobis; viam Scientiarum
Tuarum nolumus : et qui dixerunt, hæreditate possideamu-
Sanctuarium DEI. Fiat pars illorum et hæreditas igni-
perpetui cruciatûs. Cum Chorâ, Dathan et Abiron, qui
descenderunt in infernum viventes; cum Judâ et Pilato
Cayaphâ et Annâ, Simone Mago et Nerone cum quibus
cruciatû perpetuo sine fine crucientur. Ita quòd nec cum
CHRISTO nec cum Sanctis Ejus in cœlesti quiete societatem
habeant, sed habeant societatem cum diabolo et sociis
ejus in inferni tormentis deputati et pereant in æternum.
Fiat. Fiat.

*Modus exequendi hujusmodi maledictionem in die Dominico-
et quotidianis diebus in dicto Monasterio.*

Finito Evangelio à Diacono, stans Presbyter ante altare
dicat: Domini Fratres, nullus fidelium æstimet aut
credat ut hanc maledictionem quam pro inimicis nostris
ante DEUM et pretiosissimum principemque Apostolorum

Petrum, cui data est licentia ligandi et solvendi à Domino, quotidiè fundimus, ullà nostrâ temeritate aut præsumptione advenissemus; sed potestate acceptâ à sede Apostolicâ quo et ipsi potestatem hoc agendi dederunt patrono nostro S. Wandregisilio et maledictionem quam ipsi pro prosecutoribus sanctæ Dei Ecclesiæ exequebantur, congregatio S. Wandregisilii ubicumque necessè fuisset si non resipiscerent similiter fecisset. Et post hæc maledictionem istam confirmaverunt Sancti Pontifices, S. Audoenus Archiepiscopus, etc., etc.

[Here follow the names of many persons who had confirmed the right of Malediction.]

Invocatio ad Deum.

Omnipotens Deus, Qui solus respicis afflictionem omnium ad Te clamantium, Qui lacrimas pupillorum ac viduarum ad aures Tuas misericorditer pervenire concedis, respice super nos famulos Tuos, sanctissimis ac piissimis confessoribus Tuis Wandregesilio, Ansbroto, Wulfrano et Erembroto monachis [intercedentibus], et vindica nos de inimicis nostris qui villas nostras tenent et prædant, unde vestire et administrationem habere debemus. Si autem, quod totis veribus optamus, hoc etiam dare studuerint, veniat, super illos benedictio Omnipotentis Dei et retributio bonorum operum. At si induraverint et res atque prædia suprà dictorum SS. reddere noluerint et emendare pœnitentialiter malitiosè distulerint, veniant super illos omnes maledictiones quibus Deus Omnipotens illos maledixit, qui dixerunt Domino Deo, Recede à nobis, scientiam viarum Tuarum nolumus; et qui dixerunt, hereditate possideamus Sanctuarium Dei. Fiat pars eorum et hereditas ignis perpetui cruciatûs cum Dathan et Abiron, Judâ atque Pilato, Sapphirâ et Ananiâ, Cayaphâ et Annâ, Simone et Nerone, cum quibus cruciatu perpetuo sine fine torqueantur. Ita ut nec cum Christo et Sanctis Ejus in cœlesti quiete societatem habeant; sed habeant societatem cum Diabolo et sociis ejus in inferno tormentis deputatis et pereant in æternum. Maledicti, sint in civitatibus, maledicti in agris, maledicti in castellis, maledicti in insulis. Maledictus fructus ventris eorum, maledicti in domibus, maledicti ingredientes, maledicti in omnibus locis. Mittat Dominus super eos famem esuriem et increpationem et in omnia opera eorum quæ faciunt donec conterat eos et perdat velociter de terrâ. Sit cœlum quod super eos est æreum, et terra quam calcant ferrea. Percutiat eos Dominus amentia et cæcitate ac furore mentis, et palpent in meridie sicut palpare solet cæcus in tenebris, et nesciant dirigere vias suas. Omni tempore calumniam sustineant et opprimanturviolentiâ nec habeant qui liberet eos. Sit cadaver eorum in escam volatilibus cœli et bestiis terræ, et non sint qui sepeliant illud. Constitue super eos peccatorem et Diabolus stet à dextris eorum. Omnes istæ maledictiones veniant super eos et persequentes apprehendant eos donec intereant. O claviger ætherie Petre beatissime, exaudi nos famulos tuos suppliciter ad DEUM orantes et ante confessores CHRISTI Wandregisilium, Ansbrotum, Wulfranum et Erembrotum reclamantes de inimicis nostris. Exaudi nos etiam famulos tuos pro peccatis nostris talia patientes ad DEUM et ad te cum quodam singultu graviter, suspirantes et sæpiùs reclamantes de cunctis omnibus qui nobis mala fecerunt. Ergò ponantur et isti similiter ut rota et sicut stipula ante faciem venti et sicut participes omnium maledictionem, earum scilicet quæ suprà insertæ sunt, donec erubêscant et resipiscant. Quod si non erubuerint cessantes à malefactis suis et resipiscant; fac eos de cœtu sanctorum et terrâ viventium æternaliter eradicatos esse atque extorres, nunc et in perpetuum.——

Finitâ Maledictione à Sacerdote, sonent fratres campanas et cantent Psalmos et preces sequentes : " Usquequò DOMINE oblivi sceris ; " " Deus noster Refugium ; " " Quid gloriaris ; " " DEUS venerunt gentes ; " " Qui regis Israel ; " " DEUS, quis similis erit ; " " DEUS laudem meau."

Preces.

V. Obscurentur oculi eorum ne videant:
R. Et dorsum eorum semper incurva.
V. Effunde super eos iram Tuam :
R. Et furor iræ Tuæ comprehendat eos.
V. Fiat habitatio eorum deserta:
R. Et in tabernaculis eorum non sit qui inhabitet.
V. Veniat mors super illos :
R. Et descendant in infernum viventes.
V. Pone eos ut clibanum ignis :
R. In tempore vultûs Tui.
V. DOMINUS in irâ Suâ conturbabit eos :
R. Et devorabit eos ignis.
V. Fructum eorum de terrâ perdes:
R. Et semen eorum à filiis hominum.
V. Fiat via illorum tenebræ et lubricum:
R. Et Angelus DOMINI persequere eos.
V. Veniat illis laqueus quem ignorant:
R. Et captio quem abscondet apprehendet eos.
V. Proptereà DEUS destruet eos in finem :
R. Evellet eos et emigrabit eos de tabernaculis eorum.
V. Sicut ignis qui comburit silvam et sicut flamma comburens montes :

R. Ita persequeris illos in tempestate Tuâ et irâ Tuâ. turbabis eos.

V. In Deo faciemus virtutem :

R. Et Ipse ad nihilum deducet inimicos nostros.

Martene de Sacris Ritibus, tom. ii. lib. iii. cap. 3.

Solemnes Formæ Donationum.

Offero Deo atque dedico omnes res quæ hâc in chartâ tenentur insertæ pro remissione peccatorum meorum ac parentum et filiorum (aut pro quocumque illis Deus deliberare voluerit) ad serviendum ex his Deo in sacrificiis missarumque solemniis, orationibus, luminariis, pauperum ac clericorum alimoniis et cæteris divinis cultibus atque Illius Ecclesiæ utilitatibus. Si quis autem indè, quod fieri nullatenùs credo, abstulerit, sub pœnâ sacrilegii ex hoc Domino Deo, Cui eas offero atque dedico, districtis-simas reddat rationes.

Si quis voluntati meæ per quaslibet adinventiones seu propositiones (sicut mundus quotidiè artibus et ingeniis expolitur) obvius vel repetitor, convulsor etiam aut ter-giversator exstiterit, anathema sit. Et sicut Dathan et Abiron hiatu terræ absorpti sint viventes, in infernum descendat. Et cum Giezi fraudis mercatore et in præsenti et in futuro sæculo partem damnationis excipiat : et tum veniam consequatur quando consecuturus est Diabolus qui sese fallendo æthereâ sede dejectus, &c.

Si quis verò, si ego ipse, etc., iram Trinæ Majestatis incurret, et ante Tribunal Christi deducat rationes.

Si quis fortè, &c., primùm quidem iram Omnipotentis Dei incurrat, auferatque Deus partem illius de terrâ viventium et deleat nomen ejus de libro vitæ; fiatque pars illius cum his qui dixerunt Domino Deo, Recede à nobis ; cum Dathan et Abiron quos terra aperto ore deglutivit et vivos infernus absorbuit, perennem incurret damnationem. Socius quoque Judæ Domini proditoris effectus æternis cruciatibus retrusus teneatur ; et ne ei in præsenti sæculo humanis oculis impune transire videatur in corpore quidem proprio futuræ damnationis tormenta experiatur, sortitus duplicem direptionem cum Heliodoro et Antiocho, quorum alter acribus verberibus coercitus vix semivivus evasit; alter verè nutu superno percussus putrescentibus membris et scatentibus vermibus miserrimè interiit; cæterisque Sacri-legis qui ærarium domûs Domini temerariè præsumpserunt, particeps existat; habeatque nisi resipuerit archiclavum totius monarchiæ Ecclesiarum, juncto sibi Paulo, obstito-rem et amœni Paradisi aditûs contradictorem.

Vide Notas Horstii in *S. Bernardi Epistolas.*

INDEX.

A.

B.

F F

I.

J.

K.

L.

Latimer, H., bp. of Worcester, 111.
——, barony of, liv., 124.
Lawrence, S., Abbey, lay possessors of, 158.
Lee, Dr. E., archbishop of York, 109.
Leeds (Kent) lay possessors of, 197.
Leicester, earl of, his sacrilege, 259.
——, earldom of, extinct, liv.
Lennox, earldom of, liv.
Leominster, lay possessors of, 209.
Lever, on impropriations, lxxii.
Lisle, barony of, extinct, liii.
Lingfield Collegiate Church, lay possessors of, 188.
Lindores Abbey, lay possessors of, 224.
Llanthony Abbey, lay possessors of, 190, 194.

Lock, P., a persecutor, 269.
Long, Richard, misfortunes of, 271.
Longland, J., bp. of Lincoln, 110.
Lorraine, cardinal de, death of, li.
Lucian, his testimony to the abhorrence felt for sacrilege, xxx.
Lumley, John, lord. 124.
Luppet, Abbey lands there, lay possessors of, 221.
Luther, M., on sacrilege, lxix.
Lynn, corporation of, purchase of Church property, 139.
——, decline of, 139.
Lyominster, Sussex, lay possessors of, 205.
Lyon, rev. C. J., his account of sacrilege in Scotland, iv.

M.

Madoc, ap Meredith, his sacrilege, 64.
Maltravers, barony of, extinct, liv.
Malmsbury, William of, states the manifest fulfilment of judgment of God against sacrilege, xiv.
Manby, Dr., his misfortunes, 271.
Manning, History of Surrey, vii.
Mandeville, earl of Essex, death of, lii., 69, 70.
Manners, Thomas, earl of Rutland, 118.
Matham, lay possessors of, 154.
Marriages, proportion of barren to fertile, lix.
Marischal, noble family of, the decay of, 234.
Martin and Jacob, History of Soissons, viii.
Martel, Charles, sacrilege of, his punishment, xxxi.
Marmion, Robert, his sacrilege, 71.
Massingham Abbey, lay possessors of, 143.
Maximian, his sacrilege, 42.
May, History of Evesham, viii.
Megacles, sacrilege of, its punishment, xxix.
Merton Priory, lay possessors of, 173-176.
Melrose Abbey, lay possessors of, 229.
Menard, History of Nismes, viii.
Meyrick, History of Cardiganshire, viii.
Miller, History of Doncaster, viii.
Milton Abbas Church, lay possessors of, 220.
Minster in Sheppey, lay possessors of, 197.

Monasteries, the dissolution of, hurtful to literature, a loss to the poor, xi., lxxii., 129.
—— were monuments of piety and devotion, xii.
—— were means for propagation of religion, xii.
——, dissolution of, caused destruction of many noble edifices, xiii.
——, tenants of, compelled to surrender their tenures, xiii.
——, rents greatly raised, xiii.
——, the inestimable benefits bestowed upon the Church by, xci.
——, estimate of their income, xciv.
——, date of dissolution of, 99.
—— in Norfolk, particulars of various dissolved, 136.
Monk-Bretton, lay possessors of, 208.
Montague family, earls of Sarum, their possession of Sherborne Castle, 68
Montagu, viscounty of, extinct, liv.
Montegle, Edward Stanley, lord, 124.
Montgomery, caused the death of Henry II, xlix.
Montjoy, barony of, extinct, liii.
Montjoy, peerage, 124.
Morbury, earl of, his death, lxviii.
Morant, History of Essex, vii.
Mors, Rodeiick, on the Dissolution, lxxii.
Morton, Dr., bp. of Lichfield, his increase of Vicarage of Pitchley, vii.
—— History of Northamptonshire, vii.
Moray, sketches of, viii.
Munster, Treaty, provisions of, xcviii.

N.

O.

P.

R.

Radegund, S., Abbey, lay possessors of, 158.
Rankin, rev. W., acknowledgment of his help, iv.
Ratcliff, Robert, earl of Sussex, 119.
Ravaillac, Francis, murderer of Henry IV., xlix.
Religious Buildings, held to bring misfortune on lay possessors, xxvii.
Repton or (Repingdon) Abbey, lay possessors of, 201.
Retribution, instances of, from profane history, xli.
Reynerus, his *Apostolatus Benedictinus*, lxi.

Richmond, duke of, death of, lii.
—— Priory, lay possessors of, 184.
Richard I., his sacrilege, 73; his death, 74.
Ridley, bp., on sacrilege, lxviii.
Rievaulx Abbey, lay possessors of, 249.
Rock Lane Chapel, Exeter, lay possessors of, 220.
Rosington, Mr., his misfortunes, 272.
Rouèt, Mdlle. du, 1.
Rowley, F., his misfortunes, 272.
Rudder, History of Gloucestershire, vii.
Rugg, W., bp. of Norwich, 111.
Russell, lord W., death of, lii.-lxviii.
Rutland, earldom of, liv.

S.

Sacrilege, History of, when begun, i.
—— ——, first published in 1698, ii.
——, nature of the argument against, xix.
—— of Jehoiakim, punishment of, xxi.
—— of rebuilder of Jericho, punishment of, xxi.
—— of Jeroboam, punishment of, xxi.
—— of Dathan and Abiram, punishment of, xxii.
—— of Korah, punishment of, xxii.
—— ——, gradation shown in this, xxii.
—— of Achan, punishment of, xxii.
—— of Solomon, punishment of, xxii., 8.
—— of Gideon, punishment of, xxiii.
—— of sons of Eli, punishment of, xxiii.
—— of Saul, punishment of, xxiii.
—— in heathens, instances of, xxv., 31.
——, men of Bethshemesh, punishment of, xxvi.
—— of Uzzah, punishment of, xxvi.
—— of Uzziah, punishment of, xxvi.
—— of Belshazzar, punishment of, xxvi.
—— of Ananias and Sapphira, punishment of, xxvii.
—— of Elymas, punishment of, xxvii.
—— of Simon Magus, punishment of, xxvii.
——, Lucian's testimony to general abhorrence of, xxx.

Sacrilege of Nobunanga, how punished, xxxi.
—— will be attended by *temporal* punishment, xxxiii., xl., xlvii, lvi., lvii.
——, exact nature of, xl., xlii., l.
——, punishment of, extends to descendants of the guilty, xliv.
——, apparent exceptions to this rule examined, 253-258.
—— punishment of, the more usual modes, xlvi.
—— contrast between England and France in the commission of, xlviii.
—— entails terrible judgments, lxviii.
——, a discourse of, lxxvii.
——, whether the Suppression of Abbeys was, xc.
——, the punishment of, not immediate nor universal, xcvi.
—— ——, in men otherwise good and religious, cxi.
——, that it is uncharitable to inquire into, cx.
——, the curse upon not extending to utter perdition, cxiii.
—— of Lucifer, 1.
——, all idolatry is, 1.
—— of Cain, 2, 5.
—— of Time, definition, 9.
—— of Persons, definition, 10.
—— ——, instances, Pharaoh, the Benjamites, Jeroboam, Joash, Zedekiah, 10-12.
—— of Function, definition, 12.
—— ——, instances, Gideon, Saul, Uzzah, Uzziah, 12, 13.

Printed at the South Counties Press Ltd., 64, High Street, Lewes.

NOTE ON PREFACE TO NEW EDITION.

Note at foot of first page of Preface (reference at " Neale ").

Mr. Neale's fellow-worker in the editing of " Sir Henry Spelman " was (see a letter in the " Guardian " of 24th April, 1889) the Rev. Joseph Haskoll. They published a second edition of their work in 1853; and though it has been found impossible to use this as the base of the present one, it is necessary to draw attention to a most valuable point made in the preface. Very much information was sent to the editors under *injunctions of secrecy.* It is, of course, possible that if they could have investigated this, as they investigated their other matter, some exaggeration might have been found; at the same time it is a legitimate deduction that a mass of unpublished evidence must exist which, if all could be known, might probably carry conviction to the most sceptical mind.

Still, some additional information is to be found in this edition of 1853, and for the lack of it in the present work it is hoped that the present series of notes may in some measure compensate. One merit, at any rate, they may claim, that an attempt has been made, where possible, to bring them up to date. In the above-mentioned letter to the " Guardian " this has been called " invidious," but the thing must be done; for, not to mention the secondary reasons of literary completeness, and that most men are more affected by an argument before their eyes than one behind their backs, it is essential to show that the law of the consequences of sacrilege continues even now to operate. To the publication of genealogical and historical facts (most of which, indeed, are already published in ordinary books of reference) it is not easy to see any objection; and if it is ever necessary remotely to allude to other matters, courtesy will dictate delicacy of language.

Note on page v. (*reference at "direction"*).

Mr. Neale and his editors quote Spelman's account of Sir Ralph Hare's restoration to St. John's College, Cambridge, 1623, of the Rectory, etc., of Marham, in Norfolk (there are still a certain number of "Hare Exhibitioners" at St. John's) ; but he does not mention what doubtless led Sir Ralph to the act of restitution. This Church property was purchased from the Crown at the dissolution by Sir Ralph's grandfather, John Hare, who had no fewer than eight sons; the two elder and four others all died without issue, and the male line of the youngest, the Lords Coleraine, expired before the end of the same century. Sir Ralph himself had but one brother, who also died without issue, and the male line of his only son became extinct in 1764. The family of the late Julius and Augustus Hare, which (as the arms are the same) is probably connected with this, appears to have branched off before the sacrilege.—See "Memorials of a Quiet Life," i., 13.

Note on page xx. (*reference at "sacrilege"*).

The Analogy of Scripture. Two additional instances of this may be given ; one as among the earliest in date, one as the strongest which can be found, the strongest, indeed, which can be conceived to exist :—(1) Terah, the father of Abraham, as we learn from Josh. xxiv., 2, deserted the worship of the true God for that of idols, and accordingly we are told (Gen. xi., 28) that his son Haran died before him, who was probably, though it is not absolutely certain, his eldest son. It is the first instance of a son's dying in his father's lifetime, and the striking coincidence with the sacrilege of idolatry need not be dwelt on. (2) The destruction of the Egyptian first-born must be reckoned as another of these punishments upon sacrilege. The people of Israel were God's own people, dedicated to Him by Himself as no other nation has been before or since, and surely it cannot be denied that their oppression by Pharaoh was a fearful act of sacrilege. Accordingly, after the nine less grievous chastisements upon the Egyptians, comes the appropriate punishment of sacrilege as the tenth, and "in [one

moment the noblest offspring of them was destroyed."—
Wisd. xviii., 12.

Note on pages xlvi., lii. (*reference at " Goodyere "*).

For Sir Francis read Sir John Goodere.

Note on page lvii. (*reference at " apparent "*).

The easiest answer to the question so commonly put, **and**
usually considered as a fatal objection, " Have not unsacrilegious
persons died by violent means? have not the most pious of
families had no offspring ? " is to point out the false assumption on which it goes. This, though it of course underlies Mr.
Neale's discussion of the point, is perhaps not brought out as
clearly as might have been done. The false assumption, no
doubt unconsciously made, is that failure of issue, if it be the
appropriate punishment for sacrilege, is peculiar thereto; bu t
this we never have affirmed; and only if we had done
so would the question have any value as an argument. The
real point is, not whether others besides sacrilegious fami lies
have been childless, but whether failure of issue has not
been persistent in these taken collectively, and, when they are
taken individually, whether it has not occurred in generat ion
after generation, with the result, for example, that the descent,
where not failing altogether, is carried on by one son only out
of, it may be, many brothers throughout a long course of years.
Doubtless the questions above given are to be answered in the
affirmative; those who are clear from sacrilege have been
childless, or have lost their children—no one denies it, it is a
plain fact; but what we say is this, that among unsacrilegious
families persistency in failure of issue is not to'be traced as it
may be traced in sacrilegious ones. To expound further by a
homely instance: if twenty men have the 'gout, of whom
thirteen have drunk port all their lives and seven only light
claret, it does not follow because the claret-drinkers are also
afflicted that the port causes not the affliction of the drinker
thereof ; so if certain families are childless who have not committed sacrilege, this goes no way to prove that childlessness is
not the punishment of those who have. This fact is not proved

by the simple assertion, which is not denied; it would not be proved even by setting family against family and pointing out isolated cases in each; what is wanted to prove it is that the *character* of the childlessness or failure of issue should be the same, that it should be shown to continue in the same marked way in which it continues in sacrilegious families. This is what we deny, and this is what our opponents are to prove. In the illustration above given, if we prove that all or almost all the port drinkers were afflicted with gout, we should be allowed to have ample grounds for stating that the port caused the gout; so in the present case, when we show that issue fails time after time in the vast majority of sacrilegious families, we are surely justified in asserting that the sacrilege was the cause of it.

Note on page lxviii. (*reference at* "*Moodkee* ").

The dates of the events here mentioned by Mr. Neale are :—
1. Death of Lord William Russell, 6th May, 1840.
2. Of the Earl of Darnley, 12th Feb., 1835.
3. Of the Earl of Norbury (not Morbury), 3rd Jan., 1839.
4. Battle of Moodkee, 18th Dec., 1845.
5. To these, in Mr. Neale's second edition, was added the murder of Mr. Jeremie by Rush, 28th Nov., 1848.

Note on page lxviii. (*reference at* "*purposes* ").

To the testimonies of enemies, as Mr. Neale calls them, *i.e.,* favourers of the Reformation, may be added that of Dean Boys of Canterbury, a great worshipper of Queen Elizabeth and James I., who yet says, " Read the Chronicles, examine Histories, and show me but one Church-robber's heire that thrived unto the third generation" (Exposition of Gospel for Sunday before Easter). So, too, Thomas Fuller on the frequent passing of the lands, " Here I intended to present the *Reader* with the *particulars* of all those *Owners* through whose hands these *Mitred Abbeys* have passed, from those to whom King *Henry* granted them, to those who at this day are possessed thereof. A thing with very much difficulty (such the frequencies of the *exchange*) collectible out of the severall *fines* p^a.yd at their *alienation:* but having tyred out mine own modesty (though not my good friend Mr. *John Witt's* officious industry), in being beholden to him above my possibility of requitall for perusing so many *Records,* I desisted from so difficult a design "* (" History of Abbeys," p. 366).

Note on page lxxi. (*reference at "jfriends").*

To the " testimonies of friends " we add Bishop Bull of St. David's (" Nelson's Life," p. 368) :—" This design [of augmenting the maintenance of the poor clergy] he thought would be more easily carried on if some rich impropriators could be prevailed on to restore to the Church some part of her revenues, which they had too long retained, to the great prejudice of the Church, and very often to the ruin of their families by that secret curse which is the usual attendant of sacrilegious possessions. He was able to give instances of this kind in some families of his acquaintance; and in this point my lord seemed to concur with the opinion of Sir Henry Spelman."

The words of another deep and wise thinker, Joseph Mede, are also reported by his biographer (" Works," i., 71):—" He would say, ' The prohibited tree in Paradise was a sacred and a sacramental tree.' Wherefore he was positive and dogmatical in determining that the *formalis ratio* and specifical nature of original sin was sacrilege." The biographer then proceeds as follows with Mede's words :—" But now for this sin of sacrilege as God began to punish it very early, even in Paradise itself (*ut supra*), so hath He continually pursued and hounded this sin. . . . And in later ages, besides what the learned pens of Sir Henry Spelman and others have published, he had collected many rare instances of his own private observation, which upon prudential considerations I forbear to recite." On this second sentence no remark need be made; but the first will be noted as going beyond even Sir Henry Spelman's assertion that the first *actual* sin was sacrilege.

* Our copy of Fuller once belonged to Sir Francis Palgrave, and has in the margin what we suppose to be his shorthand notes. Unluckily we cannot read them.

So again Bp. Taylor ("Life of Christ"), iii., 229, ed. Heber: "Sometimes the crime is of that nature that it cries aloud for vengeance or is threatened with a special kind of punishment which by the observation and experience of the world hath regularly happened to a certain sort of persons : such as are dissolutions of estates, the punishment of sacrilege."

Note on page xc. (*reference at* "*good*").

Hooker is probably one of the most important men who have denied that the suppression of the abbeys was sacrilege (Eccl. Pol. VII., xxiv., 23). It is doubtless not easy to speak against Hooker; but we cannot see otherwise than that he can have given no deep thought to the matter, for he does not so much as mention the solemn dedication of all property which was made, and rests his case on the bare fact that the monks, as monks, were not in holy orders, and on his own argument that Bishops alone are the receivers and disposers of the Church's patrimony. He, however, makes the great exception of appropriated livings. It is a significant thing that his editor, John Keble (Pref. p. xcvi.), makes no comment on this passage, but passes by it in silence.

Note on page xcv. (*reference at* "*universal*").

The rule of punishment is not universal, but no argument can be drawn from this. "God hath not . . . broken all sacrilegious persons upon the wheel of an inconstant and ebbing estate . . . but because He hath done so to some, we are to look upon those judgments as Divine accents and voices of God, threatening all the same crimes with the like events, and with the ruins of eternity." Bp. Taylor ("Life of Christ"), iii., 350, ed. Heber.

In Mr. Neale's second edition he expanded this section considerably, instancing, among those families who had retained abbey lands since their first granting, such events as went towards proving his point. Of these families the best known is that of Russell, where he mentions chiefly the tenuity of the line of succession, and the number of violent or unexpected deaths. . His list may be increased and continued as follows :—

In 1732 the third Duke of Bedford, who was only twenty-four years old, was travelling to Lisbon, as consumptive patients did in those days, but he was unable to bear the voyage, and was landed, already dying, at Corunna, where he did not survive more than a few hours ("Historical Register," 1732).

The fifth Duke died, aged thirty-seven, in 1802, after a very severe and painful surgical operation; the ninth Duke by suicide in 1891; and his son, the tenth Duke, suddenly and prematurely, aged forty-one, in 1893.

In a younger branch; the eldest son of the first Earl Russell died before him, and an unhappy case in the law courts of some few years ago is doubtless not yet forgotten.

The Wynnes and Cottons also are similar cases. With the former, Mr. Neale gives more than one case of failure of issue, which happened again in 1878, when the eldest son of the then Lord Newborough died before him. The instance of the Cottons is a very instructive one, and must be set out at length. The estate of Combermere Abbey was originally granted to Sir George Cotton, who was father of an only son Richard, father of George, father of Thomas, whose eldest son died before him. The second son was Sir Robert, created a Baronet in 1677, whose three eldest sons died before him. The fourth son, Sir Thomas, second Baronet, had seven sons, of whom Sir Robert, third Baronet, and the five next, all died without issue. The seventh, Sir Lynch, fourth Baronet, was father to Sir Robert, fifth Baronet, who again lost his eldest son. The second son was the celebrated Sir Stapleton Cotton, created Viscount Combermere, who also lost his eldest son, and was succeeded by the second, the late Viscount, whose eldest son and successor, the present peer, has been twice married without a family. No fewer than five cases, more than one very marked, are here to be found of the premature deaths of heirs apparent and presumptive.

Note on page 30 (*reference at* " *Sacrilege among Heathens* ").

It seems to the writer almost impossible to overrate the importance of the argument to be derived from these well-proved instances of punishment on Heathen Sacrilege. It is surely a very wonderful thing that sacrilege *in a false religion should be punished exactly as if that religion were true.* At the very least it must go to establish a broad and wide principle in the matter.

Note on page 105 (*reference at* " *crown* ") (*in a note*).

Of " the calamities that happened to the Crown" it seems better not to speak at length; but a little thought will satisfy most readers that Spelman's list, continued by Mr. Neale, is quite susceptible of a farther continuation up to the present moment. But there may be mentioned the premature death of the Prince Consort, which was not only a personal calamity to the Crown, but one of the greatest State misfortunes that England has ever known.

Note on page 113.

Temporal Lords, &c. This list of the Lords who passed on the 23rd May, 1539, the Bill for the Dissolution of the Greater Monasteries, may be worked out and classified in the following table a little farther than has been done in the text :—

Title.	Extinct in Male line.	Title.	Extinct in Male line.
1. Cromwell, B., *Vic. Gen.*	1687	13. Rutland, E.	Extant [Rutland, D.]
2. Audley of Walden, B., Chanc.	1544	14. Cumberland, E.	1643
3. Norfolk, D.	Extant	15. Sussex, E.	1641
4. Suffolk, D.	1551	16. Huntingdon, E.	Extant
5. Dorset, M.	1554	17. Hertford, E.	Extant [Somerset, D.]
6. Oxford, E.	1702		
7. Southampton, E.	1543	18. Bridgewater, E.	1548
8. Arundel, E.	1580	19. Audley of Heleigh, B.	1777
9. Shrewsbury, E.	1617	20. Zouche, B.	1625
10. Essex, E.	1539	21. Delawarr. B.	1554
11. Derby, E.	1735	22. Morley, B.	1741
12. Worcester, E.	Extant [Beaufort, D.]	23. Dacre of the South, B.	1594
		24. Dacre of Gilsland, B.	1634

Title.	Extinct in Male line·	Title.	Extinct in Male line.
25. Cobham, B. . . .	1651	34. Lumley, B. . . .	1609
26. Maltravers, B. . .	1580	35. Monteagle, B. . .	1581
27. Ferrers, B.	Extant [Hereford V.]	36. Windsor, B. . . .	1642
		37. Wentworth, B. . .	1667
28. Powis, B. . . .	1552	38. Burrough, B. . . .	1601
29. Clinton, B.	Extant [New- castle, D.]	39. Braye, B. . . .	1557
		40. Hungerford, B. . .	16—
30. Scroope, B. . . .	1630	41. St. John, B.	Extant [Win-
31. Stourton, B.	Extant [Mow- bray, B.]		chester, M.]
		42. Russell, B.	Extant [Bed-
32. Latimer, B. . . .	1577		ford, D.]
33. Montjoy, B. . . .	1606	43. Parr, B. . . - . .	1571

On this list it will be seen that there are the names of 43 lords, of whom 33 have now no male heir. On this number by itself it would perhaps be rash to lay very much stress, but it is worth attention that the male line ended in as many as 15 instances before the end of the sixteenth century, in which the Bill was passed; 14 more ended before the close of the seventeenth, and the remaining four in the eighteenth. Of the 10 whose heirs still sit in the House of Lords, two (Nos. 3 and 16) still sit under the same title, five (Nos. 12, 13, 31, 41, 42) still hold it, but have been promoted, or have succeeded, to others; in three cases (Nos. 17, 27, 29) the title differs. Of these last, one case is the unique one of the Seymours, the others were caused by the passing to females of the ancient baronies· These two instances, and a few others in which a barony continued for a time, or still continues, must be considered at more length, since almost all show in a greater or less degree the failure of heirs in a way not to be looked for.

1. Audley of Heleigh. On the extinction of the male line, 1777, this barony devolved on the heir of the female line, and lasted till 1872, when it became abeyant between the two daughters of the last Lord. The Hon. William Touchet, last male descendant, then aged twenty-two, was tried 23rd October, 1844, for felonious shooting, acquitted on the ground of insanity, and confined as a lunatic. Whether he is still living the writer is unable to say.

2. Zouche. This barony was called out of abeyance in 1815 in favour of Sir Cecil Bisshopp; both his sons died before him, and the barony was again called out for his elder daughter, the grandmother of the present Lord. There is every appearance of the male line again becoming extinct, in which case the title will again pass to females.

3. Dacre of Gilsland. This barony passed, by successive failures of male issue, in 1594 to the Lennards, in 1741 to another branch of the same family, in 1786 to the Ropers, and in 1794 to the Brands, who now hold it.

4. Ferrers. This barony was called out of abeyance in 1677 in favour of Sir Robert Shirley, whose son and grandson *both* died before him: his granddaughter took the barony into the family of Compton; her only daughter again into that of Townshend; on the death, 1855, of the late Marquis of Townshend, it fell into abeyance again.

5. Clinton. This barony was called out of abeyance in 1721 in favour of Hugh Fortescue, who died without issue, and the title passed through the family of Walpole to that of Trefusis, the present holders.

6. Wentworth. This title, after passing through the families of Lovelace and Noel, devolved in 1856 on the widow of Lord Byron, who was in her turn succeeded by her eldest grandson (son of "Ada,") and he dying without issue, after a career of unenviable notoriety, by his only brother, the present Lord, now also Earl of Lovelace, who has but one daughter.

7. Braye. This title was called out of abeyance in 1839 in favour of Sarah Otway Cave; both her sons died before her and it again became abeyant: at last, in 1879, her youngest daughter succeeded, whose eldest son within two months fell in action in South Africa: the present Lord Braye is now the only survivor.

Note on page 173 (reference at " belongs ").

The first Earl Spencer, purchaser in 1762, was succeeded in 1788 by his only son the second Earl. He had four sons, of whom two were third and fourth Earls, and all died without issue except the latter, whose elder son, the present Earl, has no family, neither has his brother and heir presumptive.

Note on page 174 (*reference at* " *owner*").

Sir Alan Brodrick, first Viscount Midleton, purchaser 1661: his two eldest sons died before him; the fifth Viscount was succeeded by his cousin, and he by his brother, for want of male issue.

Note on page 177 (*reference at* " *Temple* ").

John Lord Bellasyse, purchaser 1663: his only son died before him; the grandson, the second Lord Bellasyse, died without issue 1692, and so became this line extinct. Sir William Temple, the celebrated statesman, was a subsequent purchaser; he married, as is well known, Dorothy Osborne of Chicksands,* also of a sacrilegious family (see Dr. Eales, p. 250); their only surviving child, John Temple, committed an unaccountable suicide in his father's lifetime, 1689, leaving two daughters, whose last descendant, the Rev. Nicholas Bacon, died in 1796.

Note on page 178 (*references at* " *Bonar* " *and* " *Baring* ").

The Bonar murder took place 31st May, 1813. Mr. Baring was drowned 9th July, 1820.

Note on page 186 (*reference at* " *brother* ").

Sandon Priory, p. 186. Sir John Frederick, purchaser in 1780: his eldest son died before him; the second, Sir Richard, and four others, all died also without issue.

Note on page 191 (*reference at* "*well known* ").

Mr. Neale says, " The history of the Berkeleys is highly instructive," and no less has it been so since his time. Of the two families of the fifth Earl, for the legitimacy of the second whereof the House of Lords gave judgment in 1811, and again in 1891, this became totally extinct in the male line in 1882, and the elder (with which Berkeley Castle remained) will in all probability become so also in a few years; while the junior

---

* Her letters to him were published in part in 1836, in Courtenay's " Life of Temple," reviewed by Macaulay; and in whole in 1888.

branch, now holding the Earldom, depends upon the present Earl alone : a great contrast to the flourishing state of the Berkeleys of Spetchley, who branched off before the Sacrilege. There might also have been mentioned the Grey and Berkeley case at the end of the seventeenth century, where Ford Lord Grey, afterwards Earl of Tankerville, husband of Lady Mary Berkeley, was tried for abducting his wife's sister Henrietta.* Swords were actually drawn in Court between the parties.

Note on page 196 (*reference at " almost "*).

The quotation here given from Lord Byron will be found in letter to Murray dated 10th December, 1821 (" Moore's Life "). In 1884 the eldest son of the owner of Newstead committed suicide at Cambridge. It has been stated (" N. & Q.," 3rd S., i., 94) that the well-known tomb and monument of Byron's dog Boatswain is *on the very site of the High Altar.*

Note on page 199 (*reference at " Bedley "*).

For S. C. Bedley read Sir Charles Sedley.

Note on page 201 (*reference at " Repton Abbey "*).

Sir Robert Burdett, inheritor in 1728 : his eldest son died before him ; the second son of this latter was drowned with Lord Montagu at Laufenburg.

Note on page 204 (*reference at " baffled "*).

In the last-mentioned family of Austen-Knight there were two instances, almost or quite contemporaneous, of marriage within the forbidden degrees.—See Letters of Jane Austen, i., 28, 40.

Note on page 205 (*reference at " Sir Jermyn Davers "*).

Sir Jermyn Davers, a purchaser, died in 1743 : his two eldest sons died before him.

Note on page 218 (*reference at " succeeding "*).

Sion House, p. 216. Sir Hugh Smithson, afterwards Duke of Northumberland : the male line of his elder son expired

---

* On this case were founded the " Love-letters of a Nobleman," one of the coarse books of Mrs. Aphra Behn.

1865; the second had eight sons, of whom two only left male issue.

Note on page 219 *(reference at " William ").*

Bishopsgate Priory, p. 218. The Earl of Lovelace : his eldest son, Lord Wentworth, died before him.

Note on page 225 *(reference at " alive ").*

Arbroath, p. 225. This (which is not given as a quotation) certainly might be made intelligible: for all that appears, the nephew who succeeded in 1782 is now living at the age of at least 113 ! The "son William" was Earl of Panmure; the "nephew," the eighth Earl of Dalhousie, died as early as 1787, leaving seven sons, of whom only one has now male descendants, the last descendant of the others dying in 1887. The sad and premature deaths of the late Earl and Countess of Dalhousie are within easy memory.

Note on page 236 *(reference at " mentioned ").*

Sir Harbottle Grimston, a purchaser, had five sons, who all died without issue, except his successor, the second baronet; this successor had also six sons, who all died before him except the third and last baronet, who died 1700. The estates then went to his sister's grandson, the first Lord Grimston, whose eldest son died before him, and from his second descends the present holder, the Earl of Verulam.

Note on page 240 *(reference at " fate ").*

Every published account of the death of Lord Montagu which the writer has seen makes the strange blunder that it was in the falls of Schaffhausen. These are about 90 feet high, and not even so foolhardy a man as poor Lord Montagu would dream of attempting to shoot them. It was in the falls of Laufenburg, close by, which are dangerous enough, but might be considered barely possible to pass in safety. The death by drowning of Lord Montagu's nephews, the twin sons of Mr. Poyntz, of Cowdray and Easebourne, took place on the 7th July, 1815; and the present writer may now

give, as related by his mother, whose family was acquainted
with that of Poyntz, the circumstances of the case, which were
so very sad and melancholy as to be probably unprecedented.
Mr. Poyntz was an excellent swimmer, but his sons were not,
and when the boat in which they were capsized, the boys, as is
so common in such cases, lost their heads and caught hold of
their father, so as to prevent him from using his limbs. The
only chance for any of them was that he should exert his
strength and shake them off, and this he did, but before he
could seize them again they sank, and though the unhappy
father instantly dived after them, he could not recover them
alive. This, if Mr. Neale had known it, he would certainly
have placed under his head of " Strange and unusual accidents." The effect ou the poor father was lasting: many
years after, when he was standing for Midhurst, a blackguard
of a fellow on the other side yelled out to him, " Who shook
off his son when he was drowning?" and we have been told
that he dropped, fainting, "as if he had been shot." Mr.
Poyntz left three daughters, Frances Lady Clinton, Elizabeth
Countess Spencer, and Isabella Marchioness of Exeter; these
ladies died respectively in 1875, 1851, and 1879, having sold
Easebourne in 1843 to the Earl of Egmont. He died without
issue in 1874, and was succeeded by his nephew, who himself
has no family, neither has his cousin and heir-presumptive.
Even among the descendants of the ladies failure is remarkably to be traced: for Lady Clinton left none, those of Lady
Spencer will probably expire in the first generation, while in
Lady Exeter's case, of ten children only four survived infancy
or early youth, one being drowned in Canada.

Battle Abbey (page 241) was also at one time the property
of the Lords Montagu. From their successors, the Websters,
it was purchased in 1858 by Lord Harry Vane, afterwards
Duke of Cleveland, who died without issue in 1891, bequeathing
Battle to his widow for her life, and afterwards to his great-
nephew, Francis William Forester.

Note on page 241 (*reference at* " *Lennox* ").
For Lord William read Lord Fitzroy Lennox.

Note on page 248 (*reference at* " *Pitt* ").

Cerne Abbas. George Pitt: his last male descendant, Lord Rivers, died in 1828: the estate, with a later barony, devolved on a nephew, Horace Bedeford, drowned in the Serpentine, 1831: his eldest son, the fourth Lord, was father of four sons, of whom three died before him, and the youngest, the fifth Lord, also without issue : the title reverted to a brother of the fourth Lord, who also died without issue in 1880, when it expired, and the estate passed to General Lane Fox.

Note on page 249 (*reference at* " *Duncombe* ").

Rievaulx Abbey. Sir Charles Duncombe, purchaser 1695; he died unmarried, and was succeeded by his nephew, Thomas (Browne) Duncombe, who left no sons; his brother and successor was father to the first Lord Feversham. Of the three holders of this title, including the present one, each lost his eldest son at about twenty.

Note on page 250 (*reference at* "*family* ").

Temple Newsam. Arthur Ingram, first Viscount Irvine: his elder son, the second Viscount, died without issue : the younger, the third Viscount, had *five* sons who one after another held the title, the sixth son being father to the ninth and last Viscount, who died 1778. This case is probably unique in the history of succession to titles of peerage. The eldest daughter of the ninth Viscount, who was Marchioness of Hertford, at last succeeded to Temple Newsam,.and her descendants, both male and female, became entirely extinct in 1870: those of the second had already expired in 1831, and the manor is now held by the Meynell Ingrams, the heirs of the third.

Note on page 269 (*reference at* " *Wells* ").

The Dean of Wells was murdered 10th Oct., 1646.

Note on page 304 (*reference at* " 1583.")

James Eustace, third Viscount Baltinglass, grandson of the grantee, joined in the rebellion of 1582, and died "in ve' y extreme poverty and need " (Holinshed) in 1583. Two years

afterwards the family was attainted and all the estates forfeited.

Note on page 304 (*reference at* " 1746.")

Jeripoint.   James Butler, ninth Earl of Ormond, the grantee,
died of poison 1543 : his eldest son the tenth Earl had an only
daughter, who succeeded to the estates; her husband, Richard
Preston, Earl of Desmond, was drowned between Dublin and
Holyhead 1628 ; their only daughter married her cousin James,
Duke of Ormond, and had an elder son who died before his
father, leaving two sons, James second Duke of Ormond, who
was attainted and died without issue, and Charles third Duke,
who also died without issue, 1758, last of the line.

Note on page 305 (*reference at* " *London* ").

Dublin St. Mary.   Gerald Fitzgerald, Earl of Desmond, son
of the grantee, murdered as Mr. Neale and Dr. Eales relate,
left one surviving son, the sixteenth Earl, who died a prisoner
in the Tower, 1601, without issue; his cousin the seventeenth
Earl, grandson of the grantee, was attainted, and died also in
the Tower, 1608, without issue ; his nephew, the last of the
line, died also without issue, 1632.

Note on page 305 (*reference at* " 1731.")

Down.   This family of Calvert became extinct in 1771, not
1731, by the death of the sixth* Lord Baltimore, a man of a
very disreputable character ; he was tried for a rape 28th
March, 1768 ; his sister died a lunatic.   The property, with
the rest of the estates, was sold to a John Trotter, of whom we
know nothing.   The usual rule appears to have obtained of
the continuance of the family through only one son in a
generation.

Note on page 305 (*reference at* " *place* ").

Tintern.   The grantee, Anthony Colclough, had seven sons,
of whom the three eldest died in his lifetime, and the three
youngest appear to have also died without issue : Sir Thomas,
the fourth, his successor, was father to Sir Adam, created a

* According to Burke's pedigree this last Lord was the seventh. But a
corrected pedigree is given in "N. and Q.," 2nd S., xii., 343.

baronet 1628: his male line became extinct 1702 with his grandson Sir Cæsar, third baronet, whose sister succeeded to Tintern. She also died without issue 1722, when Tintern devolved on the heir-at-law, Cæsar Colclough, grandson of a younger son of Sir Thomas. His eldest son died before him, leaving Vesey Colclough, who succeeded, and whose son Cæsar died without issue, 1842, when Tintern devolved on his cousin Mary Colclough, Mrs. Rossborough, who died 1884, leaving no son, but four daughters. The male line of this branch of the Colcloughs, which was once very numerous, became entirely extinct in 1867.

Note on page 306 (*reference at* " *Donegal* ").

Carrickfergus, etc. These were certainly not granted to the Marquis of Donegal, a title which did not exist till 1791 : it was to Arthur Lord Chichester, who died without issue, 1624 ; his brother and heir was created Viscount Chichester, and was father to the first Earl of Donegal, who died without issue, 1674; his nephew, the second Earl, was father to the third Earl, three of whose daughters were burnt to death at once; his son, the fourth Earl, was also succeeded by his nephew, who was the first Marquis; his eldest son, the second Marquis, was father to the third, whose only son died before him, and also to the fourth, whose eldest son, the fifth Marquis, has dissipated his property.

Note on page 306 (*reference at* " *Antrim* ").

Ballycastle, etc. This Earldom of Antrim expired in 1791, as also a Marquisate granted in 1789, the second title of the kind which had become extinct in the family. The present Earldom of Antrim is a fresh creation, and the connection with the old family only through the female line.

Note on page 306 (*reference at* " *Drogheda* ").

Ballylinch, etc. The family of Moore seems to occupy in the meagre annals of Irish sacrilege the same exceptional position which that of Russell, with one or two more, occupies in the far fuller English annals : that, namely, of a family which has continued to some extent to flourish. It is to be noted, however, that the fifth Earl of Drogheda and one of his sons, the Rev. Edward Moore, were both drowned in a passage to Dublin in 1758 : he had before lost his eldest son. The third Earl's eldest son also died before him. A Marquisate created in 1791 expired in 1892, the earldom devolving on a junior branch.

Note on page 306 (reference at " Thomond").

Clare, etc. In the Earldom of Thomond male heirs were, as usual, very few. The seventh Earl lost both his sons in his lifetime, and also the son of the elder, who was drowned at sea. The family (in this branch) became extinct in 1774.

Note on page 306 (reference at " Cork").

Castle Lyons, etc. There are no fewer than *four* instances of the eldest son of an Earl of Cork dying in his father's lifetime.

Note on page 307 (reference at " Kildare ").

Gray, etc. The misfortunes of the grantee, the ninth Earl of Kildare, and his family, are part of Irish history : he died a prisoner in the Tower, 1534 ; his eldest son, the tenth Earl (together with *five* of his uncles), was beheaded for treason, without issue, 1537 : from a younger son descends the Duke of Leinster, through four collateral successions. The thirteenth Earl was lost at sea ; the nineteenth Earl had twelve children, of whom only two survived infancy ; the first Duke had eighteen children, of whom the eldest son and no fewer than *eight* others died before the age of twenty-two ; one of the surviving sons was the celebrated Lord Edward Fitzgerald.

Note on page 307 (reference at " Clanricarde ").

Gormoghan, etc. The grantee, the first Earl of Clanricarde, died the year after receiving the estates : his descendants have repeatedly failed in the elder line ; the Marquisate has been twice created and twice expired, neither is there any heir to the present Marquisate or to the ancient Earldom ; the second Earldom, created in 1800, is to descend through females.

CONCLUDING NOTES.

Kirkstall Abbey. Granted to Archbishop Cranmer; by him settled on Peter Hammond, in trust for the Archbishop's younger son. In 26 Eliz., 1584, granted to Edmund Downing and Peter Ashton. Afterwards purchased by John Lord Saville, whose two eldest sons and a grandson died before him; two others also died unmarried. The third was created Earl of Sussex, and was succeeded by his only son, the second Earl, who died without issue 1671, Kirkstall devolving on his only sister, Lady Brudenell. Her only son, the third Earl of Cardigan, was father to four sons, of whom the eldest was created Duke of Montagu, but lost his only son; the second was fifth Earl, but died without issue; the third was father to the sixth Earl, and he to the seventh, who died without issue 1868. What then became of Kirkstall I cannot now say; but the title went to the heir of the third Earl's fourth son, the Marquis of Ailesbury, the owner of

Jerveaulx Abbey. This fourth son, created Earl of Ailesbury, lost his eldest son, the second being the first Marquis; his eldest son, the second Marquis, died without issue, and the second, who became third Marquis, lost his eldest son, whose only son succeeded as fourth and present Marquis, who dissipated his property; he died in 1894, aged 31, and was succeeded by his uncle.

Castle Acre. This priory was first granted, with many others, to Thomas Howard, Duke of Norfolk, whose history and that of his immediate descendants is well known. By him it was sold to Sir Thomas Gresham (whose only son died before him, aged sixteen), and by him again to Thomas Cecil, first Earl of Exeter, whose son William, second Earl, sold it a third time to his brother-in-law, Sir Edward Coke, the celebrated

Chief Justice. Sir Edward's history, especially his disgrace with the Crown, may also be considered well known. He suffered much, too, from the conduct of his second wife, the Lady Cecil. Their only surviving daughter Spelman calls " the fable of the time." She was married against her will (for the sake of Crown favour) to John, Viscount Purbeck, brother to George Villiers, Duke of Buckingham, and on his becoming a lunatic joined herself to Sir Robert Howard and produced a son, whose subsequent claims to the viscounty are among the strangest of such matters. But to return to the Chief Justice. He died in 1634, leaving by his first wife six sons ; of these the three eldest died without male issue, and the seven sons of the fourth also issueless; the male line of the sixth ended in his grandsons, and the descent was continued by the fifth son alone, and as usual only through one son in a generation, till all the male descendants of the Chief Justice became extinct in 1759 with Edward, Earl of Leicester, whose only son had died before him. Castle Acre, with the rest of the Earl's estates, devolved on his sister's son, Wenman Roberts, who took the name of Coke, and in whose son, well known in his day as " Coke of Holkham," the Earldom was revived in 1837. The subsequent history of the descent is somewhat unusual ; for Mr. Coke, as he then was, after remaining for twenty-two years a widower, without male issue, married again at the age of seventy a girl of nineteen, and became father to a second family. By the eldest of these, the present Earl of Leicester, Castle Acre is now held. (See p. 143.)

Leighs or Leese Priory, Essex. This was granted to Sir Richard Rich, afterwards Lord Rich and Lord High Chancellor. He was not a man of high character, and it seems likely that the death of Sir Thomas More was owing to a false oath sworn by him as to Sir Thomas' opinions on the question of the Royal Supremacy. He was also much of a time-server, as appears from his founding a chantry under Queen Mary. Lord Rich left four sons, of whom the three youngest died without issue ; the eldest, the second Lord Rich, lost his own eldest son, and the four sons of his third son all died without male issue. The

second son, the third Lord Rich, was created Earl of Warwick;
his wife, Penelope Devereux, left him for Charles Blount, Earl
of Devon, and they were afterwards divorced (it is to be noted
that she was aunt to the notorious Earl of Essex, of a still more
celebrated divorce case); their eldest son, the second Earl of
Warwick, was father, with two other sons, who died without
issue, to the third and fourth Earls, of both whom the eldest
sons died before them; the first of these had married a daughter
of Oliver Cromwell, and died of scrofula, aged twenty-three.
At the death, 1673, of the fourth Earl, the title devolved on
the Earl of Holland, heir male of the first Earl's second son,
and became extinct in 1759, the whole male line of the Chancellor thus expiring; but the estates passed to his (the fourth
Earl's) sisters, as coheiresses. They were Countesses of
Manchester, Radnor, and Scarsdale. The first is ancestress of
the present Duke of Manchester; the male descendants of the
others expired in 1741 and 1736. Leighs is now, and has been
for the last 150 years, the property of Guy's Hospital.

Stoneleigh Abbey (Cistercian), Warwickshire. First
granted, among many others, to Charles Brandon, Duke of
Suffolk. His eldest son died in his lifetime; his two others,
the second and third Dukes, both died in the same day of the
sweat, 1551. The heirs at law of their father's paternal aunts
then succeeded to the estates; but Stoneleigh, which had gone
to the Cavendishes, was shortly purchased by Sir Thomas
Leigh, Lord Mayor of London, and left by him to his second
son, Sir Thomas, created a Baronet. Now comes the constant
history; the first Baronet's eldest son died before him, leaving
one son, who was created Lord Leigh; he also lost his eldest
son, as did the third Lord, and the descent continued as usual
through one son in a generation till it expired in 1786 with the
fifth Lord, who was for some time before his death a lunatic.
Stoneleigh passed to his only sister, and at her death, unmarried, in 1806, to the representative of the Lord Mayor's
eldest son. In the only son of this successor the barony was
revived in 1839, and his son, the present and second Lord
Leigh, now holds Stoneleigh. His eldest son was killed in

America in 1884. The family suffered much in 1828 from groundless claims to the old peerage, and in 1848 from totally unfounded charges of felonious attempts to suppress evidence in those claims. See a suppressed publication on the subject by Charles Griffin, solicitor.

Combe Abbey, Warwickshire. This abbey (the oldest Cistercian settlement in the county) was granted to John Dudley, Earl of Warwick, afterwards Duke of Northumberland, and on his attainder and execution to Robert Kelway, Surveyor of the Court of Wards and Liveries, whose daughter and heiress married John Lord Harrington, and their only son, the second son, died without issue 1614. Combe passed to his sister Lucy, Countess of Bedford, who was a great spendthrift; it was at last sold to Sir William Craven. His eldest son succeeded in a barony his cousin Earl Craven (who was supposed to have been privately married to the Queen of Bohemia, daughter of James I.), and was himself succeeded by his eldest son, who died without issue, as did his brother the fourth Lord, and his cousin the fifth. The nephew of this last, the sixth Lord, was known in his day by the conduct of his wife, Lady Craven, who, after much disagreement, left him for the Margrave of Anspach, to whom she was married with indecent haste on the death of her husband in 1791. In their son's favour the Earldom was revived in 1801. He was father to the second Earl, whose eldest son died before him, and whose second son, the third Earl, was father to the fourth, the present holder of the title and of Combe; he was married early in 1893 to an American heiress. Combe is said to have been "more than once exposed to the hazard of the die."

Shengay Preceptory (St. John of Jerusalem), Cambridgeshire. At the dissolution this was granted to Sir Richard Long, Master of the Hawks; from him it descended to his son Sir Henry, who died 1573, leaving an only daughter and heiress, Elizabeth, wife of William, Lord Russell of Thornhaugh, ancestor by her of the Dukes of Bedford: she died in 1611, and her husband in 1613. Shengay eventually passed to their great-grandson of a younger branch, Admiral Edward

Russell, afterwards Earl of Orford, who died, without issue, 26th November, 1727. His sister Letitia had married Thomas Checke, Esq., and had issue a son Henry, who died aged eight, and a daughter Anne, who married Sir Thomas Tipping, Baronet, and died 21st January, 1727. The children of this latter marriage were an only son, Sir Thomas, second Baronet, who died, without issue, 1725, and two daughters, of whom the elder married Samuel, Lord Sandys, and succeeded to Shengay at the death of her great-uncle, Lord Orford. She had seven sons, of whom the eldest, Edwin, second Lord Sandys, and five others all died young or without issue; Martin, the fourth, had two sons, who died young, and one daughter, who married the Marquis of Downshire, and succeeded to Shengay in 1797 at the death of Lord Sandys, her uncle. She herself died in 1836, but had before parted with Shengay to her second cousin, the Hon. Thomas Windsor, son of the fourth Earl of Plymouth. He died in 1832, having again sold the estate to the third Earl of Hardwicke, who died in 1834, having survived his three sons (the eldest was drowned at sea), and was succeeded by his nephew, whose son, the fifth Earl, or rather his trustees, is the present holder of Shengay.

Grace Dieu Priory, Leicestershire. This was sold in 1539 to John Beaumont, Master of the Rolls; his son and successor, Sir Francis, had three sons, of whom the third was Francis Beaumont, the dramatist, who died without male issue; the eldest, Sir Henry, also had no sons; the second, Sir John, succeeded to Grace Dieu, and was created a Baronet. He was father to Sir John, second Baronet, who was slain at Gloucester 1644, and to Sir Thomas, third Baronet, who died without male issue 1686. His eldest daughter sold Grace Dieu to Sir Ambrose Phillipps, of Garendon, ancestor of the well-known Roman Catholic family of Phillipps de Lisle, still in possession.

A few words may also be given to the history of two titled families who once possessed (whether they were the first to do so we are not able to say) the only two convents of "Bonhommes" in England. Fuller mentions them in his "History of

Abbeys," p. 273 :—" The one is Asheridge, in Buckinghamshire,* now the mansion of the truly honourable Earl of Bridgwater, where I am informed more of a Monastery is visible this day than in any other house of England. . . . The other at Edington, in Wiltshire, now known for the hospitality of the Lady Beauchamp, dwelling therein."

John Egerton, the Earl of Bridgwater of that date (1655), appears to have succeeded to Asheridge through his mother, one of the three daughters and co-heiresses of Ferdinando Stanley, Earl of Derby.† He was her only surviving son, and had himself three sons, of whom two continued the male line. That of the younger expired in 1780 : the elder, the third Earl of Bridgwater, lost the only son of his first marriage; by the second he had seven sons, of whom the two elder were burnt to death in 1687; from the third (whose eldest son also died before him) descended the Dukes of Bridgwater, extinct in 1803; from the fifth the last Earls of Bridgwater, extinct in 1829; and the male descendants of the others expired in 1797.

The Lady Beauchamp, owner of the second convent mentioned by Fuller, was Elizabeth, only child of William Howard Lord Effingham, by Ann Lady Beauchamp of Bletshoe, and was wife of John Mordaunt, Earl of Peterborough. She had two sons, of whom the elder was father of an only surviving daughter, the scandalous Duchess of Norfolk of the celebrated Norfolk and Germaine divorce case. The male line of the younger became extinct in 1814, and the barony of Beauchamp, after being held till 1836 by the Dukes of Gordon, is now in abeyance.

We must give yet two more genealogical paragraphs, shortly to trace the descent of two portions of Church property which have remained longer than many others in one family, still

---

* A history of this foundation was written by Archdeacon H. J. Todd, and privately printed by Lord Bridgwater; first edition 1812, second edition, 1823. It is now a rare book.

† The male descendants of the others also are now extinct; those of the eldest in 1676, and of the youngest in 1789. The Egertons therefore lasted longest; they were a bastard branch of the original house of Egerton, which is now represented by Sir Philip Egerton, Bart.

remain in the same, and yet conspicuously illustrate our argument, and chiefly by failure of issue in many branches.

Chicheley. This manor, owned originally by the abbey of Tickford, in Buckinghamshire, was first granted to Cardinal Wolsey, and on his disgrace reverted to the Crown. It was again granted to a Cave, who died without male issue, and it passed with his eldest daughter and co-heiress to the Chesters. The only son of this lady was Sir Anthony Chester, first baronet, so created in 1619, and thenceforward we find the usual history to be told. Of the first baronet's five sons, the eldest son and successor alone left male issue, of which the eldest son died in his father's lifetime, and the descendants of the three younger expired in the first generation; the remaining son, the third baronet, also lost his eldest son, and after another generation collateral succession became the rule. The male line and the baronetcy became extinct in 1769, but the manor of Chicheley had passed out of the family in 1755, the seventh baronet having bequeathed it to his cousin Charles Bagot, who took the name of Chester. He was succeeded by his eldest son, he by his nephew, he by his first cousin, who died in 1879; the present owner is the eldest son of this last, and is unmarried. Of the history, apart from genealogy, of this present generation of Chesters, family reasons prevent us from speaking;* otherwise still further confirmation might be given to the argument of this essay.

St. Germans. In 1535 this priory was granted to a Champernowne, who died the next year. A rather amusing story of the way in which he obtained it is told by Fuller, "History of Abbeys," p. 337. In 1565 it passed by exchange from this family to Richard Eliot, father of Sir John Eliot, "the Patriot," who named it Port Eliot. Sir John's history, and death in the Tower, are well known; he had

---

* "What they have suffered God only knows; and even now the dark shadow of misery falls upon their path." MS. letter to the writer from Dr. F. G. Lee, who is descended from the (genuine) Chesters in the female line. Dr. Lee is believed to be the latest writer on the subject in some weighty sentences in " Glimpses in the Twilight," pp. 403-412.

six sons, of whom two died without issue, and the male line of another became extinct in the second generation. That of John, the eldest and successor, expired even sooner, in 1702, in the person of his own son Daniel, father of an only daughter, who married Browne Willis, the antiquary. Daniel Eliot, passing over the heir of the Patriot's second son, left Port Eliot to that of the fifth son, the branch which are now Earls of St. Germans. And now we come to the instructive part of the story. While the still existing descendants of the second son have spread and flourished widely (seven brothers of late all leaving sons) there is, till the present generation, *not one single instance* of two brothers leaving male issue at all in the sacrilegious branch! Edward Eliot, the first of this branch to own Port Eliot, was succeeded by his son, and he, dying at the age of twenty-two, by his uncle, whose eldest son was the first peer of the family. He lost his eldest son in his lifetime; the second, who was the first Earl of St. Germans, also died without issue; and the third, the second Earl,* though four times married, had but one son. This, the third Earl, lost his two eldest sons; the third, who became fourth Earl, died without issue in 1881, and the fourth is the present and fifth Earl. The contrast of these two descents is very striking, as in the similar case already mentioned of the two branches of the house of Berkeley.

Take again the Knightleys. The manor of Fawsley, in Northamptonshire, was first bought by them in 1415. For the next century and a half it descended through four generations from father to son; in the middle of the sixteenth century the family acquired Church property, and what followed? Collateral succession became the rule, and in spite of a partial restitution, made about a hundred years afterwards, so continued. Shortly, the history of the succession is this: At the time of the first Sacrilege, a brother (Sir Valentine) succeeded for the first time. He left four sons, among whom the line of the second and fourth

---

* By the second Earl and his son an entail was cut off about 1820, in virtue of which Port Eliot would have devolved in case of failure of issue on the elder branch already mentioned.

soon failed. The eldest, Sir Richard, left nine sons, of whom five died without issue; of the others, one had five sons and another four. All these, too, died without issue, and Sir Richard's whole male line expired in 1639. His second brother (third son of Sir Valentine) had himself five sons, among whom the line of the four youngest again quickly failed, the eldest succeeding in 1639. This Knightley again had nine sons, and Fawsley was successively held by two sons of the eldest, one of the fifth, and two of the sixth. The last of these left Fawsley to his son in 1728, and after him we have an interval of direct succession, *but short tenures.* The last-mentioned son died in 1738, his son in 1754, and now again three brothers, sons of the latter, succeed in turn. The last of these (created a baronet) died a lunatic in 1812,* and was succeeded by his nephew, the son of a fourth brother. This, the second baronet, was father of the third and present baronet, created in 1892 Lord Knightley, who has no son. His first cousin and heir is unmarried, and the whole family of Knightley, once so large, depends upon two brothers, nephews of the latter. (See p. vi.)

Thus remarkably have all the searches which we have been able to make confirmed the argument; they are but slight, merely from such ordinary books of reference as we happened to have by us, but the conclusion is irresistible that if we could have gone more deeply into the history of the families mentioned, and gone at all into the history of those which we have been obliged to pass over, our argument would have been yet further strengthened.

There are many who will call all this fanciful—some will call it fanatical—but it is difficult to believe that they who hold such language have ever seriously considered the subject, or studied and weighed the researches of Sir Henry Spelman, Mr. Neale, Mr. Joyce, and Dr. Eales. The point, it must be again repeated, is not whether such events as we call the curse upon Sacrilege, as sceptics simply call ill-luck—not whether these do not occur from time to time in families which have not com-

---

* He once attempted to murder his wife, a connection of the present writer's, who saved herself by asking time to say her prayers.

mitted Sacrilege, but whether they are not *practically universal in those which have;* and when we read—attention has not hitherto been specially directed to the rapid passing of the estates —when we read time after time such sentences as, "In 200 years 21 possessors and 18 families; in 200 years 14 possessors and 9 families; in 220 years 15 possessors and 9 families; in 230 years 19 possessors and 9 families; in 250 years 19 possessors and 8 families," so high above the general average of similar changes in landed property; when we read all this, and read, too, of the constant failure of issue even where the lands do continue for some length of time in the same family; when we consider the sad and strange accidents, the dreadful crimes,* which have occurred in sacrilegious families where none of the former punishments are found, or even where they are; when we consider all this, how can we but agree that the practical universality of punishment on Sacrilege is proved, and that the occasional occurrence elsewhere of such events as form the punishment is beside the point? Mr. Neale sums up (pp. 97, 98), after making a wide allowance for error, that the crime of Sacrilege has in all probability been punished on 600 families out of 630. We leave this fact to speak for itself.

It may seem uncharitable—it is certainly not pleasant, rather it is a fearful and shocking thing—to collect all these matters, to go over and verify and add to the researches of those who have gone before us in the task. But is there not a

---

* This latter subject is one which it is disagreeable to handle, and can only be cursorily mentioned. But we must not forget that some of the most odious crimes known to English history have taken place in sacrilegious families—the unnatural cases of Lords Hungerford and Castlehaven, the murder of Sir Thomas Overbury and the shocking Essex divorce case which led to it, the equally shocking Norfolk and Germaine divorce case. We are almost ashamed to confess that we have read through the reports of one or two of these cases in the "State Trials," and the details are so unutterably frightful and hideous that it is impossible to conceive anything worse. Here again it will be said, and of course it is quite fair to say, How do you know such crimes have not occurred elsewhere? We do not know it, and probably, or indeed certainly, they have. But what we do know is this—and the fact is of great importance—that most, if not all, of such crimes which have acquired public notice and remained on record as matters of history, have occurred—we say it again—in sacrilegious families.

cause ? Why do we rehearse every Ash Wednesday the general sentences of God's cursing ? Is it not that the hearers thereof may walk more warily in these dangerous days ? There are two reasons for the publishing of such matters as these : for the sake of those who are themselves in fault, and for the sake of others ; and here both operate, or we trust that they may operate, or we are bound to suppose the possibility of their operating. We trust that the former class may be led]to clear themselves as quickly as possible, we trust that the latter may never have the necessity of so doing. There are, of course, different degrees of responsibility for the past. A man may purchase abbey lands of set purpose, with full knowledge of| the fact, or he may do it in ignorance, or he may succeed to] them by inheritance or otherwise, but his responsibility for the future is the same. And he cannot evade this responsibility by simply getting them out of his hands as soon as possible ; no one, of course, would say that he might sell them again, and to say that he must rid himself of them in no other way is, in fact, no less a truism. In no way but one can he ',rid,'himself of them. He must make restitution ; he must restore either the lands themselves or an equivalent of some kind ;]he has not, of course, committed a new, direct, and overt act'of"Sacrilege, but he has made himself a partaker, or he has become a partaker, in the original act, and nothing is left for him but to purge himself of the stain of that act; in no other way but by restitution can it be done. Neither let it be said or thought that his responsibility is lessened or dissolved if it be by inheritance that he falls under it, for the sins of the fathers are visited on the children so long as the children turn not from them. If, indeed, he has acquired the lands in actual ignorance of their original owner, his responsibility for the past is less—perhaps it is nothing if he is not to blame for the ignorance, but his future duty remains.

The lapse of time is nothing. Even in human matters we have a maxim that *nullum tempus occurrit regi*, the king is not bound to assert his right within the time to which his] subjects are limited. Shall we deny to the Heavenly King what we allow to the earthly one ? [A claim upon a thing lasts, unless it be duly extinguished, as long as that lasts wherein the claim lies. A man's claim on his estate exists with his life, unless he divest himself of it; but the Crown never dies, and this is what gives its force to the above-quoted maxim. So the Church, even as a legal Corporation which never dies, or rather, to speak strictly, as a multitude of corporations, has her claim on her estates as fresh now as when every mitred abbot in the kingdom was in the plenitude of his power. There is no way in which it can be said that the claim was duly resigned, for even if the so-called " surrenders " of the monks would have formed such a resignation, which they would not, it is notorious and manifest that they were extorted. See J. H. Blunt's " History of the Reformation," i., 333 *et seq.* At the best these surrenders could have amounted only to a legal conveyance of the actual property then and there in the hands of the monks; they could have involved no resignation of the spiritual claim, for which a formal act of the Church must have been needful. Possibly more weight might be attached to the quasi-renunciation of Cardinal Pole when he reconciled England under Queen Mary to the Holy See; but on consideration the solemn admonition with which he ends will be found to show the real intent of the instrument: not, that is, to abandon the claim, even the legal claim, but simply to give a pledge that it should not then be enforced. As to the spiritual claim, it is not touched.

The truth, however, is that this whole question is not sufficiently recognized, if ever one was, to be of fact. The facts answer everything. They go a great way, if they do not answer it thoroughly, even to answering the question, How do you know that you have, all the cases before you? How do you know that if you had them all, the conclusion might not be just the opposite? For the rejoinder is this: All the major cases we *have;* and as to the minor ones, how is it to be accounted for that such as we have, all or almost all, lead in one way, so that if punishment is not found in one shape it is in another? Is it not in the laws of probability that if any considerable number of instances, such as might alter our opinions, remained behind, those which actually come before us would be more or less equally divided between both sides, instead of being all upon one?

Further, the individual character of the recorder of these facts cannot affect the facts themselves. This seems a ridiculous and unnecessary thing to advance, but strange to say it is not needless to give some such caution. If a writer is too credulous, it may lead him to state as a fact that for which there is insufficient evidence; and if he is too superstitious, as it has been called, it may lead him to make even from undoubted facts deductions which they will not bear. Both these things are perfectly true, and it is possible that on other occasions Mr. Neale's unsuspicious nature led him too much in the former direction, and (as in some passages in his work on the " Unseen World") his deep and high faith in the supernatural may have led him too much in the latter. But in the present case Mr. Neale's facts rest on documentary evidence, and his superstitious nature, if it was superstitious—we do not at all like the word as applied to him—can do no more than influence his own estimate of the inference to be derived from those facts. The facts are the same for others to draw their inference also, and if their inference be the same as his, this has nothing whatever to do with any valuation of his character. Yet there are some who seemingly have a difficulty in perceiving this, and think, or speak as if they thought, that what he believed not without study and research, is the less credible on account of the " superstitious " element in his character.

WS - #0023 - 310523 - C0 - 229/152/26 - PB - 9781331055440 - Gloss Lamination